A HANDBOOK ON CULTURE SHOCK:

A Cross-cultural Comparative Experience between
Nigeria (Ejaghem/Etung)
and
Upstate New York (Adirondacks)

D0879699

REV. VICTOR ACHIMA OWAN

TO: Mary Anne Youngsy,

Thanks!
God bless you!

Vic

TRAFFORD

Note for Librarians: a cataloguing record for this book that includes Dewey Decimal Classification and US Library of Congress numbers is available from the Library and Archives of Canada. The complete cataloguing record can be obtained from their online database at:
www.collectionscanada.ca/amicus/index-e.html
ISBN 1-4120-6385-x
Printed in Victoria, BC, Canada
First Printed 2005
Nihil Obstat
Fr. Ellis Kekong
St. Joseph Major Seminary
Ikot Ekpene, Akwa Ibom State, Nigeria
Imprimatur
His Grace, Most Rev. Joseph Edra Ukpo

Archbishop of Calabar Ecclesiastical Province, Nigeria

Printed on paper with minimum 30% recycled fibre.
Trafford's print shop runs on "green energy" from solar, wind and other environmentally-friendly power sources.

TRAFFORD

Offices in Canada, USA, Ireland and UK
This book was published *on-demand* in cooperation with Trafford Publishing. On-demand publishing is a unique process and service of making a book available for retail sale to the public taking advantage of on-demand manufacturing and Internet marketing. On-demand publishing includes promotions, retail sales, manufacturing, order fulfilment, accounting and collecting royalties on behalf of the author.

Book sales for North America and international:
Trafford Publishing, 6E–2333 Government St.,
Victoria, BC v8T 4P4 CANADA
phone 250 383 6864 (toll-free 1 888 232 4444)
fax 250 383 6804; email to orders@trafford.com
Book sales in Europe:
Trafford Publishing (UK) Ltd., Enterprise House, Wistaston Road Business Centre,
Wistaston Road, Crewe, Cheshire CW2 7RP UNITED KINGDOM
phone 01270 251 396 (local rate 0845 230 9601)
facsimile 01270 254 983; orders.uk@trafford.com
Order online at:
trafford.com/05-1296

10 9 8 7 6 5 4 3 2

COAST –TO-COAST COMMENTS
ABOUT THE BOOK

A Handbook on Culture Shock is far more than a handbook; it invites us to look much more deeply into the differences we might find with people of other cultures and realize the enormity of their efforts to try to reach us. In so doing we will find many more similarities than differences in what is really important. Father Victor has rendered us a great service in showing us the courage and humility of one who has worked diligently to reach the people to whom he ministers, and he does this with delightful humor and good will.
— HOWARD J. HUBBARD, Bishop of Albany Diocese, New York

A Handbook on Culture Shock denotes appreciation and understanding as the fundamentals to successful acculturation through Father Victor Owan's humorously depicted experiences adapting to upstate New York. As a native of Nigeria, Father Victor's unique perspective on western culture provokes the reader to recognize and question his or her own norms and values, while discovering some familiar facets of an African society. How fortunate we are to be able to look at ourselves through the eyes of Father Victor.
— ELIZABETH O'C. LITTLE, Senator, New York State, 45th District, Chairman Committee on Local Government

Victor Achima Owan

This book contrasting the cultures of Nigeria and Upstate New York is enlightening, fascinating, revealing, and educational. Father Victor writes in an easy to read conversational style, intermingled with humorous incidents from everyday life. The book holds your attention and makes it impossible to put down. It's a real eye-opener for anyone interested in comparing our way of life with that of another culture – in this case – Nigeria.

> – FR. JAMES M. MACKEY, Pastor, St. Mary's Church, Glens Falls, New York

I read the book cover to cover, thoroughly engrossed by this eloquent and comprehensive comparison of life in Nigeria and Upstate New York. In a world that seems to be evolving into one global, mass-marketed identity, it is a refreshing reminder of the uniqueness of our different cultures.

> – KATE HOGAN, Hudson Falls, Warren County District Attorney, New York

It's a great book! The author has a nice writing style: easy to read, extensive and accurate vocabulary. The book is very informative about the Nigerian and the Adirondacks cultures, bringing to focus some dimensions that I hadn't really thought about. It causes you to think about what is usually taken for granted.

> – VERY REV. JOSEPH ANSELMENT, Pastor, Our Lady of the Annunciation, and Dean of Warren County, Albany Diocese, New York

Rev. Victor Owan's compelling handbook about cultural differences is both enlightening and entertaining. It should prove

A HANDBOOK ON CULTURE SHOCK

to be an invaluable guide to his fellow countrymen, as well as to other foreign visitors to the United States. For Americans it affords a candid look at how our mores and manners appear to, and are interpreted by, people from other cultures. As the Scottish poet Robert Burns so aptly put it, "O wad some Power the giftie gie us, To see oursels as ithers se us!" We should thank the Lord who did "gie us the giftie" of Fr. Victor.

– NORMA H. POTVIN, Hudson Falls, New York, Former teacher, long time member of Hudson Falls Central School District Board of Education and many times president

In *A Handbook on Culture Shock,* Father Victor gives us a crash course in meeting the everyday challenges of assimilating into a foreign culture by emphasizing similarities over differences. Using his own personal experiences in the global emigration from Nigeria to Upstate New York, Father Victor articulates ways to reach out and forge bonds of friendship and goodwill across the divide of sensitive cultural differences. Drawing on his own humor and tremendous courage, Father Victor succeeded in creating a thoughtful, practical and above all most enjoyable read.

– THERESA C. MERCURE, Hudson Falls, New York

A Handbook on Culture Shock takes the reader on a grand tour of "Nigerian" and "American" cultures with provocative critical sharpness. It is truly a puzzling revelation that hides in it a great so many truths. But how many Nigerians would read it, because a great man once said: "The best way to hide something from black people is to put it in a book." What an irony!

– *THE MESSAGE,* Ogoja Diocesan Newspaper, Nigeria

VICTOR ACHIMA OWAN

Our world today needs more books like <u>A Handbook on Culture Shock.</u> Father Victor's book comfortably belongs on the shelves of public and university libraries, in the book bags of every student of cultural studies, and on every living room coffee table.

— LEO F. COTE, Hudson Falls, New York

A Handbook on Culture Shock carefully written from the standpoint of a Roman Catholic Priest, blends cultural and religious teachings with practical realities in cross-cultural comparative experiences between the author's home site in Nigeria and his newfound home in Upstate New York. There is a cross-cultural lesson for everyone in this book. Students, educators, and other professionals will find this book to be a valuable addition to their library and others will certainly learn a lot from the nuances so explicitly covered that are, for the most part, usually taken for granted in intra and cross-cultural activities. It is an eye-opener in so many ways. I seriously recommend it to all.

— DR. CHIKE NNABUGWU, New York State Educational Department, Albany, New York

This well thought-out presentation is capable of holding spellbound and thrilling a wide-ranging audience. It is a thoughtful material best for popular reading and goes beyond this to a more challenging and profound academic research on experiential cultural anthropology.

— CIE NOLIN, Hudson Falls, New York

A Handbook on Culture Shock is an informative and revealing masterpiece on the disposition, malleability and docility needed to properly plunge into and have a healthy cultural romance

A Handbook on Culture Shock

with a culture other than one's own.
— MARTHA D. BROCK, Hudson Falls, New York

This book can adequately suffice to lay a foundation for a curriculum on a holistic acculturation program or course.
— MARY BETH LASHWAY, Hudson Falls, New York

It is culturally challenging and enriching. Each chapter is presented in a way that is descriptive, intriguing, and grounded in everyday life experience.
— FR. SIMON UDEMGBA, Schenectady, New York

This book is an educating and enlightening adventure. It x-rays the inevitable hurdles, crucibles, and related challenges in their wholesome totality within the context of acclimatization and appreciation of one's native and newfound cultures and its people.
— FR. DOMINIC OKAFOR, Lecturer and Spiritual Director, St. Joseph Major Seminary, Ikot Ekpene, Nigeria

This is a classic presentation that is politely and humorously articulated, evoking and provoking thoughts and calling to question some cultural values, practices, and daily realities of life.
— DIANA D. COTE, Hudson Falls, New York

This is a daring attempt to call a spade a spade, by an honest inquirer and a reflective and curious researcher, in the face of challenging cultural differences from an experiential and comparative perspective while remaining authentic, positive and true to one's own native culture.
— FR. ELLIS KEKONG, Lecturer, St. Joseph Major

VICTOR ACHIMA OWAN

Seminary, Ikot Ekpene, Nigeria

A Handbook on Culture Shock is capable of turning mentalities upside down, upsetting preconceived notions, rewriting old headlines on global cultural perceptions, changing social ideals, and positively affecting both personal or individual and collective ideological egos on far-reaching realm of religious cum socio-cultural thoughts.

– DR. RANSOME EGIM OWAN, Washingto Gas Energy Services. Director, Regulatory & External Affairs, Virginia

In this book, the author has set the ball rolling on seminars and symposia on "The Way Forward," focusing on some disturbing and topical issues of the day viewed in the spectrum of globalization.

– DR. ANTHONY A. OWAN ENOH, Senior Lecturer, University of Jos, Nigeria

This book is a masterpiece, written with a simple, lucid, easy, and contextual flow of language that makes it readable and within the reach of both the academia and the plebeians.

– REP. JOHN ENOH OWAN ENOH, House of Representatives, Nigeria

The cross-cultural comparative ideas highlighted in this book enjoy a touch of originality, newness and awesomeness. They are backed up by a wealth of personal experiences with minimal references to already existing similar documents. Overall, this book is highly and boundlessly recommended to all peoples regardless of one's cultural background.

– DR. EMMANUEL ENU ATTAH, National Population Commission, Nigeria

A HANDBOOK ON CULTURE SHOCK

This work is fascinating, practical, and existential. The author has a unique gift for focusing in on what people are thinking, saying, and doing today. He uses extensive examples from current news stories, events, and developments to buttress his well marshaled out and beautifully articulated points.

    – PROF. EBUTA EKURE, Benedict College, Columbia,
South Carolina

A Handbook on Culture Shock is a conglomerate and a synthetic compendium of experience that arms one for a cultural adventure into a world that has become a global village. It is a must-read book for all who seek to cross cultural lines, especially for missioners and missionaries whether as clergymen, religious, or laypeople.

    – VERY REV. DR. PATRICK O. IDIKU, Administrator,
Catholic Diocese of Ogoja, Nigeria

This reflection is a "wake-up call" to some cultural and sensitive issues that are often taken for granted. It is so mesmerizing and true that it echoes not only in the mind, but also in the heart long after it has had its final say. Read it to spotlight some cultural blind spots.

    – REV. SR. BIBIANA A. IKWUN, Secretary General,
Congregation of the Handmaids of the Holy Child Jesus
(HHCJ), Generalate, Nigeria

In this book, the author has opened a Pandora's box on topical cultural and social issues with their related questions. In his well-articulated and systematic thought, he has indeed made a treasured contribution on socio- cultural literature, which addresses burning issues of the day, devoid of any academic

VICTOR ACHIMA OWAN

isolation or exclusiveness.

– PETER OKONGOR, Principal, Government Secondary
School, Ikom, Nigeria

It is hard to imagine a more painstaking, a careful and immensely constructive analysis and experiential contribution to the realism of cultural anthropology.

– CHRIS EKURISONG, (KSJ), Principal, Comprehensive
Secondary School, Bateriku, Boki, Nigeria

ABOUT THE AUTHOR

Victor Achima Owan, a native of Agbokim Water Falls in Etung Local Government Area of Cross River State, Nigeria, is a Catholic priest of Ogoja Diocese. He was ordained a priest on October 13, 1996. He holds a bachelors degree in both Philosophy and Theology from St. Joseph Major Seminary, Ikot Ekpene, Akwa Ibom State, Nigeria, an affiliate of Pontifical Urban University, Rome.

At present, he is the Associate Pastor of St. Mary's/ St. Paul's Church, Hudson Falls, Albany Diocese, New York.

CONTENTS

DEDICATION

This book is passionately dedicated to the lot of the African suffering poorest of the poor living in and amidst the squalor of rural areas. These are the people who, through no fault of their own, are condemned to the scourge of suffocating poverty, the blight of sickness and disease, the darkness of ignorance and illiteracy, the woes of immorality, unwanted and unprepared for pregnancies and the yoke of insecurity, unbridled structural corruption, and gross insensitivity to justice, equity, and related violation of human rights. For centuries, they have lain bound and bleeding at the foot of civilized and Christianized humanity, imploring compassion in vain.

These suffering poor are the innocent victims in whose name international communities give relief services, mission appeals are exaggeratedly made and for whose heartbreaking intentions the donors donate generously, but whose perennial life conditions and situations ironically and abysmally remain the same or even get worse with each passing day. But amazingly, in their excruciating poverty, they have made many millionaires of our society in this world.

Why? Because their cries fall on deaf ears, but more so because they are the *used* and the *remembered-forgotten* of our deformed society due to greedy and ravenous wolves who come in sheep clothing and in their exploitation, not only collect and feed on what belongs to the poorest but also feed on them as well.

Victor Achima Owan

"For, while politicians content, and men are swerved this way and that by conflicting interest and passion, the great cause of human liberty is in the hands of One, of whom is it said:-

"He shall not fail nor be discouraged
Till he have set judgment in the earth."

"He shall deliver the needy when he crieth,
The poor, and him that hath no helper."

"He shall redeem their soul from deceit and violence,
And precious shall their blood be in his sight."1

So, help us, God!

NOTES

[1] Stowe, Harriet Beecher. *Uncle Tom's Cabin.* Boston and New York: Houghton Mifflin Company, 1852, v.

FOREWORD

How often have we heard people say, "We have a new priest in our parish, and we don't understand a word he says! He seems like such a fine person, but we don't know what he is asking us." Congratulations to Father Victor Achima Owan for sharing with us what he has learned from his years of experience in Hudson Falls, New York. We can begin to realize more fully what would happen if we were to go to Nigeria and try to function there, not knowing what the differences were in customs as well as in language. Father Victor has rendered us a great service in showing us the courage and humility of one who has worked diligently to reach the people to whom he ministers, and he does this with delightful humor and good will.

A Handbook on Culture Shock is far more than a handbook; it invites us to look much more deeply into the differences we might find with people of other cultures and realize the enormity of their efforts to try to reach us. In so doing, we will find many more similarities than differences in what is really important.

Thank you, Father Victor, for showing us the way.

Howard J. Hubbard
Bishop of Albany Diocese, NY
December 1, 2004

PREFACE

The Ejaghem or Etung people and the Adirondack people, the former, semiprimitive, agricultural inhabitants of the semi-tropical African Savanna, and the Adirondack people, modern, multidimensional Americans in upstate New York — one could hardly imagine, much less critically compare, two so different cultures. What are the chances that the two would come into contact? Yet, they did. Father Victor Achima Owan arrived in Hudson Falls, New York on June 22, 2003. Thus began the contact and, at times, the clash of the Ejaghem or Etung and the Adirondack cultures. That is the birth date of *A Handbook on Culture Shock.*

Father Victor's book, in some respects, does not attempt the traditional textbook treatment of cross-cultural analysis. Yet, in many respects, it goes beyond such an academic approach. It is not and was not intended to be an all-encompassing comparison study of the two cultures. Father Victor does not delve into such socio-cultural topics as family structure or historical background. He presents only those parts of the two cultures with which he has had personal contact and which have presented, for him personally, the greatest challenges. Instead of a panoramic portrait of the two cultures, Father Victor presents verbal snapshots of his experiences.

The author goes to great length to present a balanced view of both his native and his newfound cultures. Father Victor's style is a combination of expository explanations of various cultural phenomena such as communication, marriage, etiquette, equality, to mention but a few, combined with a narrative illustration of his cross-cultural experiences. Shadows of African (Nigerian-Etung) oral tradition comfortably occupy the same pages with detailed scholarly analysis.

A Handbook on Culture Shock is sure to please many literary tastes. For those seeking the theoretical, the chapters on The Institution of Marriage, Death, and Funerals, Economy, and the Fruits of Acculturation Workshop will be memorable. Readers seeking a lighter vein will surely enjoy the sections on Handshakes, Forced-Feeding, Etiquette, and Static Electricity among others.

Like a scientist, Father Victor uses the literary microscope to examine the minutiae of everyday life in his two cultures, building as he does an evermore lucid, comparative picture.

A Handbook on Culture Shock is not a travelogue, not a diary, and not a how-to book on successful acculturation. Father Victor's intent is simply to shed some light — the light of knowledge. It is his wish that through better understanding of each other that the people of the world, not just the Ejaghem or Etung and the Adirondack, might achieve greater acceptance, tolerance, and indeed, love. Somehow, by highlighting our *differences,* we arrive at the inevitable conclusion that at our most basic and fundamental level we are all very much *alike.* To put it into terms with which Father Victor would most assuredly agree, we are all children of God.

Our world today needs more books like *A Handbook on Culture Shock.* Father Victor's book comfortably belongs on the shelves of public and university libraries, in the book bags of every student of cultural studies, and on every living room

A Handbook on Culture Shock

coffee table.

Leo F. Cote
Hudson Falls, New York
May 25, 2004

ACKNOWLEDGMENTS

Since no man or woman is an island, no one succeeds alone, and no one has it all or knows it all. At the end of an exercise of this sort, I am gratefully indebted to so many people. These are the people who at one time or another, especially in the course of writing this book, were instrumental to the courage and zeal I had to bring forth this brainchild.

First, I am grateful to God, in whom I live, move, and have my being. He remains my unfailing counselor and faithful provider in season and out of season, in spite of me. He directs my thoughts and gives me a positive approach to life in the midst of its uncertainties and vicissitudes. To Him I say: *Take the glory!*

Regardful of my spiritual leader and benefactor, I humbly salute with unbounded sentiments of respect, His Grace, Most Rev. Joseph Edra Ukpo, Archbishop of Calabar Ecclesiastical Province. For your unselfish love, indubitable attitude of justice, and your continuous fatherly concern, I remain eternally yours with an immeasurable sense of gratitude. More particularly, for dreaming the dream and initiating the process that brought me to the United States to begin the experience of another culture, I remain forever indebted to you and I pledge my unalloyed obedience. Thanks immensely!

I salute sincerely Bishop Howard J. Hubbard, Bishop of the Albany Diocese, New York. For your thrilling intelligence and attested simplicity, I admire you. Furthermore, for your ac-

Victor Achima Owan

commodation and pastoral paternity to all, in which I am a visible beneficiary, I give you my unwavering and unalloyed regard. For accepting to write the foreword to this book in spite of your visibly crowded schedule, I count myself privileged to have you contribute in this and other ways to navigating the course of my life journey. Along this chain of command that saw to the beginning of my U.S. adventure, I thank Fr. L. Edward Deimeke, Paula Read, and Fr. Peter Obele Abue for being instrumental to the opportunity of missioning in the Albany Diocese. At different points, each of you was such a formidable and dependable force toward the unique realization of my U.S. dream. Thanks for being there when I needed you most.

Very Rev. James Barry Lonergan, former Dean of Washington County and Pastor of St. Mary's/St. Paul's Church, Hudson Falls, New York, deserves a bunch of thanks and a bucket of gratitude for being such a wonderful person to me. To begin my pastoral experience in the United States with you and under your guidance was one of the best things that ever happened to me in my life. Your fatherly concern and your encyclopedic knowledge, which helped in reshaping my world view, positively conspired to nurse, nourish, and boost the writing of this book. You are indeed a rare gem. I never could be what I am today without you. My thanks to you are eternal. Fr. Joseph Dworak who is the incumbent pastor of St. Mary's/St. Paul's church cannot be left out in this expression of gratitude. Your timely appointment as the pastor was highly providential. Thanks for your transparent friendship and for your moral support, which gave me the final push to go to the press.

To Fr. James Mackey, I appreciate very profoundly the love

A HANDBOOK ON CULTURE SHOCK

and friendship you shared with me. Your encouragement and advice were tremendously helpful. Thanks for being there.

I must offer a special word of thanks to those special people who, at different times in the course of this work, painstakingly edited this book by reading, punctuating, offering useful suggestions, and contextualizing the ideas in this text. They are all my capable editors professionally and otherwise. For their concern and love for me, within a short period of time, they read the manuscript, corrected my grammar and expressions, suggested substantial overhaul of some sections, offered valuable input, and tracked my wavering thoughts with tutorials, which climaxed in the total improvement of this endeavor. Some of the people are Jeanie Orlandi, Cie Nolin, Mary Renaud, Mary Horrigan, Roger Hogan, Nick Phillips, Martha, Lee, & Norma Potvin, Dr. & Mrs. Chike Nnabugwu, Fr. Simon Udemgba, and Leo & Diana Cote. Leo Cote also wrote the Preface to this book. To all of you, for taking time to meticulously read and sight the blind spots of this reflection, I will always be deeply appreciative of your love, friendship, time, and sacrifice. In addition, all those who appended their authority in writing the comments for this book, such as Elizabeth O' C Little (Senator), Fr. Joseph Anselment, Kate Hogan (Attorney), Theresa C. Mercure and others, you remain so dear to me as long as I live for the additional flavor and boost you have given to this work. May God bless and reward you as we look forward to the days ahead and continue to make progress in the service of God through God's people.

Bonnie Hazelton, Tony Catone and Roger Hogan deserve a bucket of thanks for opening your doors to me always to listen to me and help in designing the cover page of this book. Your

VICTOR ACHIMA OWAN

friendship indebts me to you.

I wholeheartedly thank Sr. Therese McDonough, MMM, the facilitator of the Cross Cultural Services (CCS) at Maryknoll, New York, for allowing me to complement my illustrations in sharing the fruits of the acculturation workshop I attended under her superb supervision in the area of its **general goal** and **objectives.** I also thank Sue Philion for the trips we made to Crandall Library, Glens Falls, New York, in search for *The Post-Star* references, which helped in forming most of the References and End Notes cited at the end of each chapter of this book. To both you and Alicia Altizio, the offering of the knowledge of your computer-know-how and the sacrifice of your time in spite of your very busy schedule leave me with memories of gratitude.

I would like to thank Joan, "Nyen" Nannette, Maggie, Oliver and Jackie, Joyce Clarence, Mary Jane, Jeanne, Robert & Elizabeth, Tony & Mary, Tony & Margaret, Edward, Skip & Barbara, Pat, Kay, Dan & Peggy, Rod & Helen, Tom, and the whole Hogan and Monahan clans, represented by Roger & Margaret, "Mother" Marie & Richard, respectively, to mention but a few, for your moral and spiritual support, for your encouragement, and for always being there. I would like to thank the pastoral team — Dorothy, Margaret, Sandy, Dorothy, Patty, Shirley, Ray and Sal. To all, I salute you for providing the conducive and working environment that encouraged my reflection and boosted my appetite for the writing of this book.

Furthermore, I thank all my brothers and friends of the presbyterate of my home diocese of Ogoja. Thank you Frs. Ellis Kekong, Victor Ntui, Boniface A. Ewah, Christopher Naseri

A HANDBOOK ON CULTURE SHOCK

(Attack) Stephen Dedua (Ziga - Bobo) and others, for your inspiring and genuine friendship. To you all I say: Thanks for becoming priests in this most challenging time and age. Our friendship and priestly solidarity remains a solid bond that is irreplaceable and will carry us onward. Let us continue to encourage one another.

So, help all, God!

Finally, I thank also my beloved family, that amorphous clan of siblings, nieces, nephews, cousins, aunties, and uncles who rejoice in my small virtues, smile at my many faults, excuses my excesses, and put up with my inevitable absence and seasons of painful neglect when ministry calls me away from them.

INTRODUCTION

When things are important you put them in writing. Whether it's your birthday, day of graduation, first date, wedding day, day of ordination or religious profession, obtaining your driver's license, and lots more. It is always good to have something in writing to document the experience and remind you of your benefits and responsibilities. Besides, I believe that it is our responsibility to make sure that we preserve and document our history to inform, encourage and empower future generations.

It was precisely on January 27, 2004, that I began to organize my thoughts in gathering information for the writing of this book. This vision was to be galvanized by the periodic and frequent remarks from some of my friends and acquaintances on the need to have a journal of my cross-cultural experiences. Such remarks set a fire in me, and I began to experience a war within myself to live up to this challenge, even though I was convinced that I was not a prolific writer.

As I meditated on this challenge, I felt an obligation to share my cross-cultural experiences with others. It was my conviction that making a documentary contribution and sharing my experiences with my American friends and parishioners as well as my Nigerian people would inform and expand their knowledge of other cultures with all the variations.

This information, by my estimation, would widen the cultural horizon of my audience, enabling them live beyond the walls of their world. Advantageously, I foresaw this project as helping to retain the memories of my cross-cultural experiences, while creating and increasing awareness for others about the existence of other cultures. The result is that this would either increase the appreciation of one's native culture or challenge the need to better it.

The choosing of the title of this book, *A Handbook on Culture Shock,* came so naturally because, within the given time, it formed a major expression in my active vocabulary. No doubt, this expression, "culture shock," enjoys a primary place in daily communication that centers on cultural differences. The words that form this expression and the expression itself are very familiar to people and so are commonly used, sometimes within context and at other times out of context. The surprising thing is that, in spite of the daily use of this expression, it is relatively difficult to come across a handy definition that would tell you at a glance what it is all about. Probably because of its familiarity and wide usage, there is the fear of daring a definition that may attract the critical attention of scholars. I would not be so deterred by this timid way of thinking as not to attempt a partial definition and expound on it. I stand to be corrected and objectively criticized.

According to the *Webster's II New College Dictionary,* "culture shock is a condition of anxiety or confusion that can affect an individual suddenly exposed to an alien culture or milieu." The expansion of this definition can be elastically extensive. Consequently, it can be said that culture shock is a whole world of difference in the way of life of the people you meet in a new environment within a given time, in relation to that with which you are familiar. It is the entire gamut and the

A Handbook on Culture Shock

embodiment of the new experience in a cultural setting other than yours. This cuts across people's language, political and social organizations, beliefs and religion, literature and art, and laws and customs founded on tradition or occasioned by life's changing situations. These cultural contents also include all the material things that the people produce and use and their means of obtaining food and raw materials.

These differences could be very opposed and contrary to or slightly different from what you already know and are used to thinking, hearing, talking about, and doing. In short, the experience therein could be overwhelmingly fascinating, terribly disappointing, completely strange, entirely new, and utterly unfamiliar. It touches every aspect of life as conditioned by the circumstances and situation of your new environment. The climate and weather conditions, the effects of development and underdevelopment, the results of rural-urban drift or urbanization, the availability of resources and amenities, and the whole life milieu must come into play under this consideration, and in relation to your reactions to their attendant experiences.

Summarily, it can be said that your reactions to a new culture in terms of an encounter with strange ideas that pose some discomforts and relative inconveniences or provide overwhelming comforts and conveniences fall under the umbrella and are all within the perimeter of culture shock. Given this understanding, it becomes imperative that culture shock is an unavoidable experience and an inescapable reality for all who seek to enter into a culture other than theirs, since no two cultures in the world are exactly the same. This experience is a *conditio sine qua non* for proper and balanced acculturation.

Against this backdrop, the need to examine some areas of

culture shock becomes not only informatively relevant, but also logically and experientially imperative. My approach is far from being critical or judgmental. It is rather narrative and comparatively contrasting. However, I do not lose sight of the fact that in every comparative analysis that there is the temptation to sound judgmental, knowingly or unknowingly. But this is not my intention, and it is not the message that this book intends to convey to its respective audience.

In this presentation, when you hear or read the expressions, "my home culture," "my first culture," or "my native culture," which are used interchangeably, they do not refer to the entire culture of the Nigerian people. More specifically, they refer to the culture of the Ejaghem or Etung people who live in the Cross River State of Nigeria. Therefore, for a better appreciation of this presentation, the syllogism should be through the process of elimination, tailoring it down from the general (Nigeria)to the particular or specific (Etung) on some cultural aspects. To this end, the Etung people and their culture are more in perspective. However, true as this may be, the searchlight also flashes on and lights up some other blind spots and areas affecting the Nigerian nation as a whole. These areas would be recognized as you dare to make an adventure into my world in sharing this personal reflection on my comparative experience.

On the other hand, you would also notice expressions such as "my newfound culture," "my second culture," or "my foreign culture," which are also used interchangeably. These expressions do not refer to the entire culture of the American people, which would be highly impossible to do. This impossibility is evident in the fact that the United States is a country

A Handbook on Culture Shock

that enjoys a diversity of people of different cultures and racial backgrounds. In fact, it may be safe and proper to say that it is the melting pot of many cultures. The fact of this melting pot is brought about by a conglomerate of people from diverse and different countries and nations of the world. Hence, strictly speaking, it is difficult or highly impossible to talk about *pure Americans* unless by this you mean the pre-Columbian Indians who first inhabited this New World. At a more comfortable and safer perspective therefore, you can talk only about Anglo-Americans, Franco-Americans, Italian Americans, Irish Americans, German Americans, African-Americans, Hispanic Americans, Asian-Americans, and others. America then is, indeed and in reality, a historical New World inhabited by people of diverse origins with different cultural backgrounds. Hence, a discourse on a purely American culture may pose some problems.

To this end, this cultural reality with all its complexity increases the difficulty and somehow confirms the impossibility of drawing a cultural line that comfortably cuts across all Americans in all the fifty states of the nation. To attempt to draw such a line would obscure the glaring diversity and differences which exist among the people. These differences are buttressed racially, accentually, behaviorally, and even what I may say "climatically." More specifically, my focus in referring to my newfound culture will be on the cultural structures in upstate New York among the Adirondack people as a case in point.

1

COMMUNICATION

LANGUAGE

Language is an essential tool for effective communication. The essence of communication is the intelligibility to speak in such a way as to be understood and to understand. More often than not, this is a major source of frustration in a new culture. This does not only simply involve trying to cope with communicating in a foreign language, but it also involves getting used to the communication techniques, which convey deeper information from one person to another. Thus, the tone of voice, facial expression, body language, handshakes, winking of the eye, and eye contact are all tools for communication.

As a Nigerian, the English language is my lingua franca. Since Nigeria was colonized by the British until she got her independence on 1st October 1960, this lingua franca therefore is not a surprise. Thus, with the existence of very many dialects spoken by the different tribes, the English language is used as a medium of communication among the Nigerian people. This could be the pidgin or broken English that is commonly spoken and understood by a great majority of the people. It could also be the standard British or Queen's English that is taught in schools and used in formal education.

The U.S. culture is linguistically diverse in terms of communication. Though Americans speak English, there are subtle differences in the accent and vowel emphasis on certain words as you travel around the country. These nuances can be detected by typical Americans and identify the speaker's regional origin. Thus, some people speak very fast, others speak slowly, still others seem to swallow some syllables, and others have a heavy accent. Some speak another version of English called Ebonics (hip-hop), which I experienced for the first time spoken by the African-Americans in New York City. Some Ebonics "expressions" used in their daily communication are: "S'up?" which means: "What's up? Or "S'up ma nigga?" which means: "What's up my friend?" Ebonics is mostly expressed in the lyrics of their rap music.

Since I was based in upstate New York, I did not experience a language barrier per se. Instead, my accent and gestures, which besides giving me away easily when talking, impaired my efforts to communicate satisfactorily. What follows is an attempt to share my experiences in this regard.

ACCENT

As I have mentioned previously, the lingua franca in my native culture is the standard English, which is sometimes called the British or Queen's English that when combined with my native dialect, gives me a relatively heavy accent. In addition, the placing of emphasis on some syllables is very much different from the English spoken by the Adirondack people. You can imagine how frustrating it was when I first arrived, since

A HANDBOOK ON CULTURE SHOCK

the essence of communication was seemingly being defeated. This was more depressing since I must minister and preach the word of God to my eager congregation. Besides, I naturally speak relatively quickly. This also did not help matters because it added to my frustration in attempts to effectively communicate.

It was against this backdrop, plus other laudable reasons, that a request was made by some parishioners to have my Sunday homilies printed out and kept at strategic places in the church. The copies of these homilies were to be picked up by parishioners, who so desired, so that they could read and better understand what I was saying. In addition, these homilies were to be carefully edited by the pastor in order to put properly within context some of my grammatical, idiomatic, and proverbial expressions. This was a big help to me since it opened my eyes to a deeper understanding and appreciation of some contextual expressions. For instance, let us look at some examples of expressions that mean the same thing, but used in the Nigerian (Etung) and American (Adirondacks) contexts, respectively. First: "There are many ways to kill a rat." And: "There are many ways to skin a cat." The expressions mean that, there are many ways of doing one and the same thing that will have the same effect and give equal result. Second: "You lie like a rock." And: "You lie like a rug." These two also mean to say that someone tells lies so well, as to be described as solid like a rock or as smooth like a rug. The next two I want to talk about, I know not of similar expressions of them in my native culture, but they are contextually used in my foreign culture, they are, third: "Don't have a bird." This simply means to tell someone to calm down and not to get all upset because of what you might have said to him or her, given the situation of when you said a particular thing. In other words, the person should not take it the wrong way, because that was not what you meant. Fourth: "Don't shoot the messenger." This simply means that, if you are uncomfortable with a particular message given to you by someone who is sent to do so, you should not lay the blame on nor be angry or mad at the one who gives you the message, an instruction, a directive or an information. Thus, the one who gives you the message is only carrying out an "order" as instructed by a higher authority. Fifth: To have your ears lowered" means to have a haircut. There are many more of such contextual expressions.

The next advantage of the editing of my homilies is that, it also saved me from some public speaking embarrassments. For instance, expressions such as: "Tongues would wag." And: "The shit would hit the fan," may mean almost the same thing. The expressions: "I was annoyed." And: "I was pissed off," may also mean the same thing. They must, however, be used within an acceptable and comfortable context. Thus, in the morality and decency of public speaking, the two interchangeable expressions give the first in each of the two similarities as decent, whereas the second is considered vulgar language in polite society. Even the simple expression: "Consider the source," may be offensive to someone, depending on when it is used.

Aside from context talking in communication, as time went by, I came to discover that public speaking requires a relatively slow speed in order to be understood by a greater majority of the people. Even in speaking slowly, it was initially necessary that I spoke my Nigerian English. This was because I discov-

A HANDBOOK ON CULTURE SHOCK

ered that the more I tried to imitate the way English is spoken by the people of my foreign culture, the more I ended up worsening matters and mixing up both my audience and myself. Therefore, in order to gradually improve my English to suit the cultural expectation of my new cultural environment, I did more listening than talking. I listened more often to news on television and to people in ordinary everyday formal and informal conversations. What a great help this was to me! With the unfolding realities of everyday life, it became abundantly clear to me that, every time I listened to people talk, I picked up new things everyday. These new things were either new contextual expression or some colloquialisms such as: "Don't push it!" "Take it easy!" Pencil me in!" "Consider it done!" "Stay out of trouble!" "For the most part." "First things first." "One step at a time." One thing at a time." Yes, you never can know it all.

It is important to note also that in the idea of speaking slowly, do not expect the people of your host culture to do the same. Some of them could speak very fast when they are talking to you. Hence, as a newcomer, do not say: Yes! Or: No! when you do not understand anything that is said to you. Otherwise, you may commit yourself without knowing it. It is better to be foolish than to claim to be wise only to realize later that you were foolish. In this case,(of saying yes! or no! without understanding the implication), you make yourself a fool, who could be described by many as: "One who does not know, and does not know that he does not know, but claims to know that he knows while he remains without knowing." Your ability to politely tell the other person that you did not understand what he or she said or meant, should be a humbling experience for you, which before long will make you wise in the ways of your foreign culture.

On this note, I am reminded of my frame of mind when I first arrived in the United States. Having come to the U.S. where I thought that since all Americans speak English, so to speak, I must always do some research when preparing my homily by looking for and using high sounding words and possibly jaw-breaking vocabularies in order to impress my Church congregation. Before long, the pastor, in censuring my homilies and in his characteristic honesty, drew my attention to the fact that, I should cut down on my vocabularies and make my presentation simple by using more common, simple and familiar words. In fact, he went further to tell me that not all the members of our congregation went to school as much as we priests did. Even if they did go to school, not all of them studied philosophy and theology like us. I must say that, initially I was seemingly scandalized and taken aback at this honest information. Guided by this learning experience, before long, I came to know and confirm that Americans, including the most educated, extend their simplicity and humility even to the way they speak in their choice of words, which are for the most part, simple, familiar, accommodating, friendly, and common-place, which enjoy a more general understanding.

In very few words, permit me to say that, this mentality is different from what happens in my Nigerian culture. Over here, there is always the show-off by the educated in their use of very unfamiliar and high sounding words, (sometimes) even when addressing the uneducated people known to them. An experience of what happens when an educated person is invited to give a talk or present a paper in a symposium to

A Handbook on Culture Shock

some university students or major seminarians, will properly capture the picture I am trying to project. Without faulting the presenter of such a paper, sometimes if he or she does not sound sophisticated, philosophical and highly intellectualistic, such a person speaks below standard and risks falling short of impressing the audience. It is shamefully ridiculous that the presenter receives more cheers and applauses from the audience when they do not understand a particular cacophony he or she uses.

So, for you, the newcomer or foreigner to the American culture who may be planning to research on and increase your vocabularies and cacophonies with all their "isms, and "istics," in order to impress your audience, you have to be careful not to talk above the heads of those who may be listening to you. If you insist on using high sounding and unfamiliar words, you may become a victim of the experience I want to share with you now: The experience is all about a young foreign priest who arrived in a particular parish in the U.S. Even when he was still back in his country, he was well known by his friends as one who likes using very big words in formal and informal conversations. While in the U.S. parish, his parishioners admired him for his wonderful homilies. One day after Mass, as the priest stood in front or at the entrance of the Church building to greet and exchange pleasantries with his parishioners (as it is the custom), an elderly woman came forward and said to him: "Your homilies are very wonderful. It would be good if you could think about publishing them in the form of a book." The young priest was very impressed with these complimentary remarks. He thanked the woman profusely and then said to her: "Yes, I intend that my homilies be published *posthu-*

mously." The woman then responded: "That's very nice and thoughtful of you. Please, let it be quick and if you need help, do not hesitate to ask. I will be more than glad to help you do it fast, okay! This is my telephone number, please!" The young priest stood there with his mouth almost aghast gaping at the woman and wondering if the word, *"posthumously,"* which in this context means *"after the author's death,"* meant a different thing in the U.S. culture. He couldn't wait to get home so as to look up the word again in his dictionary to be doubly sure of its meaning. The punch line of this experience is that, big, high sounding and sophisticated words, besides complicating your communication problem because of your accent, they could sometimes yield unexpected results from those listening to you due to their not knowing their meanings, contextually and otherwise. My advice is this: "Hey 'guys!' the simpler the better!"

No doubt, my Adirondacks neighborhood seems to be exclusively white and with people who seem to talk with the same accent, to this end, I learned that my Nigerian accent easily gave me away. Consequently, in all the telephone calls that I made to people in the neighborhood, as soon as the person I was calling picked up the telephone and heard me say: "Hello!" Such a person, without even bothering to ask me who I was, responded with: "Hi, Father Victor!" This became a concern to me. I decided to ask my church congregation one day why they won't ask me who I am whenever I make a telephone call to some of them and how they easily know I am the one calling, which is not the case with me whenever they call. They answers I got were, for the most part, very diplomatic. Probably, they thought that if they told me that I have a "funny" accent that I would be offended or I might have a bird. Hence, some of them said they have caller ID, others said they are used to my voice having heard me talk in church very often, still others said they just made a guess, and so on. To make the long story short, I was pulling their legs that I had forgotten that I have an accent that gives me away.

Talking about telephone calls in another dimension of my cultural experience, it is a fact that not many people have the patience to listen to someone with a foreign accent. To this end, oftentimes I have to repeat whatever I say several times in order for some people to understand what I was saying. Sometimes, some people can be very impatient. To the newcomer with a different accent to a foreign culture, my advice to you from experience is this: Do not become annoyed, angry, aggressive, or agitated when you make a telephone call and you are made to repeat what you say several times in order to be understood. This is because your foreign neighbors, being so used to hearing a particular accent, might simply be thrown off initially by hearing anything different from that. You also need to be patient with them, even as they should with you, and gradually, in a polite way, run whatever you were saying by them again. On this note also, it is equally important to point out that sometimes you may have the telephone hung up on you by the person you are talking to. When this happens to you, you are either a victim of a transferred aggression or you may directly be the problem because of your strange accent. If it is the latter (strange accent), for security reasons, especially in this time of hyper-terrorist phobia, the telephone may be hung up on you. This can be very disappointing, frustrating, dispiriting and discouraging. If you are not careful, it could spoil or unmake your day. In the event of this, do not give up or become completely discouraged and nervous. Give it another shot. If you experience the same thing, then look for someone with an acceptable accent to help you out by way of having the person make the telephone call for you. This may help. It worked for me. In any case, to all I say, always remember that it takes the effort of two people to communicate effectively.

On this same note regarding my telephone experience, it is important to relate one of my shocking experiences. The benefit of my talking about it here is twofold: First, on a personal note, it would help to heal the wound in my mind, since it is said that problems discussed or shared are problems half solved. Second, it would be of tremendous help to newcomers into the U.S. culture not to make the same mistake or fall into the same agonizing situation. The experience is about telephone bills: I arrived in Hudson Falls, the place of my pastoral placement in the Albany diocese, New York, on June 22, 2003. Because I felt lonely and lonesome initially, I started making telephone calls to Nigeria using the telephone in the rectory. Because I thought the telephone calls were either free or the bill was to be paid by the Church, I was calling my family and friends in Nigeria almost two to three times per day. As you may guess, all these calls were long-winded at both ends, especially at my end, since I wanted to share my daily American experience with my family, friends and loved ones. Little did I know that the bills for long distance telephone calls were at my own expense. Though in fairness to the authority that be, I was given a big briefing book as soon as I arrived in the parish. But I must confess that I did not take time to read it immediately. If I had read it the telephone bill shock that I had

A HANDBOOK ON CULTURE SHOCK

probably will have been avoided.

The telephone bill shock came on July 25, 2003, barely one month after my arrival in Hudson Falls. It was to cost me $542.81. When this bill was given to me, I almost passed out. I was so confused and angry at myself that I even lost my appetite to eat. Besides the huge amount of money involved, you would appreciate my feelings when you come to know that I had no money yet coming to me from my paycheck at the time. There I was already in debt to the amount of $542.81. From this experience, I also came to know that to make a telephone call to Nigeria without using a telephone card costs about $4.20 plus tax for one minute of talk time. I was able to clear the bill after some time though. After this shock, I vowed not to make telephone calls to Nigeria again without using telephone cards.

Based on this experience, my advice to newcomers is that you may not be lucky enough to get an orientation or some tutorials or to have someone see you through your daily cultural adventure in a new culture, not the U.S. culture alone. Sometimes those who are supposed to show you the way may be presumptuous of your knowledge of things or are too busy to have time for you, which if they did would be at their own economic expense. Hence, you may be left alone to either swim or sink. To this end, you may have to navigate your own way along the path of life in your newfound culture. Yes, you may have to be both the drummer and the dancer at the same time.

My telephone bill experience enabled me to help a nun who came to the United States from Nigeria. Having just arrived to work in a business center where she needed to have a telephone, she was provided with both a landline and a cell phone

Communication

by her religious congregation. Since the plan for the cell phone with the telephone company said that from 9:00 p.m. to 7:00 a.m. is free airtime, she tried without success to use the cell phone within the free airtime to call her family members and friends in Nigeria. At the end of the day, she decided to try the same thing with the landline telephone, which unknown to her, could only be used to make free local calls. And of course, to use the landline for long distance calls, was at the expense of the one who uses it (to make such calls), but this was not explained to her by the authority that be. Because she thought that the free airtime also applied to the plan of the landline telephone, she decided to be helping herself accordingly by using the phone to call her dear ones in far away Nigeria. By the time I discovered that she was doing this, she had already incurred a telephone bill of $210.32 within a period of two weeks. I then seized the opportunity to educate her on the use of telephones in making local, long distance, and international calls.

Another advantage from this telephone experience was that, with further and proper information, I was able to use the telephone to my advantage in communicating with my sister in Nigeria. Since the charge for making a telephone call only begins to accrue when the one whom you are calling actually picks up the telephone to receive your call, I used the telephone in the United States as a beeper to my sister (in Nigeria) at no charge. Thus, upon agreement between us, each time she got an international telephone call at exactly 12 midnight Nigeria time, which would be 6:00 p.m. New York time, without picking up her cell phone to answer the call, she knew that I had sent an e-mail to her, which I could do any time and at no

A HANDBOOK ON CULTURE SHOCK

personal cost in the United States. Hence, the next morning she went to any public computer center with e-mail services in Nigeria and picked up the elaborate e-mail from me. In further using this telephone situation to our advantage, during her examination time, she told me to beep her at the same time, (12 midnight Nigeria time), so that she could get up and study in preparation for the examination. I did this throughout the time of the examination and at no cost. Can you imagine somebody in the United States waking up another person in Nigeria to study every day by using the telephone for about one month and at no cost? Yes, it is possible. Probably, this latter discovery and realization, which I used to my maximum advantage, helped in soothing or healing the wounds of the huge telephone bill that I ignorantly incurred and paid for when I first arrived in the United States.

There was also the need to have a good knowledge of the spelling of the words I pronounced or spoke when communicating. This was because, on several occasions, people who had difficulties in understanding some of the words that I pronounced would ask me to spell them. Sometimes, I spelled almost a whole sentence. Wow! No kidding! This was of great help in the sense that it helped me not only to be challenged and become very familiar with how to spell some of my new words, but also saved me from some public embarrassment. Yes! "Amidst the clouds there is a silver lining."

At this point, I remember a situation when I was telling someone that a family went to a place in the U.S. called Utah and gave me their car to use until they came back, since I had no car at the time. This person could not get my pronunciation of the name of the place, Utah. Therefore, he told me to spell it. When I did, he exclaimed with the real pronunciation of the word as: "Yutah" and not: "Uta", as I had pronounced it. Through this, I was able to confidently pronounce the word: "Utah," when I was sharing the experience of the family's kindness to me with my church congregation.

On this issue of names and spelling, perhaps it is common knowledge that different cultures of the world have names of people or things that are pronounced the same way but spelled differently. This fact is more evident in the names of places and especially people. This realization became a daily challenge to me in the U.S. culture. For instance, the following names may have the same pronunciation, but they are spelled differently: Kathleen, Cathleen, and Catelyne; Kathy and Cathey; Carol, Carole, and Karol; Don, Dun, and Dawn; Victor, Victur and Viktor; Jone, Joen, and Joan; Tud and Tudd; Lizzy, Lizzey, and Lizzee; Frank, Franc, and Franck; and thousand of others.

Usually there is the tendency to feel and presume that you are familiar with a particular name by way of its pronunciation and spelling based on the cultural context of your native culture. You may be wrong when you find yourself in another culture. In fact, this presumption is not culturally advisable. It was in light of this awareness that I came to understand why in the United States, for the most part, when someone tells you to write down his or her name, the person begins to spell it immediately for you. It could be something such as: "My name is Mary, M as in mother, A as in apple, R as in road, and Y as in yesterday." When this happens to you, do not be embarrassed. Especially for newcomers, this development could bring about mixed feelings, as if the person is doubting your intellectual ability to spell the name. Whatever your feelings may be, let

A Handbook on Culture Shock

this be a humbling experience because down the road you will come to appreciate its benefits. Among the many benefits, one of them is that, you will not be committing a double sin of mutilating someone's name in pronunciation and also misspelling it. Some people may not take it lying low or kindly (with you) when you misspell their names either when you send them a mail or at some other occasions.

Besides, some things or names are not even spelled as they sound or as they are pronounced. For instance, how do you pronounce the following words: aisle, clothed, etc? So, there is much advantage in asking someone to spell his or her name when the need arises as you step into a different culture. Avoid any presumption due to cultural disparity and other personal uniqueness. It was against this backdrop of personal uniqueness in regard to spelling of names that my next experiences are worth reading and knowing. First, one day, the pastoral associate for administration of the church where I was working in the U.S. called my attention to the fact that the spelling of a particular name on a baptism certificate was not wrong but correct. I think the name is Dian instead of Diana. I simply responded by saying to her: "Thanks for pointing this out to me! But I would not have even known the difference because in this country people spell their names the way they want to spell them." Second, I also remember an experience that was shared by a priest during an acculturation workshop, which I attended within the first few weeks of my arrival in the United States. This priest, Rev. Peter A. Mushi, an African, ministering in a parish in the Bronx, New York, related to the participants at the acculturation workshop his own personal shocking experience. He said that when he, too, first arrived in the U.

COMMUNICATION

S., he wanted to board a taxi or train to Ossining, New York. He told those concerned that he was going to Ossining by pronouncing the word, "Ossining" with emphasis on the letters "O" and the first "i." It was so difficult for those he was talking to, to understand what he was talking about, until he was made to spell it. According to him, when he did spell it, they people exclaimed and pronounced it in such a way that it sounded like: "Assning." Rev. Peter said, he couldn't understand why they should spell a word one way and pronounce it a different way.

While Rev. Peter was sharing his own experience, little did he know that, his experience reminded me of a similar one that I had, too. To cut the long story short, my experience was on the pronunciation of the word, "Albany." It was only later that I came to know that its correct pronunciation, at least in the context of the Adirondack people is something that sounds like, "Olbny." When I shared my experience with some friends on the wrong pronunciation of the word "Albany" by me at Washington Dulles International Airport, some of them said that perhaps, that was why I ended up sleeping at the said airport. Yes, my first night in America was spent at Washington Dulles International Airport in an unbearable cold and all the hazards that go with making a night very long an uncomfortable. I will never forget it! According to some of my friends, since I did not know the correct pronunciation of the word, "Albany," as at then, perhaps it was also difficult for me to understand it when they were announcing the boarding time and the eventual plane departure for Albany, New York. Even the next morning, before I flew to Albany, I was even made to spell the word, "Albany," before the people understood what I was talking about. In fact, at some point during my long night, I was asking myself whether I missed my connecting flight because I did not understand the word, "Albany," when it was announced at the boarding time. I only became convinced that I actually missed the flight in question, when on the morrow I flew together with some people who equally missed the same flight to Albany the previous day. I also recognized some of them as being in the same plane with me the previous day while flying from John F. Kennedy's Airport (acronym JFK), New York, to Washington Dulles International Airport. So I can proudly state that it was not because of the wrong pronunciation of the word, "Albany," or my inability to understand it when it was announced at the boarding time, that made me to sleep at the said airport.

On a further personal development, each time I had a funeral Mass or service to preside over, I usually asked for and received a lesson from those concerned on the correct pronunciation of certain names and words, which I would need or have to say when giving my homily. However, every now and then, either I would forget the way I was told to pronounce them or I would find great difficulties with the correct pronunciations that are acceptable and known by the people. I remember an experience where I went to a funeral home for a service. The deceased person was said to have grown the best lettuce in town and Italian dandelion. Since I found it really difficult to pronounce the word, "dandelion" in the way that it would be generally understood by my audience, before giving my homily I drew their attention to the difficulty I had in pronouncing the word in question. Because I feared mutilating it or biting my tongue in trying to pronounce it, I begged them to allow me to call it "Italian wheat." So, in the course of giving my homily when I got to where I was supposed to say "Italian dandelion", I said: "Italian wheat." The laughter from the audience was irresistibly contagious. Probably some of them must have heard "Italian weed" instead of "Italian wheat." In any case, the preparatory comments by me before the homily on the subject matter helped them to know and understand what I was talking about and meant by "Italian wheat."

Talk about a culture that likes short cuts. My American culture is a clear and perfect example. These short cuts are often reflected in the names of people. These names suffer so much abbreviations, which, too, are according to the uniqueness of those who bear or have the names. Look at the following few examples: Patricia is Patty; Patrick is Pat; Suzan is Sue; Catherine is Cathy; Richard is Dick; Joseph is Joe; Pamela is Pam; Cecilia is Cie; Chelsea is Chel; Michael is Mike; the list can go on. In fact, it is as if every name has its own abbreviation.

It is often said that "one man's meat is another man's poison" or "one man's trash is another man's treasure." These sayings in the context of accent under consideration can better be appreciated by the fact that, in the same foreign culture, while some people are uncomfortable with a funny or foreign accent, others are in love with it. This could be so much so that a foreign accent can become an attraction for people in a given cultural setting. (Oops! I almost forgot a better expression that can perfectly describe this attraction). Yes, one with a foreign accent could become like what the Adirondacks call: "The Pied Piper." This description is used to describe or to refer to someone who attracts people wherever he or she goes to. (There is story behind the Pied Piper, but let me spare

A HANDBOOK ON CULTURE SHOCK

you the trouble. You must not know everything. After all this book is not meant to be an encyclopedia of the two cultures in view). Now, such people who are attracted to a foreign accent would always look forward to hearing someone with this accent speak or talk. This realization or discovery is not just a philosophy from the blue, it is the brainchild of an experience that I had in the United States in the neighborhood of the Adirondacks.

It happened one day when I went into a certain restaurant with a family that invited me out for dinner. It was a Saturday evening. There were these two men who were talking about going to church the next day on Sunday. Of course, they did not know that I had come into the restaurant at the time. In the course of their conversation about going to church, one of them said: "I like going to the Church of St. Mary's/St. Paul's in Hudson Falls, because I like to listen to that guy with a funny accent. Besides the fact that I like the guy, I like his accent, too. Going to his Masses affords me the opportunity to hear someone else from a different culture speak the same English Language in a different way. In addition, it challenges me to pay more attention to the homily." On my own part, though I did not say a word to these men, I heard all that they were saying, and I couldn't wait to share the experience in church with my congregation.

When I eventually did share the experience, I concluded by saying: "Thank God, some people at least have a reason for going to church." From then on, I tried to keep my accent as much as possible so that I don't lose this man and others like him who may be going to the particular church because of my accent as an additional reason. At the same time however, I also kept trying to make myself understood in an accent that is close to that of my foreign culture. It wasn't an easy task. Based on this experience, it is my advice to newcomers to a foreign culture not to try to lose their native accent completely. Besides the fact that it may constitute a gravitational force that will make some people gravitate to you, someone may simply be falling in love with it. Again, always remember that you would have to go back to your native culture at one time or another and will need to speak in an accent that your people would understand.

By the way, it is difficult if not impossible for newcomers to the U.S. culture to completely lose their native accents and begin to talk exactly like the native born Americans or speak the standard American English. For them to be able to do this, they must be born and nurtured again. Of course, by this I mean, born and nurtured in America. This difficulty or impossibility is more common with adults. Remember the saying: "It is difficult to teach an old dog new tricks." The best that could happen in this attempt is that the newcomers, (though unknown to them) end up creating, developing, inventing, and finally coming up with a third accent. This third accent is usually a mixture or a combination of their native accent with that of the host cultural accent. Hence, do not be surprised that the newcomers begin to sound more funny than ever, both to the people of the host and those of their native cultures. This funny way of sounding or new way of talking becomes noticeable to the people concerned and the people of their native culture when they go back home for a visit. When I went to Nigeria to visit after staying fifteen months in the United States, each time I talked, my folks in Nigeria kept drawing my attention to the fact that I was talking differently and sounding funny. When I came back to the United States after the visit and shared some of my home experiences with my church congregation, particularly about my accent, a friend of mine in the United States gave a name to my new accent as, "Nigeriandacks," which is a combination of my Nigerian accent with the Adirondacks accent. In fact, my "Nigeriandacks" accent had some advantageous and disadvantageous effects on me during my visit with my folks in Nigeria. These effects cut across social, political, ecclesiastical, and above all economic aspects of life.

On a further observation, my home visit revealed to me that many Nigerian-Americans speak more of the American English in Nigeria than they do when they are in the United States. This is because there is always that pride and show-off by many Nigerians to project the ego that they are just coming from the United States. One of the easiest ways to do this is by talking like the Americans do. Since back home many Nigerians who have not crossed the shores of Nigeria do not know the difference, these Nigerian-Americans overwhelm them with their so-called American raps or sophisticated un-Nigerian accent and use them to their maximum advantage mostly to establish and show that they are "been-to (s)." In most cases, they could come up with anything when they are talking in the name of American English.

In Nigeria, you could tell a been-to not only by his or her phonetics (which young Nigerians called "foneh"), but also by his or her walk – quick, short steps instead of the normal leisurely gait. And most times, in company of their less fortunate friends, they always found an excuse for saying: "When I was in the U.S." "While in the States." "Unlike in America…"

and so on. Even some of their close relatives will want their own less fortunate friends to know that they, too, have a U.S. connection. And in their own case, they would always look for an opportunity to say: "My brother (or sister) in the U.S." says this or that. With the coming of the cell phone, when receiving some telephone calls in the public, such people who have American connections, speak so loud mentioning America, once in a while, in the course of a telephone conversation with their brothers, sisters, or friends, (who may be calling them from the States), even if nothing warrants it. In short, many Nigerian-Americans and their family members are real show-offs. In any case, my advice in such situations, especially to my Nigerian-American comrades is this: "Just be yourself." Yes, I mean, "keep it real."

And by the way, your U.S. been-to or connection should not be noticed only in the new way you talk or by your computer "guru-ness," but it should also be felt in your being able to practically touch and, if possible concretely change the life of the people back home for the better. Remember, those raps or slang will not satisfy the hunger of the people and will not cloth the naked among them. What it may simply do is to make them daydreamers and turn them into people living in an utopian world of ideas and fantasies, merely dreaming of America without ever getting there. In fact, if you can honestly, genuinely, and accountably bring them over to the United States to also have the American experience, this would be wonderful and very commendable.

I have a word for you again, my fellow Nigerians, resident in the United States, especially those of you who get several telephone calls and dozens of emails a day from some of your folks at home, who are always asking for money. The further advantage of bringing them over to America is that, when they come and experience America, even for a couple of months, they may go back disillusioned and would reduce or stop sending those emails and making telephone calls to you everyday. This is because it will become very clear to them that American dollars are not just picked up from the streets, but they must be hardly and deservingly earned. Again, I am convinced that even if they come to the U.S. for a couple of months and thereafter, return back to Nigeria "empty handed," both their morale and status among their equals, and of course, yours, will increase in the eyes of your people back home.

Above all, even if all else fails, one thing that is very certain is this, after a period of stay in America, those you would bring over will never be the same again in their worldviews. These worldviews in question will definitely undergo a reorientation that will, for the most part, open new possibilities and tend toward the betterment of the lives of those concerned through cultural contacts or exchange and the educational advantage of traveling. After all, it is said that traveling is part of education and maturity and growth are not only matters of chronological age, but of the wealth of experience gathered through the years via cultural pluralism and related avenues of knowledge. Finally, do you know that, it would be highly disappointing and boundlessly ridiculous that after all the years you stayed in the U. S., all you got to show for it is the change in your accent? The unfavorable gossip about you by some of your relatives and friends would be easy entertainment.

Talking about gossip – this is a reality that will always have its way not only accentually in communication, but also in

COMMUNICATION

the use of grammatical tenses and in dressing. Grammatically speaking, your use of "is" and "was" may constitute a disappointment to your people or to some of your educated friends back home. As Chinua Achebe rightly puts it in his book titled: *No Longer at Ease*, commenting about Obi (a young Nigerian from the village of Umuofia who was sent to England by the villagers for studies), Achebe says that on his return after the completion of his studies in England, in the gathering of Umuofia Progressive Union to welcome him: "Obi's English, on the other hand, was most unimpressive. He spoke "is" and "was." He told them about the value of education. 'Education for service, not for white-collar jobs and comfortable salaries. With our great country on the threshold of independence, we need men who are prepared to serve her well and truly.' When he sat down the audience clapped from politeness."[1]

Second, your mode of dressing, which may be too casual for comfort, may also be another item on the gossip agenda. Again , commenting about Obi, (the Nigerian-English boy), in *No Longer at Ease,* who appeared too simply dressed at his welcome party, Achebe says: "Everyone was properly dressed in *Agbada* or English suit except the guest of honor, who appeared in his shirt-sleeves because of the heat. That was Obi's mistake Number One. Everyone expected a young man from England to be impressively turned out." No doubt, even in today's Nigeria, among the educated elites, many people still cannot come to terms with the use of present-continues tenses when one is talking about an event in the past, not to talk of the expectation of dressing to "kill." Watch out for this and lots more as you go back home for a visit. I leave the cultural adjustment required in these areas to your discretion. In all, always know that you would be "sized up" in so many ways. Welcome home!

GESTURES

As simply understood, gestures have to do with body movements used for communication to express thought or to emphasize speech. The culture shock in this area was deeply felt as it impeded the expected results of some of my gestural communications.

One fundamental gesture, which remains ever fresh in my mind, that frustrated me is the gesture of the hand, especially the American movement of the fingers when gesturing: "Hello!" "Hi!" And: "Bye!" (my American audience will understand what I am talking about). This same gesture means a different thing in my native culture. In the Etung culture, it means beckoning someone to come to you. Putting this one gesture in the two different cultural contexts gives a picture of two very opposing realities, which also gives contradictory messages or information.

Initially, unaware of these cultural differences, when I first arrived in Hudson Falls, each time I wanted to beckon someone to come to me by the gesture of the hand, as I was used to doing it in my native culture, what I got as a response in (my new culture) was the same gesture, motioned back to me by whomever I was calling. The idea was that the people thought I was gesturing, "hello!" or "hi!" not knowing that I was beckoning them to come to me. This problem was overcome when on one Sunday I decided to share my frustrating experience in church. Thanks to my beloved congregation who after Mass explained and helped me to know the different ways of gesturing with my hand to get the proper and expected response. I can now beckon to whomever I want and get the correct reaction and expected response in my foreign culture. In the same vein, I seized the opportunity to draw the attention of my audience to the fact that, if by any chance or opportunity they find themselves in Nigeria, they should be careful with the gesture of the hand in motioning or signaling "hello!" "hi!" or "good-bye!" to the Nigerian people. Otherwise, they would have people come to them each time they make this gesture. It was indeed a very relieving experience to me and a revealing one to the congregation.

In Nigeria, the gesture to say "hello" is made by simply raising up your hand with the palm of your hand open. However, depending on the context, this may also mean "stop!" While the gesture to say "good-bye!" is almost the same as that of saying "hello!" but in this context, (in addition), you wave the palm of your hand as it is being raised up.

Furthermore, looking at gesture from the perspective of expressing an intention or attitude of concern is also culturally very revealing. For instance, it is always a good sign of courtesy when you meet someone on the street and express the kind gesture of greeting by asking: "How are you?" or "How are you doing?" or "How do you do?" and so on. These and similar expressions are questions that need answers from those to whom they are directed. If this is grammatically and logically correct, as I think it is, then: why the differences in people's attitudes in this context? The answer is not farfetched. It is because of the differences in culture. Thus, in the Etung culture, when someone greets and asks you: "How are you?" he or she makes an effort to stand and hear your response or answer to this and similar questions which express the gesture of concern.

The Adirondack's culture presents a different attitude. People here greet you and express or ask the same questions of concern as stated previously. The difference is that, for the most part, they will not stand to listen to your response or answer. Probably, since it is a fast moving culture, the people greet and ask you: "How are you?" but they will keep going or moving away from you, focused on where they are going. My question is: Why ask this question at all if you don't have the patience to stand for awhile and listen to the response? My recommendation to the people of my newfound culture is this: simply say "hi!" or "hello!" and don't ask any such questions of concern because it may be disappointing to the person to whom the question is directed, based on the person's cultural background and expectation. So, since you won't spare some time to get an answer to the question, there is no point asking the question at all in the gesture of greeting.

By my estimation and reasoning, this Adirondack cultural attitude can only be justified from the point of view of rhetorical questions. On the other hand, from some hearsays and personal experiences, sometimes it is good to express this gesture of concern and keep moving, otherwise, if you stand to get a response from some people, you may be sorry you did. This is because such people may hold you up by keeping you standing for hours talking as they tell you their entire life history. And you may not have enough time in your hands to spare nor the patience needed to listen to the whole story. In a culture of individualism, such people are not uncommon and so, once they have an opportunity to talk to someone, better still, someone who expresses concern about what is going on in their lives, they can talk forever. It is against the backdrop of this latter possibility that you would appreciate why when you ask some people: "How are you doing?" They would, sarcastically though, respond by asking you: "Do you have time?" Or: "You got time?"

HANDSHAKES

Handshakes are also other ways of communication with different messages conveyed in them. In fact, handshakes speak volumes about the people behind them. These take different forms. In my native culture, all I know about handshakes is that they are always to be initiated by a senior person. This seniority is determined by chronological age and by authority or official capacity that stratifies societal status. In other words, it is the place of a senior person to thrust out his hand first to a junior person in the greeting of handshakes, which is always gentle and soft. It is considered too daring for a junior person to initiate it. In fact, it can even be seen as a sign of one who is overly assuming and disrespectful. Women normally and usually give hugs to their fellow women and sometimes to men as well. In addition, in all the cases, there is no sign of pecking and no kissing sound is heard, unlike the case in the Adirondack culture. However, even among the Adirondack people, though you may hear the sound of kissing when they greet and peck one another, they do not actually kiss. The kissing, so to speak, is with their lips alone. So, as a newcomer, be careful when you are among them and do not misunderstand this sound of kissing and be tempted to actually kiss anyone when you are supposed to peck on the cheek or just touch the

A Handbook on Culture Shock

lips; otherwise, you will create an embarrassing and scandalous situation.

In terms of the messages handshakes convey in my native culture, it is difficult to say exactly. If at all, soft and gentle handshakes are recommended and seen as culturally acceptable and polite. Hugs are perceived as a deeper and warmer sign of welcome.

Now, my foreign or Adirondack culture has the following names of handshakes and the respective meaning behind them, as published in *The Post-Star* newspaper of January 25, 2004:

-The Winning Grip:

A firm handshake indicates confidence, and if both people's hands are vertical, it signals a balance of power.

-The Bone Crusher:

This sends the message you are trying to take control and dominate the situation.

-The Wimp:

The wimpy handshake not coming in full contact shows disinterest or indicates indifference.

-The Enveloper:

Using both hands can show extra interest, concern, care, regard, and respect for the other person, no matter the age difference or societal status.

-The Dominator:

When one person turns his or her palm downward on top of your hand, it indicates a controlling personality.[2]

Based on their meanings and messages as shown here, I must confess that initially I was a frightened victim of the crusher and dominator handshakes when I first arrived in the culture of the Adirondack people. This is because of the different messages conveyed in handshakes.

Since I was born and brought up in Nigeria, you can imagine the shock and trembling fear I had to endure and pass through in the Adirondack culture, which demanded firm gripping handshakes as culturally acceptable. In short, initially, they were not just crushing and dominating handshakes, but also intimidating and oppressive.

EFFECTIVE COMMUNICATION AS A DUAL RESPONSIBILITY OF THE SPEAKER AND THE LISTENER

It is important to note that effective communication, which benefits both the speaker and the listener, is a dual responsibility of both parties. Thus, the one who speaks has the responsibility of making an honest effort to communicate the ideas he or she intends to be put across and the information to be given. This can be done effectively by paying attention to the following areas: *context, pronunciation*, and *gesture.*

Contextually speaking, you, especially as a newcomer to another culture, should always speak and relate the subject matter to issues that enjoy a common knowledge by your audience. These issues could be recent events that have occurred or are happening at the moment in the area or such events constitute global news.

About pronunciation, the responsibility to pronounce the words spoken carefully and slowly lies on you, the speaker. No doubt, at the beginning, this slowness may appear and sound disgusting and distracting both to you and to some of your audience. In fact, some may become impatient and will wish that you were speaking faster and quicker. Remember, such

A Handbook on Culture Shock

people may represent only a very small fraction of the whole audience. In the event of this development, my advice to you is to be patient with both yourself and with the audience in question. In the end, you will achieve greater results and a wider understanding by your audience of what you are saying.

For greater results, at some point, you may even have to use gestures in your communication to buttress, emphasize, or give direction to the intended message or information. These gestures may look like "sign language" and may appear kindergarten-like and funny, but they are effective means to enhance communication.

To the one who listens, your responsibility is also enormous and challenging. Among other things, you should take note of the following: *context, lip reading, multitasking,* and *conditioning.*

The importance of context is also very vital to the listener because once the context is established, consciously or unconsciously, intuitively or otherwise, the mind can anticipate and correctly guess what the speaker is saying or talking about. Context becomes even more profitable if it is common knowledge or a familiar topic to both parties (you and your audience).

The advantage in knowing the context gives rise to the possibility of reading the lips of the speaker, and this enhances understanding in communication. It should be understood that the ability to or the exercise of reading the lips of the speaker presupposes the fact that the listener is looking at the one who is speaking. Thus, without looking at the speaker, the act of lip-reading cannot be achieved.

The knowledge of the context and the possibility of lip-

COMMUNICATION

reading can all be thwarted by the lack of attention on the part of the listener due to multitasking, intellectually, emotionally and physically. This multitasking is a form of distraction that takes different forms, such as looking at and thinking about the speaker in so many areas of life, ranging, for instance, from race or color, shape of his or her "nose," accent, educational background and capabilities, and lots of other personal thoughts that are held in the inner sanctum of the mind. This communicational multitasking inevitably divides and distracts the required and expected attention of the listener.

However, according to educational psychologists, this fact of multitasking is, for the most part, an unavoidable conscious or unconscious act of the mind. Yes, the mind is one of the most multitasking organs or parts of the human being. In a flash, the mind can cover a wide range of distance, time, and volume. Because of the floatation, flipping, and flirting of the human mind, it is hardly possible for the one who listens to remain focused and pay a clean and an uninterrupted attention to the one who speaks, beyond a certain length of time. Thus, most times, intentionally or otherwise, other related or unrelated materials or ideas flash into the mind during the course of listening to a speaker within a given space and time. This also happens during prayer. The only remedy to this situation is the direct and sole responsibility of the listener to train the mind and exercise self-discipline through the custody of the mind and the senses. No doubt, this discipline also called mortification of the senses is a difficult and challenging task.

Furthermore, one of the most advantageous positions of the listener is the idea of conditioning. In the context of our reflection, this may simply mean the ability to get used to seeing and hearing someone. It can be achieved by regularity, constancy, and familiarity. Thus, the more regularly you hear a particular person speak, the more familiar you become with the person's manner and ways of talking and thinking. This will enhance your ability to understand what he says, how he says it, and what he means. All this will result in some kind of conditioning of your sense of hearing and improve your ability to process information faster.

From the point of view of an analogy or a relational perspective, the whole issue of communication can be likened to the workings and operations of a computer. Thus, the speaker and the listener constitute a complete assemblage of a computer and so must operate accordingly for the expected results in communication. By way of a partial definition, a computer is an electronic device that accepts input as data, processes the data, and gives out information as output. It does all this under a preestablished program. Based on this simple definition, let us attempt to view the speaker and the listener from this computer spectrum.

For those of you who are familiar with the computer and its operations, you can see that the speaker is the input device. He inputs the data through the mouse or touch pad or the keyboard, represented by the spoken words and gestures.

While on the part of the listener, you can see that he/she is like the monitor or visual display unit (VDU) and the central processing unit (CPU). He gets the data through the ears (monitor), and then he processes it in his mind (CPU) in order to arrive at the correct and intended information. This final stage of information is the output or the result of the whole communication task.

Communication

Largely it is a fact, beyond all doubt, that effective and re-sult-oriented communication is the dual responsibility of both the speaker and the listener. If this responsibility is neglected or not assumed by either one of the parties involved in communication, the results are obvious: communication gaps, embarrassing misunderstandings, unpleasant feelings and negative impressions, and many other communication frustrations. For instance, as I did experience as a minister of the gospel, given these communication frustrations, it would not be surprising to notice that when the speaker says, "crop," the listener hears, "crap," and when the speaker says, "Joan," the listener hears "June." In another context, when the speaker says, "Sandy," the listener hears "Sunday," when the speaker says, "Walter," the listener hears, "Water," and when the speaker says and means, "crop walk," the listener hears and understands, "crap work," and so on.

In fact, depending on what parts of America two immigrant Nigerians live, even if they are from the same village, with time, they too would begin to have difficulties in understanding each other when they speak in English. That is why sometimes you hear even the Americans themselves talk about someone having, for instance a Brooklyn accent or a Texas accent. On this note, I remember one day having a telephone conversation with a priest friend of mine from Nigeria and even from the same diocese with me, Ogoja, (in Nigeria). He was in Orange, Texas, in America. In the conversation, I was telling him about my plan to write a book. But for sometime, each time I called or pronounced the word, "book", he was hearing, "Pope." This misunderstanding went on for sometime in the course of our conversation until we were able to establish a connection by way of a more concrete context. From this foregone explanation, it can be agreed upon that once there is a breach in communication or what I may call communication bottleneck, there can be no progress made whatsoever in this fundamental and determinant aspect of human relations. It will only amount to stagnation or retrogression. No doubt, this can be very frustrating.

QUICK TIPS

For ministers of the gospel, as priests, pastors, or any religious workers charged with the stewardship of preaching the word of God to people, I have some quick tips for you as you step on the United State soil as a missionary.

HUMOR IN COMMUNICATION

The first quick tip is all about the sense of humor. Your ability to be humorous in what you say to people is a plus in your pastoral ministry. As commonly understood, humor is the quality of being amusing or comical. It can also be understood as the ability to perceive, enjoy, or express what is comical and funny. The captivation, gravitation, attraction, and pleasantness that the keen sense of humor brings to your ministry are priceless. Humor adds spice to what you say. It helps to express a serious idea that hits back home to or on your congregation without any offense taken. It provides a suitable vehicle to transport your message to its desired and intended destination smoothly, cheerfully, and with an accommodating acceptance. For the most part, humor in communication should, as much as possible, be directed toward the self (yourself). This could be in the form of self-criticism, self-laughter, self-assessment, self-affirmation, even self-demeaning, and so on. In whatever case, always make sure that you are talking in familiar and common context with your congregation. By and large humor, especially that which really creates chuckles or loud and responsible laughter, is an icebreaker and attention-catcher, which attracts the maximum attention of your audience.

On this note of humor, the wisdom of Bishop Howard J. Hubbard of the Albany Diocese, in his book *I Am Bread Broken — A Spirituality for the Catechist,* aptly underscores its need and importance in a well and properly articulated manner. A paraphrasing reference to his reflection says that as "ministers" you must always have a sense of humor. "Very often we who minister in the church can look upon humor as frivolous, undignified, or unbecoming the grand scheme of the divine that we are privileged to represent. On the other hand, because we are often dealing with serious issues or with people having serious problems, we can tend to become overly dour."[3] After all, remember oftentimes we hear the expression: "Even God has a sense of humor." This humor of God, should be reflected in the character and expressed in the daily life of His minister.

Besides, because of the challenging circumstances of today's world, it is important that we be able to step back to gain the balance, proportion, and sense of perspective to cope with the incongruities of life and to realize that these incongruities need not defeat us. A sense of humor enables us to gain this perspective. Note well, however, that the humor, of which we speak, has to do with laughing with people. It has nothing to do with laughing at people and telling jokes; the world is

A Handbook on Culture Shock

full of people who laugh and tell jokes but who have no sense of humor. Such people who laugh and tell jokes without any sense of humor are often described as having a dry sense of humor. Rather, genuine humor, like a true sense of humility, involves a ruthless honesty about oneself without any pretense or show. It deals with those surprises, especially in relation to culture shock, that upset the way we think things ought to be, and it lightens the heaviness associated with hurt. Note that, humor does not deny hurt, but it becomes the vehicle through which anger, defiance, and pain can be handled constructively. Once you are able to develop a sense of humor that enables you to laugh at yourself as you toddle through your newfound culture with all its experiences, you can avoid that anxiety or uptightness which can impede your ministerial effectiveness. This impediment may consequently make it much more difficult (coupled with the effective communication hazards), for others to recognize God's presence in your life and your ministry. In fact, better humor comes not from books read, but from one's personal experience of life. Again, acceptable humors that are directed toward oneself should "accept" realities about yourself, and if they are directed toward another person, they should "deny" realities about the other.

With a properly developed and well thought-out sense of humor, other people can pick on you and vice versa without any offense taken by either side or party. However, you should guard against that sin which Monsignor Andrew Cusack calls "lusting of the tongue." By that, he means the terrible violence we do to others by our cruel, inconsiderate, disrespectful and cutting remarks. This does not refer to good-natured kidding or poking fun at our human foibles. As pointed out earlier, indeed, we need to laugh at ourselves and with one another. Perhaps, there has been too little of this in our postconciliar Church. Again, what should be avoided is the type of gossip and snide remarks that cut, hurt, alienate, ridicule, and isolate others, especially those that remind them of their unfortunate or less fortunate backgrounds, personalities and abilities.

On a personal note, the parishioners of St. Mary's/St. Paul's Church would agree with me that we all enjoy a good sense of humor that enables us to pick on ourselves without taking any offense. If I should recall all the instances and occasions that we picked on ourselves, the size of this book would not hold all of them. However, permit me to relate some instances that could be described as, taking a serious situation and making it light with a winning sense of humor. First, it was on Ash Wednesday, after the ashes had been distributed in the church, that I went to a drugstore to get some cards. I ran into a pa- rishioner who asked me if I also had the ashes signed on my forehead because he could not see any sign of it (on my fore- head). Furthermore, he said that if I had the ashes signed on my forehead, probably, I have had a bath since then, and so the water washed it away. I told him that, of course, I also had the ashes signed on my forehead, and I have not had a bath since then. He shook his head and said that I may need to use white chalk for my own ashes next time, that is, on Ash Wednesday of next year. Without saying anything more, he left. I simply looked at him with a smile as he walked away laughing. With- out taking any offense, I thought to myself: "If only this has made his day, thank God!"

If you think that the Ash Wednesday experience was based on racial prejudice or racially intended to hurt or attack me

A HANDBOOK ON CULTURE SHOCK

due to the color of my skin, which is "dark chocolate," then listen to my experience of a black doggy bag. My mom told me that I was born on November 23, 1968. As expected, every year at this time, I celebrate my birthday. Personally, I prefer acknowledging and marking my birthday in the quiet and solitude of my room. It is an opportunity for me to flashback, and go down the memory lane in particular or self-examination. One time on my birthday while in the United States, some dear friends in the parish of my apostolate wanted to make my day special for me. A day after the actual day of my birthday, they picked me up from the rectory and treated me to lunch in a particular restaurant. At the end of the lunch, three of us requested for doggy bags to take the remainder of our food home.

Guess what! The waitress, first came with two white doggy bags and gave them to the other two folks who were white (in skin color). Then she left and came back with a black doggy bag and handed it over to me. At this, all of us starting laughing, but we immediately came up with some ideas to the effect that I should not keep quiet about it. So as a way of giving the waitress a hard time, I called her back and pretended to be very serious, angry, and offended because of what she did by giving me a black doggy bag. I asked her: "Why did you give me a black doggy bag, am I not black enough?" While she stood there looking at me, to add more "insult to the injury," I added: "Do I need to be reminded that I am "black?" She thought I was really serious. She felt so sorry and began to apologize to me, saying that she did not intend to insinuate anything and that the black doggy bag was not intended to give any hurtful message. While she stood there looking so remorseful, I thought to myself: "Poor girl, if only she knew where we were coming from and that it was a set-up, she would have known that I was simply pulling her legs. All the time, my friends were simply listening and choking with laughter. You would not believe how much we laughed at the restaurant.

The world of humor can be found almost everywhere — in shopping malls, supermarkets, schools, and offices, on farms, and at sporting facilities or other areas such as gyms or fields. The next humorous "attack" on me was at an indoor basketball game. This time it had to do with stamping my hand. As usual, I went with some folks to watch an indoor basketball game. The woman who was collecting the tickets had a black ink stamp pad, and she was stamping others with it on the back of their hands. When it got to my turn, I extended my hand and showed her the back of my hand to stamp just like she did to others who went before me. She looked at me and said: "No, let me have the palm of your hand." Well, without any much ado or fuss, not even with the slightest objection or any question, I obeyed. While she was putting the stamp in the palm of my hand, I kept smiling all through it. She looked up at me and had no choice other than to join me in smiling and laughing as I walked away into the indoor "gymnasium." When I shared this experience with my congregation, after Mass, one of my parishioners said to me: "Thank God that the woman did not request that you stick out your tongue." Until this latter comment, I never thought that the tongue could have been another option.

I don't intend to bore you with humorous instances, but consider this: How about being pictured and described as a "black-eyed-Susan" flower? It was on one Easter Sunday Mass

A Handbook on Culture Shock

that I wore this glowing yellow colored vestment (Chasuble) on my "dark chocolate" colored skin. In this Mass, I was given the honor of being the chief celebrant and flanked by the immediate passed and the incumbent pastors of St. Mary's/St. Paul's church, Hudson Falls, New York. As it is always the case on Christmas and Easter Sunday Masses, the church on this particular Easter Sunday was packed to the doors. When we – the priests vested and were moving from the sacristy to the entrance of the church to process through the central aisle to the sanctuary, the then pastor, with his acceptable sense of humor, looked at me and said that I looked like a big sunflower. I smiled at him. Shortly before I began giving my homily, I took sometime to draw the attention of the church congregation to the description of me by the pastor as a "big sunflower." As if it was a planned action, after saying this, the pastor sprang up from his chair and said: "No! not a big sunflower, but rather "a black-eyed-Susan." The congregation got a kick out of it and cracked up for a long time. At this time, I knew little or nothing about how a black-eyed-Susan flower looks like. My immediate reaction was to keep on looking at the congregation while they celebrated the laughing session. When the laughter died down, I said in reference to the black-eyed-Susan: "Whatever that means! But I take it that the description is complementary of me." The laughter began again, but stopped after a short while.

Guess what! I couldn't wait to finish the Mass so as to go look for what a black-eyed-Susan looks like. Yes, I found one and I brought a bouquet of it to church the next Sunday. Before giving my homily again on this Sunday Mass, I carefully brought it out from under the pulpit where I hid it, and showed it to the congregation saying: "This is black-eyed-Susan. Doesn't it look gorgeous?" To tell you that this had the congregation in stitches, laughing as ever is to over flock the issue. Thank God, I now know what and how a black-eyed-Susan flower looks like. So, it can be said that out of some jokes, can come knowledge. Finally, on this black-eyed-Susan saga, I must admit that, looking at the flower, it was a vivid "typology" and the best or perfect picturesque description of me in that yellow colored vestment (Chasuble). And what's wrong with that, I mean the description? If flowers beautify the home and act as varieties that diversify the environment, thereby flavoring or spicing it up, then, how lucky am I to be a zest in the neighborhood of my newfound culture!

For the church congregation in Hudson Falls, whatever color of vestment I wore had some remarks made about it in relation to me. Do I need to tell you that, such remarks were always complimentary? They often say things like: Red is good on you! Green is so nice on you! Violet becomes you! and white so much agrees with you *because it helps!* Do not miss the message intended to be conveyed in the *color white as agreeing with me because it helps.* Just imagine the distinction and clarity between a white and a "black" color in a juxtapositional context, then, judge for yourself.

Among the many things I know about the Americans is that, once they know "where you are coming from" or "get your number", regarding the sense of humor, they can look at you straight into your eyes and say what they feel about you at any time confident that you will take it in good faith. Yes, whenever I wore a yellow colored vestment, they say I look like a black-eyed Suzan. What do they say when I wear a mellow

A Handbook on Culture Shock

yellow shirt? They say, I look like a bumble-bee. Thank God that I am neither a bug nor do I stink. Yes, this is another case of taking a seemingly serious situation and diluting it with a delightful sense of humor.

On Wednesday, May 18, 2005, I was jay walking across Main Street in Hudson Falls and a driver nearly ran me over with his car. Thanks to the intervention of a dear parishioner of mine. Based on this development, I decided to share my experience of jay walking with my Church Congregation. Within the week of my sharing the experience, I got so many reactions from people confirming the reality of my experience. Thereupon, during the next weekend Masses, I made some addendums to my experience based on the reactions. My points, which were read by some young parishioners were itemized thus: 1.) Let us be reminded that jay walking is a traffic offense, punishable by law, in case we have forgotten. 2.) When you are driving your car and you see someone at the tip or at the beginning of a crosswalk wanting to cross the street, please, stop and allow the person to cross safely. 3.) On the other hand, when you are driving your car and you see someone jay walking out of ignorance of the law or some other exigencies, Christian charity demands that you stop for such a person to cross safely. 4.) Someone said: "Besides jay walking being a traffic offense, Rev. Victor should be careful when he jay walks because at certain times of the evening, drivers may not see him." (Don't you know why?)

Now, within 20 days of sharing my thoughts on jay walking, coupled with other related worrisome developments, precisely on Tuesday, June 7, 2005, something maiden happened in Hudson Falls. What happened was the introduction of "Crosswalk Flags," the first of its kind in New York State. These orange flags have the inscription: "Stop for me – it's the law." As I mean to save you the trouble of reading the instructions on "how to use the crosswalk flags," suffice me to say that, pedestrians are supposed to use the orange flags when crossing the road to signal to oncoming drivers to stop for them as a matter of law. By way of their display: A couple of holders or buckets are installed on each strategic side of the street (where there is a crosswalk) with five or six orange flags in each. To cross from one side of the street to the other, therefore, pedestrians (as individuals or groups) are expected to pick up one of the flags and use it to control traffic by themselves while they cross the road. And when they get to the other side of the road, they leave or tuck it back into the holder or in the companion bucket provided also on the other side of the street. This is so helpful, both during the day and night, especially because of the flags' fluorescent nature.

I am not claiming to be the advocate for or the executor of the crosswalk flags law or "state law of yielding to people in crosswalk", but I must not fail in my duty as pastor of the people of God, to call attention to some possible developments, as they always happen when a new law is made or enacted. By all means, intent and purpose, this new introduction of crosswalk flags is a law that is for the benefit and good of the masses, both as car owners, drivers and pedestrians. I have no doubt in my mind that, some people may call it names. They may refer to the flags as "construction cones," "orange power," because of their orange color, and so on. Others may say that the introduction makes no sense and so may ignore the flags at their own peril and saunter through the crosswalk without

A Handbook on Culture Shock

any incident or eventuality. Though the flags do not give you complete immunity to accidents, but they may reduce the risk. Remember also that, by the time you realize their usefulness and begin to see that there is sense in them, it may be too late. Such "no sense" people may argue that they have been crossing the street by themselves for many years, and not once have they ever needed an orange flag. Why should they need one now? These reactions and many more, only serve to reveal the true nature of man as an insatiable being who finds fault with almost everything and everybody, and of course with himself. And for the "sense" people who use them, note that the flags are only helpful tools. Use normal judgment when crossing the street. Watch out for some tractor-trailers who may have no chance of stopping, even with six or eight orange flags waving in front of them.

To the initiators of the crosswalk flags idea, I say to you: "Do not mind the unfavorable remarks or derogatory comments that may be made by some people. Yours is a laudable dream that is worthy of emulation. Keep up the good work of thinking for the good of the vulnerable people out there."

It is this mentality of "no sense," insatiability and faultfinding that has made religion to become an "exiled child" or a stranger in many human affairs of nowadays. Religion, therefore, under this "attack" is being referred to as a medieval hang-up and a think of the past, no longer in congruent with school systems, social clubs, political parties, and other enclaves. And even for those who still embrace it as the centerpiece of their lives – what is their focus? Are you the type that scrupulously cares about "pettily little" thinks like morning and evening prayers, holding a grudge against someone who hurts you, masturbation, gossip, lust, romantic imaginations, etc? It is not the concerned about these private things that the scandal of the "Cross" through religious piety is experienced, rather, it is in neglecting the big picture – the granite fact that half the world goes to bed hungry every night and nobody gives a damn. Many others sleep under the bridges and flyovers, come rain come sun/shine. Still others go without hospitals, medical insurance or Medicaid, thereby, dying deaths that could have been avoided. Please, don't get me going on this painful and shameful reality! It should be noted that, to be more concerned about the former pettily little and private things amounts to *spiritual narcissism.* While the latter, that captures the big picture is the most recommended *humanitarian spirituality.*

The humorous punch line of the crosswalk flags experience is that, shortly after the introduction of this "self-shepherding" signals, someone in my parish called my telephone number while I was away and left a message for me on my answering machine. The message was this: "Fr. Victor, welcome back from your retreat. I just wanted to draw your attention to a new thing in town. It is about the crosswalk flags. Without much argument, know that the flags were introduced because of you. So you better make use of them when next you cross the road. When you get this message, do well to call the police in Hudson Falls and thank them for their thoughtfulness." Incidentally, my telephone has no caller ID, and so I did not know the person that called and left this message for me. It may interest you to know that, I kept listening to this message over and over again with the hope that I would recognize the voice, but to no avail. How could I, when all white people speak almost the same way– the young and the old, not much difference? Certainly, the person who called, did not mean what he said about the crosswalk flags vis-à-vis me. But even if he did, there is a sense of humor to it. And if there is none, then, create one, otherwise, you may become miserable.

There were many more of such jokes. The point I am trying to make here is that, with a sense of humor, people could say certain things to you or make some remarks about you and vice versa without intending any hurt. If you too, see the humorous side of every situation and learn to take remarks and jokes, not personal but with a grain of salt, then you would contribute so greatly to the world of humor. From my experience therefore, I can say that a large heart that is intertwined with a winning sense of humor and a flashing smile for all, leads to contagious smiles, which progressively generate an all-round laughter. With this lifestyle, I am tempted to say that you can get away with "anything." You will do well to know, too, that if people don't love you, they will not pick on you.

SERMONS OR HOMILIES

For religious workers, especially pastors and ministers of the Church, your mission in homiletic communication necessitated by the complexity of our society is fundamentally, to talk about what the people know, gossip, and talk about in seclusion but they cannot talk about in public because of some militating circumstances. These circumstances that militate against such talks being spoken publicly could be their life situations, conditions of living, sensitivity of the matter or issue at stake, and who is involved. You, therefore, as a minister of the Word of God has the responsibility of proving to the people that gone is the era when silence is considered golden,

COMMUNICATION

come what may.

However, in sermonizing on the "gossip" that other people do not have the opportunity, or do not have the guts or are afraid to talk about them in public, (such as the burning issues of abortion, euthanasia, contraceptives, celibacy, religious education in schools and other hot-button issues), make sure they are in line with the ethics of helping the common good, growth of the Church, development of the community, and sanitization of the secular system. It will be highly disappointing if you, too, tends to avoid talking about such issues according to the mind of the Church whom you represent. In advocating for a more vocal handling of some of these troubling developments, I am aware that some of the issues may seriously clash and disagree with your own personal ethics or views about life. Avoiding them or being indifferent to them may give the impression or message that you are complacent or you are in support of them. Remember the saying: "Silence can mean consent." To save your neck, I challenge you to address those issues as diplomatically as possible, stating categorically and clearly the Church's position on them.

While you represent the Church from the pulpit, keep your personal views to yourself and leave the burden to your own conscience at such moments, so as not to sound scandalous or become a scandal to anyone. This is no show of hypocrisy, because the pulpit is meant to be used for the proclamation of God's word, which is communicated to us through the Church's Magisterium (The teaching office of the hierarchy under the Pope, exercised through the regular means of instructing the faithful). Do not use the pulpit to communicate your own ideas, to project your own views and to inject your own ideologies into the minds of the people. Remember, you are a servant sent to do the will of the Master, who is represented by the Church through the earthly authority that ordained and commissioned you. Do I need to remind you that as a priest, for instance, the moment you were ordained, you surrendered your freedom to the Church, and from hence seized to be yourself?

After all said and done, as you discharge the ministry entrusted to you, let all you say and do be geared towards renewing the face of the Earth according to the mind of the Creator. Your vantage position of having so many people listen to you as a minister of the Word of God (not your own word) makes this mission challenging, compelling and obligatory. Failure to do this in any culture amounts to failure in your representation of the Church, and the voiceless. It might even show that you are probably timid or ashamed and so you are shying away from addressing issues of concern. All this amounts to the sin of silence compliance with the status quo.

In carrying out this onerous, challenging, and privileged pastoral duty of sermons, always remember the importance and value of contextual, short, and straightforward homilies. Avoid dillydallying or beating about the bush because of the accelerated velocity of culture where people are always in a rush to catch up with other equally important programs or appointments. Your homily therefore, should have a good beginning and a good end, keeping the beginning and end as close as possible. On this note, St. Francis de Sales "particularly impressed the value of short, straightforward and unadorned sermons, for 'the more you say, the less they will remember.' In order to speak well, we need only to love well!'[4] For St. Francis of Assisi, he opines that we should be witnesses to the gospel by deeds and when "necessary" by words.

Since we live in a seemingly capitalistic society, sermons also have their effects on the economy or finances of a particular church. Hence, this reflection would not be complete without saying a word on the economic consequences of sermons. First, uninspiring and long sermons will adversely tell on the number in the congregation. That is, the number of people who go to a particular church may drop, especially given the competitive atmosphere of other churches located in the neighborhood in close proximity. When the number in the congregation drops, logically the collection drops as well. Second, according to Roger Hogan, a friend of mine, Fr. John B. Mea once said: "The size of the collection is inversely proportional to the length of the homily." This means that the longer the homily, the lesser the amount of money contributed at the collection. This is because you either lose some people who may leave the church for other engagements and appointments before the collection time or those who stay to endure the long sermon may become too angry and so will grudgingly drop a coin into the collection basket. The results are obviously that the economy of the church will be adversely affected.

Furthermore, it should be noted that to be able to meet the demands of a short and valued homily, experience teaches that the shorter the homily that has impact on the congregation, the longer the time it takes to prepare it and vice versa. In fact, in giving a homily, "if after 10 minutes you haven't struck oil, stop boring."

Just a word or two on this topic for new arrivals, especially as priests: In your homilies or sermons, if you can share with

A HANDBOOK ON CULTURE SHOCK

your congregation some of your new cultural adventures and experiences with their related shocks, in relation to your native culture, without being judgmental, that would be very nice. And no matter how deep and sensitive they may be, if you share them with a sense of humor, this will be a plus to your sermons. To tell you that some people may even start looking forward to your Masses expecting to hear what's new, is to challenge you to give it a try. This may be your magic to breakthrough and "make it." In all this, please, "keep it real" and simple, with the Bible in one hand and the Newspaper in the other.

Besides the communication factor that one inevitably experiences in a new culture, there is also the food and eating experience. This, as well, comes with its newness, difficulties, hurdles, and challenges, as the next chapter will try to highlight.

NOTES

[1] Achebe, Chinua. *No Longer at Ease,* New York: First Anchor Books Edition, 1994, 37, 35, 36.

[2] Petteys, Martha. "The Story of Your Hello," *The Post-Star,* January 25, 2004.

[3] Hubbard, Howard J. *I Am Bread Broken: A Spirituality for the Catechists,* New York: The Crossroad Publishing Company, 1996, 50-51.

[4] Mausolfe, A. J. M., and J. K. Mausolfe. *Saint Companions for Each Day.* Bandra, Mumbai, India: St. Pauls, 2000, 38.

2

COOKING, FOOD, AND EATING

The culture shock regarding food and eating was seemingly all-round, deep, and extensive. In fact, it was a whole world of difference. In this consideration, I would like to draw attention to cooking and the combination of foodstuff used to fix particular dishes, mealtimes, meal compliments, gifts, "forced-feeding," and gifts certificates.

COOKING AND FOODSTUFF COMBINATION

In this aspect, I intend to draw attention to cooking and the combination of foodstuff in fixing particular meals. Largely, I must say that, besides my cultural orientation, my experience here was a personal habit. Accordingly, I defied all the "rules of the game" in cooking and in combining foodstuff for a meal.

In Nigeria, particularly in the Etung culture, cooking is mostly the exclusive responsibility of women. In fact, for a man to be found in a "woman's kitchen" is an insult to the woman in question, and such a man is an intruder. However, in spite of this, some men in my native culture do know how to cook. Learning to do so must have been part of their devel-

COOKING, FOOD, AND EATING

opment considering their particular circumstances of growth, ranging from family structure to other necessary and challenging situations.

On a personal note, my inability to know how to cook was again due to the mentality of parents in my home culture. Thus, it is a worrisome development for mothers who see their growing male children more inclined to going to the kitchen. The impression this inclination gives is that such male children will never marry since they are learning to do what the women should be doing and that when such male children eventually marry they would be usurping the domestic responsibilities of their wives, especially in the area of cooking. This attitude amounts to domestic territorial violation that may cause clashes and friction in the home. It would then not be surprising that I did not even know how to boil an egg. The most I knew how to do was to boil water for a cup of tea.

I remember vividly the worries of my mom in this regard when I was leaving for the United States. As a way of arming me, she made sure that I left with some soup condiments so that occasionally I could try to fix a familiar home meal for myself. When I got to the United States, after some days those condiments went bad since I did not know how to cook, and I threw them into the garbage. As time went by, at some moments I had no choice but to try fixing a meal by myself and for myself. This I did by throwing together whatever appealed to me, even if it was against dieting ethics. My conviction was that God who takes care of babies, fools, and drunks will take care of me.

Furthermore, aside having been born and brought up in a culture where it is the women's responsibility to cook, my personal inability to cook was intensified by the structure of my family, which eventually made cooking a big problem to me in my newfound culture. Besides having all the cooking at home done by either my mother or my four sisters, my training in life which involved going through a ministerial academy, particularly in terms of my formation to the priesthood, did not pose any challenge to me to learn how to cook. Thus, in the minor and major seminaries where I had my formation, there were cooks employed to do all the cooking, do the dishes, and related duties. Therefore, finding myself in my newfound culture in the Adirondacks and facing the experience of men cooking and doing related things was not only a culture shock to me, but also very difficult for me to get involved and fall in line. How difficult it is to teach an old dog a new trick!

Having said this, as far as cooking is concerned, which I had to do in my newfound culture occasionally, it was simply a case of throwing together whatever was available and appealing to me to fix a meal. This was compounded by my unfamiliarity and ignorance of the different foodstuffs found in my new culture. For instance, what do you mean by scallops and fried clam strips, hot crispy tortilla chips, pico de gallo, and jalapenos, garlic alfredo linguini, arugula, and balsamic vinaigrette, grilled marinated chicken or tuna, skewered with a fresh rosemary sprig, and topped with a rosemary balsamic butter? Given this situation, it was so difficult to explain to my sister who was always calling me on phone from Nigeria to ask me what I had for breakfast, lunch or supper. She was so worried about me since I did not know how to cook. For instance, how could I explain maple syrup, mashed potatoes, rosemary balsamic butter to her, which I did not even understand myself? In

COOKING, FOOD, AND EATING

short, not only was I completely blank in terms of the names of the different foodstuffs, but I also looked timid, confused, and seemingly stupid each time I was presented with a menu in a restaurant. On a few occasions, I had ordered dishes that sounded familiar to me, but to my greatest dismay, I got something very different from what I thought. For public decency, I endured the eating of what was brought to me.

This reminds me of my experience of *French fries* and *French rice.* I never heard of, nor did I know anything about French fries until I came to the United States. Nevertheless, when I was still in Nigeria, I was familiar with the word "French" as a language. I was also familiar with the word "rice" as food eaten by people, and it is a delicacy in my home culture.

When I arrived in Hudson Falls, where the parish of my pastoral placement is located in the Albany Diocese, New York, the pastor, Fr. James Barry Lonergan, and I one day went to see the Bishop at the Pastoral Center in Albany, about one hour drive away from the parish. After seeing him, on our way out of town, we decided to stop at a restaurant in Albany for something to eat for lunch. The waitress brought the menu to us. I went through it over and over again, but nothing on it was familiar to me. While I was still going through it, I overheard somebody at the table behind where we were sitting requesting what sounded like "French rice." Since I was familiar with the two words: French and rice, I immediately said to the waitress: "Please, give me "French rice." My thinking was that at least there is the word "rice," and so no matter how different it may look, the difference would not be much from what I was familiar with. Of course, the waitress heard "French fries" instead of "French rice." This time around, the misunderstanding in communication between us was not because of the problem with my accent. Rather, it was because she heard what she "wanted" to hear based on what she was used to hearing. Consequently, by the time she brought my "French rice," it became "French fries." Since I was hungry and the French fries brought to me looked nice, smelled good and appeared appealing, I ate it for my lunch with a glass of soda. Ever since then, I began to like French fries, and it became one of my favorite American foods.

From this experience, you would agree with me that there is no harm in giving a try to whatever food that is set before you, especially as a stranger, newcomer, or a missionary. You never know; you may end up liking it.

Because of the problems I had with food outside, I preferred to eat at home. That was why back in the rectory where I was living, whenever I had the opportunity, I made use of whatever was familiar and appealing to me to fix a quick meal. Hence, I could combine ice cream or a milk shake and French fries; bacon, scrambled eggs and a cup of tea; bread, peanut butter, banana, and a cup of hot chocolate; flavored rice, chicken nuggets, home fries, and a glass of root beer for different meals at any time of the day. At least, besides the fact that these were familiar to me, I also cultivated a taste for them. Sometimes also, I had some TV dinners, but this did not last long. Thank God for the gift of a flexible and generous stomach to accommodate all this "crazy" combination of food without developing any eating disorder or experiencing a metabolic crisis. It would be ungrateful of me to end this talk on the combination of foodstuff without paying homage to particularly bacon and peanut butter as my newfound American food. In saluting them, permit me to say that: "one can hardly get over the crispy, crunchy and delicious taste of bacon, not to talk of peanut butter with its tasty complement to any meal or great 'all by itself.' A trial will convince you."

Talking about acquired taste, from my observation and experience, I did come to the conviction that, all tastes for the different kinds of food people eat, are either acquired or cultivated. No one is born with a particular taste for some special types of food. So, one's environmental influence with its vegetation and availability of food, culturally speaking, has an undeniable role to play in the taste of food that is eaten. However, in the course of time as one lives on in a new culture that has different food, which also tastes differently from that in his or her original culture, he or she begins to cultivate a taste for the food found in the new environment, though, without losing the former (acquired) taste. Nevertheless, depending on how long one stays in a new environment away from home, there is the possibility of losing the former acquired taste for food as well and not just the accent in communication alone.

I had an experience with this combination of foodstuff, which I would like to relate. There was this day I was eating my personal combination of stuff for brunch. The pastoral associate for administration of the parish of my apostolate came into the kitchen and asked me what I was eating. I could not readily tell her the name of what it was. The best I could do was to mention all the different food items I had put together. Then I told her to give the dish a name. She said: "The name is *junk*." Having observed and noticed my foodstuff combination for sometime without being able to give names to the different dishes, and neither could I. One day she said to me: "You may have to start writing your own cookbook." Of course, it was through various combinations of foodstuffs that people came up with ideas on cooking and writing cookbooks. For instance, I was made to understand that the combination of peanut or groundnut butter with banana, was as a result of an accident of a peeled banana (accidentally) falling into a plate of peanut butter. When the person who had the accident ate the banana along with the peanut butter on it, it tasted so good. Hence, today we have the combination of banana and peanut butter as a delicacy and something delicious to eat.

There was this day I thought of giving a name to my breakfast foodstuff combination which I loved so much and ate more often. This was because some people in my foreign culture kept on asking me what I had for breakfast or other meals every now and then. Moreover, since I continuously found it difficult to give just one name to the meal, I went on mentioning all the names of the things I had put together to fix the meal. Incidentally, within this time I had developed a taste for the constant and frequent combination of certain foodstuffs for a meal. This combination was particularly for my brunch, since I was not used to having breakfast, and it was bread, scrambled eggs, banana, peanut butter, and a cup of tea. The name I gave this combination is *"the five combines."* From then on, whenever I was asked about what I had for breakfast or brunch, I would say to the person, "the five combines." That was how it was with me, and I was always fine whenever I fixed my own meal.

For my Nigerian audience, probably you are surprised that in my combinations I did not mention any of the foodstuffs or ingredients that are native to my home culture, such as yam,

COOKING, FOOD, AND EATING

water-yam, coco-yam, plantain, cassava, gari, akpu, palm oil, ogu, okassi or eruru/nfunni, melon/nkon, ogbonor/nsing, water-leaf/momongikong, bitter-leaf/ochu, green-leaf/mfai, and so forth. This omission is not fortuitous. The fact is that I could only use what was available and could be found in the groceries at the time of this reflection in my exclusively white neighborhood. However, a couple of times, I had soup and gari, native to my home culture, flown to me through overnight delivery (FedEx, UPS, DHL) from some Nigerian families living in the states of Virginia, Illinois, New Jersey, Texas, and Maryland.

Guess what! This food (soup and gari) flown to me from the various states presented a shocking experience and an uncomfortable condition to some people in my host culture. Thus, each time I went to warm and eat my Nigerian food, there was always a smell that came from it, as is the case with every food. To me, this smell was such an aroma and a delicacy that I enjoyed so much. But to others it was such a stench and an uncomfortable smell that it attracted some remarks and comments such as: "It smells awful." Without taking any offense, I went on to eat my kind of food that I missed so much. However, as a way of avoiding the making of those remarks and in order not to keep polluting the air for those concerned, each time I went to eat my Nigerian food, I would lock up myself in the kitchen and turn on the air expellant or exhaust fan called clipper ventilator. It worked out good both for those concerned with making the derogatory remarks and for me.

Naturally, in the event of this or similar experiences, one may get upset or become infuriated. There's nothing wrong with that. But, be it as it may, don't allow the anger to last too long. Cheer up and put on a smile because you never know who may be falling in love with your smile. In addition remember the saying: "Anger against a brother, sister or a friend is felt in the flesh, not in the marrow." If you are not satisfied with this saying, think about the words of Scripture, which exhorts: "...the sunset must not find you angry...do not give the devil his opportunity, stand up to him, strong in faith." If you are still not convinced of this, then be reminded that the longer you hold the anger in you or keep chewing the cud of grief, the faster you get older and possibly reduce your lifespan. Spare yourself this trouble, pull yourself together and keep moving. Don't stop!

MEALTIMES

In terms of time, my new culture, more often than not, practices and talks about specific times for particular meals such as breakfast, lunch, and supper or dinner. There is also the habit of snacking between meals.

In my home culture among the Etung people, you eat whenever you are hungry. To this end, sometimes some people eat once, twice, or even three or four times per day, but not at specific times with such names as breakfast, lunch, and supper. However, on a more advanced and wider level in some boarding schools in Nigeria, this stereotyped manner of eating occurs.

Having been so used to the eating habits of my home culture in terms of time and eating less, I found it very difficult to adjust to my foreign culture in this regard. Therefore, whenever I was able to, I ate only when I became hungry. Hence, it would not be a surprise to hear that several times the cook left my food in the refrigerator so that when I became hungry later,

Cooking, Food, and Eating

I could heat it in the microwave to eat. Sometimes, however, to keep the cook happy and give her a sense of fulfillment in her job and to keep company with the pastor, as courtesy requires, I did go for meals, but without the appetite to eat since I was not always hungry at those times.

Furthermore, due to the fact that, I usually eat less, I always feel scared when an invitation is extended to me to attend an occasion or visit with a family, especially with so much emphasis on the availability of plenty of food by my host. Such an invitation could sound like this: "There will be plenty of food, don't fail to come." Probably, besides the emphasis being a cultural practice, it may also be intended to serve as an attraction, a catcher, an enticement, or a reason for honoring the invitation. In my case, if it is the second option, then I think my host gets it all wrong. Besides my eating less, I also usually feel guilty for not eating when there is plenty of food, while others in some parts of the world do not even see as much of it to eat. Finally, I also feared making my host uncomfortable if I honor such an invitation but would not eat when others are doing so. To this end, I must confess that I made up several excuses that kept me from honoring some invitations in order to stay away from plenty of food. Whether those "affected" believed me or not, I still felt that my excuses always held together.

Still on this subject of eating, it is important to note that one's ability to eat very well with a good appetite at all times, or otherwise, may attract some remarks and criticisms from some people of the host culture. These remarks may be like a fulfillment of the comparative Scripture passage about the lifestyle of John the Baptist and Jesus Christ. In comparing these

A Handbook on Culture Shock

two figures, the Scriptures say: "Remember John: he didn't eat bread or drink wine, and you said: 'He has an evil spirit.' Next came the Son of Man, eating and drinking, and you say: 'Look, a glutton for food and wine, a friend of tax collectors and sinners." (Lk. 7: 33-34). In applying this Scriptural passage to the point under consideration, as a newcomer (to the developed country), especially if you are coming from any of the developing countries, where the general notion or idea is that there is "no food there," if you eat always and very well with a rapacious, voracious and roaring appetite, it could be said of you that, you eat the way you do because, where you came from there is no food. And so, you must have been starving ever since you were born. Hence, having come to where there is so much food, you want to eat to make up for all your years of starvation.

On the other hand, if you don't eat as often or as expected, it could also be said of you that, since you do not have enough food in your country, you are eating less so as not to enlarge your stomach, since you have to return back to your poor country at some point. These and similar remarks could cut deep and right through you. And you may feel the hurt of great insult and scorn. My advice to anyone who, anywhere and at any point becomes a victim of these cutting remarks are as follows: Always consider the source (as the Americans would say – used here in a positive sense). In addition, consider also the circumstance, situation and condition of the remark in terms of place, time and person. When you do this, then, keep moving while remaining authentic, resolute and focused on your mission. If necessary, you can have this Scripture passage for your consolation: "Fortunate are you who are poor, the kingdom of

Cooking, Food, and Eating

God is yours. Fortunate are you who are hungry now, for you will be filled. Fortunate are you who weep now, for you will laugh. Fortunate are you when people …insult you…Rejoice in that day and leap for joy, for a great reward is kept for you in heaven."(Lk. 6: 20-23).

As I gathered from some telephone conversations with some of my colleagues in other parts of America, there is another side to this food mentality. Yes, depending on which part of the U.S. you find yourself, you, as a foreigner from the developing world, may not be expected to complain about food in any way. You may not have any right to be "picky" or "choosy" or "selective." Just eat whatever that is set before you whether you personally like it or your body is accepting of the kind of food or not. After all, you come from a country where your people back home are dying of hunger, thirst and all forms of starvation. This may be true, but, naturally, it is painful to be reminded of this fact, directly or indirectly or by any kind of insinuation. Again, if you find yourself in any of these uncomfortable situations, my candid and brotherly advice to you is this: "Pull yourself together, and know that, 'this too, will pass away.'" On a personal note, I must thank God and the Adirondacks people that, for the most part, I was never given a cause to feel "underprivileged" or suffer any of these or similar agonizing remarks.

But, in defense of some Americans who may be having this derogatory food mentality about some foreigners, it should be noted that they react and respond to or behave according to the information given to them and the news they hear about Africans, for instance, from various sources. So, I hold those Americans concerned, excused for their knowledge and I do

A Handbook on Culture Shock

not fault or blame them for their consequent behaviors. Americans then only know minority communities outside America that are presented to them through stereotypes, through images in the media. If people keep being portrayed as, criminals, poor, hungry, sick, living in squalors, or as undocumented immigrants or gang members, or even as a whole *continent* (of Africa) being portrayed as just *one village*, that is what the Americans tend to believe. Hence, I'll tell you whom to blame: Blame the mass media and some Nigerians (in this context) who always project and present the pathetic picture of the African-suffering-poor to their white counterparts. Oftentimes this "brainwashing" is for some selfish material gains by those who have the opportunity to represent their countries outside their homelands. What do you expect, when you give a man a "gun" to shoot you? He may either shoot you, or run away with it, thereby, leaving you with no weapon to defend yourself when the need arises. Your present state, thereafter, becomes worse than the former, because, more often than not, the knowledge you give out to people about yourself, would be used against you. These "impostors" (excuse my language) forget that by so doing, they poorly represent their countries and belittle themselves in the face of "others." By and large, let the "host" and the "hosted" remember that every story has two sides. And so, even the most developed world has its own other side of the story.

In looking at the other side of the story regarding the situation of poverty in the most developed world, the "convicting" words of Jesus cannot be doubted. He categorically states in the Scriptures that: "The poor you will always have with you." In this statement, Jesus did not mean that these poor are

Cooking, Food, and Eating

to be found only in Africa, or Asia, or Latin America, but all over the world. So let no one be tempted to doubt this reality or global poverty by asking: "How can this be when we are and live in the 'first world'– that is politically stable, socially accommodating, and economically sound?" Even in America where people throw away so much food everyday, some people among them still go hungry, naked, homeless and hopeless. Oftentimes, you hear people who listen to stories of poverty far away inwardly exclaiming: "Thank God, there is no poverty here." Hello! Wait a minute! Take that back! Poverty, hunger, malnutrition, lack of health care and homelessness exist even in the most developed and advanced countries. Comparatively speaking, however, this may not catch the eye and it may be less threatening. It is often *invisible*. Yes, people live in poverty in the midst of affluence. This reality often goes unnoticed.

There is a revealing and an amazing idea about eating, which I gathered from one of my random chats with a friend of mine sometime in my foreign culture. This chat afforded me another understanding into the reason why some people eat. Besides the general notion of eating when one is hungry, I also understand that some people eat when they are angry and annoyed. Others eat when they are frustrated and depressed. Still more, others eat when they are just full of joy and are happy with themselves. Again, some people eat when they are free and idle. Given these arguments on the global culture of eating as stated previously, can we then categorize the eating habits in human beings into two classifications by saying that some people *eat to live* and others *live to eat?*

MEAL COMPLIMENTS

The invitation to meals in homes and restaurants is a good and an acceptable practice in almost all the cultures of the world. The Etung people in Nigeria also welcome this gesture. However, in Etung, the habit of "eating out" is not an encouraged cultural practice. Perhaps this is caused by some traditional and cultural circumstances that are considered unhealthy and unsafe to the people, especially to the guest. Be that as it may, if you have the opportunity of being treated to such a nice gesture, your reaction as a guest in this regard is not only considered important, but also culturally expected. To say that this expected reaction should be complimentary to your host is to belabor the obvious. This complimentary reaction is a courtesy that manifests good upbringing and shows pleasant morals outside the home. Although this experience was not new to me, it took a different shape in my new environment in upstate New York, among the Adirondacks.

My home culture allows for compliments only at the end of a meal. In restaurants, the servers take your order, serve the meal, and go to positions where they could easily be seen and reached. In this way, either with the tingle of a table bell or through the wave of the hand, you can call their attention if their attention or services are needed.

At the end of a meal, the exact payment is made, though sometimes with a tip. This tip usually takes the form of leaving the change (if any) with the particular person that waited on you. However, this is not an expected cultural practice in my native Etung culture, and the server does not look forward to nor even expect any tip. Now, if you must tip the server who is a girl, you have to be careful so as not to be misunderstood

COOKING, FOOD, AND EATING

as intending to give a different message. Regardless of your good intention, you may be misjudged either by the sever or by other customers as insinuating something romantic if you give the tip directly to her. To this end, it is safer and advisable to go to the counter and give the tip to the "madam" or restaurant owner, if you want to be nice and to avoid any suspicion.

On the other hand, my foreign culture allows meal compliments not just at the end of a meal, but also as the eating of the meal goes on. In other words, as you eat, intermittently or from time to time, you should make complimentary remarks to your host, if you are invited to a home or even in a restaurant. The most commonly used compliments are: "This is very good." "This is very delicious." "The food smells good." "This is so nice of you." "This is wonderful." "I am so delighted to be your guest," and so on. This attitude is not only fascinating, but also encouraging to your host. However, some questions may arise at this point, especially from someone who is new to this cultural form of gesture. Some of these questions could be: Must these complimentary remarks be made at all meals? What if the meal does not appeal to you? The answer is this: Good etiquette demands complimentary reactions, come what may or irrespective of how you feel about the particular meal. In fact, do not be surprised that in the culture of the Adirondack people, your host may even ask for it directly or indirectly by asking questions such as: "How is my cooking?" "How are you enjoying my food?" "Do you like the food?" and so on. How uncultured you would be if your answers to these and similar questions are not positive and complimentary! In short, woe betide you to say that one's cooking or food is not good.

At restaurants, the servers come to take your order and to

A Handbook on Culture Shock

serve the meal. Then, they will keep coming around to your
table, each time asking you questions such as: "Is everything
okay?" "Are you doing well?" "How is your meal?" "Do you
need anything?" and so on. These incessant and unregulated
interruptions, good as they may be, do not allow room for privacy. Therefore, restaurants are not recommended places for
private meetings that border on sensitive and confidential discussions, because you have the ears and the eyes of the servers
around. Probably, the U.S. culture of openness and transparency gives room for and permits the activity of coming and
going to the customers by the servers at restaurants.

Among other fascinating things, it is important to note that
for the most part, as it is the case in other cultures of the world,
some restaurants in the Adirondack community are very interactive. In fact, if you want to know the latest news going on in
town by way of rumor, gossip, and opinion, these restaurants
provide you with a free opportunity to be abreast on current issues. Even though sometimes you may hear different versions
of the same story, the fact remains that you come to be aware
of something going on. After all, it is often said: "In every
rumor, there is an element of truth." Just be a good listener
whenever you are in any of these restaurants, and you would
be happy you did, as you will not leave the same as when you
came in. The ideas generally expressed and discussed range
from political issues, social matters, and church concerns to
other related human affairs. In some situations, at the end of
the day, major decisions are made or arrived at and stands are
taken here in these restaurants over a cup of coffee, orange
juice, home fries, bacon, and scrambled eggs. In terms of humor, yes, they can be good places to begin your day with a

smile or laughter and make you be careful about what you say, where you go, and what you do. On this note, permit me to say that it is highly recommended to occasionally avail yourself of the opportunity of eating out in a restaurant. Furthermore, the owners of the restaurants and even the servers can be very funny, as already suggested. Their jokes and sense of humor to keep the place lively are oftentimes very entertaining while remaining sometimes too serious. I mean that they can pick on you and still keep a very straight face as they go about their jobs. Certainly, this is one of the ways of customizing their businesses.

In my foreign culture, I was a victim of one of the jokes once at a restaurant called, "Poopies Restaurant" in a place called Glens Falls. As I walked into the restaurant on this fateful morning, this man, Jerry, the restaurant owner, looked at me for awhile and then walked up to me and placed his hand on my shoulders saying: "I like this guy. I'd like to follow him to wherever he comes from because the sunburn on his body is equitably distributed and he looks well tanned." After dropping this message, the many customers, including me, were cracking up; he walked back to continue his business very unruffled. Yes, that is what you get. Be prepared! It may be your turn to be picked on when you visit any restaurant. In the event of this, "don't have a bird," respond with a smile, even if it means smiling with a broken heart. It is not intended to hurt your feelings. You are only part of the show of the entertainment galore. If others can take it, why can't you also contribute to the world of humor?

Here is another quick caveat for you the newcomer to the Adirondack culture in relation to eating out in a restaurant. It

A Handbook on Culture Shock

is important to know that the bill for eating food in a restaurant by a group of people could be the shared responsibility of all. In other words, each individual, irrespective of gender, "stranger" or "home boy," contributes to paying for the bill brought by the server at the end of a meal, including the tip. sometimes, (though it rarely happens) it may not matter whether you were invited out to eat in a restaurant by someone else or not. You might have to contribute your own percentage of the bill. So, be aware and be warned of this cultural practice. Hence, as a way of not causing any embarrassing situation, it is advisable to always have some money in your pocket, even if someone is to invite you out for a meal in a restaurant.

I am informed of this cultural practice from an experience I personally had: It happened one day that a woman parishioner invited me out for lunch in a restaurant. After the meal, the server brought the bill, which was $40.00 for both of us. The parishioner brought out $20.00 plus tip and placed it on the bill receipt. She, then, pushed the bill to me. I looked at her, and she smiled at me, without knowing why I was looking at her. Thank God, I went out with $25.00 in my pocket with the intention of buying gas for my car and some stamps at the post office. Since I was afraid of causing any embarrassment, I quietly reached my hand into my pocket and brought out the money. Guess what! Everything I had on me at that point in time was spent - $20.00 for my own share of the bill and $5.00 for the tip. This shocking experience contributed in making me become very scared of accepting invitations to eat out in any restaurant. This particular experience may be an "exception to the rule." It doesn't speak in generality. Rather, it is only recorded here to serve as a caution or a forewarning to anyone who may find himself or herself in similar situations, to be ready for anything. At times, you never know with people.

This practice of sharing the responsibility of paying bills in restaurants is not the case in my home culture in Nigeria. Over here, one person (mostly a man) picks up the bill after a meal by a group of people or friends in a restaurant. In addition, in no circumstance is one who has been invited out for a meal expected to pay or contribute any money to pay for the bill. Thus, once you are invited out for a meal, it is the treat of or by the one who invited you, no more, no less.

As if the shocking experience of sharing bills was not enough, there was to be another stunning development that intensified my phobia of eating out in restaurants. On one particular day, two priests friends of mine invited me to join them out in a restaurant for dinner as part of a Christmas treat. We all got to the chosen restaurant, and the meal was served to us. By my estimation, we all ordered and had a simple meal. But I was astonished when the server brought the bill to us. You won't believe the amount. It was close to about $150.00. What I simply did was to shake my head as I said quietly to myself: "Thank God I am not to pick up the bill nor contribute to it since I was already informed that the dinner was going to be a treat from one of the priests." This bill was not only outrageous, but also scandalous as well to spend such an amount of money at one sitting and for what I considered a simple meal with one or two glasses of wine. To say that this experience constituted another shock to me on the culture of eating in restaurants is to belabor the obvious. I must confess that these two experiences, coupled with the fact of having someone who cooked for me in the rectory, intensified my attitude of mak-

A HANDBOOK ON CULTURE SHOCK

ing excuses to some of my friends and dear parishioners who, every now and then, invited me to go out with them for a meal in a restaurant. In fact, I considered it too expensive and an additional waste of money to eat out. Therefore, in sympathy with and concern for the inviting friend or family, I looked for every means to politely say no! to the invitation. Thank God that I did not run out of the many excuses, which I had to make up. Of course, they were all "white lies."

Finally, since tipping is a natural part of my foreign culture, it is only appropriate that you give a tip to the particular server who waited on you during your meal. Yes, they even expect it and look forward to it. This tip is a sign of acknowledging the good service rendered. It does not give a different message, and it is not a bribe, but a sign of gratitude. On this issue of tips, excuse my personal thought, the following questions arose in my mind: Who is to determine the percentage of the tip to be given? Is it a "mortal" sin if you do not give the expected tip? Do the tips comprise the servers' salary? Furthermore, given that the percentage of tip is determined by the management of the restaurant, don't you see the possibility of a restriction in the grateful generosity from the very generous customers to the particular sever for a job well done and a service well rendered?

Thanks to the benefit of inquiry and thinking aloud, which helped me to gain the knowledge and better appreciation of the practice of tips and the culture of gratuities. Upon inquiry, I gathered that, contrary to my initial thinking, the true situation is that the individual restaurants do not determine the percentage. It is a national standard as a suggested percentage, usually 15% for good service, but it can be increased for superior service according to the satisfaction of the particular customers. I was also made to know that the servers receive a small salary with the expectation that tips will supplement. This then being the case, I was disillusioned, and I stopped asking personal questions in this regard. Without any bias, therefore, I encourage all to support this culture of tips and encourage the servers for the tips are great incentives. This tip culture becomes even a charitable obligation on the customers when you realize that most of the servers are either indigenous or foreign student workers who are looking for money for their education and related needs. God bless you as you encourage them in this regard.

GIFTS, "FORCED-FEEDING," AND GIFT CERTIFICATES

A gift is something bestowed voluntarily and without compulsion. It is the act, right, or power of giving something to someone as a gesture of kindness, especially in an occasion of celebration. No doubt, all cultures of the world practice the act of giving gifts to one another, especially at certain times of the year such as Christmas, New Year, Thanksgiving, or at other occasions such as a birthday, anniversary, and so on. These gifts could be in the form of any material thing such as housewares, clothes, cosmetics, or cards, sometimes with *folds in the middle* containing cash or checks for money. However, there are still some cultural differences in this practice. Without claiming to say it all, this section on gifts will take a brief look at three aspects of the culture of gifts and the act of giving in the cultural perspectives of the Etung and the Adirondack peoples.

In the Etung and the Nigerian culture as a whole, the prac-

A HANDBOOK ON CULTURE SHOCK

tice of giving gifts to people is a common phenomenon. These gifts when they are given, for the most part, they are usually not carried in and wrapped with very decorative and related attractive materials. They are always in very simple but presentable carriers. Second, such gifts are for the private knowledge and consumption of the person who receives them. Therefore, the receiver takes them home and privately opens them in his or her house at any time he or she feels like doing so. It is uncultured to open them immediately and in the presence of the giver or other people. Otherwise, the person who does this is looked upon as being too anxious and overly expecting. The attitude of getting and opening gifts immediately therefore, is culturally unbecoming among the Etung people more specifically. I also see in the attitude of opening gifts at a later time, the teaching and practice of the virtue of patience among the Etung people.

My experience of the Adirondack world so far seems to present a new and different understanding of the culture of gifts and how they are treated. Over here, it is the culture of *gift-wrap,* or wrapping gifts, which shows so much respect to the gift given. Thus, no matter the quality and worth of any gift, even if it is a piece of candy, it is always well wrapped in a decorative manner with adorning, colorful, attractive, compelling, and appetizing features. In fact, it is difficult to resist a smile when you are receiving such gifts. But on opening them, you may be disappointed to discover that the wrapping material may even appear to be more expensive than the gift itself. Second, such gifts are to be opened either immediately when they are received or sometime later, and in either case, the opening or unwrapping of the gift is often done in the pres-

ence of other people. I may be wrong. But this is my experience and I have several instances to prove my case.

As a person, then, having been used to the practice of the
treatment of gifts as it is done in Nigeria, my newfound cultural experience and expectation as pointed above presented
a shocking and challenging situation that called to question
some realities. In fact, while I lived with the beloved people of
my newfound culture, sometimes when I received gifts from
them, I tended to forget this aspect of the treatment of gifts
by opening them up immediately in the presence of the giver
and other people. Moreover, each time I forgot, I always had
someone telling me: "Open your gift! Open your gift!" When
I shared this cultural difference with my congregation, I seized
the opportunity to tell them not to hold my slowness of opening the gifts they give to me against me, but to blame it on my
cultural background and upbringing. Thanks for their understanding, as they always did! Their consequent reaction to this
was that from hence some of them, whenever they gave me
gifts, would tell me to feel free to either open or not to open
them immediately in their presence.

My personal reaction to the practice I experienced in my
newfound culture concerning the receiving and treatment of
gifts, especially based on my cultural orientation is that initially, I felt uncomfortable with it. This was because, as I mentioned earlier, ethically I believe that the knowledge of some
gifts is for the private consumption of the receiver of them, and
to bring it to the external forum may cause some embarrassments. As I reflected on this practice among my Adirondack
friends, one of the justifications I could get for it was that,
probably, this cultural practice is based again on the U.S. cul-

A Handbook on Culture Shock

ture of openness, transparency, and trust.

The third aspect of the culture of gifts and the act of giving is about those who really give and the irony of giving. By this I mean to look at the people that are actually the givers of gifts of any kind, especially money in any culture. Personally, I believe that it is in the nature of human beings to share what God has given them with others. Hence, the saying: "There is joy in sharing." I also agree with the saying: "Nemo dat quod non habet." This saying is the Latin rendition for: "One cannot give what he has not." Taking this saying literally then, it is expected that those who have should be the givers or should give more, and those who do not have, should not give or should give less. But, depending on the culture and other personal reasons, things are not always as they should be. To this end, I must point out straightaway that, in my native culture, the givers of material gifts, more often than not, are those who have. Incidentally, such people when they do give they would also have it trumpeted before people. While those who do not have, in the real sense of the word, would always wish you well and every now and then, surprise you with their widows' mite. Logically speaking and charitably understood, this culture among the Etung people is understandable, acceptable and even tolerable.

It was such an irony and a shock to me, to seem to experience something new and different in my newfound culture. Generally speaking, the Adirondacks are givers. And at first sight, it is difficult to tell who has and who has not, or apparently impossible to draw a line between the haves and the have-nots. Yes, you could be living with or sharing a neighborhood or even a yard with a millionaire, without knowing it. It is in-

COOKING, FOOD, AND EATING

deed a culture of invisible next-door millionaires, so to speak. True as this gifts and giving culture may be, the fact remains that, ironically, those that are considered not to have much, are actually the givers. Based on my experience, I always saw in them a conviction of their obligation to give and share their little resources with others. However, one common denominator among the "haves" and the "have-nots" is that, they prefer to give and or donate, as the case may be, *anonymously*. Being a beneficiary of this anonymity in one way or another, it is my sincere prayer that the God who sees all that is done in secret should reward them a hundredfold by increasing what they have, granting them health of mind and body, success to the works of their hands and eternal life in the next.

On "forced-feeding," I must begin by saying that this may not be a suitable, appropriate, or polite expression. However, for want of a better and an apt way of describing the experience herein, it came readily to mind. Perhaps I should called it persuasive feeding. In any case, I beg you kindly to accommodate and excuse my language, especially if you have a better and a more suitable expression than this, which best describes this cultural situation. My intention here is briefly to draw your attention to what appears to be an imposed, induced, and enforced feeding. It is a kind of involuntary feeding that is not done willingly or on purpose. I mean it is for the most part, not based on the conscious choice, free will, and personal decision of the one who eats. In other words, you eat food, not because you want to, but because your host or the one who waits on you, advertently or inadvertently, directly or indirectly, and knowingly or unknowingly, talks you into it, even though this may be against your will or momentary disposition.

A Handbook on Culture Shock

No doubt, my native culture in one way or the other, at one time or another, indulges in forced-feeding of some sort. For instance, children, who may not want to eat but are encouraged by their parents to do so, mostly experience this act of forced-feeding. This is quite understandable, and it is experienced in almost all cultures of the world. Even you may have experienced it when you were a child.

To some degree also, some adults indulge in the forced-feeding appeal to fellow adults. This could be by way of an appeal by the hosts to the guests, especially if some of the guests invited to an occasion are eating, while others are not. In such a situation, you may find the hosts trying to ask why those who are not eating refuse to do so. Given this situation, the guests may be talked into tasting the food at least. By all means, to refuse to eat at an occasion when you are expected to is a matter of disturbing concern to the hosts, and it is always a kind and polite gesture to talk the guests into eating the food that has been provided.

However, it is very important to emphasize that at such occasions the hosts in my native culture sometimes do not push the appeal too far, by insisting repeatedly that the guests should eat the food. In short, most times, this attitude of forced-feeding, in my native culture is not even called for, since if the guests eventually yield to the appeal, the ration may be shortened for other people present. Therefore, it can conveniently be said that, for the most part, this forced-feeding appeal by some hosts is not really intended. It may just be suggested for courtesy sake. In fact, do not be surprised that, in their minds, (the hosts), there could be a prayer going on for the guest to say "no!" to the appeal, so that those who are eating or who

Cooking, Food, and Eating

want to eat may have enough.

It was indeed another eye opening experience to notice that this tendency of forced-feeding in the culture of the Adirondack people takes a different dimension. Here, this reality, more or less, takes a further, deeper, and conscripting appeal. No doubt, food seems to be in excess in most homes and for the greater majority of the people. Therefore, it is not surprising that, among their numerous hospitalities and kindnesses, the Adirondack people are extravagantly generous with food. To eat food, therefore, to your utmost satisfaction is not a problem in this culture. Instead, the problem may be with you who may not be able to eat as the people expect you to do. You can come face-to-face with the reality of this abundance of food in so many areas.

Thus, for a walk to the supermarkets, a visit with a family, a reception after a wedding or funeral ceremony, a birthday party, eating out in a restaurant or even being waited on by a cook, the quantity of food in these and similar areas is unbelievably humongous. At such occasions, you can be sure to see and always have more than enough to eat and drink and even take home a "care package" for someone else at home or for you to have another meal, probably the next day. Sometimes at such sumptuous occasions, you hear the slogan "doggy bags." These are usually the leftovers of what one has eaten in a restaurant, for instance, steak bones meant for dogs. Hence, the name became "doggy bags," which are brought home for the dogs. However, customers under the name of doggy bags oftentimes take meat, vegetables and other foodstuffs home, which end up in the belly of human beings. The name doggy bag, therefore, has become a polite way of taking home the

A Handbook on Culture Shock

leftovers by some customers.

Characteristically, in all the areas where food is prepared and eaten, the fact of persuasive or forced-feeding is a common denominator. Thus, you would often hear some persuasive remarks by the hosts or from others present such as: "Very good, you must try this." "Very delicious." "It's good for you." "You cannot go without trying this." etc. No doubt, courtesy and politeness demand that as a guest you be a good one by eating at least a little of what your host presents to you, even if you are not hungry or you don't feel like eating at the time. Surprisingly, in the culture of the Adirondack people, this courtesy and politeness may be forced on you. I mean if you say you do not want to eat, there will be the persistent and consistent insistence by some hosts that you eat or drink something. Probably, it is considered an insult if you do not eat or drink when you are expected to do so. Nevertheless, at such occasions, whether you eat willingly or otherwise, always remember to make some complimentary remarks to your host in accordance with the Adirondack's culture.

Many people both indigenes and foreigners or strangers have been caught up in the web of this abundance of food and forced-feeding phenomena. For those who become opportunists or those who yield to every forced-feeding bidding, they can go on eating, almost nonstop, as if the food will not be there again tomorrow. This attitude in some people is either the result of greed or gluttony. In both cases, either as opportunists or as victims of forced-feeding, some of the results are obvious: overeating, overweight, obesity, laziness, drowsiness, and sluggishness.

On a personal note, the food circumstances in the culture

of the Adirondack people did not go well with me initially. My problem was not that I was an opportunist at the abundant availability of food and drink. Instead, more practically, the difficulty was in my initial inability to say "no!" to whatever was set before me or to decline any invitation to eat out because I feared offending my host (s). The discomfort I felt after every eating session and visit was extreme and "bellyaching." Initially, sometimes whenever I ate too much, I felt like a boa that had swallowed a goat. In fact, as soon as I had honored an invitation and gone out, I began to long to return home, so as to feel free and possibly lie down, since I felt tired and drowsy after being persuaded to overeat and drink. Back home, I'll be sprawling helplessly, waiting for some of the food to digest, to give me room to breathe.

At this point, I am reminded of some dining experiences I had with regard to drinks within the first few days of my arrival in Hudson Falls, while having dinner in the rectory. I am naturally not given to taking strong drinks. This dislike for strong drinks with high alcoholic content is not because I am a priest, but it is strictly a natural dislike. I hold nothing against those who drink, whether they are priests, religious or not. At dinner, the cook would usually serve a glass of wine to me. For fear of not giving the initial impression that I am selective or choosy in what I eat and drink, I did drink the glass of wine at each of such meals. Besides my natural dislike, I have a very high sensitivity to alcohol. Hence, as soon as I had taken the wine served by the cook, I began to feel dazed and dizzy. I always tried and struggled to control myself so that I do not do anything unbecoming before the pastor during and after dinner while our conversation lasted. At the end, I would barely stagger up the staircase to my suite and then lie on my bed to regain balance. Thanks for the rails at the staircase in the rectory that gave me the balance and support I needed while going up to my room. It was really a funny and learning experience. At the end of each of such meals with the staggering effect of the glass of wine, I would always say to myself: " Wow! Welcome to the U.S.!"

These discomforting situations of pressurized or persuasive eating and polite drinking were not to continue for too long, especially when I suspected that something must be wrong somewhere with my seemingly "gullible" attitude. To overcome these situations, first, I learned to accept just one and the first invitation per day for an occasion of celebration, no matter how many invitations there were. And there were really many of them. Second, being in a culture where freedom is much talked about, both at home and outside the rectory, I decided to exercise responsible freedom by standing my grounds and by being authentically myself from hence, most especially about food, drinks, and mealtimes. By this I mean, as much as possible, I tried not to allow myself to yield to every bidding of forced-feeding, though with some periodic flexibilities. At some point, I was tempted to tell the "white lie" that I am on a diet, but I did not feel comfortable with that.

This new position of authenticity was very difficult to maintain. No doubt, it was like a disservice to the cook and to people of related services. However, with some courtesy and politeness, along with a grateful and cheerful face, I was able to stand my grounds, dig my heels and stick to my guns by saying: "No thanks!" to anyone playing host to me whenever I did not feel like eating or drinking something.

Cooking, Food, and Eating

Furthermore, it was good to be myself because, largely, it paid off eventually in the sense that, in addition to feeling comfortable and at ease with myself, it helped tremendously in preventing me from blowing out of shape or becoming overweight. While I continued to enjoy my new stand of authenticity, I prayed that my hosts would please bear with me and accept in good faith whatever inconvenience I was causing to them, as a result of my decision not to be swayed by sentimentalities and related feelings that would make me yield unwillingly to force-feeding. This food circumstance, by my estimation, was not sufficient to permit the politeness or courtesy of displeasing oneself in order to please one's hosts, even though it may be a sacrifice allowable in some other situations.

There is another dimension of forced-feeding that goes on, probably unnoticed among the Adirondack people. This is in the form of "gift certificates," especially and specifically those meant for food. For the benefit of those who do not know what this means and are not familiar with this practice, this calls for an explanation: Gift certificates in this context are food certificates that are available at restaurants, McDonald's and similar places where food is sold. People go to those places to buy them and then give them to other people as gifts. If you were given such a certificate, you only need to take it to the specified food center, and upon presenting it to the staff, you will be given the food as "specified" on the certificate or any other foodstuff sold in the particular place that you prefer. And whatever you decide to get, it must be in quantitative agreement with the amount of money contained therein. This means that, the person who gave it to you has already paid for the food through the gift certificate.

A HANDBOOK ON CULTURE SHOCK

Fortunately or unfortunately, one who is a beneficiary of a gift certificate cannot just turn in the certificate at the stipulated restaurant and demand a return of the money in cash. That is, you cannot redeem the complete amount of money in cash contained in the gift certificate, especially the ones specified for food. However, you can be given some change in cash if what you purchased is less than the amount contained in the gift certificate. In any case, the point remains that, whether you like it or not, to use the gift certificate you received, you must spend either all or some of the money it is worth by buying any food of your choice found in the designated restaurant. It does not matter whether you actually care for all the different foods found there or not. The issue of freedom to use what you have been given as a gift is restricted in this case, and I suspect a kind of forced-feeding in this good gesture of giving gift certificates. I may be wrong.

Good as this gesture may be and kind and generous as the intention of the one who gives you the gift certificate may be, this cultural practice has its own setbacks and disadvantages. Thus, in addition to its disguised form of forced-feeding, as I suspect and guess, this gesture does not allow the beneficiary of such a gesture the elasticity or flexibility to enjoy the intended kindness, generosity, and hospitality of the giver. This is because such a beneficiary is already directed to a specific place and to buy just what the gift certificate specifies, no more, no less. Yes, you have no choice other than to respect the intention of the donor whether the particular donor is there with you or not.

On a personal note, this cultural practice of giving gift certificates in the culture of the Adirondack people was complete-

COOKING, FOOD, AND EATING

ly new to me, in relation to the experience of my Nigerian culture. Now, while my contact with and my stay in America lasted, the gift certificate gesture, especially in regard to food, I must confess, did not mean much to me for obvious reasons, even though I kept receiving so many of them from some of my very caring parishioners. First, my preference to be flexible and free to use the gift certificates given to me was a better option. This option was stalled by the gifts being in certificate forms. Second, in the rectory where I was living, a competent cook prepared all the meals. Hence, I considered eating out as not only unnecessary, but also wasteful and uncalled for. This second option becomes more arguable when you think of the fact that, most of the times, the different foods that are prepared and served in the restaurants around, were not so much what I really cared for. Please, do not hold this against me, otherwise, I may challenge you to take a trip to Agbokim (my village) in Nigeria, and find out if you can eat what the people eat there. I bet you, if you don't starve to death, it will be an uphill task for you to survive there.

In fact, there was a day I gathered all the gift certificates given to me. You wouldn't believe the monetary value contained in them, which if translated into cash, with its flexibility and elasticity, freedom and choice, will have helped a great deal in attending to other equally important needs of my choice, such as buying telephone cards, buying my car, and paying for its insurance and registration. Also, through them and in this way more help could have been given to the poorest of the poor, the *used* and the *remembered-forgotten* of some of our African sisters and brothers and possibly others around my foreign neighborhood, to mention but a few.

A HANDBOOK ON CULTURE SHOCK

On another note, the experience of my newfound culture gave me a cause to reflect on another phenomenon of life. This phenomenon has suffered so many literary expositions, various attacks and invasions, and practical differences in human handling and practices of it. It is none other than the topical issue bordering on the marriage institution. You are welcome to travel with me on this note, in the next chapter, as we continue this grand tour on cultural differences and similarities with all their attendant shocks.

3

THE INSTITUTION OF MARRIAGE

This chapter will attempt to analyze an important custom and relationship or behavioral patterns in the Etung versus the Adirondack cultures under the umbrella of the marriage institution. For the most part, cultures are formed and informed by the institution of marriage and the variations in its ceremony. This reality plays a vital role in the formation and information of all cultures of the world. A wide survey and critical case study would unveil and reveal many differences in its practice in relation to cultural settings. These differences, especially as highlighted and narrated below, could be fascinating, startling, revealing, and shocking.

THE MARRIAGE INSTITUTION

According to *Webster's II New College Dictionary:* "Marriage is a legal union of a man and a woman as husband and wife." Furthermore, on this pivotal institution, *The Code of Canon Law,* which is the compendium of the law of the Catholic Church, precisely in Canon 1055, in obedience to the law of nature, articulates that: "The matrimonial covenant, by which a man and a woman establish between themselves a

The Institution of Marriage

partnership of the whole of life, is by nature ordered toward the good of the spouses and the procreation and education of offspring."

Marriage is a union of opposite sexes for sharing life and love and for procreation. Ordinarily, this assertion on marriage should be understood and taken *de fide* or dogmatically and so swallowed completely. Incidentally, things are not always the same, neither are they as they seem. Therefore, the marriage institution is under siege and is being interpreted, understood, and applied to suit one's particular situation, either as an individual, a movement or a cultural practice. Fortunately or unfortunately, this marriage situation is becoming a global phenomenon in one way or another.

THE METAMORPHOSIS OF THE MARRIAGE INSTITUTION IN NIGERIA (ETUNG)

In Nigeria, as well as in all cultures of the world, every marriage begins with an attraction. This attraction is mostly personal, hence the saying: "Beauty is in the eyes of the beholder." However and whatever these attractions may be, it is a known fact that they are more or less interpreted and understood under the name of *love*. Incidentally, this issue of love could be a disguised attraction between partners of equal or unequal positions in life, by way of chronology and societal status. To the best of my knowledge, my native culture does not encourage early marriages between equals. By this, I mean that marriages between people in their teens or early twenties is not a cultural practice. More practically then, the ripe age for marriage between spouses is in their late twenties and above.

However, due to economic factors, situations, and reasons,

A Handbook on Culture Shock

there are some early marriages, especially between teenage girls or women in their early twenties and very old men, or vice versa. Such marriages are mostly considered and referred to as marriages between unequal parties. The former, that is, marriage between a very young girl and a much older man is mostly economically motivated. Thus, a family that is economically poor, may feel constrained to give away their very young daughter in marriage to an older and wealthy man in order to have economic support from him. Ordinarily, those concerned will not want to do this, but they have to, just to eat and survive, have a roof above their heads and clothe themselves. By all intent and purpose, this marriage setting is slavish and sickening. It is like trading a human being for material goods. This situation is indeed sad, though it remains inevitable for many families as the only possible means of making ends meet. The question is: Do the ends really meet? Cases abound where young girls cry aloud when the bride price is being paid and as they move into their unhappy matrimonial homes. I also suspect a kind of "forced marriage" in this arrangement.

On a more overwhelming note, another marriage culture is of late creeping in and is becoming popular among many Nigerian girls. Permit me to qualify such marriages with names that, by my understanding and estimation, best describe them: *gold digger marriages, evergreen marriages, all-ready-made marriages, and overseas marriages.* No doubt, because of the rough, tough, and hard, strangulating and seemingly hopeless economic situation in Nigeria, marriages to men with overseas connections have become a gateway to hopeful and greener pastures for many a young girl. I mean, no matter how old a man with this connection may be, especially a U.S. connection any young girl is ready and very willing humbly to accept his hand in marriage. Yes, "it is yours for the asking." Given this situation, unbelievably, cases abound where very beautiful underage teenage girls or those women in their very early twenties are married to unbecoming men, who could as well be their great-grandfathers.

In some cases, these kinds of marriages also suffer the syndrome of "overnight marriage." By this is meant, without any courtship, a man and a woman can agree to marry at their first meeting and almost instantly. From the traditional and Church statistics on marriage, this experience of instant marriage is more evident within the month of December every year. This is because many Nigerians living overseas go home during this time of the year for the Christmas celebration. This explains why the months of September through December every year (the "ember" months as they are called by many), are seen as rush months for many Nigerian girls. Within these months, there is a lot of traveling by them in search of money for shopping. Then, precisely in the month of December ("injury time," as many call it), these girls dress to kill for courting. Perhaps also, they may be lucky to fall into the hands of these overseas men, especially the **Americanas.** Given this luck, there is no question as to the choice for the old, the good, the bad, and the ugly (men).

Without any intention to be judgmental, permit me to say that all these attractions are simply because these men are materially successful. Hence, the saying: "Behind every successful man, there is a young and beautiful girl." But the question I would like to ask is: "Doing what?" Are the young girls who

A Handbook on Culture Shock

are behind these successful men, so to speak, helping to sow or are they reaping where they have not sown, gathering where they have not scattered and building on a foundation they have not laid or better put, building on no foundation at all? The consequences are obvious. Yes, all of these cases have their untold consequences that, unfortunately, are uncomfortable and unfavorable to many of these girls. Once trapped into this kind of marriage, they have no choice, but silently to endure and put up with the "papas," come what may.

Unfortunately and in utter disillusionment, many of these gold diggers and overseas marriages oftentimes turn out not as initially thought of and dreamt about by the girls. Hence, they become nightmares for those involved. Incidentally, this unfortunate dawn of reality occurs when the knot has hurriedly been tied and both parties have come abroad. This disillusionment is so disappointing to many of the girls. At this point, many of them come to realize that: "Not all that glitters is gold." They also come to know that: "It appears so green from afar." It is also, at this time, too late to grasp the benefits of the saying that: "The devil you know is, (sometimes), better than the angel you do not know." Finally, how late it is to come to terms with the saying that: "A bird at hand is worth two in the bush."

Ask those girls who have placed their hands on the "plough" of evergreen marriages how inwardly happy and fulfilled they are. If they want to be honest with themselves and true to their situations, they would tell you that their overseas dreams did come true, but their overseas marriages are, in some cases, slavish and boring, controlling and bossy, abusive and sickening, lonely and lonesome, and emotionally unfulfilling, besides

The Institution of Marriage

other deceitful, fraudulent, disappointing and heart wrenching discoveries. But, too late!

Please, do not ask me what most of these successful men do to earn a living in the United States. Otherwise, it may lead to opening a Pandora's box that may amount to the hurt and the discomfort of many. Nevertheless, permit me to say that what most of them do in terms of odd jobs in the United States is appalling. Incidentally, out of pride they will not do similar jobs in Nigeria. However, in objective defense of these men who do the odd jobs in question in the United States, it is a fact that, besides the shame and ridicule that similar jobs may bring to them in Nigeria, these same jobs back home do not pay as much as they do in the United States. In fact, most times, the take-home pay cannot take them home.

In addition to the pride of being overseas, when these men go home to Nigeria to visit, they hang out and dine with chiefs, kings, and high-ranking politicians. Please, don't ask me also how much they have to deprive themselves of by way of what they have to forego and what they have to sacrifice in order to save enough money to fly home and appear attractive and rich for a few days before their friends and others (back home). If you push this question too far, you may be uncomfortable with the answer. So, let us "allow sleeping dogs to lie." This idea of saving a lot before one goes home, becomes understandable where to home people, leave (to go home, especially from the U.S. to Nigeria) meant the return of the village boy or girl who had made good in America, and everyone looks forward to sharing, by feasting sumptuously in his or her good fortune not minding the antecedents. Yes, those with the "American post" would normally and usually be expected to do better than their

A HANDBOOK ON CULTURE SHOCK

local counterparts and other friends with the "European post." Probably this explains why some Nigerians have stayed in the U.S. for too long a time without the thought of going home, besides other factors. To such people, I challenge you to be authentic by putting yourselves together and start planning NOW to go home for a visit this summer, or winter, or spring, or fall season. Stop deceiving others and yourselves. Spare yourselves also the trouble of suffering in silence, by missing your home and people every other day. I am convinced that, right deep in your heart, you have an unquenchable hunger for home, and an immeasurable yearning to be connected with your people. I know also that, in spite of you, you are aware and you believe that, no matter what "no place like home."

The question is: Do the young girls who have become wives too early to the "Americanas" have any choice to opt for something else other than the particular marriages in question when they are in the United States? The answer is a flat "no!" Thus, having been wooed and married overnight with the promises of "for better for worse, for richer for poorer, in sickness and in health, until death do us part," they have no choice but daily to put up with the stark realities of the unhappy matrimonial union. Perhaps, some would leave if they had any opportunity of even going back home. But they cannot, and they are stuck, since these "papas" know what to do to cripple and prevent them from gaining any freedom to "elope." In fact, some of the girls who could go back home would not dare to do so out of shame, and so, they stay for the economic and material advantages. This is because the fact remains that the worst economic situation overseas, especially in the United States, in some cases is better than the best economic situation in the

THE INSTITUTION OF MARRIAGE

particular place where they have come from in Nigeria.

True and attractive as the economic situation may be, a marriage that is considered balanced, authentic, successful, and is likely to or is destined to be a union of mutual and lasting fidelity demands the compatibility of both partners. This compatibility is, more or less, at the chronological and social, physical and emotional, mental and psychological, and even the spiritual levels of life. Against this backdrop, therefore, it is a very poor exchange to sacrifice your happy, physical, psychological, and emotional matrimonial union on the altar of economic advantages and material comfort.

These poor exchanges have happened, and they still do. But in the midst of these woes of matrimonial disillusionment, some of these girls sometimes know how to make ends meet. After all: "Since the hunter has learned to shoot without missing, **Eneke,** the bird, has also learned to fly without perching," Or: "You can never shoot a moving target," so the saying goes. Yes! "When one door closes, another one opens." Again, I want to plead that you do not ask me how most of these young girls make ends meet. Otherwise, "worms would be let out of the cans" and "the old women's teeth may be set on edge" because "dry bones" are going to be mentioned in the bid to investigate and attempt to answer this and similar questions. But suffice me to say that – Eneke should be careful, because sometimes you may perch and run out of luck. This unlucky situation can be buttressed with an experience between two Nigerian immigrants in the U.S.

The story has it that, a Nigerian man in his late fifties, after marrying an American (woman) to get a green card, divorced, and later married a young woman in her early twenties from his

A HANDBOOK ON CULTURE SHOCK

Nigerian hometown. In spite of the fact that the woman was already into a serious relationship with another guy back home, the dream of America was too tempting to miss. So when this man who had visited for Christmas met her at a wedding party, and later proposed to her, she quickly agreed. When everything about marriage was done, and she came to America, it turned out to be a different ball game. Her husband was a cabbie, and she began to feel the stress of life – bills, abuses, and above all loneliness. Yes, her husband was out most nights driving the cab, and during the day, she was in school running a crash program on nursing. She was beginning to be stressed with loneliness as she spent very few hours with her husband each day. Well, young as she was, and seeing or listening to other students of her age tell their romantic escapades, she became tempted. She flew without perching for a long time, but luck ran out of her way one day. On one fateful day, she with her new American lover in her husband's car went to "another" motel. Unfortunately, her husband came into the vicinity to drop off a passenger and saw his car at the motel's parking lot. Let me spare you the rest of the story, as your conclusion may not be different from mine nor from what actually happened between the man and his wife eventually. There is more to this world than behold the eyes. This led to their divorce. Now, the question is – who is to blame, given this scenario? One lie built upon another. One deceit begot another. Unfortunately, the equation in this case, balanced out on a disastrous note.

How else do I want God to convince me that my reflection in this book is providential and guided by Providence as such! This statement is made possible because of a timely email that I got at the time. The said email was forwarded to me from

The Institution of Marriage

Lanre Yusuf on April 24, 2005 through the email medium of the Association of Nigerians in the Capital District (ANCD) State of New York. This email contains a true story of an experience narrated by Tony Agbali. The subject is: "African Migrants and Multiple Factors in Divorce Issues: Internalization and Liberalization Identity." Based on the subject, the author of the email observed this ugly phenomenon through his existential and human lenses. Hence, he continued to attempt an understanding of immigrant dynamics in general, and specifically those of African immigrants. As a Catholic priest, he said that he had listened to both married men and women share their stories, struggles and anxieties in this important aspect of life. Sometimes the different trajectories present a challenge of understanding and coming to terms with reality.

It is a known fact that immigration and special movements introduce complex issues of social and interactive relations, it shifts orders, reframes, and reconfigures simplistic and taken for granted idioms. In this array and rearrangement of data, new meanings emerge, new ideas are born, new ideologies are passed on, and new personalities are formed. Of course, new issues also beget new challenges giving rise to modalities change. The purpose of presenting Tony Agabli's experience here is, if for nothing else, to enable us view them as they are, and for what they are – as issues affecting human existence and spatial domains.

The email states that, in a key note address presented to the Igala Association USA in Washington D.C. in 2003, Tony pointed out the sad phenomenon of the rising tide of divorces among Nigerian and African immigrants. He noted from observation how the very fact of immigration and the value ingratiation or internalization, itself can become a factor for the rising tide of divorce among couples. This he substantiated with a true experience. The excerpts of the scenario goes like this: This man came to America in the late 1970s, married an American to get his "green card, (of course) divorced, then sought for a wife at home. Thereafter, his wife, who was a nurse, joined him in the U.S. But he would not allow her pursue her professional dreams of working and getting her license to practice as a nurse here in the U.S. He wanted her to be a-stay-at-home wife and mother, just making babies. He constantly reminded her that he brought her to the golden land of diamond and opportunity and so, once he speaks the case is finished. This woman was seriously demeaned by the jerkiness of her husband. In the course of time, the marriage fell apart.

It is also a known fact that many a Nigerian man in the U.S. prefer to marry nurses because of the peculiarly affirmed good income and demands for nurses. To this end, some men in this class come to this country, mess up their credits and want to rely on the assumption that they brought their wives to America, and so cultivate an ultimate culture of dependency and parasitic antennae for sucking their wives dry. Thank God, these women come over to America and make their lives and those of their family better. Amidst this betterment, however, there is also a realization of the odds in reality – they struggle to pay bills, to meet up with "home" demands and expectations and to generally survive. And for those whose wives are not nurses, faced by the glaring financial challenges, husband and wife may decide that the best route or alternative is for the wife to go to the community college, and do a two year nurs-

THE INSTITUTION OF MARRIAGE

ing to ease the pain. Cases abound where such women (nurses), having graduated, have had "scales fall off their eyes", and so decided not to live the "lie" anymore. Or alternatively, they may begin to live the lie, too. Equation balances itself.

The issue at stake is not that simplistic. But the point remains that, some African women, when they, too, begin to make good money and earn some respectability, begin to imagine things, internalizing values that are sometimes driven by western feminine paradigms as ultimate and normative cultural ideals. The earlier these women realize that this axiomatic internalization of western cultural ideals is tantamount to forcing a round peg into a squared hold, the better, both for them, their marriage and their family. Culture is a way of life that people are "born" into and not "learned" by.

When we look at the public picture of the marriage under consideration due to its attractions, the pictures of such couples in shopping malls and supermarkets, and on the streets and ecclesial cum social forums are dismally disproportionate and unequal, shameful, and embarrassing. Some of them even cause a public "stinky stir." These pictures are a social malady and contribute to increasing societal disequilibrium and related matrimonial improper fractions. Consequently, the public discomfort felt by these girls in such outings is always deeply suffocating. Many of them cannot wait to get away and leave for their homes during such occasions. In fact, do not be surprised to hear that some of the married girls introduce their husbands to others as uncles, stepfathers, grandpas, and so on, (especially when their husbands are not within hearing distances). Even among the audience who look at such couples during such occasions, tongues wag, and gossip thrive. The

A Handbook on Culture Shock

irony in this situation is that while the "gold diggers" are feeling uneasy, the "papa husbands" are showing off and having a good time hanging out with the beautiful and very young. Unfortunately, these girls are stuck in this shame until death do them part. These kinds of marriages also explain why you oftentimes see in our society, men who look so frail and advanced in years with women who look so energetic and young in years as husbands and wives. In fact in some case, especially if the "Americanas" are wealthy men, these women pray for them (their husbands) to die so they can inherit the property, which they have not worked for. Are you surprised at this?

The question now is: What must we do to balance this shameful matrimonial disequilibrium? The only remedy to this unbecoming situation would come from these *big-eye* and **aje butter** girls. They should minimize those big eyes. Parents who oftentimes arrange, push, or talk their daughters into these marriages should learn to be contented with what they have. They should realize that not all fingers were created to be equal and are actually not equal. They should take the world for what it is and not for what it ought to be. This would enable them to stop this matrimonial "slave trade" with its glaringly and stupefyingly poor exchange. Probably, they need to be catechized and made to know that this "trafficking" is an offense against God and humanity and thus, sinful. In short, they should listen to the saying: "Cut your coat according to your size and according to the size of cloth available and at your disposal."

This reflection reminds me of an experience I witnessed when I went for my visa interview. Seated by me at the U.S. embassy in Nigeria were a man and a little teenage girl. All

The Institution of Marriage

along, I thought they were a grandpa and a granddaughter or, at best, a father and a daughter of his old age. Little did I know that they were a couple. This realization came about when they were invited to the interview window. I could hear the man saying to the visa secretary who was interviewing them that: "She is my wife." The secretary asked him again: "Did you say she is your wife or your daughter?" The man insisted: "I said, she is my wife." The visa secretary who, most probably, was shocked and utterly taken aback refused to give the girl a visa. The visa secretary, who was a woman, told them to go back and bring sufficient and substantial proof of their marriage. This proof includes traditional, Church, and court marriage photographs, videotapes, and certificates. Upon inquiry, I learned that cases like that were not uncommon with Nigerian men and young girls at the embassy.

On another cultural dimension, the marriage institution in Nigeria passes through some stages before climaxing at the high point of authentic and recognized union. In the Etung culture in particular, the first stage of marriage at the traditional level is called **the knocking on door** ceremony. This is the stage of introduction of the groom to the bride's family. At this stage, the groom goes to the nuclear family of the bride, makes himself known to the bride's parents, and declares to them his intention of marriage. He goes along with his immediate family members and his close friends. When the intention is declared and accepted, then they eat and drink together. The second and final traditional stage is the paying of the marriage dowry or bride price to the family of the bride on an agreed date, day, and time. Eating and drinking, singing and dancing by both the nuclear and extended family members joyously character-

A HANDBOOK ON CULTURE SHOCK

ize this stage. At times, the whole village gets involved in the feasting. It is always an occasion of great joy and pride for the parents of the bride, especially if the groom is a promising, prominent or a successful man in the society.

After the traditional aspects of marriage have all been completed, the next stages are Church wedding and court marriage. The court marriage is a new introduction to the culture, and it has not been generally and fully accepted because of its suspected implications in relation to divorce. The suspicion is that in case of divorce after a court marriage has been contracted, the woman is always at the vantage point. Some **Nigerian-Americanas** who have suffered divorce in the hands of "American women" can testify to this. This means that the woman always benefits more than the man in any court decision to accept and end the marriage between a couple, even if the woman is at fault. Second, there is also the mentality that court marriage does harm to the family of the man, who very often becomes less concerned and disinterested in the affairs of his cradle family members. Third, there is again the suspicion that women who are married in court become too certain of their marriages and, hence, assume an air and carry about an authoritative ego and personality by becoming powerfully in charge of their spouse's property to the disregard of the family members of their husbands. Because of these and other reasons, only very few couples get involved in this kind of marriage in the Etung culture, for instance.

With the coming and acceptance of Christianity and its teachings, church weddings are encouraged in my home culture. These also pass through some preparatory stages. Thus, before the wedding day, the banns of marriage are sent to the

THE INSTITUTION OF MARRIAGE

home parishes of the couple where they are read in the church for four consecutive Sundays, if they are Catholics. Within this time, if people have any objections to the marriage in question, such people are encouraged to make their objections known to the pastor. While the time for the marriage bans last, the couple are made to attend pre-marital or pre-cana programs. Furthermore, for the wedding to take place, the fulfillment of the traditional stages of marriage are necessary conditions for its (church wedding) valid celebration. In fact, some pastors, shortly before the commencement of the wedding ceremony, may even take some time to invite the parents of the bride to testify publicly in the church that the traditional aspects of the particular marriage have all been properly taken care of by the groom, according to native law and custom. It is only after this that the pastor would proceed with the celebration of the wedding in question.

It is important to know that, as much as possible, all church weddings take place on Saturdays. Then, on the next or immediate Sunday, the wedded couple, if they are Catholics, goes to church with their family members and friends to offer a special Mass of thanksgiving. In this Mass, the couples (after a group-wedding or just one couple, as the case may be), accompanied by their well-wishers, carry the gifts of bread and wine to the altar. They also carry other gifts in cash and kind in thanksgiving to God and for the care of the pastor. Some who can may also make a special donation or contribution to the church on this day in support of the particular church. This is also another joyous occasion, and people go wild with frenzy in the church with hilarious singing, clapping, and dancing. On a day like this, people do not look at their watches, nor

A HANDBOOK ON CULTURE SHOCK

are they in a hurry to leave the church. As usual, after both the wedding ceremony proper on Saturday and the thanksgiving Mass on Sunday, there are receptions organized by the couples for all who attended the occasion.

At this point, it is worthy of note that, at some point, both in the Church immediately after the wedding or marriage rite proper has been completed, and at the reception after the wedding ceremony, there is the *spraying* tradition. This spraying tradition or custom has to do with the couple going out to dance, and the onlookers periodically join them in the dance while pasting money on the couple's faces or other ways of demonstrating their happiness for the couple.

In fact, at this high point of the wedding reception, you can't resist hitting the dance floor with the compelling rhythm of the traditional music whether you have money to spray or not. Yes, at such occasions, it is not the Rock `N Roll music, nor Blues, nor the Hip-Hop lyrics, not even the Symphony Orchestra pianos, violins and guitars nor the African high-life that awake the spirit of dance among the people. What really sends goose bumps on your body and commands the hair on your head to rise surging for a dance, is the unadulterated traditional music. The apex of it all is when the **Agaba** boys and girls take over the air with their local instruments and almost wild and warlike chants, pounding the life out of large, hide-covered drums and other metallic tinkles, traditionally known as **Ogenes.** You don't see that everyday. But the sound is convincing with its infectious, lusty beats. When they come into and invade the dance floor, if you remain seated and unmoved without, at least tapping your feet or nodding your head along with the beating of the music, then, you are either tone deaf or you are struggling to resist the natural urge and emotional challenge to dance.

The method of dancing is more or less personal as the spirit moves its participants. However, it is far from moving like triangles in an alien dance ordained for dancing in circles, which most times, hold dancing partners too close for "comfort - breast to breast and groin to groin," so that the dance flows uninterruptedly from one to the other and back again with very little real movement. Rather, when the drumming, which accompanies the singing completely warms up, the scene of the dance could be described as erratically ecstatic. Those possessed by the dancing spirit, dance apart, spinning, swaying, or doing gymnastic and intricate syncopations with their feet and waist, which strike a beautiful synchrony with the musical rhythm from the drums and other local instruments. Generally speaking, dancing is why African drumming exists. When people spontaneously dance to their music, it's considered high praise. In fact, it's the cutest to see them, even little kids cut loose, it's crazy. In short, the drumming has a spirit that takes hold of the drummers and audience.

In the Etung culture, in spite of all attempts to band the agaba chants due to its seeming wildness by some elements, it has weathered the storm and proven to be a very heated moment in the cultural and traditional display of dances. Because of its success, politicians have always used it to their advantage and so, in their political campaigns, the agaba dance is often used as a breakthrough among the young people. At such occasions, they cannot stay aloof but go with the flow. Personally, because of my personal admiration for and attachment to this kind of traditional dance, I call them (the members) "my boys" or "my people." Yes, my likeness for this form of traditional dance is not hidden. That was why at my dad's wedding ceremony, I hired their services to heat up the place during the wedding reception. And as usual, they did a good job.

Perhaps in this reflection, I have an opportunity to be an advocate for, by speaking in defense and in appraisal of the agaba dance, which I earlier insinuated that, there have been serious attempts to band it by some powers that be. Like every other song, permit me to attempt to establish a relationship and draw a connecting line between the agaba chants and the hip-hop musical lyrics. It is my belief that both of them have a historical connection and an existential similarity. Therefore, they have some elements in common, though in terms of the instruments that are used in their production and display, the former (agaba) are still local and "primitive' while the latter (hip-hop) are more modern, advanced and sophisticated along with the accompanying raps. The latter then could be said to be the result of the musical and instrumental metamorphosis and evolutionary change of the former.

It is important to point out straightaway that both types of music are not just *organized noise*. For the attentive listener, they have very useful information to give as well as historical and existential messages to convey to the world, especially in addressing the structures of society. Characteristically, they are songs of constructive criticisms, peaceful demonstrations, objective protests, and healthy revolutions that will benefit the common good. Their target or mission is the condemnation of injustice, oppression, marginalization and slavery of any kind. Again, they are chants of deliverance, liberation and freedom. They are encouraging lyrics of expectation, hope and

THE INSTITUTION OF MARRIAGE

optimism. These songs also remind us of the nothingness, the emptiness and the passing away of this material world, with all its temporary pleasures and comforts of life. And for those who tend to forget, these chants and lyrics remind us of the law of nemesis, the reality of karma and the fact of retributive justice. At the end, they are musical expressions of triumph, success and victory as well as songs of praise in thanksgiving and gratitude, first to God, then to people who supported their course. By way of gesture, sometimes while they are on stage, they tend to dramatize and mimic some real and positive, but sometimes unbecoming societal ills, especially those laced with tales of sex, drugs, and violence.

To prove that some of these hip-hop raps are designed to send a positive, inspirational message to all people, especially to kids and youths, *The Post-Star* of April 11, 2005, reports about a local rapper who reaches out with positive message. The article shows a beautiful picture of a Glens Falls rapper and songwriter T.J. Fredette rehearsing his lyrics at his family's Glens Falls home. "Fredette shared his rap performance – designed to send a positive, inspirational message to kids – for the first time Friday afternoon at Hudson Falls High School." Some of the excerpts from the inspiring article further state that: "Latter, he'll like to work in the music industry, writing or recording, but for now he's content preaching to kids the promise of staying on the straight and narrow. He tries to speak from a place that's familiar to them, sounding a lot like a wise big brother. Between songs, the sermon doesn't stop." In his own words, he says: "I have known kids that have got involved in drugs at an early age, got involved in alcohol at an early age, and I know kids that are in jail now. I know kids that

A Handbook on Culture Shock

are in prison, I know kids who died because they overdosed on drugs, and I know kids who are complete alcoholics and complete addicts and drugs and alcohol run their life." He then goes on to give his message thus: "There's nothing good about that, there is nothing cool about that." The paper further reports that: "He rapped and spoke about working hard, sticking it out until graduation and reaching for dreams. The message was cliché, but the delivery was so sincere even skeptical 15-year-olds bought into it." Finally, the rapper, in encouraging the power of positive thinking and the spirit of optimism, challenges his audience in regard to their future ambitions and careers with this question: "Does anybody want to volunteer and stand up right now and say what their goal is? Tell me what your goal is. That's right, if you can do that, if you're confident and you can stand up right now and say what your goal is in life…that's the first step."

However, in the course of carrying out their well conceived intentions in the chants and lyrics, problems do occur. This often happens when people get in their way to stop them from their mission of speaking up both for themselves as "voiceless" people and for others equally affected by the same societal handicap. As young people, most of them do not have the means to go technologically public through the media to express their views on political issues, economic matters, and social concerns. Therefore, they become provoked and are made to feel the hurt of frustration if there are attempts by some people to stifle their freedom of expression through the only means available to them. Given this interference, they become troublemakers and ramble-rousers. In fact, as a person, I am second to no one in my belief that freedom of expression

The Institution of Marriage

is a precious right that no one, should ever take away from us. Hence, for the agaba and related groups, when this freedom is denied them, the only alternative left for them is force. Yes, they often resort to using the only source of power and energy nature has endowed them with to fight their way through. To this end, they physically fight to get their message across. My candid belief, therefore, is that, if these young lads are left alone and allowed to go on with what they say in freedom, there will be peace in our homes and no fracas will be experienced anywhere. This means of expression, by my estimation, is a cultural heritage that supports freedom of speech on burning issues of the day. My humble suggestion to all concerned is this: *Just listen to what they are singing. May be there's a message in there but you don't get it. And if you get it and it directly concerns you, then examine your conscience in relation to what you hear.*

Following this line of reflection, on a wider perspective, permit me to pour my heart's content about my personal feelings on the murdering and dying of cultural heritage, with the Etung culture as a case in point. My thinking has always been that, if culture must be preserved, (and it should be preserved for the future generations), traditional dances and other cultural elements, which also form and inform culture should be promoted, encouraged, protected and preserved. For the Etung people, some of these dances include **Ekpe or Mgbe, Okumingbe, Ekpa, Moninkim, Obam, Nchibhe, Ifighe, Abon-Osenghe.** These and other forms of culture are rich cultural heritage with far reaching values, which unfortunately, are gradually being neglected, forgotten and swept away by the wave of modernity on each passing day. At some point in the

A HANDBOOK ON CULTURE SHOCK

history of the people, they constituted the centerpiece of the people's way of life. Their lives revolved around them with benefits that sustained those concerned.

Among the Etung people, it is important to note that some of these traditional institutions, the Ekpe or Mgbe in particular, long before the advent of the present legal or court system, were barons of law and order, which were exercised in justice. Without fear or favor, they rewarded excellence and meted commensurate punishments to those who deserved them. The poor and the rich, the haves and the have-nots, all had access to these institutions to seek redress or appeal for justice, equity and fair play. And the history of the people tells us that, immediate justice always triumphed or prevailed. Comparatively speaking, it will be belaboring the obvious to state that today's legal system is a worrisome departure from the cultural and traditional one. Unlike the former, our court system today leaves so much to be desired, made worse by people who conceive evil, bring forth lies and do injustice under the cover of law and intellectual wit in a compelling argumentative process, all against the conviction and victimization of the defenseless and the innocent of our society.

It aches my heart to think about and see these cultural aspects of the people's life rust away like that. It is my earnest prayer that whoever is inspired by the "god of culture" to become an harbinger for the restoration of what may be called, for instance, "Etung Heritage Foundation" should have the following that is needed to bring this dream to the lime light of historical reality. The Etung people have a past cultural history. And this past is an invaluable treasure that is suffocating daily and is being pushed to the brink due to "civilization," as it is so called.

Borrowing from the thoughts of my brother, Dr. Ransome Egim Owan, who to my knowledge, first born the idea, dreamt the dream, envisioned the vision and talked to me about the "Etung Heritage Foundation," I agree with him that, a project on "Etung Heritage Foundation," should challenge, not only the sons and daughters of Etung, but, all lovers of culture to see that it comes true. This project is all about safeguarding the tangible and intangible heritage assets of the Etung people as well as preserving who, the Etung people are as a people for our children and generations to come. Its main goal and objective is to seek to restore, maintain and extend the Etung cultural heritage beyond the geographical bounds and cultural milieu of the people concerned.

By way of stating a real cultural problem: It is indeed sad to realize that, the old folks are leaving us with no traces of their history that is captured. Everything is oral and nothing is written. Yes, the store of knowledge is based on oral history and tradition. The elderly with institutional knowledge are fast and truly vanishing without adequate knowledge transfer. As a result, a way of life and heritage is being lost to future genera-tions daily. In fact, the cultural impoverishment is most acute in children of immigrant parents and indigenes that have left the village. The result is obvious: the gradual loss of cultural iden-tity and pride. To be even more particular, among the unique heritage assets threatened are: the vernacular, history, folklore, anthropology, rites, know-how, festivals, the arts (music, song, and dance), social practices, beliefs, culinary traditions, and indigenous knowledge of medicine, nature, plants, and ani-mals. If you read in between the lines, the lamentation above

A HANDBOOK ON CULTURE SHOCK

gives a picture of a history or a heritage in flames.

The solution to the previously stated cultural crisis is not far fetched. It calls for a cultural preservation program as a mission possible. We need to band together and do something that each of us will look back and be proud of rescuing a drowning culture. I am convinced and I think you, too are, that this project may take quite some years to accomplish and many life times to safeguard. But, let's begin it anyhow and from somewhere. Friends, foundations and governments, especially from the developed world, please, encourage this "rescue project" and join in the genuine effort to contribute your ideas, talents and resources. It may be worth the while. (Sorry for the digression. But it was important to cheep this culture chip in, as a fundamental cultural option that could walk its way to and be debated on or deliberated upon at the table of any National Heritage Foundation).

Now, back on track: Finally, (on the metamorphosis of marriage) it is also important to know that there are still some cases of polygamy being practiced by some people in my native culture, especially among the so-called village dwellers. However, a church wedding can only take place in a monogamous family. A story was told of a man who once had three wives. Having gone to church one Sunday and listened to a wonderful homily on monogamous marriage as a prerequisite for salvation, he decided to arrange for a church wedding. However, for this to take place, he had to eliminate, by way of divorce, two of his wives. This man loved them all so much and did not know which ones to send packing. One day he called a meeting of his wives and told them of his plans. He then appealed to any two of them to seek a kind of voluntary divorce. None of them did. Instead, they all looked at themselves for a while and left one by one from the common room or parlor for their individual rooms.

This man was so bent on his decision that a couple of days later he came up with a beautiful idea that would help in this process of elimination. The idea was this: He brought out three sheets of paper. On two sheets, he wrote "No!" On the remaining sheet, he wrote "Yes!" With all the incontestable powers of African husbands, which more or less command trembling obedience from their wives and children, this man again called a meeting of his wives. He duly instructed them that there was going to be a secret ballot in which whoever picks "No!" would be advised to leave and would have four weeks to leave his house, while the one who picks "Yes!" would be taken to the altar for the wedding. After the secret ballot, logically, two of his wives were advised to leave, of course, not without compensation and proper settlement for them and a promise to take good care of their children. The lucky one who picked the "Yes!" went on to become his wedded wife.

If this story is true, then it is true that wonders would never end. But if we assume this story to be true and consequently find that this man's method of elimination leaves so much to be desired, may I seek your advice by asking this question: On a situation like this, what would you have done? Remember, it was like standing between a rock and a hard place (love of his wives and gaining salvation). Probably, the man's decision could be justified in the ethical application of the principle of double effects. This principle states that: "In between two evils, you choose a lesser one."

The family system in my native culture is generally patrilineal.

THE CHANGING FACE OF THE MARRIAGE INSTITUTION IN THE UNITED STATES

It is true that the U.S. culture, concerning this institution, still upholds marriage as a union between a man and woman. However, the reality of this fact seems to be coming to a crossroads. In fact, this heterosexual union is experiencing a deviation and undergoing a worrisome metamorphosis in some aspects of its essence. This changing face of marriage is provoking thoughts and arousing disturbing concerns among many people in so many quarters. From my comparative experience, the following unfolding developments on marriage in it changing face in America were not only new, but also shocking to me.

Regarding this heterosexual union, there is the growing phenomenon of marriage of convenience. This generally means a marriage or joint undertaking for political, economic, or social and recreational benefits rather than for permanent attachment. Along this line of thought, oftentimes you hear of some arranged marriages in court between a foreign female spouse and a male citizen or vice versa, for the purpose of naturalization of either partner. Thus, through this means the obtaining of a *green card* or immigrant visa, is made easy. Advantageously, this visa allows the recipient to live and work in the U.S. system and structures with all the rights and privileges thereunto that pertain to this status (immigrant visa status). However, there are specific limitations of this status distinct from the rights of full citizenship (naturalization). Thus, one with an immigrant visa cannot stay out of the country on any

THE INSTITUTION OF MARRIAGE

given trip for more than one year. Otherwise, he or she loses his or her rights or privileges thereunto. Second, such a person does not have any voting rights. A marriage contracted with this aim in view (obtaining a green card) can be a disguised intention of one of the spouses or it can be a mutual agreement between both spouses. This has become a lucrative business in the United States for some citizens who are paid by those who benefit from such matrimonial arrangements. This is indeed a *green-card-made-easy* avenue or means that undermines and over powers all immigration regulations and restrictions, which are increasingly becoming more complex and complicated than ever before, especially since after 9/11/2001.

Yes, you would recall that on September 11, 2001, an unthinkable event happened to the United States of America and its citizens: Terrorists hijacked four passengers jet airlines, with large number of passengers, enroute to destinations in western United States. The heartless hijackers who were on a murderous and suicide mission, commandeered the planes and deliberately flew three of them to points where massive and unprecedented destructions were achieved: the World Trade Center in New York City and the Pentagon in Arlington, Virginia. The fourth plane crashed in a field near Shanksville, Pennsylvania. Efforts by the hijackers to cause additional destructions were thwarted by the heroic passengers of the airliner. In this hijacking onslaught, thousands of people were killed and the destruction of property soars in the billions of dollars.

The post 9/11 effects are beyond calculation and know no bounds, both in terms of internal security and immigration related matters. Internally, the American security has been beefed up and continues to be reinforced on each passing day.

A HANDBOOK ON CULTURE SHOCK

On a personal internal observation, I am so full of admiration for the *spirit of the Americans* – the resolve of the American people has swelled to a massive crescendo of support for the country. And I am so convinced that America will achieve, persevere, stand steadfast and overcome the grievous loss it has sustained. Particularly, a heap of thanks belong to Governor George E. Pataki of New York State and his administration who remain the front liners, main actors and patriotic Americans, that sustain the *spirit of the Americans* in this context and other areas of governance. This is evident in their relentless and committed efforts to see that the dream of rebuilding the World Trade Center (now called – Ground Zero) in New York City in memory of the hijackers' victims comes true. On the whole, it must be pointed out that, the 9/11 "blood bath," or incident not only surprised the Americans as the number one world's super power, but it also shook and shocked the whole world. And all well meaning people and pro-lifers mourned with and continue to remember this day with the Americans. MY SYMPATHY, TOO!

Regarding the post 9/11 effects on immigration matters, especially in terms of the inflow of non-immigrants to America, this, too, has its toll on people. Before unfolding my personal ordeal, permit me to first, salute the Americans for being open to non-immigrants with friendliness and warmth even after the 9/11 nightmare. Now, the immigration issues and laws have continued to experience some uptightness and seeming impossibilities as a result of the hijackers' "sin." It is becoming increasingly difficult for genuine non-immigrants in some innocent countries to obtain visas that would enable them to enter the U.S. in pursuance of their careers and other life engagements. My ordeal in this regard comes from the frustration I encountered in the bid to help some struggling Nigerian students to come to America for Summer work. These Students had been employed and their accommodation certified in the U.S. With their respective letters of employment and accommodation certification, they went to the United States Consulate or the American Embassy in Nigeria for their interviews for the issuance of J-I Visa category, which is required for Summer Work/ Travel to America. They arrived at the Embassy as scheduled and quite on time, too, only to be told that they need DS2019 Forms as an additional document in accordance with the SEVIS (Student Exchange Visitors Information System) immigration requirement. My brother and I, having spent so much money already to help these students, had to tell them to leave the hotel where we had paid for their lodging and go back to their respective schools while I run the race of finding out what DS2019 Forms were all about and where they are to be generated from. The big question that remained unanswered at the time is: Are the said Forms to be generated from/in the U.S. or in the home country of the students, in this case, Nigeria?

My enquiry and chase for these Forms made me an Internet addict that kept me awake several nights browsing the internet and searching the web. I was ready to follow the instructions in this regard religiously, to leave no stone unturned and to obey the last letter of the law. This mission also brought and kept me in email and telephone contacts with so many immigration Attorneys in New York City and beyond. The different Sponsoring Agencies of International Student Exchange Programs both home and abroad, knew no peace, as I kept

A HANDBOOK ON CULTURE SHOCK

knocking at their doors for useful and helpful information on how and where to generate the DS2019 Forms. Because of the difficulty and impossibility of knowing how and where these Forms were to be generated from for the issuance of the said J-1 Visas, an Attorney in New York State, in his frustration said to me: "Father, I think it is much easier to get into this country illegally than legally." This is a very profound statement and I would like the authorities concerned to think about it. My story may only be different in context. But, spread the cards round, listen and talk to many honest foreigners, even Nigerians in this case, and you would just be adding up similar experiences that confirm this odious or frustrating reality, where many honest, sincere and transparent people have invited their family members and friends to the U.S. and met with impossible immigration huddles. What is more heartbreaking is the fact that, many of these invitations are for people with medical problems, or for the simple and honest benefits of holiday seekers, cultural exchange experiences, and all what not.

However, in my own case as narrated, I do not deny the possibility that, probably, I did not get at the right contacts at the time, even when I did everything possible to do so. This experience and similar ones, could give some credence to or make excuses for the saga of *green-card-made-easy* as experienced between couples in marriage. In fact, even the legal process of getting a green card in America would tell you that it is no picnic. Lucky and blessed, then, are you to come into the U.S. through the Diversity Visa (DV) Lottery. No thanks to the September 11, 2001 hijackers. And so, I join my little voice with the Americans in saying: "WE WILL NEVER FORGET!"

(Back to the marriage of convenient) – since the courting

The Institution of Marriage

or wooing duration for these marriages is relatively short, so also is the duration of the actual marriage itself. I mean, you could go clubbing or partying one night where you may meet your spouse with whom, through a mutual agreement, within a couple of days, a marriage can be contracted in court. The question at this point is this: Is there any way of ascertaining and verifying the validity of such marriage by the civil court before it is contracted? If there are ways, I do not know of any. The results and expected consequences after such a marriage are obvious: immediate or delayed divorce, since this is the original intention for the marriage that was, (probably), unanimously agreed upon and mutually contracted by the spouse concerned (knowingly or unknowingly). Without being judgmental, from a canonical point of view, this kind of marriage is invalid right from the beginning because the marital consent between both parties was either doubtful or deceitful. This kind of matrimonial union, for the most part, justifies and gives credit to the Church's prenuptial requirements of a couple before marriage. Within this time of prenuptial exercise, besides the need and the advantages of proper investigation and examination of related marital issues, the couples also come to know and understand themselves better. According to the teachings of the Church, this idea of matrimonial scrutiny, more often than not, promises and assures a mutual and lasting fidelity between married couples.

On another note, besides the marriage of convenience which is sometimes seen in the U.S. culture, the Adirondack people also have marriages contracted and or celebrated respecting certain steps. The first step is what I may call the *courting stage*, that is, boyfriend or girlfriend stage. In this stage, a boy and a girl become friends to the knowledge of their parents, relatives, and friends. It is not a hide-and-seek affair, unlike in my native culture where this stage is, more or less, secretive and exclusive. Such people in the Adirondack culture, hang out together, visit the parents and homes of each other, and talk proudly to other people about their friendship. Progressively, the second step is the *engagement stage* in which the boy asks the girl to marry him. This stage comes with the giving of an engagement ring by the boy to the girl. This stage is very important in many respects. Primarily, it assures the girl that the boy or both of them are in love and are serious with the affair. It is such an event of joy to the girl, who proudly displays her engagement ring for people to see. In fact, oftentimes, some of them like to not only tell you, but also show you their engagement rings, just to share the joy and happiness of their engagement with you.

At this point, permit me to comment on the economic affair or implication of engagement rings and some of the things that are involved. Sometimes, the expense of buying an engagement ring could be very high. Cases abound where some of the girls have very high taste. Consequently, the girl suggests to the boy the worth of the engagement ring she would like to have and wear. It should not be a surprise to hear that oftentimes taste and suggestion go far beyond what the boy had planned to spend for the engagement ring. The cost can be really astounding. Yes, the money can be too much just for a ring. On this note, I was thinking about a situation where an engaged couple break up before the marriage date, as it does happen. What becomes of the engagement ring, and if it was bought on credit (as oftentimes it is, being a culture that al-

The Institution of Marriage

lows a credit economy), then, what happens to the debt? To the first question, the girl could return the ring back to the boy. At other times, she could keep it, if the boy does not want it again. The answer to the last question is not far-fetched. The boy would continue the payment for the ring until it is all paid for. I wonder how happy he would be doing that. However, in some cases, if the ring is collected from the girl (which happens rarely), it could be turned in to sellers who in turn would sell it as a secondhand jewelry. Upon some inquiries, I also understand that the boy could decide to keep the ring, which initially belonged to his former girlfriend, and then give it to his new girlfriend as an engagement ring, if they intend to marry. Of course, if this must be done, then it must not be done with the knowledge of the later girlfriend.

Now, I would like to point out and shed light on a particular and fascinating wedding ceremony and tradition among the Adirondack people. Permit me to name or call it the **bouquet and garter** tradition. Thus, at one of the high points during the wedding party, the bride and the groom are expected to throw the bouquet and the garter to a group of single women and men, respectively. This is done, first by the bride, who turns her back on the group of single women and then throws her bouquet of flowers to them. Usually these single women, I was made to understand, struggle for it. After that, comes the groom, and the single men who also do the same thing with the garter (like the bride and the single girls do with the bouquet). The tradition is that whoever catches the bouquet and the garter will be the next in line to marry. As a beginning of the union, the single man who catches the garter puts it on the leg of the single woman who catches the bouquet. However, to the best of my knowledge, it does not imply that the very two (single woman and single man) who catch the bouquet and the garter must necessarily marry each other, but if it works out that way, it is always a good and wonderful thing.

On a personal note, I had an experience in this regard, and I wish to relate it here: I attended a wedding party one time. At the high point of throwing the bouquet, the bride threw it to the group of single women who were gathered at the scene. I watched carefully to see how they were going to struggle for it, but to my greatest dismay, they did not. At this I said to myself, "Oho! they are not ready for marriage." In fact, the bouquet fell in their midst, and they were standing there looking and avoiding it as if it were a taboo. Then one of the single women reached her hand down and picked it up. Incidentally, her grandmother was just behind where I was sitting. On noticing what had happened, she (grandmother) immediately said: "No! Not yet! She must graduate from school."

Second, when the single men came out for the garter, I thought, (being single myself) I could go and catch it for somebody else other than me. I was on my way out to stand with the men when I decided to find out from one of the single men if I could catch it for him. He said: "No!" and he continued by telling me that the tradition is that whoever catches the garter must, not only marry, but also be the next in line to marry. At this, I said to myself: "Oops! then I am out of here." With this, I quietly left the scene. The lesson here is that it is always a good thing to ask questions when you are not sure of what to do in a new culture; otherwise, you put yourself in trouble or you commit yourself without knowing. I mean, as a celibate priest, I do not know what I would have done with the garter.

THE INSTITUTION OF MARRIAGE

In addition to this previous personal experience, a story was once told of a young girl who in searching for a job, found herself in a foreign country with some aspects of culture different from her native one. When she applied for a job that was advertised, she was called to go for an interview. On her arrival, she was given a form to fill in. While filling in the form, when she came to where they required information about "Sex," she wrote: "Once a month." You may laugh at this, but, the point is that, the poor girl did not understand what "sex" in this context meant. This is because in her home culture, given similar forms to fill in, in place of "sex" as a way of knowing whether the applicant is male or female, it is written, "gender." So you can see that because the girl presumed to have known the meaning of "sex," which she interpreted and understood out of context, she ended up ignorantly causing such an embarrassment both to her employers and herself. If she had asked questions, this "information" about her private sex life would not have gained public knowledge. If she was in doubt, as certainly she was, she should have applied the ethical principle of: "In dubio non agere," that is, " in doubt, do not act." The application of this principle, too, would have saved her the trouble of making her sex life a matter for public "consumption."

Overall, the bouquet and the garter tradition was an interesting cultural experience, which was not just different but completely very new and shocking to me.

Converging the two cultures, by way of a similarity, both in my native and foreign cultures, there is a kind of partying on the eve of the wedding ceremony. This partying is known as "bachelors' eve" or "rehearsal dinner" in the Etung and the Adirondack cultures, respectively. The only difference is in

A HANDBOOK ON CULTURE SHOCK

their nomenclatures.

The ears never get tired of hearing, and the eyes never get tired of seeing. The conscious hijack of this noble institution of marriage has also assumed another dimension in some parts of the United States. It is the dimension of "**gayism**." This means the union of same sexes in marriage. In other words, this gayness relates to having a sexual desire or orientation toward persons of the same sex: a man with another man or a woman with another woman. The former is called homosexuality, while the latter is called lesbianism. This kind of union, for some schools of thought, is a physical and emotional revolt against the ontological constitution and reality of the human person. It also brings to question the reproductive teleology of humankind in the union of marriage, as originally conceived by the metaphysical being (God) in whom we live, move, and have our being. Please, do not ask me about the essence and matrimonial joy of this kind of marriage because I have no clue. Far from being judgmental, in fairness to those who are involved in the practice of gayism, I do not doubt that they may have their strong reasons for their desires. Therefore, for the benefit of doubt and in accordance with the fraternal morality of accommodation, our adjudication on this development should be left to God who is the ultimate and final Judge of all matters and of all human actions, as moral beings. In spite of thus disclaimer, the church must continue in her teaching on marriage, convinced of God's original intention for this institution.

It is important to know that this union, of late, has been a troubling issue in some parts of the United States and the world at large. What follows is an attempt to express some of the con-

The Institution of Marriage

cerns bordering on gay marriage. There have been a number of reactions from people opposing gay marriage. Some of the concerns of these outspoken people have been categorically expressed and reported in the mass media. Permit me to make bold to present some of their disturbing thoughts and ideas on this topical, existential, controversial, and burning issue.

To begin with, Joseph Ratzinger, who became known as Pope Benedict XVI, (elected into the Papacy on April 19, 2005, as the immediate successor of Karol Josef Wojtyla, known as Pope John Paul 11 who died on April 2, 2005), called homosexuality "an intrinsic moral evil."

The Evangelist (The Albany Diocesan Catholic Newspaper, New York), of December 11, 2003, reported the reactions of the Catholic Bishops' Conference of America as saying: "Same-sex union is a 'national tragedy.' In the opinion of the bishops, the justices who voted in support of same-sex union in Massachusetts 'have set the stage to erode even further the institution of marriage as a human reality which the state should protect and strengthen for the good of society.'"[1] The Archbishop of Boston, Sean O'Malley, called it "alarming." A Massachusetts Catholic Conference official called it "radical" and "devastating." A judge called it "an aberration." A free thinker expressed her concerns by saying: "I believe marriage throughout world history has been a permanent relationship between members of the opposite sex. I also believe that same-sex marriages weaken our health physically, morally, spiritually, emotionally and nationally. God and nature show that you need a man and a woman to create a new life — a child. Both a father and a mother are needed to bring a young life to a healthy maturity. Not every member of the homosexual community wants to steal the name marriage because they see it as a religious term. The name 'civil union' seems like an adequate name for a same-sex union. Do not steal the name marriage."

The Evangelist, again of June 17, 2004, reported that Bishop Frederick Henry of Calgary, Alberta, criticized Canadian Prime Minister Paul Martin for his moral incoherence on abortion and same-sex marriage. The paper said: "Bishop Henry said Martin's position on abortion and same-sex union is 'a source of scandal in the Catholic community and reflects a fundamental moral incoherence.'"

President Bush also expressed his concern by saying he was troubled by the issuance of marriage licenses to gay couples in San Francisco, but he again stopped short of endorsing a constitutional amendment that would define marriage as the union of a man and a woman. Bush said during a brief question-and-answer session in the **Oval Office** that he has "watched carefully what's happened in San Francisco, where licenses were being issued even though the law states otherwise." More than 2,600 marriage licenses have been issued to same-sex couples since Thursday of February 12, 2004. "Obviously, these events are influencing my decision," the President said. "I am troubled by what I've seen. People need to be involved with this decision. Marriage ought to be defined by the people, not by the courts."

Furthermore, on February 28, 2004, *The Post-Star* reported that the California Supreme Court declined a request by the state Attorney General immediately to shutdown San Francisco's gay weddings and nullify the nearly 3,500 marriages already performed. The decision marked another setback to conservatives in their fight to block the rush to the altar by gay

The Institution of Marriage

couples in San Francisco. At the prodding of Governor Arnold Schwarzenegger, Attorney General Bill Lockyer asked the justices to intervene in the emotionally charged debate while they consider the legality of the marriage. But the justices declined and told the city and a conservative group that opposes gay marriage to file a new legal brief by March. Without taking a position on whether same-sex marriage should be deemed constitutional, Lockyer told the justices it was a matter for the courts, not the mayor, to decide. Accordingly, he wrote: "The genius of our legal system is in the orderly way our laws can be changed, by the Legislature or by a vote of the people through the initiative process, to reflect current wisdom or social values." On a further reaction, Jason West, Green Party mayor of New Paltz, New York, said: "What we are witnessing in America today is the flowering of the largest civil rights movement the country's had in generations." As I carefully went through all these publications and reports on the issue, I remained stunned and shocked in my thought process and found it difficult to reconcile this phenomenon with reality. The reactions from people continue as follows.

According to Leonard Pitts, Jr., as reported in *The Post-Star* of March 2, 2004: "The issuing of licenses to gay couples by Mayor Gavin Newsom in California might well be right in the long term, but in the short term it's a dicier question." The point is that gay marriage may move forward to legality or may move backward to prohibition. The one thing that seems beyond debate is that the issue is indeed moving. To whichever direction it moves eventually, it is a fact that the endorsement of gay marriage amounts to a selective application of biblical injunctions and pious invocations of moral concern. In fact, by

A HANDBOOK ON CULTURE SHOCK

my estimation again, to rely on the courts for the justification of this sort of marriage is seriously to infringe on and clash with the values of morality and the permissivism of legality.

The Post-Star of July 16, 2004, further reported that according to the former Alabama Chief Justice, Roy Moore, who was ousted from the bench in November 2003, for refusing to remove his two-ton granite monument of the Ten Commandments from the state house in Montgomery, homosexuality is an "inherent evil. It is a violation of the laws of nature." In his view, "marriage should not be altered according to society's whim." He concluded his reflection by making a nuptial forecast statement thus: "What's next, a marriage between a horse and a group of individuals."

These disturbing concerns were not only the concerns of people who live in the United States. From far away Nigeria in Africa came this reaction, as reported in *The Post-Star* of April 16, 2004. Anglican archbishops from Africa resolved Thursday to reject donations from any diocese that recognizes gay clergy and recommended giving the Episcopal Church in the United States three months to repent from ordaining an openly gay bishop. The archbishops also said they will refuse cooperation with any missionary who supports ordaining gay priests. They said the Episcopalians, the American branch of Anglicanism, should be disciplined for the election last year of V. Gene Robinson as Bishop of New Hampshire. It is said that Robinson has lived openly with his male partner for years.

The thoughts and concerns of these archbishops were further articulated thusly: "If we suffer for a while to gain our independence and our freedom and to build ourselves up, I think it will be a good thing for the Church in Africa," Archbishop

THE INSTITUTION OF MARRIAGE

Peter Akinola of Nigeria told journalists. "And we will not, on the altar of money, mortgage our conscience, mortgage our faith, mortgage our salvation."

Without any intention to over flog the issue of gayness, it is important to state that one of the Pontiff's agendas for the year 2005 is to look into this phenomenon. *The Post-Star* newspaper of January 11, 2005, ran the caption: "Pope Vows to Fight Gay Marriage." "Pope John Paul II put lobbying against gay marriage at the top of the Vatican's agenda for 2005 and also urged politicians in prosperous nations Monday to do more for the millions of hungry people around the globe. In a speech to the diplomats accredited to the Vatican, the ailing, 84-year-old pontiff laid out the Roman Catholic Church's priorities for the new year, making clear he intended to use his energies to tackle what he called 'challenges of life' issues — abortion, cloning, gay marriage, assisted procreation and embryonic stem cell use. In an obvious reference to laws permitting marriage between homosexuals or equating the social rights of unwed couples to married ones, John Paul said that in some countries, the family's 'natural structure' has been challenged. Families 'must necessarily be that of a union between a man and a woman founded on marriage."

As you well know, there are two sides to every argument. Hence, in avoiding an argument that seems to be lopsided, prejudiced, and biased in the context of gayness, it is also important to note that proponents of this marriage culture argue for gay marriage as well. Arguing in favor of gayness therefore, *The Post-Star* of February 5, 2005, reports the ruling of a Manhattan Judge who said: "That while the Domestic Relation Law does not 'expressly' bar same-sex marriage, specific section clearly express the legislature's assumption that the parties to a marriage will be a man and a woman. Because this assumption has provided the basis for blocking same-sex marriage in New York State, the judge declared the section unconstitutional and, in effect, ordered a redefinition of terms in the statute."

According to the judge: "The words, 'husband,' 'wife,' 'groom' and 'bride' in relevant sections of the Domestic Relation Law 'shall be construed to mean 'spouse,' and 'all personal pronouns...shall be construed to apply equally to either men or women.' 'In her decision, the judge cited and relied on rulings from the last century that barred, and then permitted, interracial marriages. The judge said one plaintiff...is the son of an interracial couple who moved to California in 1966 to marry. California then was the only state whose court had ruled that interracial marriage bans were unconstitutional."

Conclusively, as the ball continues to roll and we witness the revealing and comparative experiences regarding the institution of marriage, no matter the aberrational and deviating dimensions it assumes, marriage remains a global phenomenon. From a personal point of view and assessment of the unfolding realities of this great institution in some parts of the United States, it compels me to think that the experiences therein are calling for a redefinition and a redescription of the institution of marriage. Due to its changing face, it may become necessary that when you talk about marriage in some cultures of the world that you may have to explain further what you actually mean. This is because marriage no longer seems to carry and convey the same general understanding everywhere. Probably, it is high time scholars develop a discipline on "systematic

THE INSTITUTION OF MARRIAGE

contextualization" that dwells on contextual discussions of commonplace realities or familiar ideas.

These startling experiences regarding marriage, be they marriage of convenience or gayness, were and still remain to me physical, psychological, emotional, and social culture shocks. These shocks defy all philosophical arguments and disputations, all social, political, and economic benefits, and even all theological insights to justify them. They seem to me to be a negation of the truth according to the natural order of permanent union that supports procreation.

Before I draw the curtain on this section, permit me to say that, from a comparative experience, African cultures in general, Nigerian inclusive, are more hostile and outspoken to gays than mainline American churches. Over here, (America), I observe that pastors of "souls" in some churches are very careful and even sometimes avoid talking on sensitive issues, such as the marriage ethics, issues of life and death (abortion, euthanasia etc). This "silence" could be for fear of offending some of the members of their congregations, who may be in support of a particular culture contrary to the mind and teachings of the church. To sound more specific, as at the time of this reflection, in the culture of the Etung people, the issue of gaysm does not even arise talk less of it becoming a subject of debate. For them, gaysm is a taboo, no more, no less. Yes, "the culture has spoken, the case is finished." Just like in Catholic Church matters, where we also say: Roma locuta, causa finita est," that is "Rome has spoken, the case is finished."

Death is the rite of passage of and for all mortals. And after death, come funeral ceremonies and then burials. In spite of this reality being experienced everywhere and everyday all

A HANDBOOK ON CULTURE SHOCK

over the world, because of cultural factors, there are still some strange ideas in peoples' interpretations, understandings, and reactions to the fact of death, together with differences in their ceremonies. The next chapter sets out to survey the cultural concepts of this rite of passage with its collaterals.

NOTES

[1] *Webster's II New College Dictionary.* Boston: Houghton Mifflin Company, 1995.

[2] *The Code of Canon Law.* New Delhi, India: Collins Liturgical Publications, 1994, 189.

[3] Perry, Kate. "Musician Shares a Good Rap." *The Post-Star,* April 11, 2005

[4] *The Evangelist,* "Call Same-sex Ruling a 'National Tragedy,'" December 11, 2003.

[5] *The Evangelist,* "Bishop Slams Canadian PM," June 17, 2004, 2.

[6] Kravets, David. "Court Declines to Stop Gay Marriage." *The Post-Star,* February 28, 2004.

[7] Pitts, Leonard Jr. "Marching Gaily Forward toward Civil Rights." *The Post-Star,* March 2, 2004.

[8] Randall, Thom. "Ten Commandment Judge Addresses Word of Life." *The Post-Star,* July 16, 2004.

[9] *The Post-Star,* "African Anglicans Reject Western Funds," April 16, 2004.

[10] D'Emilio, Frances. "Pope Vows to Fight Gay Marriage." *The Post-Star,* January 11, 2005, A5.

[11] Maull, Samuel. "Court Strikes Gay Marriage Ban." *The Post-Star,* February 5, 2005.

4

DEATH AND FUNERALS

The inevitable human culture of death, which gives rise to funeral ceremonies is a common place reality. It constitutes a popular talk that is, not only bandied about in academic circles, but has found its thinkers and audience in all fields and works of life. Yet, for most people, its meaning and acceptance remain vague and remote. These vagueness and remoteness are worsened by the frightening suddenness, unexpectedness, and immediacy of death. Hence, many people do not even want to spare a thought about it and shy away from discussions that border on end-of-life issues.

In his renowned and fascinating play, *Julius Caesar,* William Shakespeare writes about Caesar as saying: "Cowards die many times before their deaths; The valiant never taste of death but once. Of all the wonders that I yet have heard, it seems to me more strange that men should fear; Seeing that death, a necessary end, it will come when it will come." Scripture also has different passages that emphasize this fact of death, thus: "For you are dust and to dust you shall return" (Gen. 3:19). "Naked I came from my mother's womb, naked I shall return" (Job 1:21). "It is appointed unto humans to die once and afterwards judgment" (Heb. 9:27). All these thoughts and lots more state categorically and unequivocally as well as emphasize emphatically, the fact and the reality of that end — death, as the inevitable culture of all the earth (mortals). Remember the famous Latin saying: "Omnibus est moriendum," that is, "all must die."

This existential and eternal separation is experienced daily in all the cultures of the world. The questions of *when, where, and how* notwithstanding, *death* remains the name. The only difference, culturally speaking, is in what happens before death (antemortem), and at death (mortem), and what happens after death (postmortem). These are the issues that this section sets out to explore.

ANTEMORTEM AND MORTEM

In the culture of the Etung people in Nigeria, the average life expectancy is between 40 and 60 years. Infant mortality is very high. These two situations could be caused by the comparative poor standard of living in all aspects of life among the people. Accidents and violence also take their toll. Hence, because of these unprecedented realities of sudden deaths, the deceased person never really prepares for death by way of writing a *will*, or *personally writing an obituary*, or *personally arranging with the morticians for funeral obsequies*. In fact, to the best of my knowledge, the previously mentioned ways of personal preparation before death do not exist in my native culture, regardless of premature, mature and sudden deaths.

On another related cultural dimension, there is no question about what is going to happen to the body of a deceased person after death. This is because the Etung culture places much

A Handbook on Culture Shock

emphasis and value on the body of the dead and so needs it intact, complete, and real for the funeral ceremony and eventual burial. To this end, even if the death happens to be a case of drowning or some other accident that makes the body of the deceased difficult or impossible to find, there is always a search carried out for it (the body) by the people concerned. There is no cremation.

On this line of thought, it is also important to mention how people generally react at the death of a dear one by way of expressing emotions. From a global perspective, the expression of emotions by weeping at the death of someone you love is culturally acceptable. This is because, in addition to other things, weeping has a psychological easing and healing effect and it gives a physical balance to those who weep in relation to the grief that comes with the loss. Depending on the culture and persons concerned, some cry silently while others may cry violently. Among the Etung people, weeping is an encouraged cultural reaction or response, especially at the death of someone. This weeping emotion expresses how loved the deceased person was by the bereaved or family members and friends left behind. This emotional reaction becomes more demanding in the Etung culture because, if the one who is supposed to weep at the death of someone does not do so, such a person could be suspected of having a hand in the death of the dead person superstitiously or otherwise. To this end, some people in a bereaved family even try to out do others in the weeping emotions, so as to avoid any suspicion or accusing fingers being pointed at them.

Weeping in the Etung culture is not only reserved for those who are actually present at the death of a person. Even those who were away from the village at the time of the death, are also expected to weep when they return to the village. Such people who might have been away from the village for some number of years, on their return, they are individually escorted or accompanied by their close friends of the same age grade or group or age bracket to the village hall where they weep aloud for all those who died when they were away from the village. The idea here is that, with such public weeping in the village hall, they one who did the weeping, has wept for all those who died in his or her absence. Hence, such a person does not need to go weep at all the houses that were actually affected by the death. Though, a visit to all the family members concerned will still be appreciated. But, if for one reason or another, the one who has wept in the village hall is unable to go round to visit with the affected families, the public weeping in the hall suffices. After such weeping, if the person has the money, he or she can decide to buy some drinks for the villagers to drink in the village hall in memory of the dead. An envelope with a "fold in the middle" could also be given to the bereaved family to help offset some of the burial expenses. This will be highly appreciated.

Finally, on this weeping as a natural reaction to death, in some Nigerian cultures, there are some people called *professional mourners*. These people, as the name suggests, are people who could be hired to weep at the death of someone whom they never even knew nor had any connection or contact with when such a person was alive. Usually, their services are employed when the death occurs in a distant land and the deceased person's body is to be brought home to his or her village for the funeral and burial ceremonies. These professional

A HANDBOOK ON CULTURE SHOCK

or hired mourners are usually paid some money to accompany the body while weeping and wailing along as if the dead person is their direct relation. Yes, they could be crying out their eyes as tears gush out faster than you can ever imagine. They can be called the outsiders who weep louder than the bereaved. I don't know how they are able to do this. The advantage of having hired mourners in such situations is that, there may be no traffic holdup against the mourners. And related checks and explanations to the authorities on the road, which may cause some delays, could be avoided. To the best of my knowledge, this idea of professional mourners is not a cultural practice among the Etung people in particular.

Among the Adirondack people, the cultural practice about the personal preparation before death and at death is highly thoughtful and worthy of emulation. In this my U.S. foreign culture, I observed that there is an organized and fascinating way of taking care of this unavoidable end. Interestingly, the average life expectancy in the United States is between 60 and 90 years or even 100 years and above. This longevity of life with the fact of a relatively low infant mortality rate is so for an obvious reason: good standard of living in almost every aspect of life. Furthermore and on a general note, this is a *will culture*. Once written, its people respect the will to the letter, especially if it is a will of inheritance. The deceased person is free to will his or her property to anyone, even outside the family circle. I happened to have had an opportunity to come across the composition of one such will. For the benefit of doubt and the importance of information, permit me to give you an idea of how it reads.

DEATH AND FUNERALS

LAST WILL AND TESTAMENT

I, Victor Owan, residing at 3 Water Falls Street in the village of Agbokim, Etung Local Government Area of Cross River State, Nigeria, being of sound and disposing mind, memory and understanding, do hereby make, publish and declare this as and for my Last Will and Testament, hereby revoking all former Wills or Testamentary dispositions of my estate by me at anytime heretofore made.

FIRST: I direct all my just debts, funeral and administration expenses be paid as soon after my decease as is practicable.

SECOND: I direct that my body be buried in the Owan family lot, All Saints' Cemetery, Town of Agbokim Water Falls, Etung Local Government Area, Cross River State, Nigeria, and that a suitable marker be erected and marked if none then exists.

THIRD: I give and bequeath my electric musical organ to Hattah Enoh, Karaboard, Queensbury.

FOURTH: I give and bequeath all my winter coats to Mgbe Okon, Glens Falls.

FIFTH: I give and bequeath my computer and all other electrical appliances to Ellis Anyandi, Quaker Road, Glens Falls.

SIXTH: I give and bequeath my Carina automobile to Ntufam Obi, Nigeria.

SEVENTH: There may be other items of my personal property, which I may wish to leave to certain specific persons, and if I decide to do so, I will leave a list of the same signed by me with my executor hereinafter named.

A Handbook on Culture Shock

EIGHTH: I further direct my executor hereinafter named to sell my real property at 10 Water Falls Street, Agbokim, as soon after my decease as is practicable and deposit the net proceeds of the sale in my residuary estate.

NINTH: All the rest, residue and remainder of my estate, real, personal or mixed, of whatsoever nature and wheresoever situated, I give, devise and bequeath to the Roman Catholic Community of St. Agnes' Parish, South Glens Falls, New York, to be used for such religious purposes, at the sole discretion of and as determined appropriate and proper by the benefiting church.

TENTH: However, concerning number nine above, I suggest that half of the proceeds be directed toward supporting the African–Nigerian charitable project for the most needy through the care of Fr. Vincent Owen.

LASTLY: I hereby appoint Obi Eyyeh-Attem, Executor of this my Last Will and Testament: hereby revoking all former Wills by me made. I further authorize him to take payment on account of legal services for my estate in advance of the settlement of this account as executor.

In witness therefore, I have hereunto subscribed my name this 20th day of December, in the year Nineteen Hundred and Ninety-three.

Signature:
Victor Owan

Death and Funerals

There are also instances of people who, before their death, write their own obituaries in their own handwriting. They also arrange and pay for their own funeral obsequies. That is, they take care of it by paying for all that will be needed in advance and leave instructions on what should be done right from the time of their death. These prearrangements include delegating the responsibility to a particular funeral home chosen; arranging the church services; and designating a prepared plot with an epitaphic tombstone in a particular cemetery, which is selected by the deceased person when still alive.

The question about what happens to the body of the deceased person after death is very important in this culture. This is because before death the deceased person may write that his or her body after death should be cremated immediately or it should be given or donated to science for anatomical medical research, which is in turn cremated and later brought to or even mailed to the family of the deceased person for burial.

Probably you are shocked to hear about the cremated remains sent by mail. Though this may happen rarely, it is not a new teaching. Neither is it striking a new note in this culture when you talk about developments like this. Of course, I witnessed a shocking experience regarding this practice: As I went to check for my mail one morning, as I usually do, there was a box placed where incoming mail was kept. Without paying much attention to it, since I was not expecting any such heavy parcels, I picked up my mail and left. It was later on in the day that I was told that the said box contained the cremated remains of a onetime dear parishioner and had been mailed to the Church for burial.

Wow! Over here also, due to advanced technology and

A HANDBOOK ON CULTURE SHOCK

the availability of sophisticated medical facilities, there is the question of *living wills*. By way of definition, living wills are documents that communicate patients' wishes on medical treatments should they become terminally ill or incapacitated. There is also the *advance directive*, which is a living will that includes the designation of a medical surrogate to carry out the expressed wishes. Again, there is the *health-care* proxy, which is a document in which you name or appoint a healthcare agent or someone close to you (usually a family member or a close friend, a lawyer or even a clergyman) to make decisions about your healthcare in the event you become incompetent or incapacitated.

Thus, practically speaking, a living will has to do with prolonging or otherwise the life of a person *in periculum mortis* with medical or life equipment known as life support, such as a ventilator, a respirator, a feeding tube or a heart machine etc. In this case, with the help of this high-tech life support, if someone either wants or does not want this method of life prolongation, it would have to be written down by the particular person or sometimes to be okayed by the person's very close relative who reserves the right to do so. And whatever is written is respected religiously whenever the need arises. However, given the dynamics of some medical situations, it has been argued that, the documents (living wills) don't mean there will never be a court fight over a person's fate. They require that someone is terminally ill, completely incapacitated with no hope for recovery or in a persistent or permanent vegetative state. Those are all conditions subject to medical debate and disagreement among family members, anyway. So, in effect, a living will is only as good as your family's understanding of what your wishes are and their willingness to respect it.

At the time of reflecting on and writing this book, came the controversial issue of the culture of life-and-death, epitomized in Terri Schiavo's prolonged, protracted and agonizing health situation. Many of my American audience and possibly others all over the world, must be familiar with this issue and so will certainly know what I am talking about in Schiavo's case, since it was given an extensive media coverage with all the polemics that characterized it. Briefly, and for the benefit of information, permit me to introduce Terri Schiavo as an American, a brain-damaged Florida woman, who was confined to a hospital bed for about 15 years, unable to speak and "condemned" to death by her torturous health situation. The medical history of her health situation has it that, Mrs. Schiavo collapsed 15 years ago, presumably due to a potassium imbalance that temporarily deprived her brain of oxygen, and has received nutrition through a feeding tube. She died on March 31, 2005 at about 9:30 A.M. after 13 days of the removal of the feeding tube that was used to keep her alive, probably for all those years. The agonizing case of Terri, in what medical experts described in medical terminologies as persistent and or permanent vegetative stage, was another wake-up-call to the issue and need for living will or heath-care proxy, referred to in other states as a "durable power of attorney". Some people who are not comfortable with living wills, but prefer health-care proxy say that, the problem with living wills is that they *force* people to put in writing today what their wishes would be at some future time when they have unforeseen circumstances and difficult, complicated and unknown medical conditions.

It may interest you to know that, the battle over Schiavo's

A Handbook on Culture Shock

symbolism assumed deeper religious interpretations, profound economic thoughts, and political cum judicial controversial dimensions. Her eventual passing away may be an awakening, a symptom or a sign of a greater problem surrounding the culture of life-and-death. Terri Schiavo is dead, but the passion stirred by the fight over her life will shape and reshape debates on the culture of life-and-death for a long time to come. Such debates will certainly give rise to some urgent questions that may call for the redefinitions and reinterpretations of such terminologies and expressions as: *euthanasia; natural or ordinary and extraordinary means of sustaining life; the burdensomeness vis-à-vis the benefits of the means of life sustenance; the power of living wills and health-care proxies, legal guardianship,* you name it. By and large, my personal reaction to Terri's case is this: Without laying the blame on or faulting anyone involved in her case, making life-and-death decisions about whether to let a loved one live or die, are the most difficult and heart-wrenching decisions one ever have to make, no matter the situation or health condition. In fact, until you've seen it yourself, you cannot begin to know the difficulties and the gravity of the challenges that go with such a moment of decision making. May the soul of Terri rest in peace and may God console and comfort her loved ones left behind. And for the living, what message has Terri's death given us? How many will hear? How many will hear and would not listen? How many never will?

By way of some immediate reactions, in the wake of the controversial Terri's case, citizens were gathering in so many parts of the United States to discuss and brush up on living wills, health-care proxies and powers of attorney. This issue

DEATH AND FUNERALS

was probably the hottest topic on the news all through the month of March 2005. Before it began to die down, some people had come to the conviction and conclusion that living will and health-care proxy are good ideas and so related plans should be put in place by all, irrespective of age because you never know what's going to happen to you at anytime. And believe it or not, to save the family or any one concerned, the trouble of deciding on the path of living will to follow, some people even have decided to engrave tattoos on some parts of their bodies with the inscription: "No resuscitation!" This speaks for itself, just in case the designated health-care proxy comes to a crossroads in regard to making a decision about someone else's situation.

Furthermore, the reflection on the culture of life-and-death evidently brings us to the discussion on the culture of weeping at the death of a loved one. At the death of a dear one, (as it is the case in the Etung culture and perhaps all cultures of the world), the Adirondack people also weep. In fact, some of them, too, can be very emotional. Yes, they can let go the flow of tears from their eyes as long as they are able to. Finally, it is good to know that it is only human to weep. And it is not a sin to weep. As Christians, weeping, especially at the death of someone does not negate our belief in the resurrection. It only shows how much we love the one who has gone before us and how much we are going to miss him or her, until we meet again at the final resurrection of the dead. After all, "Jesus wept" (Jn. 11: 35) in His humanity and because of the love he had for his friend, Lazarus when the latter died. In this way, Jesus Himself gave us an example to follow.

POSTMORTEM

At the death of someone, my native culture requires that the immediate family members of the deceased person take care of the funeral obsequies. However, for easy reference and for the benefit of assuming direct responsibility, there is always one member of the family who stands out as the *chief mourner or the undertaker.* Traditionally speaking, funerals are arranged and celebrated according to native law and custom, which move from one stage to another. The first stage of the funeral consists of the body lying in state in the family compound or home of the deceased person for an all-night wake, sometimes known as sing-song-night. Thus, this night is kept busy with singing, "dancing," and praying by the mourners and sympathizers.

On the next day, if desired and as requested by the family of the deceased person, a church service is celebrated with the deceased body brought to the church. Depending on circumstances, the church service could be held at the compound of the deceased person. After the church service, the body is taken to the gravesite for burial, which, more often than not, is usually in the family compound of the deceased person. For the most part, there are no designated cemeteries, and burials are done all year round. This is unlike in Upstate New York, where at a certain time during the winter season, some cemeteries are closed because of too much snow on the ground. In addition, sometimes, too, they are closed in order to avoid accidents on the property during this time, which puts the property owners at risk of being sued for "personal injuries" by anyone who may fall on the property and sustain an injury in the course of going to bury a loved one. Burials, interments or committals

DEATH AND FUNERALS

are usually resumed sometime in spring. Hence, oftentimes you hear of "spring burials" in the Adirondack world.

The final stage of the funeral among the Etung people is what is known as the second burial. This stage consists of celebrating the life of the dead person. This may take place a couple of months or years later after the first burial. However, for families that can afford to shoulder the financial involvement, it may take place simultaneously with the first burial. In whichever case, this final stage is characterized by paying the customary debt of eating and drinking, singing and dancing on behalf of and in honor of the dead person for all his or her achievements or accomplishments while his or her stay lasted on earth. This is also the stage of paying whatever debts the deceased person may have owed to anyone or to the community, but did not clear them before death. The family members, therefore, on behalf of the dead, would have to pay the debts to all who have such claims to make. Finally, the properties of the deceased person are handed over to an uncle in a family where the children of the dead person are not of age to acquire or inherit such properties. Otherwise, the properties are divided among the children who are adults.

At this point, it is worthy to note, and I make bold to mention the cultural "window dressing" or "washing the outside of cup" malady that takes place at such occasions. Thus, both the first and second or final stages of burials are characterized by ironies, contradictions, and hypocrisy on the part of the deceased family members. By this I mean, everything is played to the gallery. Thus, there is a show of abundance of food and drink and the overnight transformation or face-lift of the family compound. In fact, the deceased person, who

A HANDBOOK ON CULTURE SHOCK

may not have had the opportunity of eating and drinking much during his or her lifetime, has an overabundance of food and drinks brought and lavished by the family members at his or her funeral ceremony. It should not be a surprise to know that such a person may have slept hungry several times in his or her life. Second, such a person may never have slept in a good and comfortable bed during his or her lifetime, but would lie in state in a cozy and very expensive bed with all the decoration that attends it. No wonder a famous Nigerian movie that depicted this situation is titled: *Died Wretched But Buried in a One Million Naira Casket.*

Third, the house in which the deceased person lived may have been squalor or an eyesore, but now is painted and electrified during the burial ceremony. In short, this stage is always a shamming or false but impressive picture. At the end of the day, it is not always a surprise to hear that some family members took a loan to pay for and project this pomp. For families that do this, it is also not surprising to know that the time for paying back the debt presents another era of confusion, disagreement and probably enmity among family members. In fact, without any disregard for traditional beliefs or native law and custom or cultural demands, or even personal opinions, if you cannot easily afford it, or even if you can, spending lots of money on a funeral is not only useless, but also wasteful. Why throw all the huge amount of money away when the star of the show can't appreciate all the hoopla? Or, are the family members stealing the show to show off?

By all means this culture and others equally affected or concerned, need an evangelization that would effectively translate the scripture passage of Matthew's gospel 25:31–46 into

DEATH AND FUNERALS

a living and concrete reality. This scripture passage is titled: *The Last Judgment.* It talks about our duties toward the living-needy and what is going to be the contents of the last judgment from God of all of us. It reads: "When the Son of Man comes in his glory with all the angels, he will sit on the throne of his glory. All the nations will be brought before him, and as a shepherd separates the sheep from the goats, so will he do with them, placing the sheep on his right and the goats on his left.

"The king will say to those on his right, 'Come, blessed of my father! Take possession of the kingdom prepared for you from the beginning of the world. For I was hungry and you fed me, I was thirsty and you gave me drink; I was a stranger and you welcomed me into your house; I was naked and you clothed me; I was sick and you visited me; I was in prison and you came to see me.'

"Then the good people will ask him, 'Lord, when did we see you hungry and gave you food, thirsty and gave you drink, or a stranger and welcome you, or naked and clothed you? When did we see you sick, or in prison and go to see you?' The king will answer, 'Truly, I say to you, whenever you did this to these little ones who are my brothers and sisters, you did it to me.'

"Then he will say to those on his left: 'Go, cursed people, out of my sight into the eternal fire which has been prepared for the devil and his angels! For I was hungry and you did not give me anything to eat; I was thirsty and you gave me nothing to drink; I was a stranger and you did not welcome me into your house; I was naked and you did not clothe me; I was sick and in prison and you did not visit me.'

"They, too, will ask, 'Lord, when did we see you hungry,

A Handbook on Culture Shock

thirsty, naked or a stranger, sick or in prison, and did not help you? The king will answer them, 'Truly, I say to you, whatever you did not for one of these little ones, you did not for me.'

"And these will go into eternal punishment, but the just to eternal life."

I challenge you who is reading this book, to think about and reflect on this Scriptural passage in respect of your family members who may be needing help now, but you are saving so much money in order to give them a "befitting" burial. Stop planning to be hypocritical!

Furthermore, if the deceased person was a married man who died leaving children of very young ages, this final stage of burial can be a turning point in the life of the poor widow with her children. Since the culture does not seem to encourage and support direct right of inheritance by widows, the concomitant ordeals of being deprived of almost all that naturally belongs to the family, haunts the direct family left behind for the rest of its life. Also sadly enough, there are other traditional or customary practices of physically and psychologically torturing and tormenting the poor and defenseless widow at the death of her husband. This is because of the superstitious belief and suspicion that, any husband who dies leaving his wife behind must have been killed by her. To this end, the cultural treatment of such a widow is seriously pathetic, very unkind, merciless, inconsiderate, and ultimately privative. Such a widow whose life (when her husband was still alive) must have been kept simply like the Americans would say *"barefoot, pregnant and in the kitchen", "seen and not heard",* is eventually made to leave her matrimonial home to go wherever she can fend for herself and her young children. In short, many of such widows

Death and Funerals

almost become objects of public scorn, societal ridicules and village taboos who consequently carry a discriminatory stigma all through their lives. This situation is very emotional and profoundly traumatic for the victims. Thanks, however, to the new wave of awareness in the elitist group, in which widows now arrange the funerals as well as acquire and inherit their deceased husbands' property, which is used to take good care of the children left behind.

On the issue of the cause of death, the mentality of the people of my home culture in this regard is worthy of note. For the most part, the Etung people do not believe in the natural death, the protracted illness of anyone, or any natural life misfortune and calamity. By this I mean that people of this culture always seem to have a tendency of pointing accusing fingers at one person or another or on a group of people as being responsible for all of these unbecoming eventualities or occurrences, especially death or protracted illness, more so concerning victims who are young people.

Probably, you are familiar with the concept and belief of the African **voodoo** known or referred to as **ojjeh** or **okpee-inon** among the Etung people. This concept is a charm, fetish, spell, or curse thought by believers to possess magic power that can put someone under its influence, changing one's destiny and even causing death. For the most part, this voodoo belief and mentality is held by a great number of the Etung people, especially among the young. Consequently, if anyone dies, it is believed that he or she must have been "voodooed" and killed by someone else through voodoo power or other related superstitious means. For whatever reason, that someone else who suffers the accusing finger is often the eldest person in a fam-

A Handbook on Culture Shock

ily: grandpa, grandma, or some elderly aunt or uncle. By my estimation, this superstition is demonic and very troubling. It would be making explicit an obvious situation to state that it has torn families apart and left generations of people in perpetual enmity.

Furthermore, the belief in the voodoo power also extends to success in life. This is in the sense that the Etung people believe that someone can use such (demonic) powers for greater achievements and accomplishments or to mar such achievements in the life of someone else. Thus, in this culture, there seems to be a *glass ceiling* in one's success in life, politically, socially, educationally, and even agriculturally. To this end, if anyone rises or goes beyond an expected position in making progress in these areas of achievements, there is always the suspicion of the use of "ojjeh" or voodoo power for such successes. This suspicion may be directed first to the living parents of the one in question who has risen so high in his or her area of life or specialty, and then the searchlight may also be turned on the person concerned. This attack on the success of a person or persons, for the most part, is gradual. Thus, as someone continues to rise, the tension and the odds against his or her family or directly against him or her also continue to accumulate, waiting for an opportunity to explode. When this eventually happens, that is, when the explosion takes place, the one accused or being suspected (of using demonic powers) becomes like a lone voice, and he or she must fight to defend himself or herself against the world that has come together against him or her. What an unhealthy conspiracy! And what a way to live!

By way of pushing the argument further on this cultural

mentality and attitude, it is important to point out that it is impossible to bring forth a tangible evidence or scientific proof that can prove the innocence or otherwise of the one being accused. Hence, it would be shocking to discover and know that there is a ritual that is usually practiced to prove the innocence or otherwise of the one accused of using voodoo power to do harm to another person and good to himself or herself, as the case may be. In my home culture, this ritual is called the **"ottee"** cult or ritual. It is literarily translated as *"talk truth"* ritual. This is a cultural and traditional means of making or forcing someone to confess the truth. Usually, it is a dangerous and health hazardous herbal concoction that the accused person is forced to drink. Your guess of the health jeopardy to the victim, is as good as mine. In fact, after taking the concoction some of them become sick all through their life, while others may die immediately, whether they were innocent or guilty. Of course, cases abound of confession by or under duress.

This ritualistic process can be likened to an incident which occurred in Lagos, Nigeria, and was discovered and uncovered by the police. To truly and vividly capture the picture, permit me extensively to quote the article regarding this incident titled: "Police Discover 50 Bodies in Cult Shrines; 30 Arrested," as reported in *The Post-Star* of Friday, August 6, 2004, by Daniel Balint-Kurti.

"Police in eastern Nigeria discovered body parts, skulls and more than 50 corpses, some partly mummified, in shrines where a secretive cult was believed to have carried out ritual killings," officers said Thursday. Some victims may have died after swallowing poison to prove their innocence.

"Two religious leaders and 28 others have been arrested

A Handbook on Culture Shock

in connection with the cult, which was feared and obeyed by people living near wooded areas — known as 'the evil forest' — where the twenty shrines were located.

"'Investigators are searching near the town of Okija for more possible remains,'" police spokesperson Kolapo Shofoluwe said. 'We must go round the forest. As extensive as it is, it may take days,' he said.

"'All of the dead found so far were adults, and at least one body and four skulls appeared to be from those killed recently,' he said. Some of the bodies were in coffins, and some were headless.

"Police believed some of the victims — businessmen, civil servants and others — were poisoned. The cult, known as Alusi Okija, is believed to practice a ritual in which people involved in disputes, often over business deals, are exhorted to settle them by drinking a potion they are told will only kill the guilty.

"Alusi Okija — which takes its name from a local, oracle god and the town — is an ancient sect of the area's ethnic Ibo people. Few details of the cult were available Thursday, but police said the ritual of swallowing poison to test guilt is believed to have been practiced for over 100 years.

"'The practice was originally intended to deter crime but has become a way for priests and their collaborators to kill and defraud people,' Ogbaudu said.

"'Investigators found the shrines after the national police inspector-general received a complaint from a man who 'alleged that his life is being threatened by a group of persons' linked to the killings,' Shofoluwe said.

"Police declined to identify the victims, and residents of the town could not immediately be reached for comment. However, reports of ritual murders regularly fill the pages of Nigerian newspapers.

"Three years ago, the issue came to international attention when the torso of an unidentified boy was found floating in the Thames River in London. British police believed the boy became a victim of a ritual killing after being brought to Britain from Nigeria.

"Some ritual killings in West Africa are carried out in the belief they provide wealth or success to a third party. Other rituals involve using body parts as traditional medicine. Such killings are widely feared and condemned by Africans, 'especially the helpless victims who have no power to stop such barbaric attitudes.'

"Naturally, as a human being I was shocked at the horrific sight in the forest and then wondered if such events can still happen in this 21st century, that people can still practice such barbaric acts,' said Shofoluwe. 'I never believed that such a thing can exist in the modern world.'"

In reaction to the incident narrated here, I would like to say unequivocally that the picture it depicts, clearly captures the culture of most African and Nigerian tribes, including the Etung people.

If our brothers and sisters in this cultural nightmare must enjoy the freedom of the children of God and all the benefits of globalization, then the sons and daughters of this culture together with any help from other concerned groups is highly solicited to free its helpless people from the shackles of this unbecoming and disturbing way of life. The time is now, and you who are reading this book, can contribute. Do you want to know how?

From personal experience, I remember vividly with tears in my eyes the untimely and unfortunate death of a very dear cousin of mine in my village in Nigeria in the year 2002, and all that attended her burial. You would not imagine, neither would you believe it, but it did happen: She died too young and suddenly at that. Because of the superstitious belief that she must have been killed by someone else other than dying naturally, there was a mass hunt by the youth to fish and dig out who may be responsible for her death. Unfortunately, all the **"dibias"** (native medicine men) that were consulted could not find nor tell them of anyone who did it. Another way of avenging her death was to bring a certain "dibia" to perform a superstitious ceremony on the body of the deceased at the graveside and in the casket before the burial. At the end of the day, after some ritualistic incantations, she was buried with a live dog, which was put inside the casket with the body. The superstitious belief and intention was that the live dog was going to look for, hunt out, and deal with anyone or all those who were responsible for her death. They even refused any form of prayers or the Christian rite of committal before the interment. The argument for the refusal was that this Christian rite of committal, with all the prayers to be offered to God, would neutralize the avenging power of the dog, render inactive its effects, and thwart its mission. I wept! This incident has remained such a painful memory to me. Yes, even as a Catholic priest, you dare not insist to offer prayers at such occasions in the presence of young men when they are culturally provoked. Otherwise, you may become a victim of physical and brutal attacks by them.

Death and Funerals

In another dimension, it is important to note that this dibia culture is not only peculiar to the dibias per se. The so-called "visionaries" and "soothsayers" both "ecclesiastical" and private, are not left out in plying this satanic trade, looking for the superstitiously gullible people as victims, particualrly those who believe in demonic powers. These people in plying their trade, which is ultimately for private or material gain and related recognition, have done more harm than good to the vulnerable, and especially some gullible Etung people and those of other cultures, who are equally trapped and ensnared by this disguised or beclouded scheme. Their (visionaries and soothsayers) works and characteristic hypnotic tendencies and strategies have not only created rifts between people (brothers and sisters), but have also implanted real and imaginary fears, psychological and physical phobias, mistrust and an immeasurable sense of insecurity among its victims. This presents a picture of a culture that has been invaded by and inflicted with the unbecoming belief in demonology.

At this point, I cannot resist the temptation to present my personal views on the whole concept of demons, devils and witches that are held by many a man as responsible for man's problems. I am sure that my views will either be confirming what has already been said on this subject, or perhaps, it will have a following. This is my stand: The belief in human problems of illness/sickness, misfortunes and failures (economic or social) or even death as caused by voodoo power, is the proper heir to the belief in demonology and witchcraft. It is this demonologic concept of human problems in living that has given rise to the therapy along superstitious, medical or psychotherapeutic and theological lines. Confronted with this re-

A Handbook on Culture Shock

alities, the aim of my thought is to suggest that the phenomena (of human problems), be looked at afresh and more simply. I mean that, they be removed from the category of voodoos and demons, and be regarded as the expressions of man's struggle with *the problem of how he should live.* These problems are obviously vast, ranging from man's inability to cope with his environment in his relationship with others and in his ambition to increase his self- esteem and reflectiveness. In these dynamics, man is craving towards liberty, self-determination and autonomy, though remaining united with his fellow men as a member of a group.

These problems in living are those explosive chain reaction that began with man's original fall from the divine grace through the sin of disobedience. This awareness brings in its wake an ever larger burden of understanding. This burden is to be expected and must not be misinterpreted. The only rational means left to us to resolve these myriads of problems is more understanding, and appropriate action based on such understanding. The main alternative lies in living, moving and acting "pantheistically." This may logically lead to pleading non-responsibility in the face of seemingly unfathomable problems and insurmountable difficulties (determinism). This deterministic reasoning cannot however, become an escape route for explaining man's problems because of the fact of freewill and choice. And that is why in man's freewill and choice, he chooses to "voodoolize" and "demonize" his existence with it attendant challenges – crucibles and vicissitudes.

Without any intention to provoke any unnecessary thought, what I am trying to say here is that, the concepts of and scrupulous beliefs in voodoo, demon, devil and witchcraft have

Death and Funerals

outlived whatever usefulness they may have had. In fact, they now function as myths. It was the function of these belief-systems to act as social tranquilizers, fostering the false and deceptive hope that mastery of certain problems may be achieved by means of substitutive, symbolic magical operations. These demonological beliefs thus serve merely and mainly to obscure the everyday fact that life for most people is a continuous struggle, not only biological survival, but for some other meaning or value, such as personal significance. Believe it or not, sustained adherence to the myths in question, allows people to avoid these litany of human problems in their various dimensions and depths. When I say that voodoo power is a myth, for instance, I mean to say that we believe in it at our own peril. By all means, this expression is a metaphor that we have come to mistake for a fact.

I will like to say it clearly and unequivocally that, the over exaggerated myth of witchcraft or devil or demon, encourages us to believe in its logical corollary: that social intercourse would be harmonious, satisfying, and the secure basis of a good life were it not for the disrupting influence of and interference by the unseen powers of the demon. However, universal human happiness, at least in this form, is but another perfect example of a wishful thinking or fantasy. It is a mirage. But this happiness, for a greater majority of people, can be achieved only if many men, not just a few, are willing and able to perceive and confront reality frankly, and tackle courageously, their ethical, personal and social conflicts. This means, having the courage and integrity to forego waging futile battles on false fronts, and finding solutions for substitute problems.

To whom it may then concern – our adversaries are not demons, witches, voodoos, or fate. We have no enemy that we can fight, exorcise, or dispel by cure through any "dibia" means. What we do actually have are problems in living – whether these be biological, economic, political, sociological, psychosomatic and psychological. From the foregone, I would like to reemphasize that my argument is to establish that our superstitious inclinations expressed in the belief in some "unseen powers" or malevolent forces, are myths, whose functions are to disguise and thus render more palatable the bitter pill of various conflicts in human relations.

This picture awakens so many questions in view of the way forward. Some of these questions are: When would this mentality be erased or changed? And when would those concerned stop chewing this cud of foolishness? The answer is handy, and it is this: When people, especially those concerned, give their lives to God and acknowledge Jesus Christ as their personal Lord and Savior. This giving and acknowledgement must be in tangible acceptance of the Scriptural fact that: "Unless the Lord builds the house, in vain do its builders labor. Unless the Lord guards the city, in vain does the guard stay awake." (Ps. 127: 1). It must also be in firm belief of the fact that, even where those "unseen" and malevolent forces exist, the weapon of the wicked fashioned against God's own shall not prosper. In his own words, the Master (Jesus) says of all who believe and are baptized, thus: "These signs will accompany those who believe: in my name they will drive out demons,…They will pick up serpents with their hands, and if they drink any deadly thing, it will not harm them. They will lay hands on the sick, and they will recover." (Mark 16: 17-18).

Given this cultural scenario of excessive superstitious beliefs and other facts, it is my firm belief that this way of life needs a reevangelization toward cultural purification and related exigencies. Such a reevangelizing task should properly sow the seed and inculcate the essence of Christianity in the lives of the people concerned. Ironically, the Etung people go to church a lot, but it is like, "the Bible is in one hand and the charm in the other hand." The evangelization in question should enthrone the total belief of all Christians in the omnipotence of the triune God. Its catechesis should drive into the mentality of the people the conviction that only God has and holds the destiny of all peoples and that this destiny may only be delayed, but not destroyed.

The methodology required in this reevangelization campaign or reevangelizing mission should be gradual but steady. It should not be an overnight delivery package that undermines the cultural context of the host culture. Rather, taking cognizance of the cultural structures that be, it should be slow but steady with a mission-oriented agenda for the common good. To bulldoze its way into a project of total and immediate replacement of what has been with what ought to be is to foment a war and a clash of cultures. If I may suggest, its agents must have or develop the willingness for a cultural-fit approach. That is, the ability to contextualize or indegenize by going into local cultures and adapting the local African culture, and then the healing and deliverance "didache" with explicit promises or coping mechanisms for various personal problems.

Without advocating for the "protestant" approach of being overly scrupulous, hypnotic, and manufacturing devils and demons where there aren't any, at the same time, the new evangelization should follow the protestant methodology at,

A HANDBOOK ON CULTURE SHOCK

not just being city-based, but must capitalize on their skill at moving into rural or the most remote areas and on the idea of directly challenging the power of the Holy Spirit.

Don't forget also that, for the evangelization to be African-based, it must not only allow, but also encourage a liturgical renewal in music and dancing, increasing the use of indigenous language where necessary and needed, and above all, putting emphasis on *social action* through voluntary and communal efforts of development – what I may call a-do-it-yourself kind of thing in accordance with the inspiring words of Mother Theresa, who once said: "Do not wait for leaders. Do it alone, person to person." This methodology becomes more relevant and urgent in a society where most people have doubts about their day-to-day survival. Hey! it sounds like I am driving towards the culture of *liberation and sustenance theology and inculturation.* Well! whatever works! If liberation theology is the solution to the existing problems, then there is nothing wrong with that, so long as its extreme agendas, contents and positions are avoided. If sustenance theology would provide a lasting solution to the impending problems, then why hesitate to introduce and preach it? By the same token, if inculturation would implant the Christian faith concretely in the people and make for a more convincing dependence and active participation in the worship of God, then let's get at it.

For the benefit of doubt, liberation theology is a movement in the Roman Catholic Church that makes criticism of oppression essential to the task of theology. The forms of oppressions to be criticized are mainly social and economic evils. Originating in Latin America as a movement inspired by the 1968 Medellin Bishops' Conference, liberation theology has held as

DEATH AND FUNERALS

its main concern the deprivation, exploitation and the "thing-nification" of the poor. It also seeks to defend the rights of minority and ethnic groups and to support women's liberation. By all means, it is therefore, a theory of deliverance from the injustices caused to people by the power structures of modern society. Not only the material liberation, but, I'll also add that, it extends to the total deliverance of the human person even from the shackles of spiritual blindness, its related vulnerabilities and substitutive beliefs. This new approach to Christianity reinterprets the Christian faith to concentrate on the main task of the Church today, to deliver people everywhere from the inhumanity to which they are being subjected, especially by those in political power. It calls for a reassessment of the main doctrines of historic Christianity in light of the changing face of Catholicism and in relation to human needs and yearnings. It challenges the church to listen, attend to and address troubling issues as human problems affecting the "universal church," and not merely look at them as "African" or "American" problems, as the case may be.

According to the *Pocket Catholic Dictionary,* liberation theology teaches the following: "Christ becomes an inspired human deliverer of the weak and oppressed; God's kingdom centers on this world, and not on the next; sin is essentially social evil and not an offense against God; the Church's mission is mainly socio-political and not eschatological; an objective divine revelation is subordinated to personal experience."

Pope John Paul 11, in addressing the issue of liberation theology endorses that its proclamation should be integral and profound. It should go above mere rhetoric and ideologies to the concrete attitudes that its proponents adopt. It should be

A Handbook on Culture Shock

contributory to the real building of the community in the form of showing care for the poor, the sick, the dispossessed, the neglected, the oppressed, the afflicted, the possessed, and the demonized. These victims represent the image of the suffering Christ. Without sounding exclusive, not only the Etung people, but, Africa at large and other parts of the world stand in need of a liberation and a deliverance of this kind for both the spiritual and material salvation of the people. Probably there should be an increase in the emphasis on the material benefits of the human person, because it is very difficult to convincingly "praise God with an empty stomach without being misunderstood."

For this movement (liberation theology) to be a lasting solution to the world's problems, I suggest that it should also envision *"sustenance theology."* By this I mean, the ability for people to self-sustain or independently take care of themselves. Hence, sustenance theology *"should teach the people how to fish, and not give them fish to eat whenever they are hungry."* Evangelization, therefore, in this context should take into consideration the undeniable and granite fact that the "umbilical cord" or "feeding tube" used in feeding the evangelized will be cut or removed at some point. This method of evangelization would consequently prepared them for the rainy day that is sure to come. Without sounding pessimistic, the questions is: For how long would this (provision) continue, especially in a world that is daily becoming very competitive and complex? Far from being selfish, I must say that this form of theology is what the African continent needs in the face of "scandalous poverty" and other "hot button" socio-political issues. Failure to adopt this radical approach would make the church to continue to witness the daily drift and lose of members to street corner evangelical and Pentecostal churches. It would even weaken its internal strength to combat the incessant struggles with Islamic fundamentalism.

I cannot help at this point not to comment on the medias' attention to the astronomical and explosive growth of the Catholic Church in Africa, Nigeria in particular. True as it may be that the Church is "crazily" growing in this part of the world, let us not lose sight of or forget the fact that, this growth is alongside the mushrooming of new religious sects, especially from the Protestant denominations. Yes, we seem really to be living in the age of new things. In Africa, as we talk about the new wave of Catholicism, we also carry in our traveling bag quite a great number of new religious realities, one of which is New Religious Movements, including, of course, Independent African Churches. If the new evangelization is to be a success on the Nigerian soil, these movements cannot be ignored, as they are certainly constituting new problems and posing new questions and challenges to the Church in Nigeria. In spite of the Catholic church's teachings on ecumenism, there still linger some concerns between and among "brothers" and "sisters" Christians, not only in Africa, but all over the world.

Historically speaking, for more than three decades or so these religious movements have littered the religious landscape of Nigeria. They constitute a new religious phenomenon for the fact that they differ greatly from the familiar orthodox Churches. Found everywhere are the Pentecostal or pneumatic types that harp on the Spirit of Jesus and the mighty works that go along with this power. Hence, many call them the "Spirit Churches." To say that the proliferation of these movements in Nigeria is quite alarming, is to make a statement of fact. Their

A Handbook on Culture Shock

presence is such that no one can pretend not to notice them. Even a newcomer to Nigeria, need not be told of the super-abundant presence of these movements in the country. Practically almost all towns and villages are so flooded with these exotic religious movements that even tend to defy statistical calculation. In just one family, for instance, there could be as many as four or more different religious bodies and in some cases one building could be found playing host to various religious groups either simultaneously or alternately. And if it is the former, (simultaneously), the confusion that arises in the "heaven-on-earth" is beyond comparison as each group tries to outshine or outdo others with "praise the Lord and Halleluiah chants." Because of their daily growth and increase, often-times they are referred to as the local industries of the people. Especially on Sundays, the picture is such that, literally, all the classrooms in school facilities, open spaces in filing or gas stations, some lockup stores, public buildings, bus stops, mechanic or garage shades, drinking parlors, etc are turned into Churches.

In looking at the motivating factors responsible for this development, some thinkers have attributed the proliferation of these movements to socio-political, religious and theological discrepancies, including economic, ethnic and liturgical factors. While concurring with some other thinkers, I am of the opinion that, the key factor in the proliferation is the failure of the Euro-American or orthodox Churches to meet the religious cum economic needs of Nigerians as Africans in their cultural context, and in view of a future "independent" Church that will cater for and fend for itself.

Undoubtedly, the Catholic missionaries who arrived in Ni-

DEATH AND FUNERALS

geria around 1885, did quite a lot for the people. From the onset, they regarded the opening of schools and hospitals as essential tools for the work of evangelization. But the question is: What has happened or what became of those schools and hospitals after they left the areas that benefited so much from their presence? Far from being an ungrateful child, or biting the finger that fed us, it must, in any case be pointed out that, the early missionaries did not take the cosmological perspective or worldview and superstitious inclinations of Africans into consideration in their noble missionary endeavors to liberate the African continent. In addition, they spoon-fed their new converts by importing from the western world almost everything needed to build the local Church without tasking or challenging the generosity of the indigenous Church. They also came to Africa with their pre-conceived ideas about this continent and its people. These ideas they had acquired from books on African history written by their white counterparts. This knowledge, for the most part, shaped mentalities and made the missionaries to come to Africa with culture biases and prejudices and were therefore, bent on exterminating and uprooting African culture in order to plant their own culture, which they considered to be superior to that of the Africans.

As they launched their mission on African soil with the intention of converting the Africans from their primitive religion, "uncircumcised" customs, culture and beliefs, the missionaries seemed to have acquired a disdain for everything African. They even rejected African names for baptism. Hence, newly baptized Africans were not free to keep even their "God-centered" names. For instance, among the Etung people, names such as "Obasi-Akare" (God has given), "Ekup-Nse" (We thank God),

A HANDBOOK ON CULTURE SHOCK

"Biriwud" (Look on us "God"), "Ekip-Obasi" (God's gift) and so on, were dropped. Thereafter, the baptized were to take such Biblical and English names as, Moses, Abraham, Jonah, John, Rachel, Maria, Emmanuel, Roland, Ignatius and the rest. Yes, local or native names were probably considered pagan and unholy, and in the missionaries' "unquestionable" logic, such names had no resemblance or prototype in heaven. In furthering their "religious colonialism," even liturgical songs became foreign and local instruments, which usually go with clapping and dancing, were not allowed to accompany the songs, since they were looked upon as capable of distracting and detracting from the holiness of God's house. According to Donatus Udoette, in an article he contributed in the book titled: *The Search:* "The Africans were literally forced to fit the moulds of an imported religion and culture or suffer the damnation of their souls forever."

Perhaps, you are surprised and at the same time asking why I had to deeply and extensively delve into the whole idea of reevangelization in the perspectives of *total belief in God, liberation and sustenance theology and inculturation* in not only the Etung people, but also Nigeria as a country and Africa as a whole. Do not forget that the Gospel message of Jesus is supposed to lead to total liberation and salvation: economically, politically, socially, culturally and spiritually. After all, when Jesus was on earth, he did not engage himself merely in verbal preaching of the awesome word of God. In his missionary manifesto in which he announced the coming of the kingdom of God and the universal salvation brought by him was not mere theory without practice. "The Master" (Jesus) knew that his preaching of the *good news* to the poor would not make any sense when the poor were not freed from their poverty. Not just poor in spirit, his understanding of the poor was holistic. Thus those who were materially poor, politically powerless, religiously deprived, socially alienated, physically weak, morally exploited, racially segregated, psychologically afflicted and superstitiously demonized fitted into his definition of poverty.

Driven therefore, by the desperate conditions of the poor that daily cry out for activism, Jesus formally launched and announced his missionary manifesto: "The Spirit of the Lord is upon me, because he has anointed me to preach good news to the poor. He has sent me to proclaim release to the captives and recovering of sight to the blind, to set at liberty those who are oppressed, to proclaim the acceptable year of the Lord." (Luke 4: 18-19). What other proofs do we want to believe that Jesus wants the total liberation of man? So, if any evangelization is to live up to its name and be good news, its message of salvation should be all-inclusive with practical solutions to the problems of the needy.

Having briefly x-rayed and flashed back on the history that was and still is, in the perspective of African culture vis-à-vis their religious indoctrination, I believe that we now share the same idea on the reevangelization proposal in the direction of liberation and sustenance theology and inculturation. (Since the contents of liberation and sustenance theology have been treated above), in its own part, inculturation (theology) should seek to expose the Christian faith and African culture to mutual interaction. It should use the resources of the culture to explain, interpret and give meaning to Christianity. By this I mean, inculturation should use the ideas, elements, structures,

A Handbook on Culture Shock

features and persons of the culture to preach the gospel message of Jesus Christ to its people. To import these features in the task of evangelization amounts to a friction of cultures, which may also give rise to vagueness of the message. Of course, this importation judges between cultures and is tantamount to an imposition of ideologies with methodologies that do not take cognizance of the inherent and "inherited" structures. It should create a new cultural identity in the society and among the multi-faceted Nigerian tribes and African cultural globe as a whole. This is the only way the gospel can become relevant and *good news* for Africans. These recommended methodologies become feasible in the acknowledgement of the fact that God indwells in every human culture irrespective of human thinking and related stereotypes.

Since "charity begins at home," for this form of evangelization, through liberation and sustenance theology and inculturation to be result-oriented, first, all hands of the enlightened and educated sons and daughters of the Etung culture must be on deck. They must all share a common purpose, common mission, common agenda and common dream, as well as be ready and open-minded, to accept and welcome the help and assistance of others outside the culture. The suggestion that enlightened and educated people must champion the course of this reevangelization becomes imperative against the background of the profound statement made by a U.S. president, Abraham Lincoln, who, from his wealth of experience once said: "Education kills the blight of disease, ignorance and superstition." That this statement is not only profound, but true, can be attested to, from an experience I want to share with you.

Death and Funerals

It was on a Wednesday morning, at about 2:00 A.M. New York time, that I had this telephone call from a friend of mind who was in England at the time. He began by saying: "Father, I have a confession to make, and I am making it to you, not only because you are a priest, but more so because, you'll better understand what I wanna talk about." And I said to him: "What's it? Say it! There's no sin that is too big which God cannot forgive, so long as we're truly sorry for it and promise not to commit it again with the help of and grace from God." He then continued, sounding remorsefully:

"It's all about the role I played when I was still back home in the village during the persecution and torture of those indicted or accused of having used voodoo powers to kill some young people in our village. I must confess that I did it out of ignorance and related peer group pressures. I have now come to believe that people die naturally and our destinies are solely in the hands of God." He went on: "What a way of life that we led back home! We strangle ourselves just for nothing, hipping guilt on people and making innocent ones to suffer. We substitute our human problems and daily struggles with other in their stead." He spoke at length, and I patiently allowed him to empty the bag. When he was finished, I then said to him: "Good to hear from you. I believe that you were serious in all that you've just said. God has actually forgiven you because you acted out of ignorance." I continued with a challenge by saying:

"Now that you've come to this realization, which I also agree with you, I think we owe our people back home a duty. We need to think about ways of educating and enlightening them, too, so that all of us would enjoy the peace and freedom

A Handbook on Culture Shock

of God's children." With this challenge, he said to me: "Father, you know better. Whatever you think we can do to help our people, both the young and the old, please, do let me know." This confession was an eye-opening experience to the reality of what education and exposure can do for the common good. It made my day. And it has remained an encouraging and driving force in me to think about the liberation and deliverance of the Etung people from the destructive hands and shackles of the superstitious.

In advocating the liberation cum sustenance theology, it is my firm belief that hunger and poverty are responsible for the enthronement of superstition and its gory experiences. As a way forward, my philosophical pragmatism is to reiterate what has been said before by many a great mind: "If you give a man a fish, he has food for one day. Teach a man to fish and he has to buy bamboo rods, graphite reels, monofilaments lines, neoprene waders, creels, tackleboxes, lures, flies, spinners, worm rigs, slip sinkers, offset hooks, gore-tex hats, 20 pockets vests, radar, boats, trailers, global positioning systems, coolers and six-packs." I have no iota of doubt in my mind that, a culture found on these "theologies" will dealt the final death blow to and bring an end to the superstitious interpretations of fortunes and misfortunes, successes and failures and even death by its people.

At this point, permit me to challenge the educated people of the Etung culture in these words: "If your education is worth its name and your exposure has anything to write home about, and your experience has anything to go by; then come, let us lead this culture out of the darkness of unbelief, the stigma of superstition, and instill in the minds of its people, a mind

Death and Funerals

that is above the fear of the superstitious and the imaginary unknown. Not to do this is to fail in our mission to enlighten, educate, and evangelize our people." The results of this failure are obvious. They can be summarized in these words from the book *Things Fall Apart* by Chinua Achebe: "Turning and turning in the widening gyre; The falcon cannot hear the falconer; Things fall apart; the center cannot hold; Mere anarchy is loosed upon the world" —W. B. Yeats, "The Second Coming."

The culture of the Adirondack people has a different approach to the reality of what happens after one's death. On a comparative note, in the United States this reality is very comfortable and accommodating of all within the culture, irrespective of status. In fact, the cultural practice here appears to be the direct opposite of what happens in my native culture. Quite practically, since it is a culture of wills, this practice of the writing of a will settles a lot of problems after one's death, concerning the properties left behind and in relation to the rights of inheritance. Attention should be drawn to the fact that in the United States, widows, with or without children, have the right of direct inheritance. They are responsible for the funeral and burial arrangements of their deceased husbands and vice versa. To the best of my knowledge, there is no second burial, and most wakes are held in funeral homes or mortuaries, unlike what happens in my home culture where wakes are held in the compound of the deceased person.

For the most part, the cultural attitude among the Adirondack people concerning death and funerals remains a fascinating cultural experience. The culture shock in this particular regard is worthy of emulation and desirable, not only for the

Etung culture, but also for all cultures of the world. Thus, as far as the right of inheritance is concerned in the culture of the Adirondack people, it is indeed the path to justice and fair play. This right upholds the fundamental human equality and respects the dignity of the human person. It also acknowledges and rewards human labor. In the short- and long-terms, this cultural practice promotes societal peace and encourages fraternal solidarity among family members with their in-laws.

Finally and on a personal note, what a staggering experience it was for me to celebrate a Mass with a cremated body for the first time in the culture of the Adirondacks people. It shook me to my very foundation. I could not imagine how nor believe that a whole and complete human being could be crushed, burned, and reduced into a handful of ashes, which are put into a portable or what I may call a small "handbox." It was profoundly stupefying, and I was so nervous that I could still see myself that first time, visibly unsteady all through the Mass. It was really a dazing experience. As a missionary who ministers to the people of this culture, I did not condemn this cultural practice, but I had to struggle to pull myself together and accept this way of life. Thank God that in a short time I was acclimated to this facet of the culture of the Adirondack people.

Another piece of startling news or information that I gathered in a discussion one day in regard to the cultural treatment of cremains is worthy of sharing. Due to the love and attachment some people have for their loved ones or pets who have passed away and have been cremated, the ashes of the cremated body are sometimes put in a box and left at designated locations or places in the house as memorials. In some cases,

DEATH AND FUNERALS

the cremains of pets are eventually buried with their owners as instructed. Furthermore, some people even get the ashes (of their loved ones) well wrapped and fancifully sealed and use them as necklaces, earrings, and other carry-ons. Can this be true?

I remember an experience that was shared by someone about a man who went to visit a widow. While visiting with the widow, this man lit a cigarette and started smoking it. At some point, he wanted to dust the cigarette of its ashes. There at the center of the sitting room on a table was a nice transparent box with ashes in it. Since the widow also smoked, he thought that the box held the cigarette ashes from the widow. As he reached out for the box to dust his own cigarette ashes into it, the widow said to him: "Wait a minute, that is Dave, my husband." Dave's cremains were kept as a memorial. I gathered that some people even open the favorite wine or drink of their loved ones who have passed away and toast it to their cremains saying: "Cheers!"

Based on the culture of the treatment of cremains, perhaps, it would be a more compelling argument and practical experience to relate a case of how an American homeless kid treated the cremains of her mom. In the book, *God Isn't Done With Me Yet – The Unforgettable Story of America's Homeless Kids,* by Sister Mary Rose McGeady, the author vividly described the pathetic and pitiable situation of one of those kids, which I would like to quote here extensively.

The chapter on this issue is titled: *"It's my mother's ashes."* It reads: "She came to our front door Tuesday morning, ragged and dirty clothes on her back, and a little aluminum paint can in her arms. From the second she stepped inside, she made it

A HANDBOOK ON CULTURE SHOCK

clear to us that she and the paint can were a 'package deal.' *Whatever she did, wherever she went, the little paint can never left her hands.* When Kathy sat in the crisis shelter, the can sat in her arms. She took the can with her to the cafeteria that first morning she ate, and to bed with her that first morning she slept. When she stepped into the shower, the can was only a few feet away. When she dressed, the can rested alongside her feet. 'I'm sorry, this is mine,' she told our counselors, whenever we asked her about it. 'This can belongs to me.' 'Do you want to tell me what's in it, Kathy?' I asked her. 'Um, not today,' she'd say, and then quietly walked off. When Kathy was sad, or angry or hurt – which happened a lot – she took her paint can to a quiet dorm room on the third floor. Many times on Tuesday and Wednesday and Thursday, I'd pass by her room, and watch her rock gently back and forth, the can in her arms. Sometimes she'd talk to the paint can in low whispers..."

"Early this morning, I decided to 'accidentally' run into her again. 'Would you like to join me for breakfast?' I asked. 'That would be great,' she said. For a few minutes, we sat in the corner of our cafeteria, talking quietly over the din of 150 ravenous homeless kids. Then I took a deep breath, and plunged into it.... 'Kathy, that's a really nice can. What's in it?' For a long time, Kathy didn't answer. She rocked back and forth, her black hair swaying across her shoulders. Then she looked over at me, tears in her eyes. *'It's my mother's ashes,'* she said. 'Oh,' I said. 'What do you mean, it's your mother's ashes?' *'It's my mother's ashes,'* she said. 'I went and got them from the funeral home. See, I even asked them to put a label right here on the side. It has her name on it.' Kathy held the can up before my eyes. A little label on the side chronicled all that remained of her mother: date of birth, date of death, name. That was it. Then Kathy pulled the can close, and hugged it."

This is a picturesque story of how cremains could be treated by some people, who were very attached to their loved ones, now separated in death. For the uninitiated to this culture, this practice may appear absurd, but it is so meaningful, comforting, and consoling to those involved.

I do not intend to provoke negative thoughts or to spoil anybody's business. But from some remarks I heard and some comments that were made, which I gathered from my random discussions with some people on the practice of cremation, permit me to raise this question: How can one be sure that the ashes, as the cremains of a dear one, are truly that of the particular deceased body? Inasmuch as we do not doubt the trusted honesty, sincerity, and integrity of the crematory operators, this question calls for an answer, at least if for nothing else, to satisfy the curiosity of the honest inquirer. This question becomes more relevant against the backdrop of an article published in *The Post-Star* of January 8, 2005, with the caption: "Former Crematory Operator Sentenced for Dumping Bodies." According to the article in question: "A former crematory operator who admits dumping 334 bodies and passing off cement dust as their remains pleaded guilty on Friday to Tennessee charges and was sentenced to 12 years in prison." In a sense of remorse, the said operator said, "I've caused much harm. I've caused much grief. I do not do my job, I can only apologize for that." He "pleaded guilty to Tennessee charges of abuse of corpses, theft of services and criminal simulation for failing to perform cremations." You can take this development as a food-for-thought, or you can leave it.

A Handbook on Culture Shock

Another and further development on this consideration of cultural variations and differences is the experience on etiquette and courtesy. In the next chapter, I will attempt a look at this important reality (of civil etiquette and courtesy) in the perspective of cultural nuances.

NOTES

[1] Shakespeare, William. *Julius Caesar.* Hauppauge, New York: Barron's Educational Series, Inc., 2002, 96.

[2] Balint-Kurti, Daniel. "Police Discover 50 Bodies in Cult Shrines; 30 Arrested." *The Post-Star,* August 6, 2004.

[3] Achebe, Chinua. *Things Fall Apart.* New York: First Anchor Books, 1994.

[4] Hardon, S.J. John A. *Pocket Catholic Dictionary,(abridged Edition of Modern Catholic Dictionary),* United States of America: Image Books Doubleday, 1980, 1985, 227.

[5] Udoette, Donatus. "New Religious Movements in Nigeria" *The Search,* Nigeria: Snaap Press Ltd., Vol. 1, No. 1, 2002, p. 37.

[6] McGeady, Mary Rose. *God Isn't Done With Me Yet...*United States of America: Covenant House, 1993, 59-61.

[7] Poovey, Bill. "Former Crematory Operator Sentenced for Dumping Bodies." *The Post-Star,* January 8, 2005.

5

CIVIL ETIQUETTE AND COURTESY

This chapter simply concerns courteous acts in relationships between one person and another or the expected behavior of a person in a group. It can also be understood as the acceptable forms and practices in social life as prescribed by social convention or by authority. The need for this section becomes more glaring and urgent when you realize that ours is a world that seems to exile good morals. In fact, it is a hot topic today. And from the look of things, there is a resurgence of interest in manners, even though not very noticeable. People striving to be cultured are more aware now that etiquette can help life go more smoothly. Hence, there are books and conversations addressing such modern issues as e-mail courtesy, online dating, sleepover etiquette, gossip habits, good sportsmanship and cell-phone decorum. The latter, (cell-phone decorum) among other things, for instance, shuns the bad attitude of hanging up the telephone on somebody, no matter what. Businesses are spending oodles on proper protocol seminars, not to talk of manner classes for children, which is becoming ever more demanding than before. These classes are so needed especially in our so busy culture where everyone seems to be rushing around and forgetting the niceties.

No doubt, caring today's parents acknowledge with lamentation that although good manners can give their children an edge in life, they are not being taught. Like in America and other developed nations of the world, with both parents working to put the food on the table and pay bills, family meals where children traditionally learned not to eat with their hands and how to hold polite dinner table conversations, are a relic of the past. On the whole, the bottom line of etiquette, experts agree, is consideration for others. This ultimate guide to manners cannot be found in any book or class. The key is that first, parents and then the society itself need to set good examples because how children see their parents act and what society do is exactly how they will eventually behave. Some of the etiquette and courtesies that enhance the culture of civility will be briefly looked at below from a comparative perspective.

ORDERLINESS AND ORGANIZATION

The sense of order is a distinguishing and laudable mark of an organized society. It is not negotiable. For the most part, it is necessary for peaceful and harmonious coexistence. It becomes demanding in a country with limited public facilities at the service of an overpopulated majority of the masses.

In relating this understanding to the existing structures of my native culture and Nigeria as a country, without mincing words, I would say, much is left to be desired. Objectively speaking, there is more or less visible disorder and vexing disorganization in many places. This is more frustrating given the glaring fact of very limited public facilities serving a teeming population. For instance, go to the banks and post offices, gas

A Handbook on Culture Shock

stations and supermarkets, embassies and public water taps or wells, and all other public places with facilities that serve the daily needs of the people, the pictures there speak for themselves: hustle and bustle, rush and stumble, kick and push, yell and quarrel, abuse and fight, break and tear, you name it. This way of life can sometimes be described as "survival of the fittest" or the jungle justice of "might is right."

I remember vividly what I went through when I went to the U.S. Embassy in Nigeria for my visa interview. My appointment for the interview was scheduled for 6:30 a.m. on Monday, May 5, 2003. Unbelievably, having been duly informed, I arrived at the embassy on that day as early as 5:00 a.m. By this time to my great shock, I arrived to find out that the waiting area at the embassy was already packed with people who were also scheduled for interviews on the same day. Upon inquiry, I gathered that some people had even slept on the embassy premises. The reason for their sleeping there was to enable them get a better position in the line and have an earlier interview the next day. Yes, the watchwords here are haste, hassle, and rush for whatever you want. However, the question is: Did this help in the eventual orderliness and organization when the time came for people to line up for the interview? The answer is a firm "no!" When the law enforcement agents came with their whips to announce that it was time to line up for the interview, the experience was mass hysteria in which the mob gathered for the exercise simply went wild in the rush to get a better standing position. Of course, the whips were used accordingly to flog and lash at random on the struggling mob. Can you imagine this?

Without trying to justify the rush culture among many Ni-

CIVIL ETIQUETTE AND COURTESY

gerians, it is important to look at some questions that should be addressed in this particular situation. Why does the embassy give interview appointments to hundreds of people on the same day and date and at exactly the same time, which they cannot satisfactorily, orderly, efficiently, and adequately manage? Don't you think that the mass appointment is also contributing to worsening the rush syndrome among Nigerians? Could the mass appointment be a smart fraud to make more money by those concerned from the anxious people who are ready to do or to make any sacrifice and to give anything that would help them get out of the tough life situation back home? Is the embassy becoming an opportunist that milks dry and increases the frustrations of the frustrated? If the embassy in question is a U.S. institution run by U.S. government through its citizens, why do they not respect the sense of time and order in Nigeria, as it is experienced and as they do in their own country? If the answer to the last question is, "when in Rome, do as the Romans do," then where lies the difference? These questions and many more are yearning for objective answers that would satisfy the genuine curiosity of all authentic and concerned inquirers about the reasons for the mass appointment for visa interviews as it is experienced almost everyday in many overseas countries' consulates in Nigeria.

Now, when I went for my visa interview at the American Consulate in Nigeria, as a priest, I was dressed in my **Roman collar.** I feared to rush and disgrace both my sacred office and myself, but soon, it dawned on me that here there was neither regard nor respect for anyone – " Jews and Gentiles were alike." Yes, "what is good for the goose is good for the gander." Hence, the saying that: "When in Rome, do as the Romans do"

A Handbook on Culture Shock

was to be immediately adopted and put into a practical effect by me. Looking at what was going on, I carefully removed the white "Roman collar" from my black shirt and put it into the pocket of my trousers. Then, with all the energy I was able to gather, I joined in the struggle to get a good position in line. When I succeeded in getting it, I then reached my hand into the pocket of my trousers and brought out the "Roman collar." I looked around to be sure that nobody was looking at me and then quickly put it back into the neck of my shirt where it is supposed to be. After tucking in the Roman collar into my shirt, I had to behave myself and maintain an appropriate decorum, since behaving otherwise would be scandalous to the people standing around me who now knew that I was a clergyman.

Surprisingly, the rush did not even speed up the process in the end. After all the embassy protocols and security checkpoints, it was at exactly 4:00 p.m. that I was granted the interview. So, I had to wait in line for about eleven hours without water or food, to be attended to together with others. It was indeed an odious and hectic day. Thank God, it paid off, and at the end of the day, I was successful at the interview. Not all were successful, though. Sad!

Overall, the picture at the embassy was that of people looking dejected and worn-out, tired-out and down, frustrated and with long faces, hungry, thirsty, paranoid, apprehensive, and slavish. But the story or the picture always changes for those people who are successful at their interviews. As they come back the next day to pick up their visas, they appear and look more relaxed and calm. In short, they become, by way of their feelings and looks, like conquerors, kings, or lords and with all the pride that attends it, and they pick up their visas and leave gallantly and triumphantly. Parties and big celebrations may be organized by and for some successful people. It is worth it considering what they go through at the embassy.

However, in all these areas that serve the needs of the masses in Nigeria, you can get what you want and be given the attention you need faster than others based on the partiality of who you know, irrespective of how late you got to the scene. The Igbo tribe in Nigeria calls it the philosophy of **"ima-madu"** (IM), which literary means *"who you know,"* while the Etung people refer to it as the advantage of **"Fon Nneh"** (FN), which literally means *"have or know somebody."* The pidgin English rendition of it is *man know man.* The Americans often express it as the advantage of knowing the right people in high places and, hence, using your connections to get away with "anything." Unfortunately, more often than not, this philosophy increases the tension among equals, thereby giving rise to delays and riots and related civil disorders.

No thanks are given to some of the law enforcement agents, such as the police, who usually come with whips to lash the people to force them to be orderly and organized in such disorderly places. What a brutal and an untamed picture this projects! The resulting effect of this scenario is that the speed of progress is retarded, healthy growth is stunted, respect and regard for one another is overlooked, and developmental advancements are completely stagnated.

It will be a serious oversight not to further illustrate this disorder with some practical and existential cases as experienced daily in some very busy commercial towns in Nigeria. For Nigerians, you will agree with me that in big cities where every

A HANDBOOK ON CULTURE SHOCK

now and then, there is the experience of very heavy traffic jam, the situation can be very chaotic and frustrating. For instance in cities like Lagos, Port-Harcourt, and others, it will not be surprising to hear that someone who closes from work at about 4: 00 P. M, and, under normal circumstances such a person will need about an hour to get home, ends up sleeping on the highway within the city due to uncontrollable traffic jam. In frustration, cases abound where some car owners simply abandon their cars just on the highway and walk or trek home. Do I need to say that such frustrated people who abandon their cars in this way, end up compounding the traffic situation? It is at times such as this, that the services of the motorcycle taxis, which we will talk about later in this book, become a hot cake, since they can meander through any available space and ride on. Their patronage goes beyond the "carless" commuters to car owners.

My admiration for the institution of orderliness and organization in my foreign culture remains overwhelming. This is experienced at all public facilities that serve the needs of the masses. Thus, people fall in line as they go to the banks, post offices, shopping malls, gas stations, and related facilities. More fascinating is the experience of order on the highways, achieved through obedience to the traffic lights and related regulations. Thus, with the aid of ever-functioning traffic lights, stop signs, and other traffic cautions, drivers religiously respect and obey them, irrespective of time, place, and traffic situation. Hence, in spite of very heavy traffic on the roads at times, the cars keep moving. Therefore, you hardly experience frustrating traffic jams. On the whole, this orderliness can best be described as a cultural structure solidly grounded on the

CIVIL ETIQUETTE AND COURTESY

morality of first come, first serve, irrespective of who and what you are in the society. And no matter how long the service takes, the person on board must be satisfactorily attended to before the next person in line is invited up. For those waiting in line, this morality of order disciplines them and helps them to cultivate and exercise the virtue of patience. In short, over here, people just know the need to take turns in an orderly and mature manner in using public facilities. The resulting effects are obvious: People keep moving in a relaxed and tension-free atmosphere, where the needs of the masses are met, leaving them with smiles and gratitude on their faces. There is virtually no haste and hassle in such places.

It is important to know that this way of life is worthy of emulation if sanity, peace, and progress must be experienced in any society. This culture of order is also necessary so that regard, respect, and honor could be given or accorded to whoever deserves them.

PUNCTUALITY

Perhaps you are familiar with the sayings "punctuality is the soul of business," "time is money," and "time is of the essence." These sayings hold much water and so are not treated *cum grano salis* in matters of serious import. In short, no serious-minded person treats them with levity. The importance of punctuality, as a determinant factor for progress, achievement, and accomplishment in any endeavor, cannot be overemphasized. For the most part, it is the first sign of commitment, dedication, and responsibility. Furthermore, in public morals, it is a mark of a gentleman or a responsible woman.

Punctuality in my native culture is not given so much at-

A HANDBOOK ON CULTURE SHOCK

tention. By this I mean that the value of time in relation to punctuality is most times not adequately respected. In fact, almost every occasion is started many hours behind schedule. For instance, an appointment scheduled to begin at 8:00 a.m. may actually begin at 9:30 a.m. or 10:30 a.m. or even later, as the case may be. Remember, I said that it took me eleven hours of waiting when I went for my visa interview that brought me to the United States. Given the general situation of time consciousness, one of the smart ways of getting an occasion started at a specific time, such as 10:00 a.m., is to make the invitation card read 8:00 a.m. With this, you have two hours grace to be at the occasion or to begin the ceremony. However, with the idea of this smartness becoming common knowledge, the aim in most cases is defeated.

This unbecoming attitude concerning the value of time in terms of punctuality is experienced in almost every sector of the Nigerian society. Even the time schedules for the celebration of the weekday and the Sunday liturgies in churches are affected by this mentality. Probably, it is against this backdrop that you often hear the slogan, "African time," which has a negative connotation in the appreciation and the value of time among Africans. However, the schools and some other more organized establishments have a sense of time, which upholds the value and importance of punctuality.

True as this idea may be, it is still possible for this mentality of time and punctuality and the cycle of lateness to be broken, especially if initiated and started by one in authority. For instance, if as a pastor or priest in a parish, you make your 10:00 a.m. service or Mass really begin at this time. Thus, whether the people are there in church or not, once it is 10:00 a.m. you start the service or Mass. If you do this for two to three times, you can be sure that subsequently, the people will come on time. Therefore, this unbecoming mentality of time is not a curse but a "conditioning" way of life.

This reminds me of a personal experience: Shortly before I came to the United States, I had been lecturing and carrying out other related assignments in a major seminary in Nigeria where the sense of time and punctuality were highly respected. While I was still waiting in my home diocese for all that needed to be put in place to enable me leave for the U. S., I found myself assigned to St. Joseph parish, Okuku in the Catholic diocese of Ogoja, Nigeria. The parishioners' sense of punctuality needed a beep or a push. Accordingly, I took it up as a personal challenge. Surprisingly, I needed to say Mass in this parish for two times right on schedule, and the news or gossip went round that: "If it is Father Victor saying any Mass, then you had better be in church on time because he will start the Mass on schedule." It worked! So, train the people, and the tradition and conditional or conditioning cycle of lateness will be broken.

On another note, the practice of appointments and scheduling visits with family members and friends at given times is not a thing to be negotiated and so is not an issue in my native culture. In other words, you can drop in at any time to visit with anyone without any prior notice, especially someone with whom you are close. When you do drop in at any time, you can be sure that you will be well received and welcomed if you are lucky to find your host at home. The handicap of not having access to telephones and other communication services makes difficult or impossible the daily scheduling and rescheduling

A Handbook on Culture Shock

of visits. Hence, at times, due to this handicap, even previous appointments may be canceled without the cancellation information being passed on to those concerned. Largely, this unscheduled dropping-in is one of the ways of expressing African communal living and sense of accommodation, goodwill and unity.

My contact with my foreign culture really challenged my value of time and gave me a deeper appreciation of punctuality. Here, time is really of the essence, and people seem to have an admirable and religious commitment to it no matter what it takes. What is fascinating is that an occasion or ceremony, for the most part, does not begin before the time scheduled for it. In fact, it starts almost exactly at the strike of the bell that announces the stipulated time. This experience always reminded me of the slogan, "American time," which connotes promptness and punctuality. However, to the best of my knowledge, if there is any lateness at any point in time, this lasts only a couple of minutes. With the availability of a reliable network of communication technology made possible by telephones, e-mails, cell phones, and other related communication services, the time for an occasion can easily be scheduled or rescheduled or completely canceled, and those concerned can easily get the information accordingly.

To some extent, the culture of the Adirondack people sometimes considers it rude, impolite, and uncultured to visit anyone without previous notice, contact, or appointment. This is usually done by the (would-be) guest, first calling the host to see if a visit is convenient. No doubt, this attitude largely is recommended for good morals, especially for the good of your host and for your own benefit. After all, civility holds

C̲ivil E̲tiquette and C̲ourtesy

that it is not a good thing to cause any embarrassment either to your host or to yourself, which may occur in unscheduled visits. However, it is very important to know that this cultural practice of scheduled visits is only possible where you have functional and dependable communication and information gadgets. True as this practice may be in the culture of the Adirondack people, in case of emergency and as the need arises, there is an understanding that tolerates and allows someone to drop in at any time in people's houses. When this emergency or need arises and you are truly sure you need help, feel free to knock on the door of anyone and be sure to be welcomed and attended to accordingly.

On a personal note, while in my foreign culture, I did drop in a couple of times to see some friends and parishioners without any prior notice or contact. At such times, I always told them that my friendship and closeness with them does not demand that I must "fill in or fill out a form" to come see them. For some of them, I told them that I have become like a member of their family, and so I can come and go at any time. I am grateful for their understanding and sense of accommodation. Furthermore, in the culture of the Adirondack people, depending on the degree of closeness, you can accept and honor an invitation from someone on the spur of the moment; otherwise, it should be scheduled some days ahead to avoid clashes of appointments and to give enough time for your host to prepare, so as to give you a good treat on your visit.

Again, on the note of accepting and honoring an invitation for a meal from someone, especially from a family, the two cultures in question have some differences. In the Etung culture, once the guest arrives at the home of the host, the meal is

A Handbook on Culture Shock

served almost immediately. At the end of the meal and depending on some circumstances of time and other engagements to be determined by the guest, they could sit and visit for some time, and such visits are short and oftentimes they do not last more than one hour.

Among the Adirondack people, however, from some personal experiences, similar invitations to meals begin with a very long visit between the guest and the host family, while snacking on some finger food or sipping a drink. Then comes the actual mealtime, after which another longer visit commences. Overall, such an invitation can take between four to five hours. Just be aware of this, if you are new to this culture. Never plan to honor such an invitation with an intention of just arriving, eating, and leaving. It may not be possible to garbage in and garbage out.

The explanation mostly given for such a long get-together is that, the art of visiting and snacking before the real meal is to make the guest really hungry and prepare his or her appetite for the main course of the meal. The art of visiting after the meal is to allow some time for digestion before the guest leaves. No doubt, there is so much wisdom in this explanation. But sometimes, such invitations and the length of time spent can, and, in fact, do at some point become very tiring, discomforting, and uneasy to the guest, especially if he or she has to catch up with some other prior or pending appointments. And good morals do not allow such a guest to have the courage to say he or she wants to leave and for fear of offending his or her host. One of the advantages of such visits is that such gatherings afford all those present to learn more about the history and culture of the people and of course become aware of some current "gossip" going on in the area. Hence, it is worth the time.

Nevertheless, the point I want to make here is that my comparative experience with this aspect of life seriously challenged my sense of time and value of punctuality. It also gave me a better insight into the importance of scheduling appointments and the benefit of previous information in this regard. Finally, my understanding of the slogans "African time" and "American time" began to enjoy the knowledge of an appropriate application and a contextual appreciation of these expressions.

PUBLIC TALKING

In this consideration, I do not mean to expound on or talk about "public speaking" per se, which has to do with the art or the process of making formal speeches before an audience. Rather, I intend to give a comparative account of the cultural etiquette of talking in the midst of friends or other people in formal and informal gatherings that trigger some general conversations.

It is a fact that one of the outstanding characteristics of human beings as rational animals is not only the possession of the ability to communicate intelligibly, but also the capability of talking methodically. No doubt, humankind realizes this gift and uses it sufficiently and beneficially. However, it should be noted that, besides the fact of the different languages and dialects, there is also the variation in the mode and modality of talking, given the circumstances of place and time. Thus, different cultures have different modes and modalities of talking in public and private places. It is important to know that these modes and modalities are not formally taught anywhere, in the strict sense of the word. They are just parts of the cultural traits that you imbibe from your native cultural setting without any particular attention paid to them. There are no special tutorials. The realization of the differences in this regard becomes culturally revealing, intriguing, and fascinating when you find yourself in a new environment that presents a different picture from the one with which you are familiar.

Far from being judgmental, it is, however, important to know that it is fittingly good to have a mode of talking that is regardful and organized, especially if this has to do with group meetings and conversations. In this way, the ideas shared, the issues brought up, and the matters discussed would be common knowledge to all present at the end of the day. This would also make room for active and contributory participation by the members. Otherwise, the essence and the aim of the gathering may not be unanimously achieved, nor equally beneficial to all.

My cross-cultural experiences afforded me the opportunity to make a comparative observation on this matter. I was seriously caught up in the web of a cultural dilemma in this regard because of the differences. In order not to be misread, misunderstood, misinterpreted, or misjudged, I decided to share the next experience regarding the cultural difference of public talking with my congregation in the church:

In my home culture, when people are talking in a crowd, only one person is allowed to talk at a time. Nobody jumps in to talk when the other person is still talking or has the floor; otherwise, it is considered rude and uncultured for anyone to do this (jump in). In fact, even for two or more other people to start a different conversation within the same crowd is cultur-

CIVIL ETIQUETTE AND COURTESY

ally unbecoming.

This manner of communication does not seem to be the case in my new culture. Here, from my observation, it is clear that people jump in at any time and talk to the same crowd of people, either on the same subject or on a different subject completely. So, it will not be surprising to notice that in a gathering where there are ten people that there could be five different conversations going on simultaneously. When I questioned this development among the Adirondacks sometime, someone said to me that jumping in, sometimes could be the only way to make the one who has the floor to stop talking, especially if such a person is either long winded or monopolistic in conversation.

Based on my native cultural orientation, I found it very difficult to get involved in this way of public talking as experienced in my new culture. In fact, sometimes whenever I found myself in a crowd of people talking at the same time, I usually got confused about to whom I should listen. The best I could do was to always look at their faces at random, without paying particular attention to any of them, which was difficult at times to do. Hence, as a way of "public decency" in a group discussion, when one smaller group, what I may call intra group, in the larger group starts laughing, I also smile or laugh with them, even though I have no clue about what is causing the laughter. It is always a very funny scene to me because, due to my divided attention, most times I end up without a proper understanding of many of the things discussed. During such gatherings, my situation is always compounded and precarious, as I try to please everybody present by lending an ear to listen to what each person is saying at the same time. This communicational multitasking did not go well with me at all due to my cultural background.

On another note, in my native culture, in a gathering of senior (either by age or authority) and junior persons, the latter group merely listens to the conversations, and if the need arises, they give very short answers to questions directed to them. In fact, the junior persons rarely talk in such gatherings. The cultural etiquette in this context can be described as: the senior persons must be seen and heard, while the junior persons must only be seen and not heard. These quiet attitudes or etiquette of the junior persons are regarded as signs of respect for the senior ones or elders. This cultural situation becomes more compelling and appropriate, when it is appreciated against the backdrop of the understanding that the art of conversation by the seniors increases the wisdom of the juniors, who, then, must listen attentively to be able to gain this wisdom. Because it is from listening to old men and women that you learn wisdom. Hence, the saying: "Words of the elders are words of wisdom." This normative saying is based on the concept of successive wisdom handed down by age.

My decision to share this cultural difference with my congregation was occasioned by the fact that, since I was not always talking in a crowd where and when the pastor was present, he, being my senior in age and in authority, I was being pestered with lots of questions by those present. Some of these questions were: "Why are you not talking?" "Are you okay?" "You are awfully quiet! Why?" Of course, these questions were borne out of the fact that I seemed to talk a lot in a gathering where and when the pastor was not present. In fact, many consider me as very long-winded. The sharing of this cultural

CIVIL ETIQUETTE AND COURTESY

difference caused people to become sympathetic to me. On my own part, I was also relieved and knew that I would not be misunderstood or misjudged by the people when I keep quiet in the future on similar occasions.

The reflection on public talking also affords me an opportunity to talk about the culture of politeness or what I may call polite talk or conversation. My questions straightaway are these: Does polite talk means telling people only what they want to hear that will make them happy? Could it, too, be said that because of the culture of politeness, people have come to learn how to always sound nice when talking to and about someone else? Don't you see in this mentality a mutual covering up of the truth of the matter? Don't you also see that this culture of politeness or of always sounding nice will make some people to be addressed on borrowed robes and thereby make them to live in fools' paradise, thinking that all is well when actually it is not? The further problem this brings is that people will not be made to realize their "mistakes" and so be challenged to improve by striving to move progressively from good, better to best? (However, I do not deny the power behind positives words said about people. This gesture, too, can act as an encouragement, a stimulator, a springboard, and a boost to the one concerned).

My questions so far do not negate the aim of politeness especially in conversations as a polished way of talking marked by consideration for others. But my argument is, critically looking at and analyzing my experience of the culture of civility, I seem to see this culture (in terms of politeness) as suggesting an attitude of one person saying to another only what the latter will want to hear said about him/her that will make him/her

A Handbook on Culture Shock

happy. This culture, therefore, seems to shun the objectivity and frankness of calling a spade a spade and replacing it with the "good manners" or tact of a sugar coated tongue, particularly when in conversation with people both about themselves and about others.

At the end of the day, given this culture of polite talk, the truth of the matter or the true picture of a situation or someone is not given and so not gotten in a group discussion when such a conversation concerns a third party. For the most part, then, truth is gotten in a one-to-one "gossip," about a third party. This is why your knowledge of one person can be perceived, understood, known and seen in so many lights and different pictures, some of which are directly opposed to and contradictory with former ideas (about the same person). In short, do not be surprise that the same person, (third party), whom you might have had a clandestine discussion about, calling him/her a devil incarnate, in another scenario, mostly in a group discussion, that same third party begins to receive a lot of praises and is painted an angel by those who initially had called him/her names. Is this what prudence is all about?

Again, to my audience – the newcomers who may be coming from what some people may called an "unrefined" culture, be aware of this culture of politeness. You may, therefore, not say exactly the way you think things are, or talk about a third party in a group conversation in an exact and true picture of the person according to your perception of him or her. Always sound nice in every conversation, even though you may know the truth and what should really be said. So, hurt no one! Step on no one's toes! Tread on no one's dreams! Poison no individual or group opinion about a third party by what you say

CIVIL ETIQUETTE AND COURTESY

based on what you think is the truth. Besides, your vision and perception of a situation or person may be wrong based on your particular circumstance, your relationship with the person and what is playing out, and of course, do not forget your personal uniqueness. All these subjectivisms can affect or blind your vision of a situation or of a person in one way or another.

To all, then, the point is, when gathered in a group conversation, for your own good, mind what you voice out or be careful about what you say and how you say it because there may be a "Judas" in the group, one who some youngsters in Nigeria will called **Amibo.** This is one of those times that you cease to be yourself in your straightforwardness and "objectivity." In fact, and better still, if you do not have anything good to contribute in talking about someone else, it doesn't hurt to just listen and not say anything. This is what I may called – politeness with style.

EYE CONTACT

To maintain a steady eye contact with someone for a long time during communication is not only challenging, but also is one of the most difficult things to do. Probably, you (reading this book) are sometimes upset that you cannot maintain eye contact in communication. Do not be worried because your brothers and sisters all over the world do suffer the same thing at one time or another. No doubt, some people are naturally very shy about maintaining eye contact in conversation and communication. Still others have a complex that would not allow them to look steadily into their neighbor's eyes during communication. While for a third group, it is a cultural orientation or demand, which makes the ability of eye contact

A HANDBOOK ON CULTURE SHOCK

seemingly very difficult or impossible. There are hundreds of other reasons that can be adduced or given for this reality.

On this note, the culture of the Etung people places so much emphasis on eye contact that is quite different from and opposed to the interpretations given by and in the culture of the Adirondack people. To begin with, in my first culture, the avoidance of eye contact is an attitude that is praiseworthy, or you may call it a weakness that attracts positive remarks or comments and yields good results. It is highly complimentary to whoever avoids eye contact at all times, especially when talking or listening to senior people, who may be your parents, teachers, or any person to whose authority you are subjected. However, during formal meetings or education of a crowd in a classroom or hall, eye contact is allowed from all those who are doing the listening. But when you are alone, either talking or listening to a senior person, to look downward and bow your head to the ground is considered regardful and respectful of the junior person. However, in order to assure attention, the junior person is expected to look up at the face of the senior person occasionally in the course of the conversation or dialogue between them. Even in this, the junior person must do it quickly and snappily. To look steadily at or to maintain eye contact for a long time by the junior person is considered disregardful and disrespectful or even saucy.

Furthermore, to talk at the same time as and with the senior person is a violation of the cultural norm of politeness, which amounts to being impudent. Worse still, a junior person who not only maintains eye contact, but also talks instead of listening is considered diabolic and "witchy." In another interpretation, such a person may be materially rich and wealthy and

CIVIL ETIQUETTE AND COURTESY

so, based on this position and status (of well being), he or she becomes disrespectful to elders. This status notwithstanding, such disrespectful attitude is an aberration that makes one appear and look culturally half-baked. In fact, any culturally well brought up person, no matter his or her societal status later in life, does not derail from this acceptable cultural practice. However, there is an exception to the rule. Thus, the culture allows a junior person who is in authority of influence and power (political or tribal) to maintain eye contact when addressing a crowd of people, even if this is a gathering of only the seniors. Even in this exception, the junior person makes eye contact with respect and caution.

My new culture presents a strange and different scenario. Here, eye contact is culturally expected and acceptable, praiseworthy, and laudable. It is a sign of self-confidence. Even the young people are advised to make eye contact when conversing with adults to show that they are involved in the conversation and are interested in what they have to say. In such conversations, they are not to give only "Oks", for an answer, but a complete answer. On another note, but in the same context, if they need to leave the conversation, it is good manners to say, "excuse me." Furthermore, if they are standing with a friend when someone starts to converse with them, they should introduce them so nobody feels left out, and so all present will have a sense of belonging. All this should be done by looking at people face-to-face and eye ball-to-eye ball. In fact, eye contact is a becoming and an expected attitude and way of life. It is even highly recommended as something respectful and regardful. Here, if you do not maintain steady eye contact, it means that you are not paying attention, and it is considered as

A HANDBOOK ON CULTURE SHOCK

a sign of shyness (timidity), or stage fright or of one suffering from an inferiority complex. Sometimes, one who avoids eye contact might be suspected of hiding something or being too secretive. From a social perspective, such a person could be seen as a social misfit and poor in public outlook and communication. From this, it can be seen that the cultural difference in this aspect of the people's way of life in both cultures is literally opposite and opposed to one another.

To tell you how difficult and problematic it was for me to adjust to the eye contact cultural expectation of my new culture is seriously to belabor the obvious. It was an uphill task. Several times, I felt visibly uncomfortable with senior people during communication and conversation and prayed for them to end, so I could get out of there to regain my freedom and be myself. I mean the steady look at my eyes by the other people made me not only nervous and uneasy, but also to stutter, possibly for lack of words to express myself because of my nervous state. It was in fact, in thoughts, words, and deeds, a challenging cultural adjustment.

TABLE MANNERS

Table manners are the expected behaviors or the way you conduct yourself at table during mealtimes, especially when eating with other people. Whether these people are your seniors or juniors, some expected table manners are required of all people. Along this line of thought, some people are taught proper etiquette regarding the conduct of oneself at the table, which, more often than not, reflects one's upbringing. This could be a discipline by the family in accordance with the wider societal expectation or a particular cultural demand.

Civil Etiquette and Courtesy

Table manners are not only a way of life that are talked about in advanced societies, but also in developing cultural settings, where people are also expected to behave in particular ways at such occasions.

When talking about table manners, in general, the wider or polite society pays attention to some "dos" and "don'ts." For instance, when eating with others, some of the following are considered as bad manners: Do not start eating before your host, rather, wait for your host to begin. If you don't like someone's food, politely decline instead of telling the host how you feel. It is bad manners to point out that someone else has bad manners. Do not eat slurping your food. Do not cough without covering your mouth with the palm of your hands. Do not sit with your hands resting on the table. Do not pick your teeth when still at table. Also, refrain from burping at the dinner table. But if it happens, say "excuse me." Furthermore, extending your hand across another person to pick up something on the same table, such as the salt or pepper container, a glass, or a plate, as the case may be, is also an uncultured way of behaving at the table. Instead, you are expected to politely request the person sitting next to you to help you get what you want, which should be passed on from one person to another, like a baton in a relay game, until it gets to you.

Finally, both at dinner table and at other times when talking with people, also remember the good etiquette of always saying: *"Yes please!" "No thanks!"* and *"excuse me!"* whenever the need arises. Besides the fact that they are good manners and signs of good upbringing, they are also magic words with great power. People who hear them are far more inclined to accommodate the person who uses these words than someone who doesn't. Parents who fail to teach their children basic good manners do their children a grave disservice, because good manners and respect for others are essential for success in life and related breakthroughs. As much as I know, in polite society, there are no penalties for the violation of these rules. They are only expected or required of you as decent ways of conducting oneself in public; otherwise, you are considered as being rude or impolite and you may become an object of ridicule and public scorn.

In my native culture, eating times are quiet moments. In other words, no one is expected to be talking during meal-times. The only sound that should be heard, is the sound of cutlery if they are being used, especially in boarding schools. However, sometimes a senior person may talk when the need arises, either for correction or to call to order an unbecom-ing sitting position or related unacceptable behaviors. The un-derstanding is that when one talks and eats at the same time, the food may go the wrong way and may cause the person to choke. This can be an uncomfortable experience, especially if the food is spiced with pepper. As a way of correcting viola-tors, especially if they are junior children, parents may delay giving them water to drink, which is considered a remedy for reducing the choking effects. In this way, such a child would be careful not to talk again during mealtimes.

Furthermore, it is expected that one feels very free before eating a meal. By this, it is meant that you release the belt that you may have on your pants (trousers or shorts) in order to give you as much allowance as possible around the waist and abdo-men. However, this should be done in such a way that it does not appear offensive to public decency. The release or undoing of the belt would allow the easy and uninterrupted movement of food eaten to go through the intestine for digestion and the smooth-sailing completion of the metabolic process. This idea is based on a legend.

The story has it that a certain police officer ate a meal without loosening his very tight belt. At the end of the meal, he discovered that he was feeling uncomfortable because the food he had eaten did not travel down properly enough due to the tightness of his belt. Therefore, he suddenly decided to loosen his belt to have the food eaten go down through the proper channels to the appropriate metabolic quarters. He immediately collapsed because the food, which was supposed to have traveled down at a gradual speed, did so with too high a velocity. This was due to the sudden loosening of the belt that consequently overloaded and stressed the intestine and, thus, interrupted the metabolic process. Whether this story is true or not, the discomfort felt when one eats with a tight belt on justifies and gives some credibility to this legend.

As I said earlier, this practice calls for carefulness so as not to cause any public distraction. Nevertheless, there is a tendency to forget belting up before getting up from your seat after a meal. Yes, I had an experience in this regard, and I would like to share it with you:

When I came to Hudson Falls to the parish of my apostolate in my foreign culture, I lost some weight initially because of the drastic change in the food and other anxieties. But when I began to acquire a new taste and my body also began to adjust to the new type of food, I kept putting on weight. On this fateful day, we were having a Lenten luncheon somewhere. I had loosened my belt, and I was eating comfortably. Toward the

A HANDBOOK ON CULTURE SHOCK

end of the meal, I was talking, and there was a need for me to get up and demonstrate a point. Guess what! I got up suddenly without remembering to fix my belt. I almost embarrassed my audience and myself. Thank God, I did not zip totally down. Probably, I would have forgotten to do the zip up as it happened on one or two occasions when I was alone.

Another aspect of table manners as expected by my native culture is that a junior person is always expected to stop eating and listen attentively, if there is need for a senior person to talk at table during meals. The junior person must continue to listen without eating until the senior person finishes talking, no matter how short or long the talk may be. My experience with this cultural practice in my foreign culture is interesting, and I relate it here:

Within the first few weeks of my arrival in Hudson Falls, whenever I was at the table with the pastor and he started talking, I would stop eating and be listening to him. Without realizing why I always stopped eating, he went on talking for quite awhile. Probably, he thought that the subject matter was so interesting (as often it was), that I was totally carried away by listening to him. By the time he finished talking, the food on my plate had gotten so cold. This went on for some time. Then one day I thought to myself that the culture over here must be different from my native culture concerning this aspect of table manners. However, I had no courage to break the standard set and what I had imbibed in my native culture. I prayed for an opportunity that would allow me to explain why I did what I was doing. God, as usual, answered my prayers. At table some day, the pastor began talking again. This time, having observed that each time he starts talking that I always stopped eating completely, he asked me why I did that. I seized the opportunity to explain to him the expected table manners from juniors in my native culture when at table with seniors. There and then, he sympathized with me and told me to keep eating whenever he is talking because it is not so in the culture of the Adirondack people. These were his words after listening to me: "Please, keep eating whenever I am talking, okay!" Then I responded: "Yes, Father!"

That evening I went up to my suite with so much happiness for two reasons: First, I felt so at ease and relieved because from hence I'll be eating my meals uninterruptedly. And second, I knew that in the future, dinner time would no longer last one hour, but at most thirty minutes, since the eating, talking, and listening could be going on concurrently.

Finally, another aspect of table manners, which I never got over, was the idea of a junior finishing his or her food on a plate and then going away and leaving the senior at table. To do this in my native culture is considered disrespectful and is tantamount to rushing the senior person or making him or her feel as if he or she eats too much. You are expected always to have some food on your plate until the senior finishes eating, even if you had dished out a smaller quantity into your plate. Without any comparative experience, this last aspect of the junior not leaving the table at the end of meals before the senior, is recommended and applauded in all cultures of the world, even in the culture of the Adirondack people.

THE PSYCHOLOGY OF SNEEZING

Generally, the dictionary explanation of sneezing is that, it has to do with the expulsion of air forcibly from the mouth and

A HANDBOOK ON CULTURE SHOCK

nose in an explosive and spasmodic involuntary action, resulting from irritation of the nasal mucosa. Ethically, this action could be regarded as an *"act of man"* or a reflex act and not a *"human act"* or premeditated act, since it is involuntary and so not under your control. True as this may be, public etiquette expects some decency in this act for your respect and the good of others.

I chose to talk about the psychology of sneezing because of the cultural similarities and variations in the belief, practice, and interpretation of this act between my native and foreign cultures. Probably, you were curious when you saw this title. I hope I would be able to satisfy your curiosity.

No doubt, the reflex acts of yawning (which is very contagious and I don't know why it is so), blinking of the eyes, and even hiccups are not strange occurrences. Certainly, you are also familiar with the tickling or twitching movements around your eyes or in the palms of your hands. These and other acts are some of the reflexes that occur in our lives, but they are not left unattended. Different cultures and schools of thought have explanations for each of these acts. For instance, my native culture explains the reflex act of yawning as a sign of hunger and tiredness or as a sign of sleepiness or of someone becoming bored with something such as a talk or lecture or a homily that is uninteresting and long. Even when you are eating and you bite your tongue, it is interpreted as people gossiping about you somewhere. When someone gives you a cup or glass of water and you choke in the process of drinking, it is interpreted as the one who gave you the water may not have given it to you in goodwill. These and other interpretations of human acts or acts of man flood the different cultures of the

Civil Etiquette and Courtesy

world.

The psychology of sneezing is my point of interest in this section. Let me return to it, else I deviate too far. This reflex human act enjoys a very positive cultural belief and interpretation in my native culture. Its understanding and interpretation positively affect the mentality and psychology of the people of my home culture. Putting this idea in perspective, sneezing among the Etung people is interpreted as a sign of good health or long life. It is also seen as a sign that someone is thinking good of you or some people somewhere are either talking well of you or wishing you well, hence, you sneeze. Whereas, in the Adirondack culture when someone somewhere else is talking about you, your ears are supposed to be burning or ringing.

On the other hand, the culture of the Adirondack people has a different understanding and interpretation of this reflex act. Over here, sneezing is, for the most part, not a good thing, and this understanding, too, affects the people psychologically and physically. It was against this backdrop that, motivated by an experience I had, I decided to share this cultural difference with my congregation. I relate it here:

In my native culture, sneezing has a positive interpretation. It is understood as a sign of good health and long life. In addition, when you sneeze it indicates that someone, somewhere is thinking and talking good of you. This is so much so that people look forward to times when they could sneeze (sorry for the repetition). That is why whenever you sneeze in a crowd or anywhere where someone else hears you, those who hear you say to you: "Bless you" or "long life." Furthermore, people do not muffle any act of sneezing because they believe that the joy of sneezing is in letting it go loud, to clear off any bacteria

A Handbook on Culture Shock

in your system that may shorten your life. In addition, by so sneezing aloud, others would hear and then wish you well. However, in cases where and when one sneezes with a running nose, then it is a sign of a headache.

The positive interpretation and understanding of sneezing as mentioned here is not the case in my foreign culture, though the recommended practice may be same. In any case, the Adirondack people realize that sneezing cannot be helped or controlled and is a reflex action, which in itself is not bad. However, they sometimes associate sneezing with a cold or allergies. It is more or less a sign of one with a bad health condition.

In fact, to widen our knowledge of the sneezing culture and to put it in perspective, *The Post-Star,* of January 29, 2004, has an elaborate article that vividly captures the description, understanding, practice, interpretation, and ethics of sneezing. Some of its excerpts state: "There is the explosive bus-honk blare loud enough to shake the dead, and there's the refined, pretend-sneeze that wouldn't make a tissue flinch. (Choo.) There's no telling what a sneeze might sound like – and you've probably been hearing a lot lately during the height of the cold season. It all depends. Are you a loud mouth-sneezer? How big are you, and how much lung-power are you packing? The more there is, the bigger the sound is apt to be.

"How comfortable do you feel letting it fly in public? Some of us don't and try to stifle our sneeze, thus, the polite socialite affectation. Not a good idea. We can all consciously control a sneeze action,' says Jay Dunfield... 'But you should let a sneeze go. A sneeze after all, is the nose's way of expelling an intruder... 'At the same time, most people reflexively open their mouths into an "ooh" as the body prepares to expel the air,' Dunfield says. For Cassius Bordelon, he is convinced 'that some people just cannot control their sneezes. It just sneaks up on them....' Bordelon thinks that sociology also has a lot to do with the sound of sneeze. Some people are taught that you are supposed to be delicate and dainty about it,' he said. Dunfield also thinks "it's truly society-driven. I think people who are countrified are more comfortable with letting a sneeze be a sneeze."

Finally, the article also points out some Fun Sneeze Facts: "Sneeze on Monday for health, sneeze on Tuesday for wealth, sneeze on Wednesday for a letter, sneeze on Thursday for something better. Sneeze on Friday for sorrow, and sneeze on Saturday, see your sweetheart tomorrow. Sneeze on Sunday, safely seek."

Based on this mentality, to some extend, it is considered polite to muffle the sneeze action by covering one's nose so as not to spread germs to others, since sneezing is a sign of the beginning of a cold or a symptom of some unhealthy health conditions. Those who do not muffle a sneeze are regarded as countrified people.

My immediate reaction to these different views of this reflex act of sneezing was to cherish and hold on to the idea of *positive thinking*, believing in the power of the mind that controls about 80 percent of our health situation. Consequently, I remained inclined to the sneezing interpretation and understanding of my native culture. With this mind-set, I never thought of reacting to allergies or having a cold whenever I sneezed while my stay in my newfound culture of the Adirondack people lasted. Instead, at all times, I kept looking forward to it. Moreover, whenever I did sneeze, it gave me such a good feeling that I am being thought about by my family and friends back home in Nigeria.

CONCERNED ETIQUETTE

Kindness, niceness, good-heartedness, and related feelings of neighborliness can be expressed in various ways. This may progressively begin from thoughts to words and finally to deeds. No doubt, individuals and cultures have different ways and manners of expressing their concerns about the life situation of others who may be in need of one thing or another, materially, spiritually, emotionally, and otherwise. On this subject matter of concerned etiquette, there will be an attempt made to mirror and capture what goes on in the cultural contexts of the cultures in question.

For the benefit of clarity, the expression "concerned etiquette" here is meant the regard for or interest in someone or something with a real or just ethical intention to assist or help in whatever way possible, especially in a needy situation.

Among the Etung people, the culture of expressing the concern in question is not uncommon. This could be in times of grief to a bereaved family or to strangers needing help. Occasionally, it could also be expressed when one is about to go shopping, especially to children, but not so much to adults. This concern can and do take the form of: How may I help you? What should I get for you? etc.

This concerned etiquette is also not foreign to the Adirondack people. In fact, over here, it seems to be blown out of proportion. Probably, besides the people's good and kind nature, ethical civility contributes to making the concerned etiquette

CIVIL ETIQUETTE AND COURTESY

household expressions. In fact, every now and then you hear the Adirondack people expressing this concern in one of the following ways: Do you need anything? How may I help you? What can I do for you? If you need anything, feel free to ask and do not hesitate. If you need anything, do let me know. Let me know what you need at any time.

It is important, however, to point out that, for the most part, in both cultures these concerned expressions are mere etiquette and so are merely ethical. Hence, they should not be taken literally or exploited to the maximum advantage of the supposed beneficiary and then to the embarrassment and disadvantage of the supposed helper who might have expressed the concern. Nevertheless, I am not insinuating that they should all be taken *cum grano salis,* and I do not doubt the fact that some of these concerned expressions really go beyond mere etiquette to real, tangible and material help. But the question is: How do you judge between the concerned expression that is merely ethical and the one that actually intends tangible material help? I guess the answer to this question is not tied down to cultural contexts. Rather, it challenges one's discretion and sense of discernment to be able to interpret concerned expressions properly from other people and within a given context. Failure in this discernment process and interpretative ingenuity may result in disappointment to one person and either embarrassment or overstretching the budget and over tasking the generosity of the other.

This discourse on concerned etiquette reminds me of some thoughts that I kept harboring in my mind whenever such concerns were expressed to me, while I lived among the Adirondack people. Having come from Nigeria, where not only my

A Handbook on Culture Shock

personal needs, but also that of my people back home are numerous, imagine someone asking me: Do you need anything?
How may I help you? What should I buy for you? Alternatively, someone may say to me: If you need anything, do not
hesitate to ask me. More particularly, when I was to buy my
car, in the event of such concerned expressions, I was tempted
to say to some people: "Buy me a car!"

Plus or minus, the points this idea sets out to establish are,
first, the fact of the existence of concerned etiquette in different cultures of the world. Second, in the Adirondack culture,
this concerned etiquette is more common and more frequently
used by its people. To this end, I cannot end this exposé without humbly sending some notes of warning or giving some
advisory caveats to the Adirondack people that, they should
be very careful about what they ask for in their concerned
etiquette, especially considering the glaring needs of the person involved. Third, they should realize that such expressions
within the context in question could result in some exploitation of the situation. Finally, by my understanding, this concerned etiquette as expressed in its varied and different ways
is tantamount to giving someone a blank check. Wow! The
implications are unpredictable and could be unprecedented,
especially involving newcomers to this culture who may feel
that, looking at the abundance of almost everything around,
the people must be having too much to manage and so want
to reach out as much as possible to reduce their excesses. This
may not be true.

With eyes and ears opened, thoughts bordering on culture
would continue to widen into other areas of life equally important. Hence, the economic situations and structures found

CIVIL ETIQUETTE AND COURTESY

in different cultures constitute a vital issue of examination and give worthy food-for-thought. Let us take a tour and see what the next chapter has to say about this aspect of life and its attendant realities.

NOTES

[1] Gutierrez, Lisa. "Aaachooo!" *The Post-Star,* January 29, 2004.

6

ECONOMY

TAXES AS ECONOMIC RESOURCES

In every developed country, governments need material resources to carry out their essential services, which include education, health care, effective transportation, communication networks, steady power supply and aid to the poor. Citizens who enjoy these services have the obligation to pay taxes to support the government. That is why taxes are generally understood as contributions for the support of a government, required of persons, groups, or businesses within the domain of that government. They can also be seen as dues or fees levied on the members of an organization to meet expenses.

These taxes are usually commensurate with the income or wealth of each person in accordance with the principle of progressivity. Therefore, the taxing of surplus wealth in order to fund public welfare programs is one way government can meet the needs of the poor and fulfill its duty to the society. This form of taxation also helps those with surplus resources to fulfill their great responsibility toward those in need. It is also a laudable government policy that those families below

ECONOMY

the official poverty line should not be required to pay any income tax, in accordance with the demand of fraternal charity.

The experience of taxes in my native culture is neither an issue nor a loud exercise. Probably, this is because of the very low and negligible percentage of people who are employed by the government or other private employers of labor. Nigerians, particularly the Etung people are predominantly self-employed and mostly live below the poverty level. Second, there is the difficulty of knowing exactly the people's income and extent of wealth, due to the unavailability of appropriate methods for gathering such information and other logistical problems. No doubt, there are tax offices and tax agents who sometimes go about in the cities and villages, especially on market days, harassing some men by demanding that they show their recent tax receipts. To this end, taxpayers must usually carry their tax receipts around to avoid any uncomfortable, unpleasant and an embarrassing confrontation by the tax agents. However, to the best of my knowledge, taxes are paid at very reduced and insignificant forms or ways that remain very unnoticeable, without any visible annual or end of the year tax fever.

This is not the case in my new American culture. Besides being careful not to commit the fallacy of overgeneralization, it is a known fact that the U.S. culture is firmly rooted and founded on a strong economic foundation of taxes. It is indeed a nation that operates a much-taxed economy. This means that all working persons and all who own business and property are taxed in proportion to their income or the monetary value of their wealth or assets. It is highly difficult, if not impossible, to live and work in the United States without paying one tax or another from your occupational means of livelihood, Catholic

A HANDBOOK ON CULTURE SHOCK

priests, pastors and all other spiritual leaders, inclusive.

These taxes range from federal to state government income taxes, Social Security, property taxes, Medicare tax, and even what I may call grocery taxes. These grocery taxes are also called "sales tax" on consumable household items. The amount of this tax is calculated in percentage and varies from county to county in the Western world and from state to state within the United States. Thus, every item you buy and pay for, is taxed with or without your knowing it. Because of this, you discover that you pay more than the amount tagged on an item when you shop for it. Therefore, it is not enough to go shopping just with the amount for an advertised item based on the tag seen on it. To avoid embarrassment and disappointment, it is advisable to have some extra money in your pocket to cover the sales tax. Furthermore, there is the money-squeezing culture of insurance policies. These insurances range from health to car insurance, business to property insurance and so on. Again, for the road users, you cannot escape the tollgate "money exit" on the New York State Thruway or on similar roads.

If those who have lived all their lives in this culture are not comfortable with this tax economy, how much more the newcomer? Yes, the indigenes are familiar with the tax situation, but not totally accepting of it. The headache because of this drives me simply crazy. However, one must not deny the fact that the taxes pay off by way of the fact that, they fund public utilities, such as good roads, effective police and other military and paramilitary services, child and related welfare programs, standard and dependable education, constant supply of electricity, dependable, safe, and clean supply of water from pipe-borne or public water systems, and lots more benefits. The provision of these services help taxpayers to seemingly overlook the crushing tax culture.

The mathematical calculation of knowing the exact percentage of tax paid annually, based on one's income or wealth, remains a mystery and a big problem to many. The trusted honesty and transparency of the U.S. culture enables many to accept whatever amount of money they are told to balance as taxes by the tax agents or those who prepare the taxes or by the Internal Revenue Service (IRS), during the annual tax exercise. Guess what! Without even bothering to know whether you were cheated or not, it is always a joyous thing when at the end of the year you have a "tax refund" check from the IRS. The difficulty of the exact mathematical calculation also extends to the extra money you have to pay as tax, when shopping for an item in a drugstore, shopping mall, or supermarket. It is against this backdrop that I would like to share with you some of my shocking experiences. The first was buying some seasonal greeting cards. The second was my "Five-Hour Driving Course," (which is necessary for you to be eligible to take the road test and get a driver license in New York State, even if you have driven a car in your country such as Nigeria for many years).

Now the first shocking experience: Within the first few weeks of my arrival in Hudson Falls, I would often go to a certain pharmacy, known as McCann's Pharmacy, to buy seasonal or occasional greeting cards. It is clearly advertised and written right on the door of this pharmacy: "All Cards — 99¢" (99 cents). Each time I went there, picked out a card, and went to the counter to pay for it, the cashier would tell me to pay

A Handbook on Culture Shock

$1.06. Obediently, I paid whatever I was told for fear of exposing my ignorance. After that, I would say to myself: "Wow! Instead of giving me change of 1 cent, when I gave $1.00 for a card, I even had to add more money (6 cents); something must be going wrong here."

This worrisome and disturbing experience went on for some time. In fact, after a while, I thought they were taking advantage of me because I was new in the area. It came to a point that I could not bear it any longer, and so I decided to share my experience with the pastor, Very Rev. J. B. Lonergan. At the end of my story, he sympathized with me and then gave me a little explanation on the economic tax situation in the United States. I also seized the opportunity to tell him that this is not the case in my native culture. Thus in Nigeria, for instance, if the price tag on an item in the supermarket is $5.00 or in Nigerian currency, 5 **naira,** you pay not more or less than this amount. They are no sale taxes on sellable items or goods.

My second experience concerns the "Five-Hour Driving Course" I took. The fee for the course was $15.00. When I went for the course, I handed over a $100.00 bill to the collector, and he gave me change of $5.00. I thought the remaining $80.00 was for tax, and so I started walking away to the classroom for the course. A parishioner was in line immediately behind me. Her name is Maggie. She saw very well the incorrect transaction between the collector and me, and so she decided to call our attention to the whole business or transaction all over again. At the end of the day, the collector apologized sincerely to me and said that he thought I gave him a $20.00 bill, as all others who went before me had done. The confusion was more so because $100.00 bills were not used so much in daily business circulation since people prefer to carry smaller bills such as $1.00, $5.00, $10.00, and $20.00 bills or simply use their credit cards for business transactions. The remaining change of $80.00 was eventually given to me by the collector. Thanks to Maggie! Had it not been for her, I would have ignorantly lost $80.00 to the collector without any fault of the latter (the collector).

Finally, on this note of taxes in the Adirondack culture, sometimes you hear very attractive business advertisements such as: "Buy two, get one free." Or "buy one, get two 50% off." You also oftentimes see price tags such as $9.99 on items. The questions that arise here are: Are you so gullible to think that these attractive advertisements are tax free or tax exempt? On the other hand, are you so naive not to know that $9.99 is as good as $10.00 plus tax?

ECONOMIC FACILITATORS (THE "PLASTICS")

One of the distinctive marks of an advanced and developed nation is the availability of reliable and dependable economic machines that can facilitate the economic process. These facilities are tools that can increase the velocity of the transfer of goods and services from one place or person to another. Their validity must meet the necessary conditions of a "legal tender" such as easy recognition and common acceptance. They must also enjoy the protection needed to uphold the security and privacy of the people in economic transactions. In addition, they should meet the convenience and safety of moving big sums of money around in one's possession at any time without risking or posing any danger or threat to one's life. Hence, they should be very portable and handy.

A Handbook on Culture Shock

I must say that the fact of the preceding economic philosophy on economic facilitators was not a familiar reality to me while still within the bounds of my native culture in Nigeria. The dawn of its awareness came in the wake of my contact with my foreign culture. Some of these facilitators are the banks and the "plastics." To begin with, it would be safe to say that my cross-cultural experiences with banks and their operations are punctuated by lots of fascinating and shocking differences, too.

In the banking economy, my native culture experiences the problem of very few banks with their consequent monopoly and overcrowding. In some places, like in the villages where the population of people is relatively small and its people, besides not having much money, are still developing, there are no banks as such. What could be found here is group banking or daily banking, **"susu"** as they call it.

In a group or "susu" banking system, people of like motives come together for a meeting at least once per week. In this meeting, an agreed or an affordable amount of money from those concerned is contributed to the common fund by each person. This can go on for at least one month, a few months, or even one year. If it is one year, at the end of which there is a ceremony known as *"the breaking of the bank,"* in which each person gets back exactly his or her money contributed throughout the year, as the case may be. Sometimes, from this same money, the individuals make an agreed contribution for some kind of feasting where they eat and drink. In other cases also, there could be a display of uniform clothes by the members as part of the end of year party.

By way of its **modus operandi,** the daily banking system

sometimes takes the form of a person who goes daily from one house to another or from one business center to another, with a notebook containing the names of all the members. This trusted person collects from its members whatever each of them is able to give at each round, either every day or once per week. The collector may personally decide to use the money collected for one business or another. He or she could loan it out to people or could use it for his or her own personal business without the consent of the group. At an agreeable time however, which the collector must be aware of, the contributors get back their money. Of course, it is not uncommon to hear that cases abound of dishonesty, fraud, infidelity, and related hazards, as it is sometimes the case with almost all of such systems that deal with money, even in advanced societies.

The question one may want to ask in this "susu" cultural practice of banking is this: What happens in the event of the sudden death of the collector, especially as in most cases, the collector is the sole *manager* of the bank? The sensitivity and profundity of this question calls for an investigation and a further inquiry into this banking system. By all means, it is risky. But you should not blame those involved in it since this seems to be the only means of saving their money. However, worthy of note is the nuance that in a more organized group banking system, there are such officials as the chairperson, financial secretary, and treasurer. While in the daily banking system per se, the collector is the sole manager of the bank.

In more populated, business inclined, and flourishing towns or cities in Nigeria, some standard banks can be found. More often than not, compared to the growing population of people in these areas, the banks are too few to effectively and suf-

A HANDBOOK ON CULTURE SHOCK

ficiently serve the needs of the masses. As if the trouble of their scarceness is not enough, there is the problem of stability, reliability, and dependability. It is not uncommon that every now and then you hear the cry of lamentation and anguish by customers due to distressed or liquidated banks. This is a big minus to the growth and flourishing of the banking industry of any nation. In fact, sometimes the village group banking and the daily banking systems are better options for the banking business in spite of the great risk of sudden mortality.

Furthermore, the more advanced or commercialized banking system operates on schedule. Customers must transact any business with the banks within the working hours, mostly from 9:00 a.m. to 4:00 p.m., Monday through Friday, and sometimes within the first few hours on Saturday. The transactions in question could be deposit or withdrawal and related banking operations. Banks are usually not open on public or national holidays.

On another note, my native culture operates on a "cash economy." In other words, almost all economic transactions in the daily exchange of goods and services are on a cash-and-carry basis. However, in very few cases, money through checks is acceptable. There are no debit or credit cards, and there is no payment for labor by the hour. The salary is a monthly payment, which even then is unfortunately characterized by delays, both in private and public sectors of the economy. The government sometimes is the worst at this delayed payment. Cases are often reported where some government workers are not paid their monthly salaries for five to ten months or even more. This unbecoming situation is a frequent nightmare experienced in some states and counties or local government areas.

For renowned economists, you will agree with me that these economic realities as found in my home culture are insufficient and inadequate. They are slow, unsafe, and risky, especially as more often than not (since there are no credit cards) people have to carry large sums of money around in their possession. Mostly, this system conspires to bring about stagnation on the wheels of economic progress in any developing nation.

Looking at the other side of the coin, I must say that my experience of the existence and the operation of the economic facilitators in the culture of the Adirondack people remains not just new, but also admirable, profoundly stupefying and excitingly overwhelming. First, there is the fact of so many banks, strategically located at different points in the villages, towns, and cities. This makes for choice and easy access by the customers. Thus, this atmosphere affords a choice banking tradition that stands over and against any banking monopoly. Consequently, the customers are given an elastic banking appetite. Interestingly, without any damaging conspiracy, the banks engage in healthy business competition through community development efforts, various sponsorship programs, friendly advertisements and related information that attract the attention of people who eventually become their customers. The existence of so many banks and the methods of customizing them give a safe, promising and secure business atmosphere that make them immune to the danger of liquidation, uncertainties, and related banking phobias.

The economic facilitation of using the "plastics" such as "check cards" or "debit cards" and "credit cards" is also another economic puzzle. These "plastics" make the daily eco-

A HANDBOOK ON CULTURE SHOCK

nomic transactions very easy and, for the most part, safe. For instance, with the check or debit card, through the help of an "automatic teller machine" (ATM), you can go check your bank statement and withdraw money from your account wherever the ATM is available and at any time. These machines are always located at places that are easily accessible to the public. They are also not limited to a particular community or locality where the banks are found. In short, they cut across community, village, town, city, and state boundaries. They are used simply by correctly sliding your debit card in the space provided on the ATM. Then you supply the necessary information requested of you, as programmed in the machine. The result is that you get all the services that you want. It is important to know that, in terms of withdrawals from these machines, you can only get money from them in $20.00 bills for whatever amount you want. These banking services are available "24/7," that is, 24 hours per day, 7 days per week. I wonder how money is fed into these ATM machines, because I never heard of anyone going to take out money from them without finding or getting the amount needed.

Talking about credit cards, it is a fact that in America, the credit card generation is getting younger. Having a credit card is not necessarily a bad or terrible thing, so long as the younger people and newcomers are educated about the ethics and the appropriate financial principles. For instance, to pay your bill in full every month is a good, praiseworthy and recommended idea, but to carry balances over, is bad and this practice by some young people has gotten a lot of their parents in trouble. To avoid this nightmare, therefore, parents of teens who use credit cards, should teach their children how to use credit and debit cards and should generally monitor their use of plastics. It is not enough to give kids credit or debits cards. This is not going to give them good money management habits. There has to be some tutorials on the interest rates, guardians on spending habits and practicing paying on time.

Another fascinating experience is that most banking operations are done during banking hours from outside the bank, while seated in your car or riding on your bicycle. This is done by simply driving or riding by the outside of the bank. You simply put your prepared check into a container provided, and the container runs through a tube in the outside facility into the bank to the desk of a bank teller. Then, in a very short time, you get a feedback in the same container, running through the same tube with the correct information of your lodging transaction. This was not only mesmerizing, but also fascinatingly amazing to me when I first arrived in my new culture. To this day, this facility and its operation remain a big puzzle and a stupefying technology to me.

Furthermore, the inconvenience and the risk of carrying about in your possession large sums of money are also taken care of by the "plastics." Thus, the debit card holds the information about all the money that you have in your bank account. With this card in your possession, you can purchase and pay for goods or items, and the amount of money spent will be deducted from your bank account immediately through the help of a machine or computer operated by the salesperson or cashier in the business area where the transaction is made. The credit card also offers its own credit economic advantages in the daily purchase of goods and services. This simply requires proof to your business partner that you are able to pay for the

A Handbook on Culture Shock

services rendered in due course. Once this proof is confirmed, you are eligible to use your credit card when purchasing goods or services, and you will receive a monthly statement of purchases charged to you with their equal reduction from your bank account. Be reminded also that each time you use your credit card, make sure that you record the reduction in your bank book or teller so as to always keep track of how much money you have left in your bank account. Depending on the terms of agreement between you and your business partner, the complete payment for any good, particularly the purchase of a car, can be spread over a period of five years.

However attractive and convenient as this economic atmosphere may be, it is important to sound a note of warning that the gullible and greedy understanding of the elastic and limitless purchasing power of the credit card can be quite tempting, particularly to a newcomer. Usually such a person does not have the proper insight into the workings of the credit card system with all its huge interest implications. Before one plunges into the easy use of the credit card, it is advisable to begin with a cash-and-carry business policy as you gradually adjust to the use of the plastics. This will give you time to ask questions and get answers that will help in your proper understanding of the use of the latter (credit card) option. This advice helps!

No doubt, these economic make-easy facilities and facilitators are culturally overwhelming and mind-boggling. Thus, the banking industry here is dependable and reliable. It is non-monopolistic and elastic. This fact is enlarged especially when you consider the tremendous and the unbelievable economic power behind the "plastics" with their limitless space and purchasing power.

266 •

Do not forget that, unlike what happens in the Nigerian culture, in the culture of the Adirondack people salaries are not usually delayed. People in regular jobs (schools, banks, and offices) are paid weekly, semimonthly, or at times monthly. These salaries or the payment to the employee for work done or services rendered is calculated and sometimes paid by the hour. At other times, when a job is negotiated, it comes with the option of payment for completion of the particular job, regardless of the length of time it takes or so much per hour. For example, this payment could be $100.00 for the job or $10.00 per hour. Payment usually would be at completion of the job in either case, especially in specific jobs such as roofing, painting a house, editing a book and so on.

By way of some objective criticism in the hourly payment, the question here is: Who determines the amount of work done by the hour? Is it the employee or the employer? In other words, is it the person rendering the service or the person who is to pay for the service that determines the number of *active* hours put into a particular job? If it is the first option, do you not see a possibility of some fraudulent acts? If it is the second option, do you not see a possibility of some incommensurate payments? Think about this! No doubt, it can be argued that some establishments have facilities that can measure the quantity and quality of work done in an hour, to correspond to the hourly payments. For instance, many people who work by the hour belong to and work for unions. These unions set standards of performance for their members (per hour) and negotiate agreements or payments with employees. In this way, the employers can be assured of the productivity of the employees, at least by the union's standards. True as this may be, this

A HANDBOOK ON CULTURE SHOCK

argument cannot be pushed too far without discovering some **lacunas** or loopholes.

This section on economy would be incomplete without giving a thought to the structure of the U.S. economic system as a whole, as it appears to me. I may be wrong. No doubt, every economic system should be for the good of the country and its people. It should be designed in such a way that it is sustainable. This sustainability is best if the economic policies and structures are self-sustaining through internally generated revenues and international trade. This ideology (of sustainability) is the driving force of the U.S. economy, which helps the country in funding internal works, financing international projects, and generously giving aid to needy nations around the globe.

Not only because of its sustainability, but also because the system is faithful and pays better than what is obtainable in other countries, there is the global attraction and rush to the United States by people and job-seekers from all over the world. This is so much so that immigrants do not mind whatever jobs they have to do in the United States to earn a living, even if such jobs are far below their educational qualifications or outside their areas of specialty. This argument can be substantiated from an article in *The Post-Star* of February 9, 2005, by Thom Randall titled: "Foreign Worker Program Takes Off." Some of its excerpts report that a foreign worker "washes dishes at the Log Jam restaurant in Queensbury (New York). Washing dishes at the Log Jam pays better than working in his home country as an accountant intern." Besides the good pay, the foreign worker also states that: "I'd rather be working in accounting, but washing dishes is good work and I'm doing it as a different experience — to learn about the American culture and to meet new people," he said. "It's better pay than I'd make back home as an accounting intern, but the money is really secondary."

The article goes further to talk about, comment on, and applaud the disposition and work ethic of foreign workers, which constitute the attraction by U. S. employers. It says: "Dozen of area businesses are hiring more and more foreign workers because of their strong work ethic, dependability, and intense motivation even for entry-level work." Richard Funk who works with the **Connection** and acts as an advocate and problem-solver for foreign workers in Lake George gives a brief historical background of the Connection. He says that the Connection was started as a clearinghouse, which has become such a tremendous success that other resort towns now want to know how to set up similar programs. "Employers in Lake George and surrounding communities have in recent years been starved for reliable workers," Funk said. The work includes jobs like lifeguarding at municipal beaches, clerking at gift shops, and waiting or bussing tables in area restaurants. Employers throughout the area said Monday they're increasingly turning to foreign workers because local college age people typically shun the menial work — regardless of good pay and steady hours." According to Tony Greco, manager of the Log Jam restaurant: "Foreign workers will consistently show up (at work) and work hard bussing tables, washing dishes and prepping food. We'd love to use local workers, but kids nowadays don't want to work up the ranks," Greco said. "Others are unreliable and work only when they want to."

For Sandy Abbenante, personnel director at Fort William

A Handbook on Culture Shock

Henry Hotel in Queensbury: "Foreign workers are productive and enthusiastic at not only menial jobs like chambermaid, but administrative, technical and customer service posts. They have a great work ethic and they're willing to do anything you'd ask them to," she said. "They'd work 24 hours per day if you let them."[1]

True as it is and attractive as the U.S. economic system may be, newcomers have to be careful and prudent in the spending and saving of money. I am sounding this caveat and calling for caution because the system seems to be designed in such a way that the movement and circulation of money simply rotates within the system. This economic monetary rotation, which more often than not is unnoticed by people, makes it difficult for immigrant or foreign workers to save enough to be of tangible help to their people back home. It also makes it hard for newcomers to stabilize in the system and begin to think of establishing themselves back home in their native countries. If you are not careful, you may end up living from *paycheck to paycheck*. In other words, it can also be expressed as living from *hand to mouth*, with nothing left for the pocket. In more concrete terms, this economic hypothesis is evident in the reality of house rents, electric, water, telephone, heat, and related bills and finally in the inescapable culture of taxes.

For clergy and religious who are provided with room and board in the United States, hold your breath, redirect your thoughts, and do not begin to celebrate that you are off the hook in this economic system as I mentioned earlier. I was in the same boat with you until I got disillusioned. Initially when I first arrived in the United States, I thought that as a Catholic priest I was free from paying taxes and so would escape the

annual tax fever and bite on my income. It did not take long
for me to know that no alibi or immunity could enable one to
escape the demands of this economic system of "no sacred
cow" taxation. When I got my first W-2 Form with all the state
and federal government tax reductions, I was shocked. I could
not wait to call some of my family members and friends in
Nigeria to tell them that I now pay tax in the United States.
They, too, were shocked to hear me talk about paying taxes. It
took me almost two years to also know that even my room and
board as a priest were not free. When I learned of the yearly
amount, (for my room and board) it was unbelievable. However, I thank the Church for taking care of this financial aspect
of room and board. But the tax for the annual amount of room
and board is the responsibility of the clergy or religious worker since the amount for the room and board is calculated as
part of his or her income. I'll tell you something and it is this
– the only escape route from the room and board tax is to opt
out of the Social Security system. By so doing, you are opting
out of all the benefits that the Social Security system gives you
at retirement. After all, I am sure you don't intend to remain
working in America up to your retirement age. Or do you? If
your answer is in the affirmative, I hold nothing against you. In
that case, I would advise then that the earlier you get involved
in the Social Security System, the better.

In light of this exposé, on the economic monetary rotation,
for the most part, whatever money you make in this system
goes back into the system to service it and keep it alive. And
the proportion is – the more money you make, the more you
pay into the system. Yes, every convenience you have, every
comfort you enjoy, and every euphoria is paid for, except the

A Handbook on Culture Shock

air you breath.

Finally, note that I did not intend by this economic observation or hypothesis to criticize the U.S. economic system. Far be it! My intention, backed up by my experience, is primarily to create awareness, especially for the benefit of newcomers as foreign workers in the United States. So, as you step onto the U.S. soil, it would do you much good if you bear in mind how the economic system works for the good of the country as well as yours.

On another development, in the dynamism of culture there are means by which people of different cultures move about from one place to another, either for leisure or for business. The availability and means or ways of obtaining these means of movement vary from one culture to another. This is evident in the next chapter, which treats transportation and means of transport.

NOTES

[1] Randall, Thom. "Foreign Worker Program Takes Off." *The Post-Star,* February 9, 2005.

7

TRANSPORTATION AND MEANS OF TRANSPORT

The importance of transportation in the conveyance of passengers and goods or materials from one place to another cannot be overemphasized. If my guess is correct, in all nations of the world some of the transportation vessels and vehicles are privately owned and used accordingly. Others are privately owned by individuals and commercialized as a public means of transport. Still, some of them are owned by groups and organizations or companies and corporations and could be used strictly for the need of the group or for the commercial service of the public. Furthermore, some transportation is owned and operated by various levels of government such as the federal, state, county, or local government. In this chapter, I intend to look at the means of transport and how they are acquired and used by people in a comparative case study.

MOTORCYCLE TAXIS (OKADAS, ALA-ALOK, AKA-UKEH, INA-AGA)

The idea of motorcycle taxis may appear or sound very

strange to some people, while it is a familiar phenomenon to others. For those in doubt, this is a means of transport that is provided by motorcycles for commercial purposes. If I am correct, it is more common in developing countries where a majority of people cannot afford to buy and own cars, in addition to other factors. In some countries, this means of transport has a national recognition, and therefore, the people who provide it are unionized or structured in a kind of union. In fact, in some places, these unions are so strong that they can stagnate or upset the whole transport network of a nation, state, county, or local government or city or town, as the case may be.

For my Nigerian audience, you would agree with me that this means of transport has become very dependable for the common person who patronizes it all the time. This patronage has given credibility to their rights and legality, which keep growing stronger and stronger from strength to strength and from day to day. In addition, in a country where the rate of unemployment is alarming, motorcycle taxis have become a major transport occupation and means of livelihood for so many people. They are found in almost every nook and cranny of the nation, and their services are, in most areas, provided 24/7, that is, 24 hours per day, 7 days per week. For the most part, they are dependable, trustworthy and safe. In Nigeria, this means of transport has many connotations and is usually referred to with such interchangeable or synonymous names as Cyclist, (English language), Okadas, (Origin is unknown), Ala-alok and Aka-uke, (Ibibios and Efik tribes), Ina-aga, (Igbo tribe) and so on.

In praise of them, you can be sure of their services even during an acute gas shortage, traffic jam, or congestion on the city roads. In the latter situation, you can be sure of an Okada meandering through any available space in the congestion or traffic jam to bring you to where you are going, not only on time, but also most often they will take you to your doorstep, even if this is on terrible terrain with muddy, unpaved, and dirt roads. Just pay the transport cost, and you will get the services that you want. However, not all these services go without the risk of accidents or possible attacks and a walloping nightmare, especially on lonely city streets or on dirt roads that lead into villages in the woods.

There are two sides to every coin, as you well know. Therefore, in spite of the advantages of the Okada, it is a known fact that they can and do become a big nuisance. For instance, they are an annoyance in gas stations, especially when there is a shortage in the supply or availability of this very essential commodity. Their characteristically disorganized butting in line and their meandering tendencies of jumping the queues so as to get the product faster than others, irrespective of when they got to the gas station, can either stagnate or seriously impede and slow down the selling speed of the product to consumers. Furthermore, since the gas stations are not self-service, the troubles caused by the Okada riders do sometimes cause the person pumping the gas to leave for his or her safety, in case a fight begins among customers in the struggle for position to buy the product. Consequently, this can cause a gas station to stop the sale and completely shut down for an indefinite length of time. Your guess of the frustrations and discomfort of commercial motor vehicle drivers and commuters who may be stuck in the cars given this situation would be as good as mine.

TRANSPORTATION AND MEANS OF TRANSPORT

The cyclists' nuisance can also be experienced within the cities as they struggle to compete with so many cars on the roads. In fact, without considering their vulnerability, they even claim the right of way on very busy roads or highways, especially since more or less, there are no traffic signs or unified driving codes. Not to talk of the fact that a cyclist can cross the road without looking back or giving any signal.

However, in spite of their unruly behaviors, be very careful not to run over any of them with your car, even if the fault may not be yours. To run them over is to run the risk of losing your car, which would be set ablaze and possibly cost you your life as well. This is because other motorcyclists, in what appears like a planned speedy operation, will most certainly arrive at the scene of the accident like angry bees and hungry lions to carry out the jungle justice of a guerrilla attack on you. Each of them arrives from nowhere and takes his "pound of flesh" from you by a hit-and-run scenario. In fact, even if they run into your car and thereby cause an accident, please, don't stop. The best you should do is to keep driving to a police station to report or turn in yourself.

And when caught in this unfortunate nightmare, your appeal to civil justice, more often than not, amounts to the denial of justice. This is due to the indefinite delays that characterize the civil order of justice or the judicial system, which goes through a series of investigations and related abortive fact-finding measures. In most cases, justice could be denied to the innocent person with the application of the unbecoming philosophy of ima-madu (IM) or Fon Nneh (FN). As earlier stated, this philosophy can also be explained thus: "You can get what you want, not because you deserve it, but because

A HANDBOOK ON CULTURE SHOCK

of what you are, what you have and who you know by using your connections." But in using this philosophy, every now and then there arise tensions among equals who seem to have the same powers and connections.

What probably, has not been given a serious thought is the fact that the "Okada" means of transportation also contributes in upsetting the order of morality, especially among city girls and university or campus students. This fact is swept under the carpet or it may be unnoticed and unknown to many people. Thus, since this means of transport is available 24/7, late night-keepers and twilight risers, popularly called **quarrangidas,** who have no means of transport of their own, will always have a way and a means of sneakily returning to their homes whenever and from wherever they may have spent the night. Don't ask me with whom! In this way, their return remains unnoticed by onlookers along the road or even by next-door neighbors. Sometimes, by some kind of special negotiation, you can have the "Okadas" at your beck and call wherever and whenever you need their services.

To say that this convenience provided by the motorcyclists does harm to societal moral values is to state a real moral problem that should be addressed as an issue of concern. Cases also abound where female late night-keepers and twilight risers have suffered some molestation by the "Okadas," while rendering the services for which they were duly paid. Largely, this side of the coin under consideration in relation to the motorcycle taxis reveals that, their services promote indiscipline and related immoral behaviors, especially among city dwellers and campus students where they are mostly in demand.

On another aspect, wherever the "Okadas" are in high demand but their availability is limited, one Okada can take four people at a time. Certainly, you may be wondering how many people a normal taxi car or bus can take at a time, if one Okada takes four. Do not wonder too much. The factual experience is that, for instance a normal taxi car that should take four people can take nine at a time. This may seem unimaginable and sound impossible to people not familiar with this phenomenon. But for those who are daily confronted with this reality, this situation is difficult and discomforting but not impossible. In fact, cases abound where people even sit in the trunk or boot of a taxi car. In this case, the number of people may increase from nine to eleven, twelve, or more.

For most Nigerians who have had the experience of the nocturnal travel by luxurious buses from the east to the west and vice versa, you would agree with me that these buses are always so heavily laden that the commuters have no room to hang their legs down. Some of them sit on the uncomfortable "attachment seats" and others sit with their feet on the same level as their buttocks, their knees drawn up to their chins like roast chickens. Surprisingly, the people do not seem to mind it. Why should they, since they have no other options? Yes, sometimes when the people are faced with no other choice, this overloading experience becomes inevitable. At its worst, when and where they are not available at all, some people walk long distances everyday to their farms, neighboring villages, and other places. Probably that is why they are hardly out of shape, coupled with other living conditions of the majority living below the poverty level.

In the Adirondacks, the motorcycle taxis or the Okada syndrome is not an issue. In short, they do not exist here. If they do, I have not seen them nor heard people talk about them. However, there are motorcycle clubs for social and philanthropic advantages. These motorcycles in question, comparatively speaking, are big, fanciful, and imposing. This picture comes full blown at the amazing sight of the annual "Americade" motorcycle touring rally held at Lake George, New York. This Americade is considered the largest of its kind in the world. At such times, motorcycles dominate traffic on the Thruway, the Northway and related routes all over the United States and beyond up to Canada, leading to Lake George. The thousands attendees are not only the bikers themselves, but also other Americade enthusiasts from far and near. In order to maintain peace and order during the rally, Sheriffs always stood at the corners shepherding Americade motorcycles into the resort's driveway. By way of numerical estimation, the annual rush is up to 50,000 motorcycle enthusiasts who usually descend on Lake George, nearly doubling the population of the entire county.

To add more zest or fun to the rally, the attendees participate in guided tours, boat cruises, technical seminars, shows, banquets, contests and fireworks displays. Historically speaking, the rally now known as "Americade" began as "Aspencade," a gathering of motorcycles in the little town of Ruidoso, N.M., which is tucked far away in the mountains. Several hundred sport-touring bikers and some café racers would annually travel to Ruidoso in the 1970s and early 1980s to see the beauty and enjoy the natural metamorphosis of the Aspen leaves turn bright yellow in late September or early October. William Dutcher, the event founder, changed the name to "Americade" in 1986 when his Lake George event survived the withering of

TRANSPORTATION AND MEANS OF TRANSPORT

the Ruidoso event.

To ask the question whether the rally has any added advantage to the economy of the area is to belabor the obvious. Many of the authorities concerned in the area have always cited the six-day rally's economic impact of more than $20 million to the region, according to *The Post-Star* of June 6, 2005 in an article titled "Americade '05: Bigger than ever" by Thom Randall. Yes, the motorcyclists kick off the summer season and boost employment during this critical time of the year.

On a personal encounter, I had an occasion to bless the motorcycles of one of the clubs in Hudson Falls, where my parish of apostolate is located. Looking at the sizes, I told to the riders that if they take their motorcycles to Nigeria to use as motorcycle taxis, each of them can conveniently take seven to eight people at a time. Do not ask me about the possibility. When the time comes and the need arises, you would know.

Furthermore, on a personal observation, while I was blessing the motorcycles, it appeared as if all the riders were tattooed. You could even see these tattoo marks on their hands or legs. The idea that immediately came to my mind was to think that the tattoo mark was like a "trademark" or a sign of identification of the motorcycle club members. That was why a couple of days later, when I came across one of the motorcycle riders, who stopped by to say hello to me while I was taking a walk, I then seized the opportunity to talk with him about the tattoo. I said to him: "In case I decide to become a member of your motorcycle club, would you have a *white* tattoo for me, since I am black or dark chocolate?" This person looked at me for some time, a bit confused about what to say to me, and then he said: "You can have the tattoo on the palm

A Handbook on Culture Shock

of your hand." However, before he left, he promised to find out for me if there is a white tattoo anywhere. Until this day, I never heard from him again. In any case, it was a very funny encounter, and when I shared the experience with my church congregation, they could not stop laughing for quite awhile.

This tattoo culture remindes me of a similar practice by the Etung people, especially among the womenfolk. Over here, the name for tattoo is called **Mbim.** It is a kind of body arts or black patterns, which some women make on their bodies with the juice of some special kinds of trees. With the "ink," or juice that comes from those trees, they could write either their names, make a special drawing or whatever they want on their bodies. Most of them prefer to write or have the mark on their hands. Some of the ink or marks are indelible or permanent while others are temporary. My cultural experience in this regard then is to establish the fact of a similarity between *tattoo or indigotin and "mbim"* among the Adirondacks and the Etung people, respectively. The only difference is that, the tattoo or "mbim" marks are more visible or pronounced on the bodies of the Adirondack people than on that of the Etung people. Don't you know why?

Furthermore, here in the culture of the Adirondack people, aside from the mind-blowing experience of personal car ownership, which is going to be our next area of reflection, there are commercial buses and certified taxicabs (not motorcycle taxis) with appropriate signs and telephone numbers inscribed on them for transport purposes at the service of the public.

CAR OWNERSHIP

This section addresses the issue of the legality of owning or possessing a car with all the rights, responsibilities and privileges that go with it. Of course, the means of acquiring a car will be highlighted, too.

The Nigerian economic policy is established on the economic tradition of "cash and carry." In other words, to own and possess a good, you have to pay the complete cash for it. There are a few occasions where payment by installment is allowed. This installment type payment is not a generally accepted economic policy. It can only be brought about through a healthy and trusted negotiation between the business partners, otherwise the economic system has no provision for it. To that end, to buy a car you have to pay the complete amount for it to become yours and consequently drive it home. Considering the economic situation in the country, it would be stating the obvious to say that very few people can rightly claim ownership of cars. So, for one to own a car, it is looked upon as a sign of wealth and luxury. And, as it is typical with Nigerians, those who have cars seem to belong to an exclusive club (of car owners), whose members greet one another with: "How's the car behaving?" "What party is your car insurance?" This setting gives a picture of a culture where people mostly walk or trek or hitchhike from one place to another on a daily basis.

In the cultural scenario of the Adirondack people, car ownership is a given cultural expectation and practice. Here, almost every person gets a driver license at the age of 16 years and can legally own and drive a car at the age of 18 years. In fact, many at the age of 20 years and above do own and drive their own cars. This makes the means of transport so easy and common in this area.

As I earlier stated, this Adirondack cultural experience is

A HANDBOOK ON CULTURE SHOCK

not only mind-blowing, but also presents an overwhelming situation, vis-à-vis the Nigerian phenomenon in this regard. To say that I was not affected by the economic system of my foreign culture is tantamount to some passivity, insensitivity, and indifference, but since I was sensitive and actively involved in the daily lives of the people of this culture, I could not have remained insulated and untouched by what economically plays out here. However, the economic adjustment process was to take such a bite of me that it even took me quite awhile to buy my own car, even after getting my driver's license some months back. Precisely, I got my driver's license on Thursday, December 18, 2003, while I got my car on Wednesday, April 21, 2004. So mathematically calculated, it took me about ten months and four months between the date I first arrived in the United States and the time I got my car, and between the time I got my driver's license and the time I got my car, respectively.

This delay to some extent provoked, caught the attention, and awakened the concerns of some of my parishioners who could not understand why it was taking me so long to buy a car. In spite of the many questions from them in this regard, I tried to remain unpressured and not stampeded. In fact, I kept thinking that if only they knew where I was coming from, culturally speaking, they would bear with me. Some of the people, who in the course of time came to understand, did appreciate my cultural background and praised my resoluteness not to be carried away by the scenario of my foreign culture so soon in terms of getting a car on credit or going to a bank to obtain a loan. Thanks to the parishioners who helped to chauffer me around in carrying out my pastoral duties during the time that

TRANSPORTATION AND MEANS OF TRANSPORT

I had no car.

Based on the credit economy in my new culture, car owner-ship is as easy as walking into a car dealership and coming out with whatever kind of car you want to drive. This is possible as long as you are working and earning a salary, as well as having a good credit history. Your working situation will guar-antee that you are capable of paying in due course the com-plete amount for the car of your choice, given that you are not able to pay the agreed and complete amount immediately. This means that the buyer would be paying an agreed percentage of the total cost of a car monthly. Its complete financing, includ-ing the huge interest, may spread out for a maximum of five years or more, depending on the agreement reached between the two business partners. In fact, it would not be surprising to hear that some dealers may not be very happy if you want to buy a car and pay its complete amount at once, since there would be no interest money gained by them.

Sometimes, you may not see the need for something until you are face-to-face with a situation that may warrant the need of it. I am talking in particular reference to the need for one to have and use a credit card. Initially, having come from a cul-ture, which for the most part, deals only with cash in business transactions, I found it very difficult to adjust to the American culture of having and using credit cards. My difficulty and re-luctance was to avoid the temptation of being in debt. In fact, at some point, I had said that nothing would make me get in-volved in using credit cards. But hey! the time did come for me to tender or show my credit card history before getting a loan from the bank in view of the publication of this book. Since I neither had nor have ever used a credit card, I had no history to prove that I am a good "debtor" who would pay back the loan in accordance with the terms of loaning. And of course, I had no property to mortgage. Thanks immensely to the dear parishioner who accepted and did cosign for me to enable me get the said loan from the bank.

The point I am trying to make here is that, even as newcomers, it is good to have and at least, once in a while, use your credit card. This is because, you never know, down the road, you may need to show your credit card and its history to quality you for a benefit or to help you get what you may be looking for. Do not wait to learn from your own personal experience. Remember the saying: "Learn from the mistakes of others, you may not live long enough to make them all yourself." Or by the time you make your own mistakes, it may be too late to fix the situation.

In another dimension of car ownership, there is also the leasing policy. In this case, you can get a car from a dealer to use for a period. Within this time, you also pay some agreed amount of money per month for keeping and using the car. This agreement can be renewed if you want to extend the time for keeping and using the particular car. At the end of the duration, you return the car to the dealer who inspects it to ascertain that it is still in good condition. If not, you will pay some charges for rough handling of the car.

Now, for newcomers, the picture presented by car ownership and related welfare in the culture of the Adirondack people can be misleading and misinforming. Thus, your instant reaction regarding your interpretation and understanding of the general economic standard of living among the people could blow your mind. The immediate impression you may have is that of thinking that every person is rich and wealthy in this area. This impression is possible and excusable, if based on where you come from; car ownership is considered a sign of richness, wealth, or luxury. Here you are now in a new environment, where you see almost every person, even young boys and girls of 18 years, driving big cars such as the Lincoln Navigator, Jeep Cherokee, Pathfinder, Limos, Cadillac, Lexus, and so many others. To put this in perspective, in my Nigerian culture, these and similar cars are owned and driven by very highly-placed politicians or other "bigger boys" with well paying jobs, business magnets with flourishing business empires and possibly overseas connections.

My schooling and gradual understanding of this economic system in the course of my stay in the Adirondacks was very revealing and disillusioning. This was intensified more so, based on my further personal experience, as I discharged my pastoral responsibilities and obligations to the beloved people of this area. On reflecting on this and related facts, first, I came to the conviction that not every person here is rich in the real sense of material wherewithal. Second, I also discovered that as an economic tradition, the people in this culture are not only familiar with being in debt, but also are comfortable with being in debt as an inevitable or an unavoidable way of life. In fact, it appears as if not to be in debt is tantamount to "singing outside the choir."

Interestingly, this credit economic system is not limited to the buying of cars alone, but also extends to the ownership of other goods and services, even houses. Furthermore, being a moving culture in the sense that people are always on the move from one place to another such as to their workplaces, schools, or business areas, the need personally to own a car becomes a necessity and not a luxury.

On this note, I want to conclude by saying that the culture of car ownership as found in my foreign environment is very praiseworthy. Among other things, it provides convenience, encourages independence, and promotes a sense of responsibility. It also reduces transport frustrations and accounts for punctuality. For the most part, it checks and regulates the idea of sneaking in and out of places for unbecoming affairs and behaviors. This is because, when caught by the police or some other people, it is more difficult to tiptoe or run away with a car into the narrow roads in the woods, as oftentimes is the case in my home culture. Hence, in Nigeria it is very easy to get away with misconduct or misbehaviors by using motorcycle taxis and escaping onto roads that are not motorable. My Nigeria audience can better appreciate this reality.

Furthermore, car ownership not only promotes careful driving, but it is also safer in the sense that many commuters' lives would not be at the mercy of some reckless commercial bus drivers or the motorcycle taxi drivers on a daily basis, as it is in Nigeria. Do I need to say that in the event of accidents in these Nigerian commercial means of transportation, the aftermath situation often results in mass incapacitation of people for life, mass deaths, mass funerals, and mass burials, sometimes burial in mass graves.

Besides transportation and the means of transport that are essential for human existence, there are also other necessities equally important. In the next chapter, there will be an attempt to look at electricity, water, roads and gas as not only wanted, but as essentially needed by all people, irrespective of cultural

Transportation and Means of Transport

structures or definitions. No doubt, since not all fingers are equal, the next chapter will throw more light on these essential realities from a comparative point of view, putting in perspective the four amenities or utilities of electricity, water, roads and gas or fuel.

8

PUBLIC UTILITIES

ELECTRICITY, STATIC ELECTRICITY (STATIC ZAPS OR SHOCKS), WATER, ROADS AND GAS (GASOLINE) OR FUEL, OR PETROL

Public utilities are mostly private business organizations subject to governmental regulation that provide essential services and commodities to the public. The most essential of these services include electricity, water, roads, and gas among others. The existence and functionality of these services are a source of pride to any nation. A government that is able to provide such for its citizens is one whose priorities and scales of preference are well placed and properly drawn to arrive at an excellent governance. On these also lie the conditions that determine a developed nation and a true democracy. In short, the nitty-gritty of the point here is that, these amenities could also be considered arguably the fulcra, and the hub that every nation's nifty life should revolve.

The provision and availability, serviceability and functionality of these utilities are the rights of the citizens, especially as taxpayers. Incidentally, for one reason or another, these

Public Utilities

utilities are neither found nor are they equally distributed all over the world. These imbalances are either blamable on the governments that be or on the availability or unavailability of resources, in addition to other reasons.

The availability and enjoyment of the utilities in question in Etung, and in Nigeria as a whole seriously fall below average. Not only are these public utilities not found all over the country, but also even where they are found, most of them have simply decayed and become like monumental wastes due to lack of maintenance and related governmental aberrations. It is not uncommon to take a tour of the nation and find tilted electric poles with draping electric cables, which have suffered the catastrophic syndrome of abandoned projects. It is also possible and abashing to find the monuments of water systems (pipe-borne) located here and there, supposedly meant for public water supply. The hazardous realities of dirt, bumpy, and muddy roads are a very familiar phenomenon.

ELECTRICITY

Talking about electricity, it is worthy to note that in Nigeria its provision and functionality as a public power supply is a nightmare. Oftentimes, it is as good as not having it at all. Most times, if you are able to have a complete haircut in a salon or iron one pair of pants or trousers without a power outage, then you are lucky. Furthermore, whether it is predicted or unpredicted, announced or unannounced, power outages can last a few hours, days, or even weeks and in fact, it may stretch to some months before power can be restored. The cause for the outage may be the blowing of a transformer or simply a car running into and knocking down an electric pole. In any case, the general supply of electricity where it is found can be very erratic. Hence, as an alternative, there are private power plants or backups popularly known as *standby generators*, owned by those who can afford them. For the most part, these two sources of power supply (public and standby or private or backups) seem to have swapped or exchanged positions. The public power supply has become a standby means of power supply, while the alternative of private generating plants or backups have become the main supply of electricity for those who have access to both of them. No thanks belong to the National Electric Power Authority (NEPA) of Nigeria.

Regarding electricity, the culture of the Adirondack people enjoys this utility almost uninterruptedly all year round. Being such an essential utility, it is found everywhere in the area, including all the cities and villages. Over here, electricity is such a hub, live-wire, and a nonnegotiable necessity because 95 percent of the daily activities engaged in by the people are dependent on it. To this end, any power outage brings to a complete stop the 95 percent of life involvements and activities that are carried out by the people and operated by electricity.

Thanks belong to Niagara Mohawk and the New York State Electric and Gas Company (NYSEGC) for the public supply of energy or this source of power with all that it takes. More thanks to their swift and almost immediate attention and response to any electrical problem that may cause an outage for some people, even for very few minutes. Just call them, and they are there. Certainly, they are very much aware of the fact that in the event of power outage everything seems to come to a sudden and an abrupt halt even to the endangerment of people's lives. Thus, some people may be trapped in elevators or stuck in trains in the subways or on railways; medical attention or operations in the hospital that are in progress may cease, which consequently puts the lives of patients at risk. Furthermore, computers may shut down, and communication by telephone may become impossible. Shopping in malls and supermarkets may be adversely affected, and televisions may be off. Also, the sale of gas at gas stations may have to stop as long as the outage lasts.

This constant power supply is more necessary against the backdrop of the fact that people here in the Adirondack world, for the most part, do not have private power supplies like stand-by generators. Nevertheless, in most hospitals and related sensitive areas, they have backup generators. In such places, the source of power in question comes on automatically as soon as the public power supply fails or is interrupted.

Besides their sensitivity to people's need for energy, the power companies are more up and doing their jobs because they are aware that, in this culture consumers have the right to sue them in court in the event of an unexpected power outage that lasts too long before its restoration and such consumers can possibly claim damages as a result. This claim could run into hundreds of thousands or even millions of dollars. On the whole, it is indeed a thrilling and an overwhelming experience that, at all times, you only have to reach out and turn on an electric switch and you get what you want (light).

Wait a minute, even the rich do cry. Thus, within a so-called perfect culture, there are also occasional moments of imperfection, lamentation, and darkness. This shocking and disillusioning experience within a perfect culture, in my experience

A Handbook on Culture Shock

can be described as, *"a culture shock within a culture shock."* I want to explain this point by saying that, initially I was so naive as to think that in the entire United States there is never any experience of power outage at any point in time. This mentality was based on hearsay from people about the perfection of things over here, as if everything over here is "made in heaven," not "made in China, Japan, the United States," and so on. In the course of time, this idea and indoctrination was to be challenged and consequently changed due to the advantage of a personal encounter and experience of the U.S. culture and its society. So, my new mentality in this regard is now based on my personal experience.

The disillusioning experience in question occurred during the second month after my arrival in the United States, at a time when I was still struggling to settle into the culture of the Adirondack people. Precisely on August 14, 2003 on a Thursday evening, an unprecedented general power outage brought about a total blackout. The report later said that there was an explosive sound heard coming from one of the power plants in New York City. Whatever the explanation, the point was that this power outage was a shock that took me completely by surprise based on my indoctrination. Moreover, in Hudson Falls, the blackout lasted for about four and one-half hours; while in New York City and other places that were also affected, it lasted much longer, even all through the night.

Further reports on this development confirmed that a large swath of the eastern United States was brought to a shuddering halt by this nation's worst ever blackout. Stoplights went dark. Trains stopped cold. Stranded commuters by the thousands, were left wandering the streets of New York City, drinking

PUBLIC UTILITIES

warm water and warm beer. It extended to almost the complete northeast coast affecting other states such as New Jersey, Pennsylvania, Vermont, Ohio, and others. On a personal and reflective observation, I feel that the blackout also revealed some glaring weaknesses in the nation's power grid and in emergency preparedness in hard-hit cities like New York. However, unlike New York City's 1977 blackout, with its arson and looting, the August 14, 2003 blackout only generated many fond recollections for New Yorkers. As a way of looking forward, the blackout led to a broad analysis by the utility industry of how electricity is transmitted and what could be done to prevent or at least minimize a repeat.

In short, it would amount to a negation of the truth if I say that I was not seriously shocked by this incident. When I e-mailed some of my friends back in Nigeria informing them of this power outage, their reactions were not different from mine. Indeed, it was a culture shock within a culture shock. It was very disillusioning, hence the sayings *"even the rich do cry"* or to some degree, *"it is not better in the Bahamas."*

STATIC ELECTRICITY (STATIC ZAPS OR SHOCKS)

Static zaps are some uncomfortable electric shocks that you experience when you encounter some objects at certain times of the year in the Adirondack environment. The discomfort created by this is so unpleasant that you may become very scared when touching people, objects, and related things at those times. The gravity of this startling discomfort is more intense when you are taken by surprise, that is, when you are unaware of it out of either ignorance or forgetfulness.

As much as I know, in Nigeria, electrical shocks are not

A Handbook on Culture Shock

uncommon. This most often occurs when the electric power is on and your body is exposed to an electric wire or cable that is not insulated. In some serious cases, this shock can cause electrocution, especially if it involves someone coming in contact with a high-voltage or tension wire or cable. Electric shocks can also occur when one is exposed to a defective or malfunctioning metal that transmits electric current such as a ring boiler or an electric kettle.

Electricity in upstate New York has an additional dimension of shock or zapping experience. Here, the weather that determines the atmospheric condition comes with a zapping experience during the winter season, known as static electricity. Scientists say static electricity is more common at this time of the year, since the air gets dry from the cold temperatures.

An article in *The Post-Star* that addressed this issue at the time states that: "Dry air is a poor conductor of static electricity. When the air is moist in the summer and people sweat, the electricity naturally discharges without the person knowing it, but when the air is dry in winter, the static electricity stays on the body until that zapping contact comes when you touch a switch to turn on or to turn off the light. It also comes when you touch clothes or meet objects, such as carpets and rugs, or even by handshakes. About contacts with carpets and rugs, the friction created by rubbing two materials together generates static electricity. Thus, walking across a carpet results in friction between the fibers of carpets and rugs and the shoe soles, thereby building up a charge of static. So, this and similar contacts discharge the electricity."

Therefore, with the coming of the winter season, besides the trouble of trying to put up with the chilly and freezing cold and

Public Utilities

the foggy and snowy weather conditions, the zaps or shocks present an additional hazardous winter discomfort. Given this situation, even those who choose to hibernate are constantly reminded of the season by these zaps whenever they touch their electric switches, similar objects, clothes, or people.

On a personal note, these shocks were a painful discomfort to me. So, as a way of avoiding them, I developed a habit of using either a pen, pencil, or a piece of dry wood (toothpick), which cannot conduct electricity to turn on and turn off the light in my suite. At one of my Sunday Masses, after sharing the experience of my new discovery with my congregation and upon inquiry, I further understood that these zaps could be avoided by tying a rubber band on your hand or by quickly hitting several times on the object you intend to grab, before finally grabbing it. In the former, the static electricity would be absorbed by the plastic rubber band. In the latter, by hitting on the object several times, the static electricity is discharged automatically (before you grab it).

There is another way I discovered or found out from personal experience about avoiding the zapping discomfort. Having been born and brought up in a relatively poor family and economically tough environment in Nigeria, the first body cream or pomade that I grew to know and use was what we called in my native dialect **"aku mbang"** translated as "kennel oil." This oil is obtained from palm nuts. The process of obtaining the oil involves getting the palm nuts, drying them under the sun, and cracking open the shells to bring out the nuts. After this, the nuts are dried under the sun again. The nuts are then fried on a hot firewood fire in a frying pot or pan while constantly stirring them. At this frying stage, the oil begins to come out from the nuts, known as kennel oil.

Many growing children in my home culture begin with this kennel oil for their body and hair cream or pomade until they are of age to decide for themselves what they want to use for their body cream. Besides, there is also a traditional or superstitious belief that, kennel oil can protect children from demonic or voodoo attacks. For my Nigerian audience, particularly the Etung people, it is believed that, the **"Ogbanje"** or "water spirits," what the Bible calls Legion, can be rendered powerless with the use of the oil in question. This belief also fuels and encourages the use of kennel oil as cream for children who are considered defenseless and vulnerable to demonic or "spiritual" attacks.

Still on this personal note, the second kind of body cream I graduated to using was Vaseline or petroleum jelly. For whatever reason, I decided to stick with this, even until date. Guess what! This Vaseline or petroleum jelly is another magic aid in overcoming or avoiding the zap from static electricity. Thus, its soothing effect on the palms of hands greases and insulates someone's palms, thereby preventing and helping in absorbing the static shocks from objects or other people's hands when you are exposed to them.

In fact, generally speaking, this new dimension of electric shocks called static electricity is so discomforting that I doubt if anyone enjoys it or really gets used to it. The most I can guess is that, people just become aware of and familiar with it and remain conscious of it while the season lasts. It becomes one's personal challenge to do whatever you can, as previously suggested, to reduce the discomforting zapping experience.

Public Utilities

WATER

Concerning the Etung people, it is again worthy to note that the rivers, streams, and springs form the main source of water supply for the people of this culture. These sources of water are, for the most part, all-purpose. However, in some villages and neighborhoods, it is not uncommon to find boreholes and wells that serve to provide this essential need for the people. In any case, I don't think that any of these sources of water supply is treated with any of the chemicals needed for water treatment. The consequent risks that endanger the health and life of the people of this area because of the all-purpose source, and the use of untreated water are obvious: dysentery, e-coli, guinea worm, cholera, and other waterborne diseases.

On a wider reflection, it is a fact that the value of water cannot just be measured in liters. Without fear of exaggeration, more than one billion people, including millions of children, lack access to safe drinking water. This is a crisis. Incidentally, as in Etung villages, children are often the primary collectors of water. It is bad enough and a sorry sight to see them (children) walk many miles each day in search of water for the family, through muddy and slippery, stony and rocky areas and amidst dangerous creatures like snakes, insects, and other biting and poisonous animals. Given these hazardous and dangerous situations, cases abound where children returning from collecting water from long distances fall on the way, and the water collected pours out from the containers. Of course, they have to go back to the source of the water to fetch fresh water since this water is needed at home for one thing or another. This situation takes the time that could otherwise be spent in school, study, or play for those children whose parents can

A Handbook on Culture Shock

afford to send them to school. What is even worse is that the only available water is frequently unsafe. Again, this leaves children vulnerable to disease and infection.

Buttressing the need for safe and clean water, an excerpt from UNICEF Finance Development's "Invest in Children" from *Time* magazine of April 7, 2003, states, "Safe drinking water and sanitation are basic to human survival, dignity and productivity. Lack of these fundamentals is one of the main underlying causes of malnutrition, disease and death in children." In this same magazine article, UNICEF's column titled: "Children, Our Bridge to the Future," contains a message from Nane Annan, children's author and wife of UN Secretary-General Kofi Anna. She says: "I believe education is the road to the future, for boys and girls alike. But what if there were no safe drinking water or sanitation facilities along that road, threatening the very health and safety of the children who are supposed to thrive? For millions of children, most of them girls, the lack of clean water and safe sanitation in schools is one of the reasons they are prevented from taking up their right to basic education." Touched by this pitiable situation, in her passionate appeal she challenged all those concerned in these words: "The World Water Forum gives us a wonderful opportunity to unite in a common cause – to ensure that every primary school in the world has the safe water and separate sanitation facilities that boys and girls need, together with good hygiene education. Their lives depend on it. So does the future of our world."

Furthermore, in describing the problem of pure water for the world, the Rotary Club agenda to alleviate this problem states that it is a worldwide problem. This humanitarian club, from

PUBLIC UTILITIES

its wealth of experience observes: "Nearly one in five people have no access to clean drinking water. Diarrhea, the second biggest child killer, causes 1.3 million deaths per year. These deaths could be prevented — 80% of those without access to clean drinking water live in rural areas of the world where, in many cases, water is collected from remote locations."

The experience of pipe-borne water or the public water system in the Adirondack environment reveals that it is ever sure and the people are free of any related anxiety. In addition to the fact that the water is treated with necessary chemicals, such as chlorine and other water treatments that make it safe, you just turn on the tap at any time, and it is always "bingo!" That is, there is neither disappointment nor anxiety, as you will hear the gushing of water from the tap for your use, unless there is a plumbing problem. Furthermore, depending on what you want at any point, you can have the water cold, warm, or hot. Again, aside from a few public outdoor taps, the rest are mostly indoors. This saves you the inconvenience of going out in search of or to fetch water from the rivers, streams, and springs or even to pump from boreholes or draw from wells with all their concomitant hazards. It is also worthy to note that this pipe-borne water, wherever it is located, is all-purpose for drinking and washing both dishes and clothes. The washing of clothes also comes with its own convenience. Thus, there are machines to wash the clothes and machines to dry them. As much as I know, there is no scrub boarding. That is, there is no washing of clothes on a stone in the stream.

I must confess also that the practical experience of the wash machines was new to me, too. Hence, I had some initial problems and accidents in an attempt to use them. These accidents

A HANDBOOK ON CULTURE SHOCK

cost me some losses of some of my wool trousers or long pants. As I was not used to reading the washing instructions on the label of clothes before washing them while I was still in my native Etung culture in Nigeria, this negligence or ignorance or overlooking tendency, was to take its toll on me in my new-found culture. I remember with a nostalgic sense of loss two of my lovely wool trousers or long pants that I threw into the wash machine. Guess what! By the time I unknowingly completed the damage in the dryer, they came out shrunk almost to the size of short pants. That was how I ruined them and so could not use them again. Through this experience, I came to better appreciate the saying: "If you think education is expensive, try ignorance." From thence, before throwing any of my clothes into the wash machine, I began to take time to look for and read the washing instructions.

ROADS

In Nigeria, without denying the fact that there are roads that lead to different parts of the country, the question is about the condition of the roads. You can experience and enjoy good roads in some of the big cities, but as you leave the cities for the suburbs and villages, the picture changes dramatically to dirt and bumpy roads. This change is just like when you fly an aircraft from the U.S. to Europe and then from Europe to Africa. You would discover that the convenience, comfort and safety of flying change as you begin to enter the African continent. The risk and anxiety of being in the air keep on heightening and increasing because of the unpromising and scrappy looking nature of the airplanes. This is very sad. Poor Africa and Africans! What did we do to deserve this? What can be done to help us? What can or should we do to help ourselves?

Now, even in places that have good roads, because of the low premium paid for their maintenance, their present state has become worse than the former. This makes traveling short distances within the country longer than necessary, as well as risky and hazardous. These bad roads also make the passengers vulnerable to armed robbery attacks. Cases have been reported where thieves have laid in ambush around the very bad and muddy parts of the roads to wait for luxurious buses with commuters who may be traveling that way. This is because when commercial buses get to these bad spots, they either are slowed or are stuck in the mud or at worst even break down. Then comes the attack and robbery of the commuters by thieves who may have been waiting in the area for an opportune time to strike. This is a very scary and frightening situation. Isn't it?

As a way of taking care of and preventing this ugly situation of robbery, many luxurious buses have well-armed military escorts on board whenever they are making trips during the day or at night, especially from the east or southeast to the west (Calabar, Port-Harcour, or Onitsha to Lagos in Nigeria). The presence of these military escorts gives protection and assures some kind of security to the commuters on board. However, every now and then, you hear of stories where the escorts were overpowered by armed robbers, who seem to have more sophisticated weapons than those meant to check them. In spite of these periodic accidental attacks and overpowering, the fact remains that this security measure has been tremendously helpful to commuters and has done so much known and unknown good for the safe transport system in Nigeria. Thanks

A Handbook on Culture Shock

for this idea and initiative and to its initiator or originators.

On a more particular note, Agbokim Water Falls is the name of my village in Nigeria. The road that leads to this village was paved so many years ago, but without any maintenance, its present situation has become regrettable and a death trap, in fact, even worse than the former. Cases have been reported where sick people, who were being rushed to the hospital from the village to the nearest town, Ikom, for proper medical attention, died on the way because the cars were stuck in the mud at some point on the journey. So they could neither get to the hospitals on time nor get there at all. It is in these kinds of condition that the motorcycle taxis are useful. Since they can manage favorably on these roads, many people prefer to ride with, climb on, or go by them, especially in cases of emergency.

I remember a time during the rainy season when the roads become impassable. I would drive my car to Ikom, the town nearest to my village. Then I would park the car in this town and look for a motorcycle taxi to bring me to my village. It was such a shame. It is more shameful when you realize the fact that, this (my) village, Agbokim Water Falls, has natural and beautiful waterfalls that could make it one of the tourist attraction centers in Nigeria. Hence, the name: Agbokim Water Falls. This natural gift is left in the woods unattended to and undeveloped. When developed, there is no doubt in my mind that it would bring employment opportunity and yield revenue to the government and people of the area. It is indeed very sad to overlook such a natural gift of God. This situation of insensitivity, misplacement of priority, and negligence calls for a prayer to God to come to our aid through human instrumentality. These people as instrumentalities and God-sent, should have and be provided with the means necessary to enable the development of this natural endowment so that, particularly the people of this village would use what they have been given by God to get what they want for the common good. Ironically, among the tourist attraction areas, not only in the state, but also in the country, that feature prominently on pictures, is the Agbokim Water Falls. What a hypocrisy!

In talking about roads, the experience in the Adirondacks presents another episode. It is a known reality that the entire United States enjoys an attractive and an unbeatable or incomparable network of roads across the country. Whatever government that dreamed of this utility as an essential vehicle for accessibility and related developments, deserves to be honored by all generations of this great nation. By way of retaining this laudable tradition, the current government cannot be outdone in the practicality of enhancing the maintenance culture. Hence, there is the continuous existence of good roads today, which also give hope to the future because its usefulness has been tested and proven.

GAS (GASOLINE), FUEL, OR PETROL

By gas, fuel, or petrol, I mean gasoline as a volatile mixture of flammable liquid hydrocarbons, derived chiefly from crude petroleum and used principally as a fuel for internal combustion engines. So, the expressions "gas," "fuel," and "petrol" are only matters of nomenclature and, therefore, are sometimes used interchangeably depending on where you are in different parts of the world. In all cases, they are used either to generate energy for electricity or to assist internal combustion that

A HANDBOOK ON CULTURE SHOCK

enables locomotive engines or machines to function.

Nigeria is one of the oil producing countries of the world. The reality of this fact is very evident and is stated or attested to in so many publications for global information. For instance, *The Post-Star* of Thursday, June 10, 2004, carried an article by Dulue Mbachu (Associated Press) with the headline: "Fuel Rates Spark Strike in Nigeria," and subtitled: "Production, Exports Not Affected So Far." Some portions of the article state: "Children played soccer in the deserted streets of Lagos and stores shuttered their doors across Nigeria on Wednesday as unions representing millions of workers launched a general strike over fuel price hikes.

"The strike, which began Wednesday, threatened oil exports from Nigeria, *Africa's largest producer and the source of a fifth of the United States' oil imports*.... Don Boham, a spokesman for Royal Dutch/Shell, which accounts for half the country's production of 2.5 million barrels a day, said 'Some workers in the commercial capital of Lagos were unable to come to work because buses and taxis were not running.'... Deji Haastrup, Nigeria spokesman for Chevron Texaco, said, 'The company's employees hadn't joined the strike yet and that production and exports remain unhindered.'...

"Nigeria is the world's seventh-biggest oil exporter and the source of one-fifth of U.S. oil import...

"The government insists the increases in the government set price are necessary to stop shortages and prevent massive smuggling of fuel to neighboring countries, where prices are higher.

"At fuel stations on Tuesday, gasoline sold for $1.44 per gallon — up from $1.17 before the May 29 increase.

PUBLIC UTILITIES

"Critics argue the inflationary burden is too much for most citizens of oil-rich Nigeria, more than 70 percent of whom live on less than $1 daily."

Given the previous scenario on Nigeria's global oil production position, gas, fuel, or petrol for the running of vehicles and related machines should be, if not affordable, at least, at the disposal of all who need and can afford it. Unfortunately, there is a glaring irony surrounding this sector of life. This irony adversely affects the day-to-day activities of the citizens in the country. This is in the sense that, the availability of crude oil or petroleum on the rich Nigerian soil, notwithstanding, Nigeria mostly depends on imported gasoline. This situation is made worse in the smuggling out of this imported product by some citizens, to other neighboring countries through the porous borders. This story of smuggling becomes a scandal when you realize that even some high ranking people in the Nigerian nation are involved in this mess. Sad enough, these people who should protect the resources of the country and use them for the common good of its citizens, have turned out to become invaders and ravenous wolves who go about in sheep clothing.

The refineries that were once efficient and ego monuments and sufficiently served their purposes in the early 1960s and brought about the heyday of the oil boom in Nigeria, have today, literally become gigantic monumental wastes. This is due to the catastrophe and syndrome of lack of maintenance, intensified by the unavailability of capable technicians and engineers who can professionally maintain the equipment and correctly attend to all the workings of the machines. Sometimes, some people argue that the correct diagnosis about the refiner-

A HANDBOOK ON CULTURE SHOCK

ies' nightmare is the unavailability of money to procure new equipment and modernized machinery. I beg your pardon! I am totally disagreeing with this later diagnosis considering the natural resources that this country has been endowed with and how much money is privately owned by the powers that be. As if the aforementioned problems are not enough setbacks, there is the managerial problem that kills incentives and slows down effectiveness and efficiency. In this way, there is the twisting of the hand, kickback, kick-forward, and various organized *pecks at the elbows*, which thwart every goal-oriented operation.

Unfortunately, this disturbing issue of lack of maintenance extends to other important projects and areas of interest. For instance, a trip to and a tour of the National Theater at Lagos in Nigeria, will give you a vivid view of the picture of neglect, abandonment and carelessness. It is a tearful sight to see this gigantic complex, which cost millions of naira to erect, decaying and rusting away. No doubt, sometime in history, this facility was the pride of the nation. But today, it stands out there with an imposing picture of a culture that overlooks and pays no attention to the laudable priority of care for and maintenance of public facilities.

I am tempted at this point to say that, probably, privatization of essential commodities in Nigeria may help alleviate some of its problems. But I fear the fact that, those who would have the money and connections to buy the essential commodities to be marketed and privatized, are only the politicians and others who are already a problem to the system. Hence, the exploitation of the poor masses would only take a different dimension, perhaps, it may become more aggressive, especially without any government regulation. In this case, those con-

Public Utilities

cerned will use their whims and caprices to their maximum material advantage and to the disadvantage of the vulnerable, thereby leaving the poor poorer. It may be arm-twisting and neck-racking. These suspicions bring the nation into a real crossroads situation that makes the making of a decision in favor of privatization very dicey and risky, too. Many Nigerians can attest to the fact that the bill or the option for privatization has been a long standing and debated issue that has been put on hold (by the Legislature and other decision making bodies) in so many sectors of the economy because of its cloudy and uncertain consequences. The clouds that hang on this economic policy of privatization make the vision of bettering the situation for the good of the poor masses very unpredictable. At the moment therefore, Nigeria seems to be standing in between the lion and the deep-blue-sea or a rock and a hard place.

Regarding the issue of gas, it is also a reality that the troubling issue of real and artificial scarcity and shortage of this product is a frequent nightmare. This unfortunate and frustrating development is frequently experienced during holiday seasons and festivities of global recognition or of national importance, such as Christmas and New Year celebrations. The effects of these nightmares terribly affect the transport sector of life in some states or even nationwide. Sometimes, hoarding of the product, known as "artificial scarcity," could cause the artificial scarcity, or it could be a real scarcity, known as "fuel shortage."

In the event of any of these shortages, the resulting effects are numerous. Thus, commuters will be seen standing or sitting helplessly and hopelessly at motor parks and on the streets, since there are no vehicles running. In short, the transport sys-

A HANDBOOK ON CULTURE SHOCK

tem will be crippled because cars cannot move, and some who dare to, more often than not, run out of gas on the way to their respective destinations. This is more so because the taxi drivers may be driving on fumes without knowing it, since most of their cars do not have functional fuel gauges that normally and usually enable you to know how much fuel or gas you still have left in the gas tank of your car. The picture you often see, therefore, is that of many cars parking by the roadsides with commuters standing or sitting by them on the ground, merely dreaming of their respective "homes".

There is also an astronomic hike in the pump price of this product per liter or gallon by the government. This situation is worsened by private fuel dealers who also fraudulently adjust their pumps to make them pump less fuel into the gas tanks of motorcars with the meter reading faster than normal. The quantity of fuel, therefore, pumped into cars, for instance, most times does not agree with the amount of money charged for it.

Oftentimes, according to Federal Ministry of Labor and Productivity, the argument by the government for the hike is that it wants to attract more money to care for the poor masses of the country, who ironically continue to live on less than $1.00 per day income as earlier stated. Unfortunately, the story is that Nigerian government officials and patrons continue to junket major cities of the world equipped with staggering sums stolen from public funds under the eyes of the Economic and Financial Crimes Commission, the Anti-Corruption Commission, and the Code of Conduct Bureau. Do we need to say that these unbecoming attitudes of embezzlement and related misconduct constitute crimes against God and humanity?

Public Utilities

In the face of this hard and tough life, the fascinating thing is that Nigerians have a way of surviving in any given situation or circumstance. Therefore, in the event of scarcity or shortage of gas at the gas stations, the *"black market"* selling of the product arises. This is a kind of market that is mainly championed and engaged in by some street boys who seize the situation of scarcity to become independent and uncertified marketers of gas. Along the highways and street corners, you find them plying their trade, selling the product in rubber containers or even in waterproof or zip-lock plastic bags. These opportunists get this product mostly from gas stations at night. They and the dealers are nocturnal partners in business. When they go get it at night, they punch or mix it with similar liquid products such as kerosene to increase the quantity and make more money when selling it.

Naturally, in accordance with the effect of mass production, as the quantity of the fuel bought by the black market marketers increases overnight, the quality decreases, and the engines of cars suffer from this adulteration and infinite dilution. Thus, many cars are ruined either by catching fire or by engine failure, expressed by Nigerians as *knocking of engines*. During this time, car owners who are wise, prefer to walk long distances or go by commercial taxis or buses to their destinations. In this way, their cars are saved from the nightmare associated with these circumstances and situations of fuel scarcity and adulteration, even though the owners may suffer some inconveniences. Others who live in the same neighborhood and work far away from their homes, especially in the same place or within comfortable proximities, take turns in carpooling to save cost and reduce the risk of massively ruining their cars.

A HANDBOOK ON CULTURE SHOCK

Given this troubling and frustrating Nigerian situation, we ask the question of the psalmist: *From where shall come our help?* When even high-ranking government officials and law enforcement agents patronize these black marketers without any questions regarding the source of the product or their qualification to sell it. The belief of the common man is that at the appointed time, though through human instrumentality: "Our help shall come from the Lord, who made heaven and earth." So, help us God!

The Adirondack environment presents a culture where this essential commodity is given its place of importance and is treated as such. I mean that you can always find gas in the gas stations. This product is also at the service of the populace twenty-four hours per day, seven days per week. With so many gas stations, within a short time, you can drive into a gas station, get the quantity of gas you want through self service, pay the corresponding money to the cashier, and leave. At all times, you are sure to get the high quality gas that is free of adulteration. Over here, there is no black marketing of the product whatsoever.

This reality becomes more challenging when you come to think of the fact that, America does not feature prominently in the count of oil producing nations of the world. This is not because America does not produce oil, as such, but, its production is minimal compared to the rate of its internal demand and consumption. With a few oil wells here and there, America depends more on imported oil to meet the day-to-day need of its people. Thanks to the admirable and emulating ingenuity of American leaders and those concerned for their rich oil reserves and bunkers.

PUBLIC UTILITIES

As a way of explaining the reason for this America's cultural status quo in this aspect of gasoline and related comforts and conveniences, some people may argue that it is so
because of the long period of civilization and independence
since 1776. Hence, they would take solace in the reasoning
that Nigeria would one day come of age, too, since it got its
independence in 1960. True as this may be, this argument is
what may be called ***argumentum ad misericordia,*** that is, argument that appeals for or to self-pity. Thus, those who hold
this pitiful argument would say that the Nigerian situation
would be better sometime; after all: "Rome was not built in
a day." People of such mentality should be made to understand that though, "Rome was not built in a day," it was neither built in one thousand years of procrastination, worsened
by structural bribery and high profile corruption; crippled by
unbridled and unchecked embezzlement; "impostorized" by
empty pride, hypocrisy, and pretentious impressions; damned
by social insensitivity, denial of justice, and gross violation of
human rights; and finally, "phobialized" by boundless insecurity, and related imbalances.

Moreover and unfortunately, when called to question, all
these unbecoming attitudes and behaviors commonly found in
Nigeria and among some Nigerians, are attended to with protracted, expensive, and abortive investigations. But hey! wait
a minute, structural corruption is not only a "Nigerian child"
even in the western world it is there today. Whether it is re-
baptized and christened in some situations as *kola nut, lobbying, smartness, a peg at the elbow* or carried out in *fund raising gimmicks*, the crime does not change. In whatever case,
it is called a bribe and so it is corruption. Or does the crime's

A HANDBOOK ON CULTURE SHOCK

name change because it is of a higher standard and done by the "civilized" and more developed world? No one can deny the fact that all over the world there are lots of hush-hush dealings mostly involving hush money.

On this exposé about public utilities, it is sad to note that their unavailability and dysfunctional situation constitute parts of the problems in the Nigerian nation. In fact, and in deed, this nation is suffering from a sort of national psychosis. Thus, political and military leaders are corrupt, many see crime as a legitimate avenue for advancement, and people in search of solutions are turning inward to ethnic prejudice and religious bigotry. Without leaving one in doubt, there is a complete split between power and moral right, and unless you have access to political power, you have "nothing," not even the right to share in the "National Cake." Because of this atmosphere and sickening cultural climate, which is compounded by charac-teristic instability and uncertainties, politicians are short-term thinkers, and everyone is seeking instant gratification mostly by cutting and eating a lion share of the national cake, which most of them did not bake.

No wonder in his book, *This House Has Fallen: Nigeria in Crisis,* Karl Maier captures the shameful image of Nigeria and thus extensively states that: " TO MOST OUTSIDERS, the very name Nigeria conjures up images of chaos and confu-sion, military coups, repression, drug trafficking and business fraud," 'christened 419'. The international media generally shun Nigeria because it is a difficult place to work, and it is not easy for journalists to sell the story to editors in New York, Atlanta, or London."[1]

However, in acknowledging Nigeria's rich natural endowments and related potential, Karl Maier's optimistic recapturing of its image puts Nigeria on the threshold of hope. Accordingly, he states again in his book that: "However deep it has sunk into a mire of corruption, repression, and economic dilapidation, Nigeria remains one of the world's strategic nations. It is the biggest trading partner the United States has in Africa. It is the fifth largest supplier of oil to the U.S. market...As the world's tenth most populous country, Nigeria represents an inherent sizable market that could provide trade opportunities for North America and European companies. Its '125' million people are an extraordinary human potpourri of some three ethnic groups that represents one out of six Africans."[2]

In addition, "Nigeria could, however, follow another path. Its potential is huge. Its tremendous wealth, if properly channeled, holds out the hope that a stable government could unleash the unquestioned energy and talent that pulsates through the rich ethnic mosaic. The human potential is there. Thousands of Nigerian professionals are well educated and skilled enough to drive the country forward...'In fact,' Nigerian professors grace university campuses across the United States and the world."

No wonder Olusegun Obasanjo, the president of Nigeria in the 2005 World Economic Forum of the G8 (USA, UK, France, Germany, Japan, Italy, Canada, and Russia) held in Switzerland, with the theme "G8 and Africa", with the aim of tackling and reducing poverty in Africa, laments that many Nigerians who would have helped to move the country forward are overseas. He seized the opportunity during the Forum in his remarks, to challenge and invite Nigerians abroad to go home and help build the Nigeria of our dream. Touchy, emotional

A Handbook on Culture Shock

and patriotic as this challenge, call and invitation may be, besides the poor economic situation, the insecurity in Nigeria is
another bottleneck that would make this clarion call to fall on
deaf ears. It is my conviction that, once security is guaranteed,
political stability is assured, and the general economy begins
to improve, pioneered by the government that be, by honestly
and selflessly harnessing and using its rich resources and potentials for the collective growth of Nigerians, then, Nigerians
abroad would be willing to make the sacrifice of going home
to build their own and one nation into one people with a sense
of hope for a better tomorrow.

My reaction to the laudable theme of the G8 in the World
Economic Forum is this, if America and the developed world
are serious about their stated intent to tackle poverty, most of
which in Africa, then we thank them for this dream and for
recognizing the fact that they cannot overlook or ignore the
home of 20 percent of sub-Saharan Africa's people. Yes, it is a
tough question for anyone who has ever been assaulted at the
airport in Lagos, Abuja or Port Harcourt just trying to enter
Nigeria, or hit up for a bribe by Nigerian government officials,
or struck dumb at the sight of orphaned and abandoned children, drinking dirty water and picking up crumbs of food on
the street as the only means and alternative for survival. What
a picture! It's a shame! With the preceding observations, it is
a pity to say that, on a general note, this nation is speedily and
swiftly drifting into social fragility, political apathy, and a general state of insecurity.

Unbecoming as this image may be, besides the power of
positive thinking, the good examples of a few Nigerian leaders
should not go unacknowledged, left unrecognized and tossed

Public Utilities

away unmentioned. Through these very few, there is hope in this land of dashed hopes. We pray O Lord!

Furthermore, in talking about the struggling spirit and attitudes of Nigerians everywhere, Karl Maier observed that: 'Back home,' anyone who has visited Nigeria's markets and witnessed its people endure the constraints of bad government and the sinking economy can testify to the country's resilience."[3] And based on my personal experience of the Nigerian situation, I totally agree with Karl's observation. For instance, in the case of the gas situation, let the problem not be that there is no fuel in the gas stations, rather, let it be that, there is fuel but the pump price is way too high. This is where and when you would see that, Nigerians will not stop moving. They will definitely look for the money and buy the gas, though with lots of complains.

By the same token of hope and optimism, Chinua Achebe in his book, *The Trouble with Nigeria,* as quoted by Karl Maier, states the Nigerian problem and expresses a conditional but confident hope about its situation. He says: "The Nigerian problem is the unwillingness or inability of its leaders to rise to the responsibility, to the challenge of personal example which are the hallmark of true leadership.... I am saying that Nigeria can change today 'for the better' if she discovers leaders who have the will, the ability and the vision" for true and authentic governance."[4] And I add: this vision should envision electricity for all; safe and clean drinking water for all, and accessible roads for all. It should also take into consideration the availability of essential commodities and equal employment opportunities for all, a sustainable, payable, and reliable minimum wage for all, and the provision for the care of disabil-

A Handbook on Culture Shock

ity cases. Of course, it should also not undermine stability in government and finally and perhaps most important, it should guarantee security for all, which would consequently attract and encourage foreign investors to invest and do business in and with Nigeria. With all these structures put in place and functional in a country, what else can the people ask for?

Because of the importance and sensitivity of the present Nigerian situation, I make bold to say that Nigeria needs a radical cleanup exercise to restore the bartered image of a country of fraudulent men and women, especially among those within the corridors of political power and those who hold related mandates. This fight against indecency in high places must be made a priority in Nigerian polity and policies, not only in the political arena per se, but also in the national educational system and others entrusted with the education of our young ones who will become leaders of tomorrow. This sanitizing exercise should be total, having no sacred cows, and rolling like a stone that gathers moss.

The leaders of this great country should realize that embezzlement, corruption and all forms of indecencies are actions that violate all known norms of good governance, progressive leadership, integrity, credibility, accountability and trust. By and large, with this ugly status quo in Nigeria, the question is: What moral right does Nigeria have to seek for debt relief from foreign creditors? You can accuse me of sermonizing or sounding preachy. To those concerned, I say to you: "Don't spoil your name and soil your image and integrity just for a few years of power. Always have it at the back of your mind that, justice or nemesis will certainly catch up with you. Remember the famous words of Dele Giwa (a one time Nigerian editor with *The Newswatch Magazine,* who was murdered in cold blood): "Every evil done by man to man will most certainly be redressed! If not by man, then certainly by God, if not in this world, surely in the world to come!"

Furthermore, in sympathy with this Nigerian situation, Karl Maier, in making a historical flashback on this nation, says: "Designed by alien occupiers and abused by army rule for three-quarters of its brief life span, the Nigerian state is like a battered and bruised elephant staggering toward an abyss with the ground crumbling under its feet. Should it fall, the impact will shake the rest of West Africa."[5]

In his objective criticism of the role of the West in helping the Nigerian nation out of this messy situation, Karl Maier unequivocally states again in his book, *This House Has Fallen: Nigeria in Crisis* that: "So far the West has done little to help and has often made matters worse. It is hypocritical of the West to blame Nigeria for corruption, fraud, and drug running and to demand that Nigerians own up to their foreign debt while at the same time allowing the funds garnered from such nefarious dealings to be deposited in Western banks." 'A man who receives stolen goods is called a fence, but what do you call a country that is in the business of receiving stolen goods?' asked Dr. Folarin Gbadebo-Smith, a U.S. educated dentist and businessman... They lend Nigeria money, somebody here steals the same amount of money and gives it back to them, and then they leave these poor Nigerians repaying what they never owed."[6]

Thus, Nigeria's leaders, like the colonialists before them, have sucked out billions of dollars and stashed them in Western banks. The role of the Western powers, therefore, leaves them either as sadists or partners in crime or accomplices in Nigeria's nightmare. Yes, given the second-highest proven oil reserves in Africa, Nigerian officials spent oil income on lavish estates in Europe and America instead of decent schools and water systems back home. What an irony that, the country that produced the Nobel laureate Wole Soyinka and arguably Africa's best author, Chinua Achebe, was better known for the cruel, thieving and embezzling dictator of many people like Sani Abacha (a one time Nigerian military leader). Without attempting to pass judgment on him, may the merciful God rest his soul! And may other leaders learn from his unbecoming example of leadership. His successors should seriously look into and address such areas as discipline, responsibility and accountability in government.

Based on the series of catastrophic end of many prominent Nigerians, especially military leaders and politicians who failed to improve the lot of the masses when they had the opportunity to do so while in office, I have a word or two to the power that be:

"Death is a leveler. No houses and foreign bank accounts will be buried with one when the inescapable final trumpet is blown. Remember the existential and piercing words of Job in the Bible: 'Naked I came from my mother's womb, naked shall I return.' (Job 1: 21). Let those in government ask themselves what legacy they will like to leave behind. Perhaps you have been chasing the shadow all the while, it is time to stop awhile and think. Realize that it is not too late to rearrange your scale of preferences and amend priorities. God bless you as you contemplate this. Why not you recontextualize and be challenged by the words of a one time American president,

PUBLIC UTILITIES

John F. Kennedy, who said: "Do not ask, what can America do for me? Rather ask, what can I do for America?" In fact, it is my believe that, together with other laudable ideologies and personal sanity, these questions and their positive reactions have resonated and guided the leadership agendas of Americans. Hence, in a very healthy conspiracy for the common good, they have contributed and will continue to contribute to the development of the American world.

As a way of escaping Nigeria's painful reality, millions of Nigerians, including much of the cream of the educated and business elite, have fled their country to escape impoverishment and political repression. Most live in the United States and Europe. Besides, even today, every young man or woman in Nigeria is exploring opportunities and seeking avenues that would enable him or her to leave this troubled motherland to go overseas in search of greener pastures, security, and related better means of livelihood.

On another development, a deeper look into the cultures of the world would reveal that some natural phenomena play a fundamental role in shaping the different lifestyles or ways of life of people. Most important of these natural occurrences are the seasons, the climatic and weather conditions for a given people found within a geographical location of the globe. These natural phenomena, which may be taken for granted in the treatment of cultural literature, play a determinant role in cultural differences as reflected in the daily practical lives of the people concerned, even in the way they think and reason, especially in "conquering" the hazardous conditions brought about by the weather and climatic changes. Chapter 9 of this book opens up a discussion on some of these phenomena in

A Handbook on Culture Shock

relation to the points of interest that this book sets out in its adventure to deal with – to educate, inform, challenge and possibly to set free from mistaken beliefs.

NOTES

[1] *Time,* "The Value of Water Cannot Just Be Measured in Liters," April 7, 2003, 8-9.

[2] "Water, Water Everywhere, But Not a Clean Drop to Drink. It Is a Worldwide Problem." *Pure Water for the World,* 2004.

[3] Volke, Matt. "Cold, Dry Weather Sparks Static Zaps." *The Post-Star,* January 30, 2004.

[4] Mbachu, Dulue. "Fuel Rates Spark Strike in Nigeria. Production, Exports Not Affected So Far." *The Post-Star,* June 10, 2004.

[5] Maier, Karl. *This House Has Fallen: Nigeria in Crisis.* Harmondsworth, Middlesex, England: Penguin Books Ltd., 2000, xviii, xix, xx, xxiv, xxvii, xx, xxii.

9

THE SEASONS AND RELATED DEVELOPMENTS

Since this book is more or less a comparative case study or presentation, the description of seasons will also suffer a "culture-textual" definition that properly situates them within their given environmental and climatic conditions. In relation to the tropical climate of Nigeria, a season is one of two divisions of the year: *rainy* and *dry* seasons. In the Adirondack region of the United States, a season is one of four divisions of the year: *winter, spring, summer,* and *fall* or *autumn.* These periods are full of expectations and are marked by certain activities, celebrations, and vegetation. The later, (vegetation) is usually noticeable in the availability or unavailability of certain crops. The expectations of these seasons affect the life of the people in varied ways, mostly contingent on the meteorological conditions. This fact will be explained under the considerations of climatic and weather conditions, clothes and accessories, time difference and siesta or nap time.

THE SEASONS AND RELATED DEVELOPMENTS

CLIMATIC AND WEATHER CONDITIONS

Climatic and weather conditions are the meteorological conditions that prevail in a region at a given time and place. The state of the atmosphere within that given time and space is described by the specification of variables such as temperature, moisture, wind velocity, and barometric pressure. These conditions may be unpleasant and violent and affect the way of life of the people concerned.

Nigeria lies at the extreme inner corner of the Gulf of Guinea and is the largest geopolitical unit in West Africa. The country is located entirely within the tropical zone. It occupies a position where the western parts of the African continent meet equatorial Africa. Nigeria extends northward from the coastline for some 1,170 kilometers. The country extends in the south from the Atlantic Ocean, which washes the coastline for about 900 kilometers, to the Sahara Desert in the north. The Republic of Niger borders Nigeria on the west. On the east, Nigeria shares a border with the Republic of Cameroon.

Although Nigeria is within the tropics, the climate varies from the typical tropical humidity at the coast to the subtropical farther inland. There are two well-marked seasons: *the rainy and the dry seasons.* In the south, the rains last from April to October, starting later and ending earlier in the north. The dry season lasts in the south from November to March, extending up to June in the north. In the coastal area, rainfall varies from 125 centimeters in the southwest area to nearly 500 centimeters in some parts of the southeast. In parts of the north, it may be as low as 50 centimeters. Temperature at the coast seldom rises above 90 degrees, but humidity is high. Farther north the climate is drier, and extremes of temperatures are more common, sometimes reaching as high as 110 degrees and falling to 50 degrees and even below at certain times. During the dry season, the harmattan wind blows in from the desert, causing extreme dryness and carrying with it the fine dust particles that form the haze common all over the country from November to January, though with greater intensity as one moves south to north.

The gradation in vegetation and climatic condition is the result of wide variations in rainfall produced by the seasonal inflow of humid air from the south Atlantic. In many instances, the zonal differences in soil fertility and food crops resulting from this natural differentiation have produced complementary economies. For example, Nigeria can produce all its food requirements through exchanges between the zones.

The weather and climatic conditions do not affect much what the people wear all year-round, and the clocks, in terms of setting the time backward or forward, remain the same throughout the two seasons and all year-round. There are certain times when the country experiences relatively longer days and shorter nights or vice versa. However, the time difference responsible for this experience of longer days and shorter nights is hardly noticed, since the days remain almost the same in terms of when the sun rises and sets.

Unlike Nigeria, which has two seasons, the Adirondack region of the United States has four well-marked seasons. These seasons are *winter, spring, summer*, and *autumn* or *fall*. Accordingly, following the calendar year, they run thus: winter: December 21–March 20, spring: March 20–June 21, summer: June 21–September 20, and fall: September 20–December 21. All these seasons play a fundamental role and generally affect the day-to-day life of the people. This cuts across their vegetation, outdoor clothing, daily engagements (sports, school, and related activities), and even the time difference, in terms of setting and resetting of clocks at certain times of the seasons. It was really an eye-opening and fascinating experience to see what goes on among the people during the different seasons. Some of these experiences are worth talking about.

CLOTHES AND ACCESSORIES

The wearing of clothes, hats, or caps and the putting on of shoes are phenomenal realities all over the cultures of the world. In certain cultures, however, there are particular tribal outfits. There are also clothes peculiar to religious groups, confraternities, and organizations that distinguish and set them apart from others as marks of identification. True as this may be, there are also cosmopolitan cultures where, due to intermarriages and intermingling of diverse cultures, there is a crossbreeding of cultures and so the issue of clothing is no longer a distinguishing mark of identification. This cultural polarization that shuns or ignores all dichotomies has brought about uniformity in clothes which takes for granted and accepts the wearing of particular clothes by its people without questioning. In such situations, there can be the problem of identity crisis. This cosmopolitan setting, in terms of clothes, can also be brought about by climatic and weather conditions as found and experienced in a given environment, which affect all its dwellers, as is the case in the Adirondacks.

The Nigerian nation is a conglomerate of many ethnic groups, various tribes, diverse religions, and other enclaves. This gives rise to differences in the clothes worn: tradition-

A HANDBOOK ON CULTURE SHOCK

ally, tribally, religiously, and otherwise. These clothes can give you away easily wherever you go, especially within the geographical ambience of the country. To this end, it is extremely difficult, if not impossible, to talk about clothing in the Nigerian cultural context in a common or single entity. However, strictly speaking, there seems to be a textural constant and similarity in the type of clothes, hats, caps, and shoes worn all year-round. Despite this fact, there is a little variation in areas that are colder than others, or muddier than others, especially when it rains or gets hot in accordance with the environmental condition of the two main seasons.

In the North Country, the dwellers or people in Upstate New York in the Adirondacks come from different countries and places. For instance, you have the Irish, Italians, French, Germans, Hispanics, Ghanaians, Nigerians, African-Americans, and others living together in the neighborhood. Incidentally, due to the environmental situation and other related factors, the cultural experience here is cosmopolitan. Consequently, their clothing is so common that you can hardly tell who is who, especially conditioned by the weather and climatic situations of the four seasons of winter, spring, summer, and fall.

Among these four seasons, winter and summer are so at the extreme of each other that you barely have a choice other than to wear what would make you comfortable in each of them. One is extremely snowy and chilly, and the other is extremely humid and hot, respectively. The other two seasons, spring and fall, are more or less the same in their atmospheric conditions, though with usually more rain in spring. However, they also have their differences in the sense that trees lose their leaves in the fall (season). They remain leafless, (except for the ev-

328 •

ergreens), all through winter and get them back in the spring
(season). It is also important to be aware that, characteristically, the weather condition in the spring is very unpredictable.
In fact, during this season, in just one day it is almost possible
to experience the four seasons. Thus, it may be sunny in the
morning, hazy at noon, warm in the afternoon, and very cold
at night. You never know what to expect.

In accordance with the atmospheric conditions of the four
seasons, it is a known fact that almost every dweller in the
Adirondacks has four wardrobes or closets, each containing
clothing and other accessories or necessary incidentals for each
season. The shopping malls and the people's shopping appe-
tites are also affected by each coming season. Thus, depending on the season, the daily newspapers have advertisements
for the available clothes and accessories in shopping malls
at low rates or prices, as a way of customizing their goods.
The people also react accordingly. Hence, you often hear of
winter shopping, spring shopping, summer shopping, and fall
shopping. Therefore, as the shopping malls prepare for each
season, by what may be called a "replacement process," the
people also open their wardrobes and get them updated with
the latest clothing through various shopping trips. Yes, given
the season, you find people dressed and looking winterized or
summery, as the case may be.

On a personal note and observation, among all the clothing,
the winter clothes and accessories remain very strange and fascinating. What a difficult adjustment and shock it was to me,
not only to see the people, but also, having no choice, than to
see myself wearing several layers of clothes, bundling up with
very thick jackets and winter coats. That is not all. I also had

A HANDBOOK ON CULTURE SHOCK

to put on very heavy boots, gloves, ski masks, hats, mufflers, earmuffs, and insulated underwear. All this "bundling up" was to help me put up with the extreme cold weather conditions at the time. For newcomers, this cold weather during the bad winter season can be a real killer. Be warned! The contrast and the apparent need for this metamorphosis in accordance with the weather condition, which was very difficult to me, can be better appreciated when you compare the difference here with the tropical weather conditions of my country, Nigeria, where I was born and brought up. What a glaring and sharp difference it is. It would be a statement of fact to say that I was very uncomfortable in these clothes, since I was not used to them. That is why, whenever some friends say to me: "You look good in your winter attire." I would immediately respond by saying: "Ask me how I am feeling in it." It was not fun at all. I needed to be free and dress lightly. In fact, I could not wait for the season to be over so that I could go back to my Nigerian light way of dressing.

Furthermore, during this time, the pictures of people you see on the streets, especially on a blizzard day, can be very bizarre and frightening because of their monstrous and masquerading looks. I mean that the people kind of look so disguised with all the different layers of clothes, thereby making it difficult and somehow impossible for you to recognize whom the person approaching you might be. To put this picture in perspective, they constantly remind me of how armed robbers dress in Nigeria when they are out on an operation during the day or at night, covering every part of their bodies including their faces with hats except for the eyes.

Another fascinating, surprising, and shocking winter experience is about sunshine and its ironic effect. In Nigeria, sunshine makes the weather hot and brings about the effect of sweating because of the warmness or hotness of the atmosphere, depending on the intensity. My Adirondack's winter experience in this regard presents a different effect and feeling. Over here, during winter season, sunshine can be deceiving. This is in the sense that it could be very sunny on a winter day outside looking through the window, but the temperature at the same time could still be "below zero." To this end, the sunshine notwithstanding, the weather remains very cold. Of course, when I first arrived in Hudson Falls, New York, I was deceived by the sunshine and I did go out several times from my suite during the winter season without wearing a coat. No sooner had I gone out than I began to really feel the cold, in spite of the sunshine. The best way, therefore, to enjoy winter sunshine is either from inside your room through a glass window or from inside your car with the windows wound up. I called this experience, "the irony of sunshine." So, just as it is often said: "Not all that glitters is gold," based on this irony of sunshine, it could also be said that: "Not all that is sunny is hot."

With the coming of spring, the heavy and suffocating clothes gradually give way to something relatively lighter, and the sunshine begins to become warm. The summer season finally brings an almost shaking-off of airtight clothes, and the sunshine begins to become hot with its uncomfortable high humidity. Thus, having braved the cold and snow over the past several months, the people are happy to put the shovels, snow blowers, heavy boots, coats, and gloves away for another year, as they joyfully welcome the warm months of spring and

A Handbook on Culture Shock

summer. There is also the joy of welcoming back and reuniting with those (mostly retired people) who, during the winter season, might go south and west to places like the Carolinas, Florida, Utah, Arizona, and other places experiencing warm weather at the time.

To say that the culture of clothing among the Adirondack people usually experiences what may be called a "revolution" is a fact that is depicted by the clothes the people wear during the summer season. They want to be free, as much as possible, after several months of airtight dressing. They want enough air and to enjoy the free summer sunshine and breeze coming from the surrounding rivers and lakes. There seems to be a conspiracy to avenge the suffocation endured during the winter season with its blizzard weather conditions. Some people push this "revolution" so much that the picture could become too revealing and obscene, projecting an environment of "nudity" or a moral revolution. When you begin to experience this by seeing some people dressed in ways that may be unbecoming, do not be judgmental. Remember the popular saying: "Do not judge anyone until you have walked in his shoes." However, this saying does not justify clothing that is offensive to public morality and does not compromise the laudable etiquette of modesty, public decency, and decor, especially in sacred places.

During this hot season of the year, I have a word or two for you, the newcomer. If you are from a developing world where it is always thought that the weather there is hot all year round, be careful about your reaction in your new environment when it becomes hot, humid and the heat is high. Yes, if you, too, begins to complain that it is hot and the heat bothers

THE SEASONS AND RELATED DEVELOPMENTS

you, you may be reminded of your "unfortunate" background or where you are coming from. In fact, why should you complain, when where you are coming from, you have neither fans nor air conditioners to help in/during the hot weather, which is always "120 degrees" with its accompanying high humidity? Do you even have swimming pools to cool off when the heat becomes unbearable or very uncomfortable? True as this may be, (to whom it may concerned), it should also be noted that the newcomer does not become culturally acclimated to the new environment only in the way he reasons and talks or in the gradual changing color of his skin "to whatever." His body system or sensitivity also becomes adjusted and used to the prevailing weather conditions experienced in the new environment. And before long, the expression: "What is good for the goose is also good for the gander," begins also to apply to him in terms of the popular reactions to weather conditions, be they hot or cold.

Regarding the restrictions and frustrations of the winter season, people outside this environment (as in faraway Nigeria) find it difficult to understand what you may be experiencing during this season. It is a season that is characterized by lots of weather uncertainties. Yes, you may wake up one morning and your are unable to go out of your house because you have been snowed in. In most cases, all attempts to explain any frustrating snowy experience to someone who does not have the slightest knowledge about the winter season, often ends up in failure to convince him or her. In fact, sometimes the person may think that you are just making up an excuse.

For instance, some time ago I was supposed to send my sister, Joy, in Nigeria, mail by overnight delivery through FedEx. But it happened that it was not possible to do it within the time I had planned. She waited for the mail for three days beyond the expected day of arrival, but to no avail. Eventually, she called me on the telephone to find out what was wrong. All attempts to explain to her about the frustration of the blizzard weather condition that prevented me from going out to send the mail, seemed to have been ignored. From the way she responded as I spoke with her, I suspected that she thought I was just making it up for want of an excuse. I didn't blame her because of her lack of experience.

Faced with this inclement weather condition, shortly after my arrival in Hudson Falls, I remembered complaining that it was very cold, when the temperature was 50 degrees above zero, and the pastor said to me: "You haven't seen anything yet." He further went on to tell me that a time would come when 20 degrees above zero would be considered very warm, and I would celebrate it as a heat wave. The time did actually come. I saw! I experienced! I believed! Like the Biblical doubting Thomas, I said: "My Lord and my God." Things were never the same again. No kidding!

Furthermore, on this note of the changing weather conditions and the people's response to it, I had an interesting experience. During the spring season, with the coming of the sunshine and relatively warm weather, some people in upstate New York stay out in the sun to sunbathe. At the end of the day, they have a natural tanning, and some people experience sunburn. Now, within this time, I had an opportunity of going into a Faith Formation class to field or answer some questions and share some thoughts with the second graders who were between seven and eight years old. One of the children kept looking at me intently. He then raised his hand and asked me this question: "Do you also experience sunburn?" I answered the question by saying: "No!" Then I added by saying: "Even if I do, it will not show." Still curious, he asked me this follow-up question: "Why?" At this time, the bell for the end of the class was rung. I said: "Thank God!" I told the teacher of the class to explain the last question to the children in their next class. The point here is that besides the relevance of the question, you never know with children! especially, the American children. In their innocence and curiosity, they can ask you any question. So, be prepared if you are to meet with them, (at any point in time) for any embarrassing question that may put you on the spot.

You will understand the love of the sun by the Adirondack people when you live with them for a year or more. Since they experience the beauty and warmth of the sun for only a few months during the year, they always try to stay outdoors and enjoy it whenever they have a sunny day. Hence, on sunny days, I always had several telephone calls from friends asking me to go out and enjoy the gorgeous sunny day. In fact, I vividly remember an occasion when a very kind and dear family invited me for breakfast on one Sunday morning. It was indeed a sunny morning. On my arrival, they requested that we sit on the deck and enjoy the sun. While out there, they kept on saying: "Wow! It is a gorgeous day. The sun is so nice and warm." I must confess that it was not fun for me. Besides, the sun on this particular day and place was directly on my face, and it was so hot. Well, I had to endure it for the sake of pleasing my kind hosts throughout the time of my visit with them. However, all along, I kept on saying to myself: "I don't think I need this natural tanning. I have had more than enough sun in Nigeria." Thank God that the long and uncomfortable visit ended eventually. Yes, at certain times you have to endure some inconvenience to make your host happy. This I did several times, and I hope very well, too.

Generally speaking, concerning the seasons and their related weather conditions as experienced in upstate New York, I must say that it is an interesting experience. This interest is in the sense that, *weather monotony* is replaced by *weather variety*. The beauty of the weather variation is that, in what seems like a rotational circular movement, within one year, you see the winter snows give way to the spring flowers, and the summer's heat and humidity give way to the autumn's briskness with its colorful leaves on trees. This is another beauty of the "North Country" besides the beauty of its people.

TIME DIFFERENCE

It is worthy to note that the time difference between Nigeria and New York is either five or six hours, depending on the current season in the United States. In either case, Nigerian time is always ahead. The actual difference is six hours; so when it is 10:00 a.m. Nigerian time, it is 4:00 a.m. New York time. However, something called "daylight saving time" in New York is in effect from early April of every year. During this time, clocks are pushed one hour ahead. This lasts until late October, when the clocks are pushed one hour back again. This gives people an extra hour of day light in the nice weather months to enjoy outdoor activities. With daylight saving time, when it is 10:00 a.m. in Nigeria, it is 5:00 a.m. in New York. This explains the five or six hours difference as

THE SEASONS AND RELATED DEVELOPMENTS

mentioned previously. Putting this idea of hourly time difference within the context of the different seasons, therefore, it is obvious that during spring and summer seasons and during autumn and winter seasons that the time difference is five and six hours, respectively.

Again, regarding the setting and resetting of the clock time at specific times and seasons of the year, as already stated, during fall season, the clocks are reset one hour behind and are left that way until the end of the winter season. Hence, the name "fall," that is, the hour falls behind. Then, during spring season, the clocks are reset one hour ahead and are left that way until a certain time in the fall. Hence, the name "spring," that is, the hour springs ahead. Also, another source of the names "spring" and "fall" is that leaves fall from the trees in fall or autumn season, while grasses, trees, and plants spring to life in spring season.

With this time difference as explained here, my contact with the new environment in the Adirondacks was almost like moving from one extreme to the other. Thus, my usual active hours in the afternoon and evening or morning seemingly became my passive or less active hours because of the different time range over here. Sometimes depending on the time and calculation, my initial afternoon and evening become my current morning. For instance, during daylight savings time (April through October — spring and summer seasons), when it is 2:00 p.m. Nigerian time, it is 9:00 a.m. New York time, (five hours difference). Again, during regular time (November through March — winter and fall seasons), when it is 2:00 a.m. Nigerian time, it is 8:00 p.m. New York time. This was another difficult and challenging cultural adjustment to cal-

A Handbook on Culture Shock

culate, understand, report and explain to my family members and friends in Nigeria to enable us also change and adjust the different times of making telephone calls at both ends.

Within the first few weeks and even months of my arrival in Upstate New York, I had very many sleepless nights, and so I had to make up by sleeping many times during the day. My nights were sleepless and frustrating, not only because of the change in time, but, also because of the many telephone calls I had from Nigeria. These calls were mostly made during the dead hours of the night in New York while it was daytime in Nigeria, considering the time difference. Though I was happy to hear from home, these telephone calls affected my productivity adversely the next day. Sometimes I was tempted to take the telephone off the hook, but I feared missing an important telephone call from my family if I did that.

By the same token, it is interesting to note that the whole idea of time difference revealed another difference even within the United States. This time difference within the same country was another experience of what I referred to in this book as "a culture shock within a culture shock." In other words, it was very strange to discover that the fifty states in of the United States do not all share the same clock time at any time of the year. This is because America has four different time zones - Eastern, Central, Mountain, and Pacific. For instance, at no time of the year would it be 1:00 p.m. all over the United States at the same time. It was a shock to me to hear, for example, that the state of Texas is always one hour behind New York time, which is in the Eastern time zone in the same country. While the state of California, is three hours behind New York time in the same country, to mention but a few.

THE SEASONS AND RELATED DEVELOPMENTS

These ideas of "intercontinental," "international," and "interstate" time differences with their related setting and resetting of the clocks were really strange and new to me. Of course, several times I became forgetful and got confused about the actual time of the day because of the brightness of the day, even when the time is in the late evening or very early in the morning. Particularly, there was this morning during the first few days of spring after the clocks had been reset one hour ahead, that I had a telephone call from Nigeria, and the time was 10:00 a.m. Nigerian time, which was 5:00 a.m. New York time. As I looked through my window after receiving the telephone call, it was already very bright outside and the sun was rising. I thought I was late for morning Mass, which was at 7:30 a.m. In fact, I became visibly very confused, thinking that the clock I had in my room was running late. In order to be sure of the exact time, I decided to look at my wristwatch and then walked through and took a look at all the clocks in my suite. They all reported the same time: 5:00 a.m. I then had to go to bed again for another two hours before I got up at 7:00 a.m. to prepare for the morning Mass. In fact, I even had to look through my window to see if there were any cars outside that belong to the regular people who come to morning Mass. I did this to be doubly sure that something was not wrong somewhere. Imagine what the Adirondack culture was doing to me.

During the spring season also, as expected, I removed my hat from my head, which I often used to cover and protect my head from the winter cold. This was because of the fact that a lot of heat is lost through the head, and so the head needs to be covered more tightly during the snowy and chilly weather

A Handbook on Culture Shock

conditions. So, as I took away the hat from my head with the coming of spring, my hair was once more exposed for people to see. Within this time, I had a second opportunity of being in another Faith Formation class, and again, a child asked me if the hair on my head would grow longer than it was. I responded: "No!" He again asked me: "Why?" This was easy to answer. Accordingly, I said: "God made it so." Once more, I say to you: "You never know with children's curiosity. Be prepared! Do not take offense or take it personal when they begin to ask you similar questions. It is not an *argumentum ad bacculum,* that is, arguments or questions meant to attack your person.

That reminds me, you don't have to blame the child who asked me the question about my hair because within the time I had just had a haircut and so my hair was very low. And it may interest you to know that, the story of my haircut was another issue I had to battle with as I lived among the Adirondacks. Being an exclusively white neighborhood, it was difficult to find a barbershop in the area that any barber could cut my kind of hair. Therefore, my search for a place that I could have a haircut of my choice was quite an adventure. I was not satisfied with the first one that I had, which was given to me by a white guy who even promised to do a good job before its commencement. At the end, his best was not good enough. However, as demanded and required by good etiquette and politeness, I thanked him very profusely before leaving his barbershop. But I was saying to myself as I was leaving: "I am out of here and never to return."

For those of you who are familiar with the area, my search for a better place that I could have a haircut of my choice

The Seasons and Related Developments

brought me to Saratoga, to Clifton Park, to Albany city, and to Schenectady, all in New York. Finally, it was during one of my trips to New York City that I discovered that, the boys (African-Americans) there could really do a good job. I was however not surprised nor shocked that the barbershops in the typically Adirondacks area could not take care of my hair because they are not used to cutting my kind of hair. This situation of not readily having someone who could cut my hair when I needed it and the way I wanted it, made me to start carrying so much hair on my head. This was a surprise and a shock to some of my family members and friends in Nigeria, who saw my hair in some of the pictures that I took at the time and sent to them. In short, some of them thought that, it was part of my Americanization to leave my hair grow wild.

I remember one time that I left my hair to really grow beyond the usual level, some members of my congregation called my attention to it. I simply told them that I was "gonna" leave my hair to grow to afro (style) because I wanted to look different. One parishioner on hearing me say this, simply said to one of her friends as they walked away from me at the end of Mass after exchanging pleasantries at the door: "Does he not look different enough?" You will appreciate the importance and relevance of this question when you come to know that my American neighborhood was exclusively white, and in my congregation I was almost always the only "black" person. Yes, you never know what people are thinking not until an occasion comes up for their inner thoughts to be laid bare or made known, even if in passing. Of course, this question reminded me of a reality that I was taking for granted.

By and large, the experience of the climatic conditions and

all the dynamics that go with it, among other things, increased my knowledge about the rising and the setting of the sun at different times. The time difference also took another dimension and has its own story, in terms of its adverse effect on me regarding my habitual siesta or routine naptime, which I was so used to taking while still in Nigeria. What happened?

SIESTA OR NAPTIME

As it is widely known, a siesta or nap is a short sleep usually taken after the midday meal. If you agree with the assertion that the best form of rest is sleep, then the need for siesta becomes a necessary exercise to be worked in, within one's daily busy schedule. The body and the intellect need some rest during the daily schedule, so as to recharged and become more productive in facing the physical and mental challenges of the day. You cannot underestimate the refreshing power of sleep. In most cases, a denial of this form of rest (sleep) becomes counterproductive. This may affect you physically, or you may experience a diminishing return in work-related activities. However, depending on one's cultural orientation, this napping exercise or siesta option may or may not be a necessary daily routine with any value placed on it.

In Nigeria, in some sectors of life, especially in boarding schools, siesta is an exercise that enjoys a prominent place in the daily timetable of the curriculum. This usually takes place between 1:00 p.m. and 3:00 p.m. Siesta time is not treated lightly. Any violation of this rule by any student is tantamount to seriously breaking one of the school's rules, which is punishable and viewed with consternation. In fact, the worst punishment given to recalcitrant students is to make them miss their siesta by having them do some manual labor while others are having this form of rest.

Believe it or not, if you grow up in a siesta culture of this sort, you would become so conditioned or "addicted" and would definitely become used to a siesta or naptime. This is because, besides your bodily adjustment, it would also become a mind-set, which may also affect your psychological constitution. So, for you to be denied this exercise in future, in any place and at any point in time and no matter what the circumstance may be, would be very worrisome. In my own case, having been brought up in a siesta culture, it seemingly became habitual. As you know, habits are so easy to form (sometimes unconsciously), but very hard and difficult to break. This would not be surprising when you come to know that, throughout my formative years to the priesthood in the minor and major seminaries for about fourteen years, siesta was a daily routine. Even as a priest, my pastoral placements for about seven years were in institutions that, for the most part, afforded me the opportunity for napping or snoozing because of the daily plan of the school timetable, which always had room for such a refreshing exercise.

This routine was not to continue when I came to the United States to live and work within the Adirondack culture and its people. Besides the time difference factor and telephone calls, which as earlier mentioned, affected my night sleep, my siesta time, which would have made up for my sleepless nights, was also seriously thwarted. The culture in itself has no room or provision for siesta or naptime. It was an unbelievable, surprising, and shocking experience to come to know that the Americans do not seem to place any priority nor do they have

A Handbook on Culture Shock

any programmed time for siesta. Up until now, I thought that the U.S. world was a culture of eat, drink, relax, go partying, go clubbing, hang out with friends, and have a good time, all year-round. Believe it or not, this mentality of always having a good time in the United States is still the belief and mentality of many Nigerians back home, especially among young boys and girls. How disillusioning this was to me within a very short time of my arrival and stay in the U.S. culture!

In reality, it is a culture of workaholics where people are worker bees or beavers. Over here, life is: "Speed up! Quick! Fast! Fly! Keep moving! Do not stop!" It is a culture that is filled with drive-thru windows and overnight delivery. Its people are always on the run or running out of time. They need something done ASAP (as soon as possible), and even when their friends are sick, they wish them a speedy recovery. It is a supersonic jet age with never a dull moment.

In her book *The Time Bind – When Work Becomes Home and Home Becomes Work,* Arlie Russell Hochschild, beautifully captures the modern American culture of work and time. In picturesque illustrations, which may be difficult to imagine, she explains each picture accordingly. In picture one, she shows how in his 1936 classic *Modern Times,* Charlie Chaplin depicts a speedup on the factory floor. The result is that the hapless Charlie fastens bolts onto machine parts at a faster and faster rate.

Picture two turns the searchlight into an era when few women worked outside the home. The result here, too, is that the speedup was confined to the workplace (by those who worked outside the home.) And consciously or unconsciously, now that the majority of women and mothers are employed, the speedup extends to the home with the tendency of "cloning" or "bi-locating" in order to achieve more results within a given space and time. True and laudable as this tendency may be, the earlier we realize our limitation, keep in mind and remain conscious of the fact that we cannot be in two or more places at the same time doing different things, the better for us in so many ways.

You and I can only be in one place at any given time because we are bound by space. Right now, I am at my desk in my home. As much as I might like to be with my parents, brothers and sisters in far away Nigeria, I can only be in one place, and for now it's right here, in my study, working at my computer.

I will tell you who it is who can be everywhere. That person is God. He can be everywhere at once. In His omnipresence, God is present with Africans seeking to glorify Him in the midst of an earthly hell. He is in Bosnia trying to keep the unity of the spirit in the midst of generations of division. He is in Iraq trying to grant democratic freedom in government. He is present with my beloved mom in Nigeria struggling in her farm in the woods for what to eat. He is with my dad groping about to find his way as he struggles with his blindness. He is with my paternal Aunt, Christiana Oyonghe Enoh, in her last days as she is tormented by Parkinson disease and gets weaker and weaker on each passing day. He is with me, as I write this book, and with you as you read it.

Humanly speaking, some of the fruits of realizing and accepting our human limitations, especially in terms of our presence are as follows: Life will be less stressful; our lives will be much more simpler; our works will be more effective and

A Handbook on Culture Shock

efficient; our productivity will be more qualitative than quantitative; our domestic responsibilities, particularly the care for our God-given children will fundamentally get all the attention and attentiveness needed to be good stewards.

In an era of automation, it is not surprising that in picture three, Charlie is trapped to the Billows Automatic Feeding Device, which is a machine introduced to save work time by feeding workers more efficiently. The imagination needed here is to see an automatic fork rapidly feeding the startled Charlie steeling bolts for lunch. The feeding device referred to here applies to the act of eating the principle of efficiency introduced by the time and motion expert Frederick Taylor. Today, it is a reality that workers efficiently eat lunch at their desk or at fast-food delis. They even begin the day at home in the spirit of the Billows machine where certain jobs are begun, carried out and completed automatically in their minds or imaginations.

Sorry to further challenge your imaginative powers, picture four captures a recent advertisement for Quaker Oatmeal, where a working mother feeds her child in just under 90 seconds. If the Billows Device mentioned previously hurried the factory workers, it is the mother who hurries her child. And indeed, left with no option, it is the child who hurries himself. The virtue of hurry becomes internalized and acted out unconsciously as a way of life.

What do you expect, in a culture where speed is the order of the day, many accidents occur and the effects of such are either injuries to others or personal injuries or malfunctioning. To this end, picture five brings us to the scene of a film where the speedup drove Charlie crazy. He began dancing around, chasing his secretary, and tightening imaginary bolts on her dress.

THE SEASONS AND RELATED DEVELOPMENTS

He is at last carted off in shame and disgrace to the insane asylum. But, thank God, no one today is hauling the speeding worker off to a mental hospital, otherwise, many of us would be patients. Indeed, in modern life, speed and "efficiency" are not associated with insanity, shame and disgrace, but with sanity, pride, and heroism. And the encouraging slogan is "keep up the good work." Do we need to be reminded that, it is not when we get "there" but how well we do, that really matters? Do we also need to reminded that, it is better to be late than "never" or "the late?"

Here is what really takes place nowadays, in a cartoon that represents picture six, when a boss reminds workers to quit at five, they think he's either insane or has gone mad. By my estimation and reasoning, the picture also explains the *law of diminishing returns.* It also reminds us that no matter how workaholic we become, we cannot solve the world's problems in just one day, if at all. The best or worse thing that may happen is that, we would discover more problems and possibly create many more. No wonder, Pope John XXIII, (during his Pontificate), after working so hard and seemingly endless one day into the wee hours of the morning, as he thought about convening the Second Vatican Council to address the problems of the Church, before going to sleep, was purported to have said something that ran like this or to the effect that – *God, the Church belongs to you and you will take care of your Church.* Both in the Church's life and secular affairs, how many of us realize that actually everything belongs to God and we are just the visible instruments in his hands to bring about his designed or designated purpose?

Picture seven invites us to listen to the world's daily cry that

A Handbook on Culture Shock

hinges on the complain of – there is either no time, or we are running out of time. Hence, a cult of "efficiency" moves from the workplace to home. Consequently, the business world with its expertise on reading and interpreting market psychology rises to the occasion, and so foods are advertised according to how little time they take to cook – a five-minute lunch or an eight-minute fajita feast.

In our keyboard or push-a-button technological world, there are also other ads that feature computers by e-mail or telephone calls that enable people to order groceries, which are brought to our doormat. This is the message that picture eight sets out to give.

"Express" connotes speedup, run on a fast lane, and get "there" or get "it" done in little time. Hence, the commercial world with its commodities or items have inciting logos or trademarks that can wed the appetite of customers and persuade them to patronize the goods with the belief that the logos would live up to or act out their names. In the last picture that challenges your imaginative powers, I invite you to build up a mental picture of an iron called Handy Xpress as its logo. In a humorous depiction, this iron, while performing its function with the intent of living up to its name, is touted as going so fast it gets speeding ticket. The question is – who should get the speeding ticket? Is it the iron or the person using it? It can only be the former (the iron) if the argument is that, it is its fault because of the logo – Xpress, and so the user had no control over its speed.

The different imaginative picturesque illustrations above, are meant to show and prove beyond doubt that, in the American culture, (perhaps also in other parts of the world, like in

The Seasons and Related Developments

Europe), the allure of speed enters the culture. Doing something "fast" becomes a virtue in itself. Indeed, to say that today, it's not simply the premium on efficiency and speed that has been transferred to most homes; corporate ways of thinking about time have become part of home life, too. Once again, to make the obvious explicit. It would not be striking a new note to say that, even in leisure, time is divided into carefully measured segments, which amounts to a domestic version of "office hours" allocated to each member of the family.

Meanwhile, in many workaholism situations, men don't simply transfer a work orientation to the home, they may even forget they have a home; they may forget, not only the names, but also that they have children, too. When they are back from the "office," they may even walk pass their wives into their "office-home" with just the following dispassionate, "programmed" uncaring and inattentive words: "Hello, dear. I had a very hard day at the office, and grabbed a bite on the way home. I've brought home some work, which I'll be doing in my study. See you in the morning. Good night!"

The results in family life of such behaviors where people are practically glued to or married to their works are obvious – deprivation, divided allegiance, immoral temptation and finally, divorce. The names too are clear – idolatry, "goddism," and secular monasticism. It is an arguable thought that, what may possibly give vent to this ugly reality in family or married life is a culture where you have a commoditization of everything in the commercial, social, and political life of the people — their time, their space, and their experiences.

In modern American culture, it is like work, work, and work until you drop dead. Yes, you work for every dime you own.

A HANDBOOK ON CULTURE SHOCK

Hence, creditably, I would say that the people deserve all the comfort they have and enjoy because they spend almost all their entire lifetime working for it. If you must live in this culture, you have to be not only awake, but also active and fast, so as to meet up with each day's official work, related demands and personal challenges. Furthermore, this working culture is more so because you must be able to pay your bills so as not to suffer any eviction or be denied any service or medical attention. It is an inescapable culture of bills. The fortunate and good thing about it is that, you get and enjoy the adequate services that you pay for in accordance with the principle of commutative justice. Thank God! and the governmental structures that be.

Yes, it is not surprising in this culture of bills to find many people doing several or more than one job per day so as to be able to pay their bills, besides other reasons. Therefore, you will not be hearing something new when you hear two Americans talking on the telephone in this way: "What is new with you today?" "Me, I've just been sittin' at work. Goofing off. Surfing the Internet. Calling people." Multilaboring they call it, and multitasking is the name.

More thanks to this cultural system that calculates and allows the payment for jobs done by the hour. This provides an incentive to people to work hard since the results of hard work are obvious and are reaped almost immediately. Without fear of repetition or sounding hyperbolic, permit me to say again that the U.S. culture is, in fact and in deed, a superlative and supersonic jet age. It is a culture where, what is to be done today or tomorrow, the people would want it to be done, "yesterday." Ask a typical American, who wants something done for

The Seasons and Related Developments

him or her, a question such as: "When do you want it done?" Or: "When do you want to have it done?" The response you get would be equal to saying not just "now" but "yesterday." This is because whatever and however the response may be, it is more or less like saying: "I want it now" or "I wish I had it already." How about: Welcome to tomorrow?

Given this cultural setting, it is not a matter of saying: "If you can't beat them, you join them." It is rather a glaring fact and a stark reality that you cannot beat them, so you join them immediately, if you must stay here or you quit. You simply do not have a choice. It is against the reality of this speedy and fast culture that one comes to understand and appreciate the American culture of Domino`s drop off or home delivery food caps; takeaway houses of Pizza or Pizza Huts; Dunkin` Donuts houses and fast food centers – called McDonalds, and even Stewart's Shops, which are flooded all over the country with their related "drive-thrus." Of course, the speediness and no-time-to-waste way of life of the Americans explains the technology and convenient of express car wash drive-thrus and lots more.

On a personal note, it was against the backdrop of the speedy experience of this culture, which I became part of, that I had this encounter with someone. When I was looking for a car to buy, I went to a dealer who asked me this question: "How soon do you want a car?" I said to him: "Yesterday!" He looked at me and probably thought that I did not understand the question, but I knew what I was saying based on the given cultural mentality of, "yesterday."

Still on the topic of work and time in relation to siesta deprivation, I found that because I could not take a siesta, my daily

A HANDBOOK ON CULTURE SHOCK

weakness and unproductiveness were like nightmares. Several times, I did experience drowsiness and headaches as I tried to stay awake so that I could accomplish my pastoral duties of the day and related exercises. It was a tough cultural adjustment. I thought I was going to the United States for endless enjoyment galore. I got it all wrong. As a way of satisfying this siesta urge, I availed myself of any personal free minutes that I had during the day to snuggle under my comforter for a snooze. Though these naps were very short, comparatively speaking, they paid off a great deal, at least on the psychological level. Wow! Welcome to the U.S. culture of "workaholic!"

Most times, I had ask myself when the people actually wake up from sleep every morning. From this line of thought, it is safe to say that the Americans rise with the chicken. Don't ask me when they go to bed because I have no clue. My suspicion of this early-rising by the people come from my experience. And it is this: Every time and no matter the hour of the night I got a telephone call from Nigeria, besides the natural difficulty of going back to sleep immediately after each of those phone calls, the noise from the constant movement of cars, the banging from the garbage disposal trucks, the receiving tones from the Fax Machine and related activities in the neighborhood, "helped" to keep me awake for a much more longer time.

In a discourse of this magnitude and sensitivity, as a contribution to cultural anthropology, not to look into and talk about human perception of one another in terms of their sexuality or gender treatment and in relation to the place accorded other creatures by way of equality, amounts to a serious oversight. Particularly, the treatment of sexes or genders and animals by people of different cultures, is a burning issue that "newcom-

THE SEASONS AND RELATED DEVELOPMENTS

ers" grapple with and so it thus occupies the minds of many scholars of cultural literature. Without saying it all, let us see what the next chapter has to say about this subject matter. It may be quite revealing, shocking and stunning to many. At the same time, the content of this chapter may be a vivid capturing and confirmation of some ideas and realities for others, who are already aware of and familiar with these phenomena.

NOTES

[1] Hochschild, Arlie Russell. *The Time Bind: When Work Becomes Home and Home Becomes Work,* New York: Metropolitan Books, Henry Holt and Company, 1866.

10

EQUALITY

The subject of equality between men and women is becoming a very controversial issue in cultural anthropology and other philosophical fields of life. This controversy is also a cultural phenomenon or reality that enjoys a disparity based on people's way of life. My approach to this matter is to address the idea of equality from the point of view of people and creatures having the same rights, privileges, and status and treated as such. Depending on cultural situations and other collaterals, the subject of equality as understood here could be fascinating, stunning, shocking, and very revealing.

GENDER EQUALITY

Created in the image and likeness of God, man and woman, although different in some aspects of body composition, are essentially equal from the point of view of their humanity and teleology. This makes them enjoy an equal personal dignity, inalienable rights, and responsibilities proper to the human person in all spheres of life.

Unfortunately, some African customs and traditional practices deprive women of their rights and the respect due to them.

EQUALITY

For instance, the rearing and dometsic upbringing of children, for the most part, seems to be an exclusive responsibility of the women. Domestic activities such as cooking, keeping the house, and staying "always at home" are the nonnegotiable jobs of women. The typical African woman is basically a housewife or homemaker who must go to the farm, take care of the home, always stay in the house, and be at the beck and call of her husband. As expressed earlier, she is kept barefoot, pregnant and in the kitchen.

Concerning the rights of inheritance, the treatment of African women who become widows is appalling. In general, at public gatherings with men, women are mostly to be seen not heard. Hardly ever do they assume high political positions. In short, they are victims of societal marginalization and related irrelevant appendages. However, with the struggle for and growing awareness of women's rights, polite society is gradually recognizing that women can also have something to offer for the betterment of all and in all fields of life. This recognition or realization is made more obvious, compelling, and challenging through the work of evangelization in the contextual and hermeneutical preaching of the gospel and the enlightenment from education that creates awareness. This method of evangelization, for instance among other things, upholds and talks about the fundamental human equality of all peoples, irrespective of sex, race, nationalistic distinctions, and related chauvinisms.

Comparatively speaking, the issue of gender equality among the Adirondack people, as it is experienced in the daily life of the people, is not as troubling in the sense that, fundamental human equality is upheld, respected, and recognized among its people and by its dwellers. Though there may be some "red tapes" or lines drawn here and there, these lines (of inequality), are not easily seen or detected. No doubt, the present environment of equality in the United States as a whole passed through a lot of "tinkering" in the relentless struggle for women's liberation. It is against this backdrop that you can come to appreciate the philosophy on which the U.S. foundation was built. Thus, every now and then, you run into pieces of information that talk about the U.S. tradition which is rooted on a solid foundation of equality, freedom, and liberty. Outside of some lapses here and there due to human imperfection, comparatively, this great nation truly upholds this noble tradition.

In fact, the saying that, "whatever a man can do, a woman can do 'better'" holds much water in the Adirondack culture. Here, the domestic activities that revolve around keeping the house, cooking the food, and the care for and general upbringing of children, even babysitting, are the shared and collective responsibilities of the men and the women. Furthermore, education is a right, and its opportunity is equally afforded to both men and women on the same competitive ground.

Progressively, over the years, career opportunities have opened up for women. Hence, there is no barrier to one's choice of a life career. Yes, there are more or less no "glass ceilings" for women. Consequently, given the opportunity, they can rise to any appreciable height and position in the economic and engineering fields of life, in the medical and jurisprudence professions, in aviation and military careers, and even in the political corridors of power. Most stunning is the fact that the jobs of driving taxis, commercial or school buses, as well as trucks and trailers, thought to be strenuous and so not for "the weaker sex," so to speak, are not restricted to men alone, but women also do them very well. Again, the jobs of mail carriers, carpenters, electricians, automobile mechanics, restaurant owners, and related businesses are open equally to both genders. In all these areas mentioned and lots more, there are no exclusive considerations, and the competition therein between the men and the women is healthy in an atmosphere of healthy gender permissiveness, gender friendliness and gender equality.

On this note of equality between men and women vis-à-vis the history of women liberation in America, I must not fail to mention that, on the side of women, their deserved liberation, so to speak, has been an experience that has kept growing stronger and stronger and increasing in its strength by the day. In America, it is indeed a woman's world. Now, this increase in women's strength is mostly experienced and felt in the home between and among married couples.

In marriage therefore, if one is not careful, the picture could be such that seems to suggest a shift in power from the men to the women in the keeping and running of the house. Over here, you could hear of "honey-do-lists" prepared by the women and given to their husbands to go shop for some items for the home even in groceries and supermarkets. This is more common among retired men. By all means, it is good to keep them, in fact, all retirees, busy with domestic affairs. Otherwise, having been workaholics for such a long time in life, on retiring, they may have too much time in their hands without knowing what to do with it. Do I need to tell you that this state of "idleness" may be dangerous to the family, to the community and even to the society as a whole? Or have you forgotten the ad-

A HANDBOOK ON CULTURE SHOCK

age that: "An idle mind is the devil's workshop?" On this note, I want to salute and thank the Adirondack's retirees for volunteering in various places, such as helping the young people in schools, in faith formation classes and other Church help, in the soup kitchens, and other community development efforts. You are the best! You are the winners! Keep up the good work! Don't stop moving! Remember, work is not just a logical necessity, but, a practical need so as to keep young both in mind, heart and body.

To my shock, the power and strength of American women is to the extent that every now and then you hear stories of women who have kicked their boyfriends or husbands out of their houses whenever they feel such men are not behaving themselves. On this note, I had an experience of a man who came to the rectory one day to complain that he was thrown out of the house by his girlfriend the previous evening. And he had to sleep at the bus station. This man needed help with some money (handout) to travel from upstate New York, back to New York City.

Based on my native cultural experience, where men seem to have all the power in the home, I listened to this man with an unbelievable shock while he narrated his story to me. Perhaps, he wanted me to sympathize with him. But it was not funny to me. In fact, I was saying to myself: "Is this man not ashamed of himself to be telling me that his girlfriend whom he had lived with for almost a year with the intention of marrying her, threw him out of the house?" But hey! it is the culture. Experiences such as the one just narrated are not uncommon, and there is nothing wrong with a woman kicking a man out of the house. If men could do it in other cultures, then, why should women not do the same where they can do it? After all, "male and female, he created them" (Mt. 19: 4), and whatever a man can do, a woman can do, too.

What is more fascinating and mind-boggling in this comparative experience is not so much the variables nor the differences and similarities in the domestic responsibilities of the genders. It is not even in the power of women, but rather in the gender life careers. For instance, to the best of my knowledge, driving taxis seems to be an exclusive job of men in Nigeria, not to mention the carpentry, electrical, mechanical, cobbling, and masonry jobs. This status quo seems to me to be unjustifiable and troubling, questionable and unbecoming in a nation where the majority of its citizens are, comparatively speaking, economically very poor, and living in devastating and horrifying conditions. Hence, given this circumstance of comparative poverty, they (Nigerians) all should be doing whatever job is available to earn a living, gender difference, notwithstanding. This comparative experience, therefore, reveals a ridiculous irony. This irony is in the sense that the poor people of Nigeria should be the ones to do whatever work is available to earn a living instead of the Americans. Overall, there appears to be a kind of selection or exclusivity in life careers, particularly among the Etung people of Nigeria. No doubt, this selectivism in jobs contributes to the loitering, idling, and redundant lives of many, especially among students during holiday seasons. During this time, it is wasteful and sad to know that many students just stay at home doing nothing, or they just keep on traveling from one place to another waiting for the holiday season to be over so they can go back to school. For some of them, long holidays can become very boring and tiring.

A HANDBOOK ON CULTURE SHOCK

But given an organized society or a culture where there are holiday jobs of any kind and the young people are ready to take them, the results are obvious: Crime rates will be checked; loitering will be curtailed; poverty will be reduced; idleness may become a thing of the past; working for one's daily bread will be more fulfilling; there will be continuity and increase in production; and the rate of unemployment after school will give way to self-employment opportunities, to mention but a few. Not until the Nigerian government or society is able to appreciate and create opportunities for holiday jobs, the speed of development and related advantages will continue to remain far-fetched. This idea of creating holiday jobs can be done by the government encouraging individuals and organizations to create job opportunities for students who are out of school during the holiday period. Those willing to do this, should be given loans for agricultural programs, kindergarten or head-start education, building technology, road construction, restaurant business, you name it.

This idea of holiday jobs is a known phenomenon among the Adirondack people. Some students, during this season, even work for their parents, brothers, sisters, and relatives in their establishments or businesses, and they are paid for it accordingly.

This section on equality allows me to philosophize on another aspect of life that promotes and fosters the culture of equality. This aspect is on the *culture of titles.* By title here I mean, a formal appellation attached to a person or family by virtue of office, rank, hereditary privilege, noble birth, attainment, or as a mark of respect. From life experience, titles of this nature that are conferred on people and made to be recognized as such or as a must, create barriers and gaps between people. They separate and distance people both psychologically, physically and otherwise. They make room for the feelings of some complexes, be they superiority or inferiority complex. They breed and allow the mentality of worthiness or unworthiness, and the sense of belonging or not belonging to thrive. In general, the culture that overemphasizes or places very high premium on the recognition of titles in calling or addressing those concerned, is one that could be said to consciously or unconsciously stratify society into the feudalism of lord and vassal, master and servant. For lack of a better expression, permit me to say that this mentality of titles pushes the envelope too far on the recognition of the right of "freedom" or "freeborn" and the "son-of-the-soil ego." In fact, an excessive call for titling undermines equality and may be building walls than constructing bridges between and among people in their day-to-day interaction.

After all, titles are only "accidents" of birth and the privilege of opportunity. For the most part, they only tell people *who is who* and not *who is what*. They are many in our society today who are titleholders of one kind or another, but who do not actually deserve them. These undeserving titleholders range from kings, chiefs, mayors, doctors, lawyers, honorable politicians, engineers, the list could go on. Yes, our world is flooded with undeserving titleholders in almost every aspect, field and all works of life. Besides, come to think of it, when a title person dies, his "anklets" of title are cutoff so that he will return as he came with no excess luggage.

Before I rest my philosophy on the culture of titles, else I be read wrongly, permit me to make a disclaimer by sounding

A HANDBOOK ON CULTURE SHOCK

clearly and categorically that I do not intend to condemn any culture that upholds the mentality of title recognition. If any particular culture or some people in a given culture allow, accept, love, and expect you to recognize their titles when calling and addressing them, please, by all means, do it. In this way the path to respect and peace will be maintained by "giving to God what belongs to God, and to Caesar what belongs to Caesar." However, in the discipline at home, I advocate that the *mom* and the *dad* titles remain and should be recognized as such in all cultures of the world. Come what may, they deserve these titles and all the respect, obedience and honor that go with them, in spite of some circumstantial aberrations regarding some parents.

Now, having stated my personal thoughts and expressed my ideas, as much as possible on the subject under "siege," it is now time to illustrate and situate this philosophy within the cultural contexts of this book.

Generally speaking, Nigerian culture is a culture of titles. By this I mean, people are called and addressed by their titles and treated accordingly, especially in secular and ecclesiastical gatherings. At such occasions, you could hear those concerned being addressed, for instance as: "Your Excellency, Ambassador, Engineer, Doctor, Doctor, Professor John Akobi." Note that, all these titles are referring to just one person. Or in an ecclesiastical forum, you can also hear something such as: " His Lordship, Most, Right, Reverend, Doctor, Bishop Emmanuel Akor. All these titles are according to the offices and degrees such a person has attained and obtained. Moreover, do not be surprised that if in any gathering, one's title is skipped or omitted by the master of ceremony (MC) in introducing such title freaks, first, the title maniac will be highly offended. And then, he or she may call the attention of the MC to the one title that was omitted, even if they had called as many as six of the titles already.

As a Nigerian, who grew up in a culture that celebrates and excessively promotes titles, it was such a culture shock to me when I came to the U. S. and discovered that, over here, titles do not mean much to the people. In fact, for the most part, the Americans prefer to be called just or only by their first or last names, without any titles attached, such as Mr., Mrs., Dr., Barr., Engr., Mayor, Prof., and so on. For instance, Mayor John Lee, may prefer to be called, either John or Lee. By all means, this does not mean that they do not respect offices or recognize the achievements of each other. They respect and honor each other and give honor to whom honor is due. The point here is that, one's place or position in the society due to his or her chains of degrees does not matter much to the people and it does not affect the freedom and fundamental equality of all persons. I must say that this form or manner of address as experienced in my foreign culture, reduces and closes the gap, psychologically and physically, between "unequal" persons.

In addition, in order not to offend you or make you feel disrespected, as a newcomer into the Adirondack world, its people will usually ask you what you want to or how you prefer to be called. At least, I experienced this when I first arrived in America, from the parishioners of the parish of my apostolate in New York. And once I told them that I would prefer to be called, "Father Victor," that was it. From hence, I was known, called and addressed as such by all. However, every now and then, you find some people who just call me "Victor." I do not

A HANDBOOK ON CULTURE SHOCK

have any problem with this, since it is a culture that does not place too much emphasis on titles.

On a personal adjustment process, it was really difficult for me to adjust to the culture of calling people who were much older than me just by their first or last names, as they so desired and preferred. Initially each time I did, I felt some kind of guilt of disrespect that haunted me for sometime. But guess what! it did not take long, I joined the chorus and went with the flow.

On this American experience on the culture of titles, a friend of mine shared a troubling experience with me, which he had when he went to Nigeria to visit. Incidentally, this friend of mine had a girlfriend back in Nigeria, called Glory. During his visit, at one time he brought Glory to where he wanted to make a telephone call to the U.S. to say hello to some of his American friends. In the course of the telephone conversation, he kept on addressing the particular American whom he was talking to as, "Betty" without any titles as Mrs. this or that. Meanwhile, Glory kept listening attentively with such a discomfort. The discomfort was because of her suspicion that Betty must be her boyfriend's girlfriend in the U.S. especially as the telephone conversation ended with: "I love you honey!" This "I love you Betty," was like the last straw that broke the Camel's back. Glory became visibly sick, emotionally heartbroken, and looked as enraged and confused as ever. To cut a long story short, my friend told me that it was not possible to explain and convince his suspicious girlfriend that Betty was not his American girlfriend as such. What seemed to have calmed Glory down was that, when next he made another telephone call to Betty, he started addressing her (Betty) as

EQUALITY

Mrs. Jerry. He even had to ask her (Betty) about her husband (Jerry) in order to prove to his Glory that Betty was a married woman and he was simply a family friend to Betty's family. The point here is that, the problem of my friend's suspicious girlfriend was a cultural problem due to cultural discrepancies in regard to titles, and in terms of when they are to be used.

It was against the backdrop of my friend's experience that, when I went for a visit to Nigeria, I was very careful with what I said and how I said it in the presence of my Nigerian folks, each time I brought them to a public telephone booth to make a phone call to my U.S. friends. This was because I did not want to either scandalize them (my Nigerian folks) or make them begin to have different unbecoming ideas in their minds. For instance, whenever I was ending a telephone call with my American friends, as usual, they will say: "We (or I) love you!" I in turn, instead of saying: "I love you, too." I would rather say: "Me too." Or: "Likewise." Or: "I do, too." Yes, you gotta be smart, otherwise, you may need to explain yourself.

To my countrymen and women, therefore, I say to you, as you enter the United States be aware of this culture of no titles. And when you happen to be back home in Nigeria either for a visit or for a complete or final return, be conscious of the recognition of titles and be mindful of what you say and how you it. Failure to do this, may bring about untold consequences, not only like that of my friend's experience (just narrated above) but also at the level of respect, regard and honor among your people. Like I said and I recapitulate: "Give to God what belongs to God and to Caesar what belongs to Caesar," so that we would all enjoy peace in our homes, in our families and on earth.

A Handbook on Culture Shock

Perhaps, the foregone on the culture of titles gives me another opportunity to turn the searchlight of my reflection to another aspect of life that encourages or discourages the mentality of titles. This aspect has to do with how people of different cultures all over the world accept or do not accept *old age*, and how they feel when others think or say of them as old or young, as the case may be. It is an arguable fact that in some cultures of the world, some people like to be regarded or be referred to as old even though they may be young in chronological age. While in some other cultures, it is the reverse. In this reverse case, those concerned want to remain young forever and expect others to think about and look at them as such.

The Etung culture and its people in particular, are more inclined to the first option. That is, they are more accepting of old age and all that goes with it. That is why oftentimes, you hear people from this culture cautioning anyone who tries to insult them by saying or making such remarks as: "Be careful, I am your senior." Or: You gotta respect me because I am much more older than all of you here." Or: In my old age, you should all listen to me." Yes! the Etung people believe that: "Habet senectus autoritacem," that is: "Old age certainly has great influence."

In another context, someone introducing himself or herself may say to you: "I am chief (**Ntufam**)" this or that, or "I am His Excellency, His Eminence" His Royal Highness" this or that, or "I am Mr., Mrs., Madam" this or that, or "I am Dr., Barr., Engnr." this or that, and so on. Such people feel so good when they are referred to as the oldest in a group with their appropriate titles accorded them. This acceptance of old age, besides the fact that it is more honorable and people get excited getting old, it becomes more graceful when you come to understand that *old age connotes wisdom and it is regarded as the reward of a well led/lived and beautifully spent youthful life.*

True as it may be that comparatively speaking, the Adirondack people really keep, look and feel young even when some of them are far advanced in years, for the most part, the acceptance of old age is not a cultural practice. As someone rightly said: "They are afraid to get old." Oftentimes I had asked some of them who told me how old they were, to tell me what really makes them look so young. Some say it is genetic, others say it is in the mind, and still others say it is good medical environment, and so on.

In my deductive thought process in this regard, I am tempted to ask the following questions: Could it then be that because of the non-acceptance of old age in this culture, that is why its people do not want to be addressed by their titles? Is that also why even when some of them are introducing themselves to you, they just say their first or last names? Do they think that titles will make them look and feel so old? Would the knowledge of their titles make people to begin to guess how old they may be? On the other hand, is the non-acceptance of titles, a mentality that indicates and encourages personal humility? Could this phobia of getting old be responsible for why some of them get upset when they forget something?

Yes, in the Etung culture people do not pay attention to forgetfulness, or if they do, it is interpreted simply that the one who must have forgotten had so many things to think about at the same time, hence he/she naturally tends to forget some things along the line. In the Adirondack culture, forgetfulness

A Handbook on Culture Shock

is interpreted by some people as a sign of old age. It may even constitute a disturbing concern and a great source of worry. Hence, you often hear some of them whenever they forget something lamenting: "Oh! I am losing it." By my own thinking, I believe that forgetfulness is a natural human tendency that affects the young, the middle age and the old, at any place and time, though, it could also be a "senior moment."

Whatever is the reasoning, the point here is that, many in this culture do not want to be seen, referred to, or even thought of as old in spite of their chronological age. In fact, you can make someone's day when in the course of a conversation (and when the need arises), you tell the other person that he or she looks and sounds much more younger than his or her actual age. One commonly used expression to tell someone that he or she does not really look as old as his or her actual age is: "You don't look it." After saying this, watch out for a smile and expect to hear from the person: "Thank you!" To whom it may affect, sorry, as I have no choice than to speak up and sound this blunt truth to newcomers who may not be aware of this cultural expectation: "Always tell "them" that they look much younger, even if this amounts to 'flattery, mutual deceit; or addressing someone 'on borrowed robes.'" Of course, it doesn't cost anything to say a person looks younger if that would make the person's day or keep him or her happy. This is one of many simple life courtesies.

The bottom line message here is that, never you tell anyone that he or she is old, worse still, that a person looks older than his or her real age. Before continuing our travel and tour of these cultures, from the foregoing expose`, I invite you to reflect on the next question with me: Could this abhorrence to old age and its consequent conversational expectation, in addition to the culture of food compliments, concerned etiquette and other related matters, (as experienced in my foreign culture), constitute some of the justification for the "keep it real" mentality? This "keep it real" mentality is often expressed by some African-Americans in their daily conversations. And for them, anyone among them who tries to act otherwise, such a person is often referred to as "Uncle Tom." Yes, there is a story behind Uncle Tom. Go read the book: *Uncle Tom's Cabin* or ask those who know it or your "elders" and they will tell you. The scope of this book does not allow me to delve into that. But suffice me to say that, sometimes those concerned stretch and push this mentality (of keep it real) way too far.

On this issue of titles and their consequent names, if you are becoming bored, please, be patient with me, as I am presuming your permission again to point out another cultural practice among some Adirondack families, which I admire so much. I want to talk about the fascinating and thrilling practice and experience of the keeping, retention or retaining of maiden or family names, especially as it applies to women even after marriage. Straightaway, you would agree with me that in some cultures of the world, once a woman marries a man, she drops or loses her family name and takes that of her husband. For instance, former Miss Gina Lonergan, becomes Mrs. Gina Okonkwo after being married to Mr. John Okonkwo.

But in other cultures, the dropping of the family name by the woman even after marriage, is not encouraged. Thank God, that we are all entitled to our opinions and for the freedom of speech or expression. Hence, my reaction or reasoning to the dropping or losing of family names (especially after marriage), amounts to a personal provocation, irrespective of cultural practices. I see this mentality as "serfish," subjugating, unequal, regardless, overly controlling, domineering, exterminating and "deadly" to the woman and her family's name. Don't you also see a losing of genealogical connection and a breaking of related family bonds between the woman and her other family members? Does the woman become a piece of property sold to the man, which amounts to change of ownership and so allows for change of name? Certainly not! The best I can think and make of any authentic matrimonial union in this aspect is that, the woman only adds another name to her original family or maiden name in respect to and in honor of her husband. To this end, from the example above, Miss Gina Lonergan, should become known or addressed as, referred to and called Mrs. Gina Lonergan Okonkwo. Since in the mathematics of marriage, one plus one is one and so, *two* become *one*, in addressing John Okonkwo and Gina Lonergan together as husband and wife, (say in a formal gathering or on an invitation card), they can be addressed as: "Mr. & Mrs. John and Gina (Lonergan) Okokwo."

The advantages of the retention of maiden name, by my estimation are numerous. First, it is a sign of equality. Second, it makes the man (in this case husband) constantly aware that "Gina" did not just fall from the sky. She came from and has a family to return to from time to time. Third, there is the possibility of tracing family lines and connection to so many generations once the name "Lonergan" is mentioned anywhere. Fourth, I also see the free acceptance, the humble spirit of belonging or the proud connection, on the part of the woman, with her original family through the retention of the maiden name. These attitudes (of pride, no matter what) are very commendable. Fifth, if I need to remind you that common names, especially as occasioned by family connections, are links and rallying points of unity, oneness, togetherness, courage, strength, solidarity, (you name it), then be reminded. As I am "downloading" this reflection, I have no doubt in my mind that some people would feel uneasy with my ideas. Forgive my philosophy if it hurts you. It is not my intention to cause you any discomfort by stirring up a riot or inciting a feminist revolution in your culture.

By way of situating the discourse on the culture of dropping or retaining maiden or family names within the two cultures under consideration, in an economy of words, the fact is, the Etung culture completely falls within the first option of totally dropping the family name of the woman after marriage. While the Adirondack culture, for the most part, falls within the second option of retaining the family name of the woman even after marriage, especially among the elitist groups.

What an admirable and captivating experience it was and remains to me to hear of such names as the Hogans, the Potvins, Monahans, the Woods, the Murrays, the Loffredos, the Rockefellers, the Leobrunos, and so on! I am personally challenged by this cultural practice as experienced in my foreign culture. And I look forward to when I can break the ice, introduce the mentality and vanguard the culture of retaining family names among the Etung people, so that we, too, can begin to talk about, for instance, "the Owans." Perhaps, I would be able to present and argue my case from the standpoint of my personal philosophy on this issue as previously stated. Who knows, I may have a following.

On another note on this subject of equality, in the Adirondack culture, there seems to be an extension and a push beyond the borderlines of humanity to the inclusion of other creatures, such as animal pets.

PETS

Pets are animals kept for pleasure or companionship. No doubt, pets such as cats and dogs, birds and rabbits play an important role in the daily life of people. As much as it is known, it may be safe to say that, as either culturally permissible or as personally desired, some people have and keep pets that they very much cherish. Among other reasons, such pets may be kept for pleasure and companionship, to provide recreational and caring opportunities, or to keep one domestically busy. Of course, pets such as a special breed of dogs are also kept for protection, hence, the police dogs that are specially trained and used as detectors for investigative duties, such as searching for drugs and other criminally related crimes and offenders. On the other hand, pets can also be kept as mementos or souvenirs, as well as memorials to serve as remembrance of persons or events. These and so many other laudable reasons allow and justify the culture or practice of keeping pets.

Talking about police dogs and their detective abilities, I came face to face with this reality in the U.S. culture. Here, Canines, German shepherds, which can detect scents several thousand times more than humans, are trained to snoop in search of or to find marijuana, hashish, crack cocaine, heroine and amphetamines. Due to the unbecoming behaviors of some students in schools, there is a periodic drug sweep where canines (dogs) are used to sniff out boxes containing dangerous pills, controlled substances and contraband. These dogs search student lockers for illegal drugs and paraphernalia. The sight of a drug-sniffing canine homing in on the contents of a locker can be intimidating for students. This culture of canine search was such a shock to me that I praise the wisdom, ingenuity, and the ability of those concerned with training the canines. I also praise the canines for their conditional responses that yield the expected results of sniffing "contrabands."

True and praiseworthy as the idea of having and keeping pets may be, the Etung culture has a different concept, understanding, or view of this phenomenon. For instance, to the best of my knowledge, cats are kept in some homes to chase the mice and similar creatures away from the house. The English rabbits and birds such as parrots, are kept just for fun and related domestic engagements. Dogs are kept primarily to provide security for the home as watchdogs. Hence, some night security workers who believe in the fastness of the dogs and their high auditory senses use them as coworkers and hunting companions.

Talking about high auditory senses, the point is this, since dogs naturally and usually lie with their ears very close to the ground, they can easily hear the sound of movement from a far distance through the vibration of the ground. Hence, they howl or bark to alert people about a strange movement around the neighborhood, which may be dangerous, especially at very late hours of the night. With this alertness, brought about by the barking of the dogs, those concerned get ready for security actions. Of course, the barking also awakens the night security workers in Nigeria and other places, who most times are asleep. Some hunters also use dogs for gaming activities because they run very fast. They can very easily pursue, overtake, and catch their prey.

As far as where the pets lie down or sleep, especially at night, is concerned, they do not enjoy any particular privilege or special attention in my native culture. To a large extend, they do not enjoy any medical attention. Except in very rare cases, they can pick up food anywhere. The cats and dogs roam about the streets and eat grasshoppers and lizards, feces, and related wastes. Among all this, the English rabbits and birds, particularly parrots, enjoy a more caring attention in the sense that they are mostly protected in cages outside the houses and fed with selected foodstuff. These latter are the pets that really provide the companionship and fun for some people who care for them.

At this point, I remember a conversation I had sometime with someone in my host culture. Since the conversation was centered on the culture of pets, I mentioned to the person that, in my native culture we don't keep pets as such. Without looking at it as a cultural circumstance, this person said to me that, the reason why we don't keep pets is that, since my people do not have enough food to eat themselves, they cannot afford to feed the pets. Does this reasoning remind you of similar possible remarks mentioned in this book? Yes, sometimes people will always attempt to give interpretations and explanations to cultural attitudes and behaviors whether it is their own culture or not, and irrespective of how others concerned will feel (about the remarks). These are some of the culture shocks that this book talks about and sets out to expose with the hope that people will become more culture friendly, in what they say and do to others.

EQUALITY

What a shocking experience it was for me to discover that in some parts of the world, pets are not just pets, but they have been humanized with almost all the attributes and characteristics of human beings. To put this experience in perspective, the Adirondack culture afforded me the opportunity to see beyond "pets" to something of "children" and "real friends," "true companions" and "compatible associates" that may even become rivals in relation to the treatment of human beings.

Unbelievably, pets are treated more or less like human beings with all the rights and privileges that go with such status. Thus, they live inside the houses and sleep in very carefully made areas, or in some cases, they sleep on the same beds with their owners. They eat very good food and drink well-treated water. In fact, though rarely because of its expensiveness, in extreme cases, they are covered by insurance policies. No doubt, they enjoy good medical attention with special doctors or veterinarians, who keep their medical history. From all indications, they also suffer from all the sicknesses and diseases that human beings suffer, and so are treated accordingly. It is not surprising, therefore, to hear someone in this culture telling you that his or her pet is suffering from diabetes, dysentery or upset stomach, hyperthyroidism, high blood pressure, migraine, and other related health conditions. At the end of the day through medical recommendation, these pets can be placed on daily medication that costs a fortune. In serious cases, they can have X-rays and undergo operations or surgeries by special veterinarians, with prayer request by their owners. There is no gain in saying that, even in the United States, some pets receive better medical care than poor people without health insurance do.

A Handbook on Culture Shock

In relation to family structures, these pets are more or less counted among the children of the family, or they are the only children of some families. In the obituary announcement of some deceased persons, the list of survivors may include the names of their pets. Depending on the gender, a pet is referred to as, "he" or "she" and not "it." Depending on the seasons, some of them have clothes to match and fit the weather conditions. In fact, every now and then, you run into somebody on the street with a pet wearing matching clothes. Perhaps, one may think that I am simply making this up or exaggerating my point. In *The Post-Star* of March 13, 2005, it is reported that: "The wildly successful world of canine couture is nothing if not outrageous. How else to explain the global popularity of doggy dresses, vests, bikinis, kimonos, hoodies, booties, rain slickers, tennis outfits and tuxedos? How else to explain a $5,000 alligator-skin dog collar and leash set or a $350 Fido-sized Burberry trench coat? 'It's phenomenal. Absolutely phenomenal', says owner of Dog & Friends, a Florida boutique. 'We sell a dozen pieces of clothing a day now.'" The article even shows a picture of a dog, with the followings words written under it: "Rizzo wears an outfit from a line of dogwear made by Orlando designer Kara Kono. Dog attire is becoming a large industry as more owners – of small dogs, especially – dress up their four-legged friends." This argument becomes more compelling when you come to know that boldly colored doggy dresses and vests are making their way to Hollywood.

Guess what! pets generally can also be adopted like human beings with all the necessary inspections and paperwork. Some people have entertainment rooms for their pets where they have a television or radio to keep the pets company when the owners are away from home. They also enjoy the care and attention of babysitting or pet sitting, sometimes with the provision of pee-pee pads. On this note of care and love for pets, I remember having a chat with a friend who said that, in some obsessive cases, some people have been tempted to write their wills in favor of their pets. Personally, I consider this an overstatement.

Over here, too, it is not difficult to know those who have and keep pets, such as dogs and cats, whether they have the pets with them or not at the time. Yes, the hairs from dogs and cats on the clothes and the inside of cars of some people who are "parenting" or "befriending," them cannot be hidden. These hairs are oftentimes, a visible "betrayal." I am not saying that, these hairs cannot be picked up by "innocent" people from other homes with pets. But the hairs remain an indication, or evidence and the first sign of "suspicion."

This brings me to a personal experience: I was in the rectory one day, and this telephone call came in for me. It was from a parishioner who was traveling south to Florida for a winter getaway. He needed someone to baby-sit his cat (pet sitting, they call it) while he was away in Florida. With all good intent and genuine purpose, he wanted to find out if I could do that for him since he felt that I was always alone and so I may need company. Initially, I thought he was joking, but before long it dawned on me that he was serious. I politely told him that I was not a pet fan and begged him to excuse my cultural orientation if my declining was offensive to him. That ended the negotiation. It was on this line of thought that I came to know of the culture of boarding pets when the pet owners are away from home for some time. Pet boarding, then, must have been

A HANDBOOK ON CULTURE SHOCK

what the dear parishioner in question did eventually, or he may have found someone else to help baby-sit the cat he wanted me to pet-sit for him. Besides my cultural orientation, I do not feel comfortable carrying pet's hairs around, on my clothes or in my car, which would have been unavoidable had I accepted to pet-sit the cat.

Listen to this! A story was once told of a new associate pastor in a parish where the friendly culture of pets was the order of the day. At a very late hour of the night, he got a telephone call from a dear woman parishioner. This woman wanted a priest to go to her house and administer the Sacrament of Anointing or the Last Rite to her only "child," Tom, who was at the point of death. The zealous associate pastor quickly rolled out of his comforter and hopped down from his bed to get ready to go to the woman's house. Incidentally, the pastor was awakened by the sound of the same telephone ring. While he was still trying to go back to sleep, he heard the associate pastor opening his door to go out. Being so caring and protective of him, the pastor came out of his suite to find out where his associate was going at that late hour of the night. As the dialogue went on between them, the pastor knew who the parishioner was and told his associate to go back to bed because the said "child," Tom, was not a human being, but a dog. However, he told his associate to return the woman's call and to say that he would say a prayer for Tom since it was such an "unholy" hour to go out. This was pastoral diplomacy, (by the pastor), and it is necessary in some circumstances, such as the one in question concerning the woman parishioner who was in need of some pastoral care for her only "child," Tom.

Unfortunately, Tom died, and a prayer session was organized for his burial with all the memorial flowers. Did I hear you say "crazy?" Please, take back that word and be open-minded. This is a way of life of some people, and a cultural practice that has stood the test of time, and has been of great help to many people, given their life's situations and circumstances. Remember the sayings: "Do not judge someone until you have gone with him two miles." "It is he who wears the shoes that knows where it pinches." "One man's meat is another man's poison." Finally, "one man's trash is another man's treasure." An old Indian proverb also says: "You should not judge unless you have walked in another's moccasins." Yes, most times we have no idea of another's pain, another's struggle, or another's battle with personal demons or human faults and failures. These pieces of advice need to be borne in mind as you work in and walk through the pathways of the ways of life of other people. After all, to hit the point home on this culture of pets, it is worth knowing that even the President of the United States, George Bush, takes his dog on many of his official trips. He is often photographed with the dog. What a lucky dog! By and large, bear in mind that no culture is superior to another; rather, every culture is superior unto itself with all its practices.

The next story may sound funny to some people, but it did happen. It actually threatened the relationship between a boy and a girl who were in love with each other. The former, my nephew, hails from the Etung culture in Nigeria, and the latter is from England. One day, I had a telephone call from him while he was in Europe. He said to me: "Father, my girlfriend and I have a serious problem, and I'm going to end the relationship if she does not stop doing what she is often fond of

A HANDBOOK ON CULTURE SHOCK

doing." At this point, I asked him: "What's it that she does that you do not like?" He continued: "Father, she has a dog as a pet. She kisses this dog mouth-to-mouth. Each time we are together, she will kiss the dog and immediately come to kiss me. Sometimes, she even wants me to kiss the dog. I have told her repeatedly that this attitude is not culturally acceptable in the culture where I come from, but she will not listen. I have, therefore, come to a point where I can't stand this any longer, and so I am no longer interested in the relationship. Father, to tell you the truth, I love this girl and I don't wanna lose her. Please, what do I do?" Advise!

This question really put me on the spot. I thought of saying to him: "When in Rome do as the Romans do," but I immediately discovered the contextual flaw of this statement. In fact, this saying was **non sequitur** in this particular context. At the end of the day, I did advise him to go with his girlfriend to see a priest for counseling or to attend an acculturation workshop with his girlfriend where issues of similar cultural differences are usually addressed. I hope he did because I did not hear from him again on this issue.

From what has been said, it would simply be stating the obvious to say that whatever applies to the treatment of a human person also applies to the treatment of a pet. For instance, to abuse, maltreat, or treat carelessly and even endanger the welfare of a pet could result in prosecution. No kidding! This fact can be proven from an article in *The Post-Star* of Thursday, May 13, 2004, titled "Woman Jailed in Animal Cruelty Case." It states that: "A 45-year-old Lake George woman was arrested Wednesday on animal cruelty charges after her two dogs died of heatstroke in the back of her pickup truck while she worked,' police said.

"She was charged with two misdemeanor animal cruelty charges under state agricultural and market law, for failure to provide proper sustenance for the two dogs, one male and one female.

"Police said that since December she had been leaving her two border collies in the back of her pickup truck in the parking lot of Glens Falls Hospital. The dogs were kept in separate crates and the back of the truck was covered with a cap.

"'The dogs died from heatstroke when the temperature in Glens Falls reached 87 degrees,' police said."

True as it may be that animals or pets should also be treated with some feelings for them, the issue of their death, either deliberately or out of carelessness on the part of their owners, does not attract any prosecution in Etung culture. At least, none that I am aware of. Therefore, the case of prosecution just related here was both shocking, revealing, startling, and profoundly thought provoking to me.

I just cannot help not mentioning another group of pets that may also send goose bumps on your body for those not familiar with or not acceptable of it. Would it surprise or shock you to further hear that some people even have snakes as pets? These snakes are also cared for and often fed with frozen rats and other food items. Please, don't get me going on this. Based on my native cultural orientation, this realization had a shuddering effect on me. Of course, every now and then you hear of accidents between snakes and their owners, the latter being the victim or sufferer.

Without denying the reality of domesticated snakes in some homes by some people in Nigeria, I must say that the scenarios

A Handbook on Culture Shock

and reasons are not the same in both cultures. More specifically, some Nigerian magicians do keep snakes and similar creatures, which they use as sources of their magical powers. Snakes are not kept as pets per se. The occasions of their mesmerizing magical displays with snakes are full of charm, filled with and marked by signs and wonders in the totality of their awesomeness.

On another gradation, all cultures of the world admire and cherish environmental decency, recreation and relaxation. Consequently, people do whatever they can to avail themselves of these exercise or realities. Because of cultural differences occasioned by development or advancement through the availability of recreational facilities, these realities are not the same and or not found everywhere in the world. A closer look at some of them and what goes on would be of enlightening importance. This is what the content of Chapter 10 is all about, particularly in the revealing experience of my newfound culture, which I consider worthy of emulation.

NOTES

[1] Santich, Kate. "Fetching fashion: Canine couture becomes the norm." *The Post-Star, March 13, 2005*

[2] Reiss, Stephen. "Woman Jailed in Animal Cruelty Case." *The Post-Star,* May 13, 2004.

11

SANITATION AND RECREATIONAL ENGAGEMENTS

In every culture, there are some personal or group engagements that are equally important and useful to the people concerned. These may not be strictly cultural demands but are perceived by individual members of that culture as worthwhile for their personal good in terms of good health, physical fitness, up-keep, and relaxation. This personal good is hygienically, socially, and psychologically profitable. The latter two (social and psychological) become more important and necessary in a culture of individualism and "workaholism," where people become worker bees and their jobs keep them separated and apart from each other. This is a daily reality, especially in America, where work becomes home and home becomes work. Even parents flee homes invaded by the pressures of work, and the workplace seems transformed into a strange kind of surrogate home. This chapter will explore two areas of importance, which allow people to take time off (work) for personal clean-up exercise, engage in socials and have some recreational moments.

ENVIRONMENTAL SANITATION OR CLEANLINESS

"Cleanliness is next to Godliness," so the saying goes. In another instance, it is often said: "First impressions always stick with you." Furthermore, in an epistemological context it is said: "From the known you go to the unknown." I am imploring the implicative benefits of these sayings and expressions to give just one message that: The cleanliness of an external environment of someone can, for the most part, tell you how the whole home may look, including the inside. No wonder Anne Graham Lotz in her book, *The Joy of My Heart,* in "Meditating Daily on God's Word," gives a personal reflection on cleanliness thus: "I am not a good housekeeper. But motivated by the thought that my house is His home also, I try hard to keep it clean and neat. It is not professionally decorated, but it is as pleasing to the eyes as my time and budget would allow. I want those who walk through my door to know that the Lord God lives here. And I hope the reality of His presence is evident to all by the beauty of the outward appearance and an inner atmosphere of warmth and love."

To a large extent, the cleanliness of a people can be seen in the cleanliness of their environment. For this decency to be achieved, there must be first, the *thought* and then programs, vehicles, and tools that would help in the realization of a litter-free environment. In this way, waste, junk, and related materials are properly directed and thrown away through recommended and available disposals, such as garbage disposals or trashcans. These facilities can be for both private and public services or use. In the end, they ensure a clean and welcome environment for the hygienic condition and steady health of the people and for the attraction of onlookers or passersby. Remember, a clean environment ensures a healthy and wealthy life, hence the saying: "Health is wealth."

The Nigerian culture encourages and promotes the lifestyle that ensures clean environments. Hence, there is what is known as a weekly or monthly "environmental sanitation" program. As much as I can remember, some time ago this exercise was a unanimous and simultaneous national concern, which was being observed accordingly. But for now, while remaining a national recommendation, it has become the concern of individual states in terms of its implementation and execution. In addition, at a limited level concerning the private practice of environmental cleanliness, you can find garbage disposals in some homes and at the entrances of some supermarkets, at some gas stations, and around some government offices.

As much as I know, there are no garbage disposals in or along the streets and they are rarely seen at motor parks and parking lots. Even in places where these disposals are found, the question about where all the mess is eventually emptied or dumped in an organized and acceptable system would be very difficult to answer. At least, I know that in some places, they are dumped anywhere, especially in gutters, where during the rainy season they are transported or carried and left to litter other environments. At worse, they are emptied into streams or rivers from which many people drink. Your guess of water pollution and its consequent health endangerment may be better than my own. Without a systematic and organized way of disposing of the waste, more often than not, the waste still comes back to the environment. The picture is like that of a vicious circle or the proverbial **"Abiku**,- coming and going."

The Adirondack culture also takes environmental cleanliness and sanitation very seriously. Being a more advanced culture, the collection of garbage and eventual disposal is well organized and planned. Here, besides the private effort for the cleanliness of homes and houses, there are also facilities that encourage and promote public sanitation. Thus, at street corners, parking lots, and other public places, you would find large garbage containers, and into these containers, the public is allowed to drop "whatever" waste needs to be disposed of. In addition, on a very fascinating note, people bring out the waste from their houses and leave it in containers by their driveways on a weekly basis. These containers, containing waste are in turn, picked up by the garbage collectors from the garbage companies and taken to big facilities called "trash plants." There the wastes are dumped and are eventually disposed of by burning.

It is against the backdrop of the culture of environmental sanitation that you would appreciate why even a dog's poop, is usually scooped by its owner. Thus, dogs' owners who take out their dogs for a walk also carry along with them pooper scoops or baggies to pick up the mess by the dogs left on peoples' lawns, driveways, streets, yards and compounds. And it is against the law of environmental cleanliness for one not to *pick up*. Offenders or violators can be sued or prosecuted. Even car owners have garbage bags or trashcans in their cars into which they put whatever waste there is. It is also against the law of environmental sanitation to throw away any garbage through the window of cars. Even though, every now and then you see some people, especially cigarette smokers throwing away the bottom of cigarette sticks through the windows of their cars, it still remains an act of indiscipline.

A Handbook on Culture Shock

Interestingly also, it is important to know that in Nigeria, garbage, such as glass, plastic, tin, and paper are thrown carelessly almost everywhere. Sometimes, however, you may come across some scrap collectors of particularly bottles, who go from house to house to buy them from people. For the most part, this situation is different in the United States. It was among the Adirondack people in Upstate New York that I came face-to-face with the conservative and useful culture of *recycling*. The practice is this: Glass, plastic, and aluminum, which are considered as garbage, are recycled in gigantic recycling plants for further use. In this way, the original raw materials used to manufacture the containers that carry such goods are not wasted. In fact, some people even go along the streets and roads in search of and to pick up such garbage (glass, plastic, and aluminum), either in fulfillment of their duties in the responsibility of *"adopt a highway program"* or in order to bring them to a collection point and claim a few cents. Even used engine oil from motor cars are used for recycling purposes but at no charge.

Along this line of recycling, there is also the culture of shredding papers in shredders or shredding machines. The shredded papers also go through the recycling process. In this way, the papers are eventually used again. Personally, I was simply in love with the shredding machine because it helped me to get rid of any unwanted paper or document that I no longer wanted to keep around, such as junk mails, which were always coming through my mailbox. This could be because such documents either littered my suite or they were pieces of information that were unnecessary or useless, or still, too sensitive to live hanging around for too long, else they fall

Sanitation and Recreational Engagements

into wrong hands or someone stumbles into and sees them, thereby getting my private information. I remember that each time I was exercising the culture of shredding, one of the parish staff would say to me: *"Shred the evidence."* Of course and perhaps, little did he know that I always took that remark seriously. And I would quietly add to the remark by saying: "Always shred the evidence because, you never know what could happen tomorrow or what the future holds for you." After all, we all have our secret lives and no one can deny this fact. Who can be saved? So, if you have it, always use the shredder. And if you don't, then, go get one if you can afford it. It helps! either immediately or down the road. You never know!

True as this may be, before shredding any document, be it a junk mail or whatever, try to double check it to make sure that it is not or it is no longer a relevant piece of information. If you fail to do this, you may end up shredding an important document or mail that you may regret later. I am saying this because, there was a time I almost shredded my tax refund check that was mailed to me from the Department of the Treasury Financial Management Service in a thick khaki envelope. When I got it on my mailbox, it looked like one of those junk mails. While I was heading for the shredder, I decided to take a second look at the envelope to find out what it was all about. Behold! it was the very thing I had been waiting for, for weeks – my tax refund. So, for your own good, always double check your documents or mails before sentencing them to death by shredding.

Advantageously, the recycling process reduces the manufacturing hazards and saves the cost of production, more or less. Overall, it can be said that the economic advantage of the

A HANDBOOK ON CULTURE SHOCK

culture of recycling is that, the manufacturing of the recyclable materials is made cost-effective. The sanitary good is that the garbage is not littered along the streets so much, therefore, ensuring a clean environment.

True and attractive as this method of waste removal may be, do not forget that the people pay heavily for all the services. They are not free. Yes, if you want convenience and an easy life, you must pay the price. The implicative demand or cost for this service properly fits into the musical context of an American musician, Syleena Johnson, who sang this phrase in one of her songs: "You wanna play the boss, then you gotta pay the cost; You wanna be the king, then you gotta wear the crown," and so on.

Finally, since more often than not, it is the first impression that always sticks with you and based on the philosophical wisdom of moving from the known to the unknown, the external outlook of an environment has a lot to say about the overall cleanliness of a people. This becomes more urgent considering the fact that many who see the outside may not have the opportunity of seeing the inside. Therefore, the outside speaks for and bears an eloquent testimony to the inside environment. This cultural attitude remains challenging and worthy of emulation.

BALLOON FESTIVAL

It is probably against the backdrop of one who is a bookworm or bookish and overly studious that this saying came about: "All work and no play makes Jack a dull boy." Again, from an economic point of view, the economic "law of diminishing returns" can be paraphrased and interpreted in this context as: With so much time and manpower, you experience a decline in productivity. This is because the physical and mental energies needed for the job are waning due to overuse and related multitasking engagements. When this begins to happen and you realize that you are becoming less productive, you should then know that it's high time you got away to get some fresh air. You cannot keep moving all the time in one direction or doing the same thing; otherwise, you experience boredom and burnout. You cannot keep staying at one place, especially indoors, or you experience claustrophobia. Remember also that variety is the spice of life. It is in the realization of these facts that all cultures of the world have various recreational engagements, sporting events, and facilities where people meet and hang out for some fun and relaxation. It is also against this understanding that the busy Americans can't wait for summer seasons to get away from work, relax, travel places, and have fun.

At this point, as suggested by the subheading, **Balloon Festival**, I want to relate what this is all about and my experience of it in the Adirondacks culture, on their annual Adirondack Balloon Festival celebration. This festival has to do with flying hot-air balloons as aircraft from airports or from other open areas that have good landing space and comfortable topography. By way of description, these particular aircraft are solidly woven big baskets with big balloons tied to them with strong ropes. Between the baskets and the balloons, there are carefully built and suspended propane tanks, which when operated make enough hot air to fill or inflate the balloons. With this hot air, the balloons are inflated and made to fly. While airborne, with the pumping of more hot air into the balloons by the pilots through a device, (propane tanks), the balloon aircraft rises higher and flies faster. Depending on the volume and space, each basket onto which a balloon is tied has a capacity of carrying four to five people. They are ridden or flown by standing inside the baskets and holding your hands on the ropes that bind the baskets and the balloons together.

Until I came to the Adirondacks, I had never heard of nor seen anything like a balloon festival where people are airborne in balloon baskets. Here was I in Upstate New York, not only to hear and see, but also to have a personal experience of flying in one of them. This development took place on Sunday, September 21, 2003. On this wonderful and thrilling occasion at the grand finale of the Adirondack Balloon Festival, I was talked into trying the experience, and I found myself hopping into a balloon, in the company of two others including the pilot. Guess what! We were to fly to an unknown destination contingent or depending on the direction of the wind. Wow! My feelings were rather mixed. Before even hopping into the designated basket, I was visibly very nervous and uneasy. Within a short time, my initial state of heebie-jeebies turned out to be very exciting when we were airborne. Though it was cool, it was also very frightening and scary to look downward from the balloon.

The landing of this particular balloon was to be another very frightening episode. While trying to land, the balloon almost got tangled up in the branches of a tree. I prayed to God to help us land safely. At this point, I was wondering what I would tell my parents or my bishop in case I survived an accident. As if that was not enough, a car pulled over at the corner of the road on the very spot where we were to land. Trouble!

We started yelling at the driver and got very close to it before the car was driven away from our landing spot. My thanks go to the expertise of the pilot, Robert "Bob" Dick. O boy! Talk of roller-coaster experiences; this adventure was one of them. When we disembarked, I breathed a sigh of relief and said: "Thank God, it is all over and I am out of here!" On the whole, this development was quite a shocking exercise and a delight to me to have personally had the experience of flying in a hot air balloon, a thing that even many "Adirondacks" have not done. Again, you never know with the U.S. high-tech. Thanks to the Monahans and the Hogans for arranging and affording me the opportunity to have this experience.

SPORTS — FOOTBALL VERSUS SOCCER

I would like to acknowledge as well as draw your attention to the fact that the word "sports" has so many connotations. In this section on recreational engagements, I intend briefly to talk about sports as an active involvement involving physical exercise and having a set form and body of rules. Particularly, I would like to point out a nuance in the nomenclatures of "football" and "soccer" that posed some confusion to me when I first arrived in the United States.

In Nigeria, the most favorite and common sport is soccer. And many Nigerians are either soccer players or its great and "fanatical" fans. As a person, I played soccer for about 18 years, and so, soccer is one of my favorite sports. I know its form as being played with the foot, leg, or feet, as the case may be. That is why, for many Nigerians, they call it either football or "soccer." The name soccer becomes another synonym when you also understand that "football" means a game played on a

A Handbook on Culture Shock

rectangular field with net goals at either end in which 2 teams of 11 players each maneuver a round ball mainly by kicking or butting or by using any part of the body except the arms and hands in attempt to score goals.

In the United States, as it is becoming the case in other parts of the world, sports as a recreational engagement is not a pastime exercise. But over here, it is simply blown out of proportion. I think it would not be an overstatement if one says that sports has become like a religion. For most people, because of their fanaticism, it is even the first religion. Its material benefits and related advantages are seriously attractive and overwhelming. In fact, many multimillionaires in the United States are sportsmen and sportswomen. My concern here is not to dwell on a reflective or intellectual gymnastics about the economic advantages or dividends of U.S. sports. This section has been necessitated by the shock and confusion I had in understanding and accepting the expression *"football"* as it is used in the U.S. context vis-à-vis "football" or soccer in the Nigerian context.

Having been born and brought up in Nigeria where the expressions, football and soccer are used interchangeably or synonymously, this posed a problem to me when I first arrived in the United States. Thus, what the Americans call football is quite different from that in Nigeria, both in terms of its form and rules of the game. To put the picture in perspective, what the Nigerians call, football is generally called and commonly known as soccer, in the United States. As much as I do know, the form of football played in the United States is not played in Nigeria, and so it is not known by most Nigerians.

It is because of this initial ignorance that when I arrived

SANITATION AND RECREATIONAL ENGAGEMENTS

in Hudson Falls, New York, and a family wanted to find out from me what kind of sports I like, I immediately said to them: "Football!" As if that was not enough, I went on to tell them that I even played football for 18 years. Little did we know that we both had different understandings of the concept or name, "Football." A couple of days later, I had an invitation from the same family to go out with them and watch a football game. I was all excited because I thought it was a soccer game. To my greatest disappointment or dismay and disillusionment, I got to the field of play and realized that the kind of football I meant was not what was being played. It was only then that I understood what the Americans call "football." I then said to myself: "Thank God, they call it American football. Yes, only in America!" So, for newcomers into the U.S. culture and based on where you are coming from, be mindful of the distinction between "soccer" and "American football." Finally, one question that I have still not been able to answer is: Why do they call it football, when 95 percent of the game is played with the hands? Well, my only consolation is that it is called "American football." "They better!" Yes, only in America!

Ideas become ideologies when they are communicated from one mind or person to another. And they have consequences *only* because they are created, embraced, and lived out in *persons*. Knowledge becomes experience when one person shares it with a wider audience. It is through the combination of ideas, ideologies, knowledge, and experience that we can move the world forward for the better. It is because of my personal conviction of this philosophy that I feel bound in conscience to share some of the fruits of an acculturation workshop I attended when I first arrived in the United States

A Handbook on Culture Shock

in preparation to immerse myself into the American culture. The workshop was not only revealing, but also armed me for future eventualities as I made my way through the paths of the U.S. soil with all of its cultural complexities. The fruits of this workshop are dealt with in the next chapter of this book.

NOTES

[1] Lotz, Anne Graham. *The Joy of My Heart: Meditating Daily on God's Word.* Nashville, TN: J. Countryman, 2004, 16.

12

FRUITS OF ACCULTURATION WORKSHOP

PREAMBLE, GENERAL GOAL, AND OBJECTIVES

PREAMBLE

By way of historical origin, in this context, an acculturation workshop is a workshop that arose from **Maryknoll's Cross-Cultural Services** (acronym CCS), which began about twenty five years ago as the *Center for Mission Studies* to be of service to the USA Church engaging in and promoting education, research and communication of *mission*. Since its inception, it has effectively and efficiently responded to the needs of the time in light of the changing face of mission. Presently, CCS is a dependable resource for missionary organizations, dioceses, religious congregations, Catholic Universities, Lay Volunteer Organizations and individuals who seek a smooth and balanced cultural immersion. The services offered here include, preparation of candidates for overseas mission, cross-cultural immersion experiences, international field placements, and re-entry programs for those returning to the U.S. (after years of missionary work away from home). These services also take into consideration and organize cultural diversity workshops for groups desiring to grow in inter-cultural sensitivity, and acculturation workshops to facilitate the adjustment process of those who have recently arrived in the USA.

A number of experiences shared by some international priests brought to America either to minister to immigrant parishes, or to make up for the shortfall in American priests, or for training in advanced university programs, strengthen the urgency and need for acculturation workshop. Besides the fact of its benefits in cultural immersion, it also helps in proper inculturation. To this end, the religious worker for instance, becomes better equipped to, not only understand and assimilate the changing face of American Catholicism, but also to give the American faithful a better vision of the universality of the Church, and possibly introduce new liturgical styles in parish life. In this scenario, numerous voices in American Catholic community speak of some problems with foreign-born priests. Among these problems are the arguable difficulties in spoken English, cultural differences, which sometimes cause misunderstandings with American priests and laity, and an ecclesiology which is often termed pre-Vatican. Quite apart from any of these arguments, given the relentless pressures on bishops to find priests, more internationals will most likely, be brought here in the future.

Granted this, if international priests are brought in, there is need for some guidelines and orientations. It is not enough that international priests be endorsed by the sending bishops, major superiors, and given a written contract that spells out du-

A Handbook on Culture Shock

ties, salary, and duration of service. In agreement with others of like minds, I suggest that they be given some acculturation period on arrival before beginning ministry. In addition, there should also be an orientation program sponsored by the diocese or religious community for foreign priests and religious when they arrive, and if possible, everyone should be assigned a mentor or the one concerned should look for a mentor for the first few years. In reality, many of those concerned with flying in international religious workers do not provide much orientation and mentorship. It is my conviction that, the adoption of this program will have far reaching and priceless benefits for both parties, such as the improvement in the understanding of the American culture and of the local diocese or parish. A second benefit is that it will help with language and contextual preaching skills. And third, it will have successful and satisfying ministry. To allow the new arrivals to find their own support network, is risky both to the neophyte and the benefiting "Church."

In this chapter, I intend to make a partial presentation and share some of the fruits of an acculturation workshop I attended when I first came to the U. S. It is my hope that it would be culturally informative, historically revealing, and realistically preparatory, especially for newcomers to the U.S. cultural environment and other cultures of the world. My approach will be to relate the day-to-day issues that were handled and matters that were discussed by the presenters in all the stormy, exciting, and interactive sessions. Nevertheless, this presentation is far from being a verbatim reproduction or a Xerox production of the ideas of the facilitator and presenters at the exercise.

Based on what I gathered from this exercise, permit me to

FRUITS OF ACCULTURATION WORKSHOP

boldly say that the need for an acculturation program or workshop for neophytes (newcomers), cannot be overemphasized nor traded in for any other option. One of the worst things that can happen to you is to bump into and interact with a foreign cultural structure or setting, uninformed and so unprepared for the unexpected but inevitable culture shocks. Without any doubt in my mind, you will be surprised and taken completely unawares by some cultural enigmas. The unavoidable shocks therein could appear like a double-edged sword, cutting sharply and deeply on both sides. They may be so overwhelming that you may be left either completely frustrated in the face of disappointment, dumbfounded in excitement, or lost in some kind of ecstatic euphoria. They could be deeply devastating or profoundly confusing. You may even look stupid before your audience. Furthermore, these initial feelings could result in the development of some complexes and unwarranted phobias that may conspire to give rise to some funky or depressive moments.

For missionaries, especially priests or any religious worker, an acculturation workshop is not only necessary, but also a "MUST." This program, which facilitates the acculturation experience, should not be negotiated as a choice. If it is subjected to any negotiation at all, it should be preferred as a necessary exercise and a fundamental and compulsory cross-cultural program for the newcomer. This exercise should be carried out or attended before the actual and concrete encounter with the host culture. Though this program does not promise complete culture shock avoidance, it deals with culture shock by preparing the participant for the expected and unexpected cultural differences with all the realities that are involved. The partici-

A Handbook on Culture Shock

pant is also assisted in identifying, building, and developing healthy culture shock absorbing valves, attitudes, and tools to help him or her move with and through culture shocks, as he or she navigates his or her way in and through the newfound cultural environment.

I thank the pastor and the beloved parishioners of St. Mary's/ St. Paul's Church, Hudson Falls, New York, who provided me with the wonderful and priceless opportunity for the acculturation program in perspective. This exercise took place from August 17–22, 2003, at Ossining, New York, in the community house complex of the Maryknoll Fathers and Brothers. I thank also the facilitator of this program, Sr. Therese McDonough, MMM, through whose coordination and tutorials from her wealth of experience the exercise was worth the name. I thank also my fellow participants who provided the company and fraternal fellowship throughout the course of the workshop. They were Rev. Joseph Kabali and Rev. Athanasius Kasekende, both from Uganda. Others were Sr. Norma Pocasangre from El Salvador and Sr. Sia Temu from Kenya.

With the permission of the facilitator of the workshop, I boldly state the general goal and carefully thought-out objectives of the program.

GENERAL GOAL

- To assist religious and priests in adjusting to their new environment and their ministry in the United States of America (USA).

OBJECTIVES

- To offer a forum for sharing recent ministerial and cultural experiences in the USA.

- To increase an awareness of the way one's culture has shaped him or her and to identify some common elements of all cultures.
- To assist in becoming critically conscious of both one's own culture and the USA culture(s) in which they now live and to deal with differences effectively.
- To facilitate a personal integration into a Church and society that has cultural complexes.
- To understand the acculturation process and identify how it affects one personally.
- To look at ethnocentrism and the challenge this presents.
- To deepen one's understanding of what it means to be a missionary in the USA.
- To realize that acculturation is an ongoing process of personal and cultural transformation.

To be able to appreciate and make good the aforementioned goal and objectives, the primal vision recommended by John V. Taylor for new arrivals is worthy of attention. Paraphrased accordingly, this primal vision recommends that: Our first task in approaching other people, another culture, and another religion is to take off our shoes, for the place is holy, else we find ourselves treading on people's dreams and ideals. Furthermore, let us not forget that God was there before our arrival, according to the Christian anthropological thought of Karl Rahner.

The profundity of this cross-cultural vision is so deep that, once objectively analyzed and taken seriously, it would help in a great number of ways in any cultural adjustment process, especially in the perspective of evangelization. Advantageously, on the part of the neophyte, with this vision, prejudices and

A HANDBOOK ON CULTURE SHOCK

biases can be avoided and malleability can be made possible. In addition, it can give a boost to the power of positive thinking and create an environment of a healthy accommodation, accessibility, interaction, and even generous interpretation of remarks and perception of ideas. Above all, this vision would instill in anyone concerned a spirit of humility and submission. All these preparatory dispositions would successfully conspire in building up a nonjudgmental personality in relation to the cultural differences that exist. This approach of working with the consciousness of this cross-cultural vision would profitably assist in the process of a balanced cultural adjustment. The experience thereof would nurture and promote minimal culture shock, while the individual gradually and cheerfully passes through the crucibles of cultural adaptation. At the end of the day, you (newcomer) would become someone with a dual cultural orientation and would be enabled to live within the different cultures, given the circumstances of place and time.

However, while you consider this option, in imbibing and undergoing this cultural metamorphosis, it is important that you remain true to yourself and authentic, especially in terms of ever appreciating your own cradle culture. This authenticity agrees with the philosophical thought of Soren Kierkegaard, in his attempt to propound the philosophy of authentic existence. To recapitulate: Below is an attempt to give you a grand tour of the day to day issues that were looked into during the acculturation workshop exercise in addition to my expanded personal reflections on them.

DAY ONE AUGUST 18, 2003

CULTURE

Culture is a way of life of a people in a particular place and within a particular historical context. In *A Handbook of Catholic Theology,* edited by Wolfgang Beinert and Francis Schussler Fiorenza, culture is defined as: "The specifically human way through which persons perceive and shape their reality, that is, their own selves, their fellow human beings, and the world they share. Human beings, therefore, are creatures who possess and produce culture."[1] Within the gamut of culture are traditions and customs, norms and needs, thought patterns and concepts, perceptions and practices, beliefs, values, and worldviews.

Every culture is informed and formed by such institutions as its marriage system, religious beliefs and practices, climatic and weather conditions, social stratifications and economic situations. Most of these institutions and related cultural conditions have provided and still provide tools and vehicles for cultural interaction. They also help to pass on or convey information or messages from one person to another within a given culture. In most cases, these tools avoid verboseness or the use of too many words. Thus, they strive to maintain an economic use of words, but with a wide range of contextual information embedded in them, and by all means, they satisfy the curiosity of people within a given cultural context. This abundantly explains the use of proverbs and myths in all cultures of the world to give explanations to some recurrent phenomena while maintaining an economy of words.

A Handbook on Culture Shock

TERMINOLOGICAL NUANCES

Sometimes, in the course of reading a write-up that is culture-related or culture-based, students of cultural literature come across a twist in some cultural terminologies. This twist, more often than not, grammatically conveys a particular and contextual meaning, which may inject a problem of ambiguity that beclouds the easy understanding and intellectual assimilation of the subject matter in question. Some of these familiar and recurrent twists are:

-*Enculturation:* This refers to one's native, first, or primary culture of socialization.

-*Inculturation:* This is primarily a concept often used in faith and evangelization-related discourse. It talks about the contextualization and concrete actualization of the Gospel message in and within another cultural milieu or setting. It takes into consideration the culture of the people but without compromising the essence of the Gospel message per se.

-*Acculturation:* This is the process by which one culture is affected by another. It refers to contact with a culture other than yours (one's own). This expression is best suited in discussions that border on cross-cultural experiences.

END OF DAY ONE

In a very challenging but worthy task of going down memory lane, the participants at the acculturation workshop were made to dig into and recapture the pictures of their own individual native cultures. This enculturation exercise involved an examination of the cultural circumstances of one's birth and the particular historical developments playing out at the time.

FRUITS OF ACCULTURATION WORKSHOP

This was very interesting, since it helped in the recapturing of one's almost forgotten past.

The high point of this endeavor came during the interactive sharing of the fruits of this exercise by all the participants. It was, in fact, an eye-opening session beyond the walls and myopia of one's world. It was also an opportunity for a personal discovery and rediscovery of the necessary and all-important knowledge of one's yesterday. In short, it was a reflective moment that gave a taproot to one's present auxiliary roots of life. This recapturing session can better be appreciated by the saying that: "A person without the knowledge of his or her past is like a tree without roots." By my estimation, this recapturing exercise, which also calls for cultural appreciation carries along with it a more challenging call for cultural patriotism.

By cultural patriotism here I mean, the genuine, "naked" and shameless love, unflagging support, and unpretentious devotion that one continually demonstrates towards his or her native culture. This attitude should be orchestrated alongside an objective, unbiased and honest defense of one's original culture with all the people who share one's life in that culture. This is a steppingstone for global cultural appreciation. For even Scripture says: "If you do not love your brother whom you see everyday, how can you love God whom you do not see?" Again, Daniel Jenkins once said: "If a man cannot love his own kith and kin whom he sees, how can he love the international community...whom he does not see?"[2]

Accordingly, cultural patriotism is concerned with love of a people within a given cultural milieu, who have a sense of their distinctiveness, people with a deep sense of identity with others in a recognizable group. Enlarging this point further, it

A HANDBOOK ON CULTURE SHOCK

could also be said that this kind of patriotism has to do with appreciating one's culture *just as it is,* and as it has been loved by God in Christ, and then doing one's level best to: "Bring to birth what it is lacking at this point in time; Recognize, cherish and encourage its strengths and achievements; and Acknowledge its weakness and confess its guilt."[3] This acknowledgment with its concomitant confession of guilt must be ignited by a fervent commitment to positive change of those people in a given cultural environment whose plight gives them little outward cause to be grateful for living "here."

In this context then, a true patriot is one who takes full share of public responsibility in his culture with an intent to leave the office of service better than "you" met it. Such a person exhibits pecuniary disinterestedness while in office either by appointment, or election or by personal life opportunity, instead, devotes his or her lifetime to the promotion of the common good. He or she works to the bone to cure the culture's defects and develop the nobler side of its character. A cultural patriot should brace up with fixity of purpose and strength of will to discover the culture's distinctive qualities, potentials, and special capacities and ensure the exercise of these by his or her compatriots, beginning with himself/herself. Finally, all culture enthusiasts and patriots should stop asking what the culture can do for them, and start figuring out what they can do, (both as individuals and as collective groups), for their cultures. This thought, I reemphasize, is a mission that agrees with the sound thinking of a one time American president, John F. Kennedy, who is popularly quoted and known to have said to his fellow citizens: "Do not ask, *what can America do for me,* rather ask, *what can I do for America."* The benefits of such a philosophy will be progressively overwhelming in all aspects of life, human endeavors, systems and sectors.

DAY TWO AUGUST 19, 2003

CULTURAL PERCEPTION OF POWER

This concept helps in explaining and giving a better insight into the understanding of the *"power distance"* cultures and their varied and various cultural perceptions. More authoritatively, it is developed by Geerst Hofsted to describe the different understandings of inequality across cultures. Thus, this power distance is about how people from various cultures perceive their personal power. In this school of thought, there are two main perceptions of power: *high power distance and low power distance.*

The high power distance culture is a culture of maximization. Its perception has the following cultural characteristics:
- Existential inequality is how life is and should be.
- Power holders are by right entitled to privileges.
- These power holders are few; the middle class is small; and the majorities are intrinsically powerless, poor, and uneducated.
- Opinions are expressed; ideas are held; and thoughts are respected hierarchically in the descending order of societal status and importance.

According to Eric Law, people of a high power distance culture should pray for the "miracle" of tongue, so that in their high and elevated positions, they do not sound "goddish," imposing, intimidating, and oppressive to the "have-nots." On a personal reflection, I also recommend that they pray for the

A Handbook on Culture Shock

gift of the virtue of humility that acts as a check and balance on pride, so that they do not fall. Otherwise, it may be said of them: How are the mighty fallen? And how great will their fall be! Remember the saying that: "He that is humble need fear no fall...he shall always have God to be his guide/guard."

The low power distance culture holds contrary views and opinions. As opposed to the former, it is a culture of minimization. Thus, the belief here suggests that one's personal quality of life should be minimized in order to inculcate a sense of belonging as well as to accommodate all peoples in a given culture. On its own part, this perception holds the following cultural characteristics:

- Existential inequality should be minimized and reconstructed.
- Essentially speaking, all peoples have and should have equal rights and privileges.
- In this culture, the majorities are educated, the middle class is high, and the economically poor and uneducated are few.
- Hierarchy is established to get things done for the greater good and benefit of the majority of the people. Therefore, any existing hierarchical structure is not for the convenience of a selected few, to the insensitivity, exclusion, and detriment of the weak.

According to Eric Law again, people of a low power distance cultural vision should pray for the "miracle" of ears, so as to hear properly, understand correctly, and discern objectively what is good or bad without any biases. It is even suggested that they should pray not to hear certain things that may be upsetting and so make them develop a phobia or any other unhealthy complexes (inferiority) and related imaginary or psychological syndromes. If both the prayers for the "miracles" of the tongue and ears are sincerely offered in the different cultural contexts of high and low power distances, it is hoped that there would be a mutual transformation of any cultural status quo for the harmonious existence of all. Such an existence would respect the fundamental equality of all people and minimize all other manmade and societal driven incongruence.

THE BLACKS' ANTAGONISM

The session that centered on the blacks versus the blacks intra or in-house fight in some parts of the United States was not only historically and existentially revealing, but also shocking, staggering, and dumbfounding. Thanks are due to the able and gifted presenter of this session, Dr. Carolyn N. Williams, an African-American and an expert in community and child psychology.

In a cheerful, humorous, and characteristic conviction of one speaking from the chair of a long-lived experience, she systematically and prudently exposed us to the historic antagonism of blacks versus blacks. Incidentally, the tension and begrudging friction go on amongst blacks unnoticed by many people. These two camps of blacks are in the divide of the *African-Americans* and the *immigrant Africans* living in some parts of the United States. Without daring to claim the capability of expressing the ideas exactly as the presenter did in what I may call a Xerox production, I would attempt to paraphrase some of the points of departure in the existing contention between the divide.

A HANDBOOK ON CULTURE SHOCK

Most African-Americans are not happy with the immigrant Africans because of the ugly and painful, "dramatic" and historic nightmare of the slave trade. The point is that the African-Americans feel that the immigrant Africans centuries ago sold their ancestors into slavery to work bestially in the sugar cane plantations of the Americans. Consequently, this has become like a generational sin with a generational effect. Hence, at present, there seems to be a tendency for some African-Americans to look at any immigrant African they come across as one who, directly or indirectly, overtly or covertly, and historically contributed in selling them into slavery.

Through this unchristian and inhumane human trafficking, the exported Africans, who are today known as African-Americans, have come to remain in the United States as a people in a foreign land, still suffering marginalization, segregation, and racism, which may be real, systemic, and psychological. In this human trade, they were stripped and raped, reaped and ripped of their historical identity (culture and language, geographical origin and tribal affinity); they suffered painful separation and detachment, estrangement and alienation from their own kith and kin, flesh and blood, brothers and sisters; and they have become a people without a reliable knowledge of their authentic family tree. Consequently, their genealogy is more or less speculative with no rooted, concrete, dependable, and solid reference base.

Worse still, for whatever reason, today in the American culture of workaholics, some people see the African-Americans as weak, redundant, and loiterers. All these mentalities and lots more aggravate and intensify the tension and revive the nightmare of slave consciousness, which has probably affect-

Fruits of Acculturation Workshop

ed the mentality and worldview of some African-Americans. To this end, this setting witnesses more intra-group differences than inter-group differences, or more intra-racial tensions than inter-racial conflicts and tumults. That is, concerning peaceful accommodation and cohabitation, there are more "blacks" that are more similar to the "whites," or in some cases, the "blacks" have become "more Romans than the Romans themselves," so to speak. The consequences of this mentality are far-reaching in adversely affecting the transparent brotherhood of all blacks in some parts of the United States. The situation is susceptible to an ongoing silent or cold war and a hidden tension among people of the same race, probably of the same tribe, village, and family. These people are far from "home" and are living in a "foreign" land. Like the Biblical kingdom that is divided against itself, it cannot stand in the midst of this "unspoken" rivalry.

But wait a minute, let us look at the issue of slavery from a more extended/extensive base and historical perspective. On this note, permit me to cite a theological and scholastic statement made by a one time lecturer of mine in the Major Seminary, Rev. Fr. Dr. C. Ifeanatura, who once said: "Before the Bible, there was a bible." By this he meant that before the written Bible, as we have it today, there was a bible in the form of oral (bible) tradition. Therefore, logically speaking, the written Bible is a product of the oral bible handed down from generations to generations through stories told by parents or ancestors to children or the younger ones.

Against the backdrop of the wisdom of this profound theological statement, therefore, and in relating it to the issue at stake, it is a known fact that from some African stories

A Handbook on Culture Shock

and experiences, it is also possible to say: *"Before the slave trade, there was a slave trade."* In other words, before the international or trans-Atlantic slave trade, there was the internal slave trade among the Africans. This was chiefly brought about through intertribal wars and related conquests in which some war captives ended up in another tribe, village, or land as slaves. To this day, this mentality still holds sway in some African cultures. If this is not true, then how do the Africans or, to put it in perspective, some Nigerian tribes explain the **"osu caste"** among the Igbos in eastern Nigeria? Even for the Etung people as the case in point, what is the explanation for **"nshoong"** (singular) or **"ashoong"** (plural), as the case may be? The two preceding expressions (osu caste and nshoong or ashoong) simply refer to slaves in the two Nigerian tribes cited, the Igbos and the Etung people, respectively. To this end, even the immigrant Africans may not be too sure of their own origins. After all, even in America itself, the history of slavery in general tells us that even before the black slaves arrived in America, there were white slaves among whites.

Again, would it be scandalous to know that there was the slave institution in the Bible? The experience of the Israelites in their different captivities and the vivid experience of Joseph who, was sold into slavery by his brothers to the Ishmaelite, are practical cases in point as recorded in the Old Testament. The slave institution, therefore, is more or less a human institution as old as humanity itself. The burning issue at stake is how to stop and get over it inside of cultures, within the structure of religion, and in the hearts and mentality of people.

Now, as a way forward in healing the wounds of sin and division in the hearts of the African-American brothers and sisters, the presenter spoke of an African bishop who beauti-fully addressed this situation. The bishop recommended that the immigrant Africans must "role-play" and apologize to the African-Americans for what the African ancestors' fathers did to the African-Americans' parents. Following the same line of thought, from a personal reflection, I also wish to advance a solution to the impending problem in another dimension of a pastoral approach.

Before I express my view about the pastoral solution, it is important to know that, believe it or not, it is a fact that today the United States has become a world power and the land of abundant goodness. It is like the earthly promised land of our time, where almost every African in the African continent is praying and looking forward to, one day coming to (America), possibly even to be brought over as slaves. This is because of the plights of the African nations with the increasing reali-ties of today: abject poverty, sickness and disease, tragic mis-management of available scarce resources, political instabil-ity, incessant assassination, social disorientation, nervous or trembling insecurity, and other heebie-jeebies. The results are obvious: hunger, misery, wars, and visible despair.

The situation seems to be getting worse and worse every day. Could this be a curse for selling a brother or a sister to a stranger for a bottle of whiskey, a piece of candy, a gun, and a mirror? Alternatively, could this miserable status quo be the responsibility of the government that be? Only God knows the answers to these questions. On the other side of the coin, the existential question is: What is the present situation of the "brothers" and "sisters" that were sold into slavery and taken to a foreign land in America, I mean the African-Americans?

A Handbook on Culture Shock

For the most part or in some cases, it is far better off than that of the ones who sold them, so to speak.

Now, let us look at the pastoral solution I promised to proffer: If the picture of the present situation of the divide (Africans and African-Americans) is accepted as well-painted and depicted here, then on both sides of the divide lies a responsibility for charting a way forward. On this note, there is a challenge to both camps to imitate and relive the Biblical episode between Joseph and his brothers, who sold him into slavery in Egypt, as recorded in the book of Genesis, Chapters 37, 39, and 41–50. This passage by my estimation and description, offers us the divine mystery of the economy of salvation in what I may call "the dramatic comedy of redemption." And this in the sense that, in ways well planned by God, Joseph, the rejected brother, and the slave became the bread winner of the ones who sold him. Yes, here the biblical statement also had a unique fulfillment: "The stone which the builders rejected has become the cornerstone. This was the Lord's doing; and we marvel at it." (Matthew 21: 42).

By way of a contextual application of the Biblical passage (of Joseph being sold into slavery by his own brothers), and the contextual hermeneutical approach just narrated above with its crystallizing effect in the "cornerstone" analogy, permit me to appeal to the African-American brothers and sisters to see themselves as the "Josephs" that were sold into slavery to and in the United States. Consequently, they should behave toward their African kinsmen and kinswomen as Joseph did: with forgiveness, mercy, consideration, accommodation, and acceptance. All these recommended "Josephite" attitudes should be founded on the conviction that the trade was the brainchild of ignorance.

In another light of pantheism, it could possibly be seen and interpreted as God's design that Africans should also become bona fide occupiers and owners of this New World, and in ways best known to God, the slave option was chosen by Him as a means to bring about His plan for the good of all. Unfortunately, some Africans went through a lot of excruciating crucibles to realize this plan. To them, we remain ever grateful and appreciative of their "sacrifice," though they did not know that they were the sacrificial lambs. Hence, the African-Americans can even go an extra mile in saying and living the ultimate prayer of forgiveness, following the perfect example of Jesus, when He hung upon the cross as the innocent victim for our salvation: "Father, forgive them for they do not know what they do." (Luke 23: 34)

On the other hand, the Africans should also see themselves as "Joseph's brothers who handed him over to foreigners." Consequently, while remaining remorseful for what they did, the Africans should be sorry and apologize to their African-American "family members." My conviction is that this awareness is a step in the right direction that can heal the wounds and make for peaceful cohabitation.

On another way forward, the African-Americans should realize how much they or their ancestors have put in and contributed to the building of America. Therefore, in a nonviolent, polite, reasonable, peaceful, and gentle negotiation with the authorities that be in America today, they (African-Americans) should begin to negotiate for a commensurate or at least charitable compensation in the sharing of the national cake, to also help build their own motherland in Africa.

A Handbook on Culture Shock

By and large, I must confess that the session (during the acculturation workshop) that exposed the silent tension and quiet antagonism among blacks in some parts of the United States was a startling and shocking revelation to me. It positively changed my worldview on this and related cultural issues. I thank again the erudite and impeccable presenter for the exposé on this delicate and sensitive matter.

DAY THREE AUGUST 20, 2003

STAGES OF INTERCULTURAL DEVELOPMENT

Our reactions to situations, people, and things differ in manner and approach, in methodology, in depth, and in view. Hardly do you find two people who respond or react to a given situation in the exact same way. For one thing, there could be some similarities and sameness which, plus or minus, do not hold much water. Hence, for the most part, differences abound in people and their reactions to a given situation, occasioned by the innate, intrinsic, and ontological uniqueness of each individual human person. For instance, some people can take a greater amount of cold than others. Some people also can resist the attack of one illness or another more than others due to their body immunities. These varied and different reactions and sensitivities can also be the results of cultural and environmental influences and of course one's power of the mind.

On this note of differences, Eric Law presented a case study that tries to look at the different stages and reactions in cultural adaptation and advancement of people in a given culture. The stages he presents are as follows.

ETHNOCENTRIC STAGE

This is the first stage in the cultural appreciation of every person, consciously or unconsciously. This stage runs throughout life, helping to shape and bring one to a fully developed and balanced person in his or her first, home and native culture. At this stage, without a choice, everything is seen from the status quo of one's native culture, which progressively molds his or her cultural perception and shapes its perspective, since there are no competing cultures. Thus, in this monopolistic cultural environment, one's native culture tends to become the only spectrum and yardstick of viewing and of measuring other cultures when in contact with them. This stage provides the cultural parameter and the excellent paradigm for a comparative analysis of other people's ways of life. In fact, for extremists, it may become a determinant and supreme reference-base to the extent that whatever does not fit into this spectrum is wrong. Furthermore, this stage may give rise to an inclination to use one's set of cultural values to judge all people in a juxtaposing consideration.

At this stage, there could be the serious danger of extremism in which, for others to exist, there must be a nonnegotiable conformism to your worldview. This unconditional and "conformistic" expectation creates a feeling of cultural supremacy and superiority. The effects of this are culturally unaccommodating and uncomfortable to the block or divide of the *subordinate* and *inferior culture,* so to speak (if there is anything like that).

On a positive and generous note, however, there is nothing wrong in being ethnocentric. Among other things, it can be seen as a sign of patriotism, which shows the acceptance

A HANDBOOK ON CULTURE SHOCK

and appreciation of one's native culture, regardless of what and how it is. This is because every culture is superior unto itself and has something to offer to its members and to those of other cultures who are malleable and docile without any cultural prejudice. Be that as it may, ethnocentricism is a basic human intercultural survival response. After all, psychologists say that in all people there is an egocentric natural proclivity. Moreover, this proclivity or propensity lays the foundation for related centricisms, which philosophers laudably interpret as self-affirmation.

This self-affirmation has to do with the ego of "I am." Hence, for others to affirm my existence, I must first assert or affirm that, "I am." This self-affirmation again, is in line with the philosophical dictum of Socrates, who, in his methodic doubt in the affirmation of his existence, affirms this existence by saying: "I think, therefore, I am." (Cogito ego sum). In fact, on a wider hermeneutical approach, even the Bible suggests this self-affirmation in the summary of the love command-ment: "You shall love your neighbor as yourself." (Mark 12: 31). And so, in accordance with this Socratic sound teaching and the biblical injunction on self-affirmation, I agree that to act otherwise, in the context under consideration, (ethocentri-cism), is to give room for others to deny your existential and existing culture. Therefore, in this culture-related discourse it is not sinful to be proud of your native culture. Rather, it may be sinful if you are not, since it may amount to denying your own existence, forgetting your taproot or biting the hand that fed you. True as this ethnocentric promo may be, it is a matter of disturbing concern to become insensitive to other cultures of the world. This causes friction in cultural appreciation and adaptation.

DENIAL STAGE

This stage takes into account and examines the initial and instinctive reaction and response to a foreign culture. For the most part, due to ethnocentric orientation, there is first a denial response, consciously or unconsciously. That is, this stage denies the existence of other cultures and is blind to differences. This may be due to physical isolation or psychological estrangement from other cultures. To avoid or get out from this myopic or ghetto mentality, you have to recognize the existence of other cultures and open-mindedly interact with them without any prejudice or preconceived ideas. Otherwise, you create a blockage that would hinder the positive and creative assimilation of new cultural ideas, which may be of benefit to you, either immediately or sometime and somewhere down the road.

DEFENSIVE STAGE

Even when one enters into a new culture with the expected and recommended open-mindedness, there is always a natural tendency or human proclivity to be defensive of oneself and protective of one's native culture. This attitude can also be interpreted from the point of view of the instinct of self-preservation. Furthermore, this defense that favors cultural patriotism may take the form of rationalization in the bid to justify one's cultural values vis-à-vis the values of the host culture. This attitude of defense may even affect the way one speaks in generalities. This can be seen in expressions such as "those northeasterners," "those Nigerians," "those Africans," and so on. In this way, one uses a particular situation to make a general assertion or statement about people living together without cognizance of their varied cultural backgrounds and other personal uniqueness. More often than not, this and similar assertions amount to the error of hasty conclusion and the fallacy of overgeneralization. If not carefully and prudently handled, it may give rise to a judgmental approach that is against intercultural etiquette and the ethics of cultural immersion.

Oftentimes, at this stage there is an attitude where one feels that other cultures exist, but yours is superior. People can become very defensive, angry, and aggressive at this stage. There may also be a feeling of insecurity, fear, and suspicion. These reactions, according to experts, are caused by the lack of a convincing cultural self-esteem of one's own home culture. However, in the course of time, with more openness, you may gradually reverse the order and begin to romanticize the new culture while remaining appreciative of yours.

MINIMIZATION STAGE

This is the stage of appreciating equality and recognizing sameness. Thus, as you hang on in the host culture, you gradually begin to experience the minimization of culture shock due to familiarity with the culture in the unfolding realities of each passing day. In this way, you begin to know, to understand, and possibly, to personally answer the entire *why* questions arising from a given cultural setting. As you forge on and move along, there is a conscious and even an unconscious reduction of the fear of cultural differences. You begin to become acclimated with contextual application and expression of ideas and behavioral manners and other ways of life. You become more relaxed and almost at home with the structures that be and people that are.

At this stage, you no longer deny other cultures, nor are you defensive any longer. You simply move into another stage of saying: *"Sure, the other might look different, but deep down we are all the same."* However, people at this stage do not see the deep surface culture, which can only be acknowledged and appreciated from the iceberg analysis of culture. They are on the superficial and surface level of the "romantizing" relationship between their home and the foreign cultures.

Paradoxically, silence, quietness, and little talking or talking sparingly initially and often characterize this stage of minimization. This is because of the fear of being misunderstood in communication and the readiness and eagerness on your own part to learn correctly the way of life of the host culture. Thus, you become like a student who must pay attention to the teacher in order to understand properly what is being taught. In this context and at this point, it is worthy to know that you may have very many teachers since every member of the host culture (even children) becomes like a teacher to you. Do not be surprised, however, that there may be some conflicting ideas and clashing of information in this teaching and learning process. So, ask questions when you do not understand something or when you experience a clash of information or contradiction of ideas along the way from your *too* many teachers.

Finally, it should be noted, that this stage is also very problematic in the sense that your silence can seem unbecoming and your quietness can become confusing and worrisome to your host. Therefore, while it is the stage of minimization or partial openness for you, it is enthusiastically and fully the stage of complete openness by your host(s) who are delighted to be open and want to teach you more about their culture, since you have shown an interest and a willingness to learn more about their ways of life. True as this may be, there is still the possibility of your being misunderstood by the people of the host culture because of your silence or partial openness, which they may not understand that it is a learning technique. To avoid this development, it is important that, as the need arises and the occasion comes up, you try to explain your new and present situation to those concerned. This would make your host feel comfortable and patient and even become sympathetic to you and even be disposed to guide and teach you more since you are ready to learn.

ACCEPTANCE STAGE

This stage is a practical manifestation of the "serenity prayer" which says: "God, give me the serenity to accept the things I cannot change, courage to change the things I can, and wisdom to tell the difference." In this stage of acculturation, what one is accepting are differences. These differences, therefore, become part of life in your intercultural enhancement and should not be seen as cultural substitutions. Thus, they should be added to what you already know, culturally speaking, and not serve as replacements. After all, grace does not destroy nature, but builds on it. The disposition at this stage is that you are willing to live in the cultural uncertainties of your new environment without being judgmental.

ADAPTATION OR "INTERPATHIC" STAGE

This is the stage of healthy flexibility and honest accommodation of the host culture. It goes beyond sympathy to empathy in which you simply move out from your ethnocentric or monopolistic worldview into a pluralistic one. There is a kind of forgetfulness of the ego, to allow a conscious step into another person's shoes and the world therein.

The expectations of this stage call for and amount to a commitment to "cultural pluralism." This pluralistic disposition allows for a healthy "one-size-fit" mentality, which breeds a generation that could scarcely be imagined. Consequently, differences are included in your view as an ongoing process. This crystallizes into a complete or a more advanced and balanced intercultural immersion, bearing in mind that acculturation is an ongoing process like every other process of acquiring knowledge, especially of the growth of an institution.

No wonder it is said of the Church: "Ecclesia sempe reformanda est." That is, "the Church is always in the process of becoming or ongoing reformation." And this also applies to culture, hence the saying that culture is dynamic. There is no culture that is frozen otherwise, there is a problem. Cultural evolution therefore, is an ongoing work of far greater complexity and subtlety. Its dynamism stretches from decades into centuries having more than one architect. Albeit, it is important to note that, the many architects of a single, identifiable culture are those whose contributions to the overall plan of a cultural structure are consistent with the original image. This is where the Christian culture stands out as a pathfinder and a "numero uno" of a culture that is consistent with the original image, of the person of Jesus Christ, understood as fully divine and fully human. This image is safeguarded in all the consequent doctrines that illuminate and legitimately develop it. Every au-

A HANDBOOK ON CULTURE SHOCK

thentic culture then, must be built, both in its larger structure and in its finer details, according to the original image.

Furthermore, at this stage of adaptation you leave the "I" and move into the "I-thou" relationship. By implication, this involves a temporary suspension of the "I" frame of reference for the sake of moving into the "thou" cultural frame of reference. However, you do need to reestablish yourself at some point. By this time indeed, you have expanded your cultural identity because of the journey you have made to the other's worldview and perception of cultural ideas. The end result is that the "I" can fully come to understand the feelings of the "thou" and embrace and finally accept what is uniquely true of the "thou" cultural situation. This cultural progression suits the philosophical and epistemological imperative of Socrates who said: "Man know thyself" and "an unexamined life is not worth living." Thus, in knowing thyself and examining your life as the "I" in a cultural context, you come to appreciate the "thouness" of the other.

It is worthy to note that the first step to be culturally adaptive or "interpathic" is to esteem and appreciate your own native culture. Then progressively, you put aside your ethnocentric views and temporarily embrace the other with a refined cultural docility and malleability. Given this disposition, there would be a conscious and an unconscious ongoing cultural mixture that would arm you with a deep knowledge of cross-cultural experiences. At the end of the day, among other things, you would most certainly no longer be the same in your worldview and way of thinking and in your manner of doing things, understanding of people, and perception of ideas and interpretation of events. All this will occur because of your wide range of cultural perceptions and perspectives gathered from your cross-cultural contacts. I may call this new position a positive "cultural damage" that reshapes your initial world-view and upsets your entire life because things are no longer and will no longer be the same.

INTEGRATION STAGE

This is the final stage of intercultural development. It involves learning to do contextual evaluation and application of the intercultural knowledge acquired over time in any given cultural milieu. The ability to do these tasks challenges your "spirituality of creative marginality," that is, a cultural spirituality that fringes on your experience and conscious acceptance of cultural differences and learning to live with them. Thus, it is no longer an "inventive marginality" from a distance or knowledge based on theoretical data and hearsay. It is rather an experiential, tangible, and creative marginality with you as the main actor, "hero," and "architect."

Do not forget that at this final stage, in the course of time, you will become a perpetual foreigner and an intruder even to your own native culture and people. At all times, from hence, you need to be more or less consciously aware of the fact that you are always on an intersection or cultural crossroads whether at home or abroad. This is where the challenge of cultural maturity and experience come into play. This maturity is seen in the proper placement and contextualization of your way of life, determined, conditioned, and occasioned by where you are at a given time, whether in your native or in your foreign cultural environment. Thus, you have to be aware of your audience and the cultural expectations therein. This is where and when the saying "when in Rome, do as the Romans do" is applied, so that you do not become too loud and outstanding in cultural oddness and unfitness, otherwise you remain a cultural "stranger" to both cultures.

It is a fact that a proper intercultural mixture, growth, and experience make one culturally tolerant, culturally accommodating, and culturally perceptive of others. You would also come to know that you are not alone in the world and that not *everybody* is equally opportune. These others (*everybody*) are primarily those who may not have had the opportunity and privilege of a cross-cultural contact of any kind. So, their ways of life, often expressed in the questions they ask and the way they feel about cultures other than theirs, can be strange and appalling. In answering these questions, explaining facts, communicating or sharing your experiential knowledge and lots more, all these challenges would call for patience, tolerance, and accommodation on your own part. Above all, be always ready to give the inquirer the benefit of the doubt, and as much as possible, as many times as demanded, speak in a calm and polite language in explaining a cultural situation that you know of.

DAY FOUR AUGUST 21, 2003

THE MISSIONER VIS-À-VIS FAITH DEVELOPMENT

Generally speaking, the idea here is to look at one who comes into another culture as a "missioner," especially in relation to the faith development of the people to whom he or she ministers. According to the presenter, Fr. J. Walsh, it should be established straightaway and unequivocally that as soon as you

FRUITS OF ACCULTURATION WORKSHOP

cross cultural lines geographically, ethnically, and otherwise, you are a missioner. It matters not whether your mission is politically motivated or educationally opportune or economically driven. Neither does it matter whether it is religiously oriented or occasioned by asylum, or made possible by the search for greener pastures and related adventures for a better standard of living.

This well articulated session made it abundantly clear that the missioner as a guest, more often than not, has a cross-cultural advantage over the host culture and its people. Consequently, on you (the missioner) lies some responsibilities and expectations from your host and then, later on, from your native culture because of your vantage position, which empowers and enables you to acquire and then relate a comparative cultural experience of both cultures.

Now, to state the point more clearly, one ought to know that as one steps into another culture that the individual meets people who know their own culture better than the newcomer does. The undeniable advantage you, as a newcomer, may have is that down the road you would have a practical experience of two cultures. Through this contact, you are equipped to have a comparative cultural knowledge of the native and the foreign cultures. The challenge here is that you must realize and come to terms with a double heritage.

Putting this argument in a ministerial perspective, it is a dogmatic or an unquestionable fact that the advantage of this cross-cultural experience cannot be overemphasized concerning religious missioners. In this case, you have an experience of Christianity from the point of view of inculturation from two insights. Hence, on you lies the incumbent responsibility and charitable duty to educate, expand, and widen the knowledge of your congregation or audience. In this endeavor, not only do you let them know the fact of the existence of other cultures, but also on another fascinating note, you can point out the similarities and differences of the one and same universal Catholic Church, as it is practiced in both cultural milieus given the circumstances of time and related exigencies. This opportunity and your ability to impart the necessary knowledge and give the required information are tremendous and cost-effective for your audience.

It is cost-effective for your audience in the sense that they do not need a passport to go beyond their cultural bounds by traveling thousands of miles by air, land, or sea in order to get the knowledge of another culture. Rather, you bring the knowledge to their doorstep. In addition, on your part, it is a challenging apostolic and ambassadorial responsibility because in you is realized the *mobility of culture*. This is in the sense that your home or native culture is carried on and moved by you to a new cultural environment. Consequently, you become the harbinger and bearer of your native culture and the representative of your brothers and sisters therein as you find yourself in your new cultural environment and wherever you go and are functioning.

Therefore, in the context under consideration, as an apostolic "nunctio" or ecclesiastical ambassador, the need to be authentic and sincere is important because you may be the only source of information and the only cultural "bible" to be read by your host in many ways. But be warned and avoid the temptation of becoming an *opportunist* by taking advantage of the cultural ignorance of the people of your host culture and so feed them with exaggerated, nonexistent and wrong information. This could be done either by presenting what is not actually existing in your native culture or blowing certain things out of a comfortable proportion for your immediate or delayed advantage. Remember and do not lose sight of the fact and effects of globalization, in which the whole world is becoming a global village or as small as a conference hall, as some people say. This is made easy and brought about through information networks and related vehicles, which facilitate the culture of globalization. This challenge, therefore, to be a true and authentic witness by what you say and do becomes more urgent when you realize that you may become a paradigm for a general cultural assertion and conclusion by your host in regard to your native culture and its people.

Without any intention to over flog the issue of authentic and sincere missionary work, in case you do not know or perhaps you have forgotten, do permit me to draw your attention to the technological possibility and reality that *the world of truth is only a click away.* And from life experience, it has been observed that to tell one lie "successfully," you have to be ready to tell nine more lies to support the first one. The result is obviously a chain of lies being told. Woe betide you, if one of the connecting links on the chain becomes weak or even breaks up completely. And this "accident" always happens before long. What a shame!

By and large, as a religious missioner in all you do, always remember that you are a messenger and a prophet, a celebrant and a disturber, a consoler and a healer, a hero, a victim, and a visionary. This is what it means to be a missionary with a sense of mission. Furthermore, from an extended point of view, as a missioner in the general sense of the word, you are like a coin with two sides. On the one side, you are a learner, a student and a listener, an observer, a questioner and an inquirer, a seeker and a searcher, a philosopher and a criticizer. On the other side of the same coin, you are a teacher, an instructor and an informer, a representative and an ambassador, a disturber and an intruder.

CHALLENGES OF ACCULTURATION

THE ICEBERG THEORY

For a balanced growth and holistic intercultural development, it is not enough nor sufficient to have color vision, but over and above this, there is the need also to have *culture vision*. This simply means the ability to see the multiple worlds of others. Incidentally, from a cultural standpoint this culture vision can never be exhausted. It is because of the inexhaustive nature of any given culture that the theory of culture as an *"iceberg"* was developed. This illustration of culture as an iceberg helps for a better appreciation, understanding, and humble acceptance of the culture of others.

The theory of culture as an iceberg explains that in any given culture you know little compared to what you do not know. In other words, you should realize that the history and the unconscious of any culture is very huge and extensive, very massive, deep and large and even more profound compared to the conscious. Incidentally, this conscious cultural knowledge, for the most part, is very shallow and superficial. The point is that there is always a lot more going on inside every cultural iceberg than what goes on and appears on the outside level.

FRUITS OF ACCULTURATION WORKSHOP

Hence the saying: "There is more to this world than behold the eyes." The knowledge and awareness of this fact, therefore, to a large extent, makes you as a missioner not only humble, but also anxious and curious to know the inside level of the culture where you are missioning. Through historical research, by reading or by oral tradition in the forms of folklore and stories, this in-depth knowledge buried in the iceberg theory can be acquired. But, you can never know it all.

To recapitulate: As already insinuated, as you struggle with these challenges, bear in mind that there is always pain when you encounter something different. This pain cuts across the emotional, physical, and even psychological levels of life. Consequently, you may be forced consciously or unconsciously to develop some defenses in order to protect yourself from the strange elements, which may not only be new facts, but also opposing ideas and realities. The path to these defensive techniques could be through withdrawal or rationalization, which only helps to minimize or overcome the momentary culture shock. At this point, you may sometimes become avoiding and unfriendly, angry and judgmental, ashamed, funky and bored, but do not throw in the towel. It is only natural that you pass through this stage of cultural adjustment. But the question is how can one minimize culture shock?

MINIMIZING CULTURE SHOCK

Culture shock cannot be completely avoided. At most, it can be minimized. Therefore, to engage in a thought process or an exercise with an intention of developing a way of avoiding and overcoming this shock in its entirety is an uphill task that is tantamount to an effortless endeavor of one who is overly expectant. In other words, such intellectual gymnastics may be irksome, fruitless, and futile in the end. Your best bet, then, is to target or to aim at advancing some ways of reducing or minimizing the culture shocks as much as possible. One school of thought suggests *curiosity* as a way of comfortably going through culture shock.

CURIOSITY

According to the conviction of philosophers, everyone naturally desires to know. This desire to know as a way of acquiring knowledge is rooted in and founded on curiosity of some sort. With this tendency of curiosity, as a newcomer into a new culture, you are challenged daily with the desire to know more. You may become so preoccupied with this desire that you never actually pay attention to the culture shocks along the line that come as a result. As it applies to other fields of knowledge and from a cultural perspective, to be able to satisfy your curiosity, you should ask questions on subject matters to expand conversations. For instance, such questions might be:
- Can you, please, tell me more about that?
- Please, what do I need to know about this subject matter?
- Can you, please, explain or throw more light on this subject matter?

These and similar questions would not take a simple "yes!" or "no!" for an answer. They would need a better and further explanation for more clarity. In addition, on this note avoid questions that would warrant a simple "yes!" or "no!" as an answer, such as:
- Is it good?
- Is it bad?

Fruits of Acculturation Workshop

- Is it right?
- Is it wrong?
- Is it true?
- Is it false?

Such questions do not give any in-depth information, nor do their answers expand the conversation for a better insight on a subject matter. Furthermore, avoid *"why"* questions, such as:

- Why do you do this or that?

These and similar questions appear defensive, judgmental, and emotional.

Without fear of repetition and for the benefit of emphasis, in rounding off my reflection on this section, I wish to reiterate the significance and effectiveness of acculturation workshop by making the following catchy statements: *1). The significance of acculturation workshop lies in the arguable fact that it is culturally informative, historically revealing, and realistically preparatory, especially for newcomers to the U.S. cultural milieu, and other cultures of the world. 2). Acculturation workshop arms you with the necessary tools, such as mental preparedness, psychological disposition, and even physical "fitness" to weather the cultural storm, shocks and related enigmas found in a foreign cultural environment. 3). The effectiveness of acculturation workshop is seen in one's ability to translate and apply the rich fruits of the workshop into the concrete realities of the daily unfolding of the foreign cultural structure. This can be effectively done by being contextually alert and vigilant, disposed and malleable, open, ready-to-learn and curiously unbiased, nonjudgmental and humble. All these attitudes however, should be solidly rooted in and found-*

ed on cultural patriotism, which is the cultural appreciation of one's native culture. These attitudes prepare the way for an easy adaptation to a foreign culture.

In conclusion, permit me to say that, to the best of my ability, the ideas addressed in this chapter, represent some of the fruits of the acculturation workshop I attended. I do not claim to sound very exhaustive and precise on the whole matter. In short, these ideas are not without my own personal input based on my understanding of the various subject matters on which the searchlight was directed to while the acculturation exercise lasted. If this information leaves much to be desired in content; linguistically and otherwise, do excuse my language, and I take the blame for any errors in presentation.

Whatever has a beginning has an end. It is only God who transcends the limitation of time and to Him alone belongs no beginning and no end. This book, *A Handbook on Culture Shock,* certainly had a beginning and, therefore, would have an end. Hence, having established the premises in the aforementioned chapters, the end of this reflection though momentarily is in view. Chapter 13 concludes this work with, among other things, some important messages under the heading: "For Your Information." It then pulls down the curtain on the facts of the inevitability of culture shock, a call to the recognition of our fundamental sameness, culturally and otherwise, and an invitation to accept cultural pluralism as a way of life in the awareness and the daily encounter with people from different cultures of the world.

NOTES

[1] Beinert, Wolfgang, and Francis Schussler Fiorenza. *A Handbook on Catholic Theology.* New York: The Crossroad Publishing Company, 2000, 158.

[2] Jenkins, Daniel. *The British: Their Identity and Their Religion,* London: SCM Press, 1975, p. 18.

[3] Obi, Nick. "Patriotism and Us" *The Search,* Nigeria: Snaap Press Ltd., Vol. 1, No. 1, 2002, p. 23.

13

FOR YOUR INFORMATION
(ACRONYM FYI)

As I take the risk and commit myself to the task in this section of **FYI,** I must acknowledge that ours is a world that seems to be characterized by too *much information*. This phenomenon has been propelled and sped up within the last twenty or ten years of increased age of information technology. This has resulted to periodic clashes and sometimes contradictions in information channels and contents, among other things. Given this reality, so many questions arise, such as: Which information do we take or reject as junk? What are the criteria for judging an authentic information? What is the lifespan of a particular information between when it is given and when it would outlive its usefulness? What sources of information should be trusted and taken seriously? Due to these and other inquiries, contemporary persons must hedge on these questions and their answers to be able to regain the freedom from information slavery.

My intention here is far from crying wolves where there aren't any, neither do I intend to raise false alarm and so run the risk of being labeled an alarmist. I intend rather to state realities as confronted by many people everyday. My vision is that, perhaps this would help in one way or another to assist the newcomer into a foreign culture in watching out for new experiences, and so help serve as antidotes in the shocks that lie ahead. On the other hand, this information may also act as reminders and reinforcements to those who already have the knowledge. As I lead you into the gist of the matter, permit me to say categorically (in answer to one of the many questions above) that, the best and most trusted source of information is from the experience of the informant himself or herself.

To Catholic priests and religious who are newcomers into the U.S. Catholic culture, especially in terms of clerical and religious clothes, sacramental ministration, and liturgical celebrations, you would probably experience something different from what you were used to seeing and doing. Your experience in this regard, as mine was, could be new and shocking. Permit me to draw your attention to some of the things you may come across. I did experience a surprise and a shock in them, too.

SOUTANES OR CASSOCKS AND HABITS

I come from a culture where priests and religious such as nuns still wear their soutanes, or what some people call cassocks and habits, respectively, both at official and unofficial times and within the parish and convent premises and other areas such as along the streets, in the market or malls, and all other places. In short, the soutanes and habits constitute the uniform of those concerned and are worn by them everywhere, especially when they are leaving their "homes." Also, in Nigeria, priests can also be seen in their Roman collars.

But this is not a common practice because more often than not, it seems to constitute an "identity crisis" between Roman Catholic clergymen and pastors of other Protestant denominations. The soutane, therefore, makes for an easy identification of who is who, though not who is what.

My U.S. experience in this regard initially presented a picture that is different and surprising to me. Over here, for the most part, priests and religious do not wear their "uniforms" as is the case in Nigeria. In the United States, priests are mostly seen wearing their Roman collars, especially during official hours and at other times when they are carrying out their pastoral duties.

For the nuns, or reverend sisters, the wearing of habits is no longer a common practice. I understand that this change came in the 1960s, especially after the Second Vatican Council that took place between 1962-1965. This Council has been a turning point or a point of departure, which has turned things upside down or perhaps inside out in the life of the Church. Hence, some people refer to its spirit of reformation and transformation as the *war* of the Council. Things, in respect to the life of the Church were never the same again. It is mainly in accepting or not accepting the spirit of this Council, among other realities, that today in the Catholic Church, we hear of terms such as *liberals* and *conservatives, or orthodox* and *progressives,* respectively.

According to James Davison Hunter, in his book, Culture Wars, these terms "orthodox" and "progressive" may be familiar to many, they have a particular meaning depending on the contexts. Consequently, James offers some elaboration by saying that: "The words, orthodoxy and progressive, can describe specific doctrinal creeds or particular religious practices. Take orthodoxy. Within Judaism, orthodoxy is defined mainly by commitment to Torah and the community that upholds it; within Catholicism, orthodoxy is defined largely by loyalty to church teaching – the Roman Magisterium; and within Protestantism, orthodoxy principally means devotion to the complete and final authority of Scripture (sola scriptura – mine). Substantively, then, these labels can mean vastly different things within different religious traditions."[1] Be it as it may, what is common to all three approaches to orthodoxy is the personal commitment on the part of adherents to an external, definable, and transcendent authority. Such transcendent authority defines a consistent, unchangeable measure of values, teleology, goodness, and identity, both personal and collective. It dictates and tells us what is good, what is true, how we should live, and who and what we are. It is an authority that is incontestably sufficient for all time.

Within cultural liberalism or progressivism, by contrast, religious and moral authority tend to be defined by the spirit of the modern age, a spirit of rationalism and subjectivism, which more often than not, is a conspiracy and a metaphysical revolt against the transcendent authority. With this spirit of modernism, moral ideals tend to be changeable. From this standpoint, truth tends to be viewed as a process, as a reality that is ever unfolding. Again, be it as it may, what all progressivist worldviews share in common is the tendency to redefine and resymbolize historic faiths according to the prevailing assumption of contemporary life. This is so much to the extent that, people are encouraged to interpret the Scripture for themselves in ways that suit them best, by justifying their acts with rationalization that accommodates them as children of God, too.

The general point here is that the traditional sources of moral authority, be there Scripture, papal pronouncements, or Jewish law, no longer have an exclusive or even a predominant binding power over their lives (progressivists). For these people religious tradition has no binding address, and no opinion-shaping influence. Rather, the binding moral authority tends to reside in personal experience or scientific rationalization and proofs, or either of these in conversation with particular religious or cultural traditions. From the foregone, these impulses toward orthodoxy and progressivism aspire to describe in shorthand a particular locus and source of religious and moral truths and the fundamental moral allegiance and personal dispositions of the actors involved in the culture, in this case, the Catholic cultural beliefs.

In fact, this contemporary cultural divide in the context of religious communities highlights the historical novelty of the contemporary situation, which pictures vividly the ongoing culture war in the Catholic church today. To this end, without judging the spirit of *aggiornamento or* adaptation, in conformity with the spirit of the Council, many Catholics and Religious Congregations in responding to this transformation "spirit" have ever since, seized to be the same again.

This Council not only gave rise to liturgical changes, it was also the birth date for the adoption of civil clothing among various religious congregations. Today, therefore, you find a good number of nuns or reverend sisters belonging to some religious congregations in the United States dressing like every other woman in the secular society. As a newcomer, these experiences may throw you off or overboard initially. When this begins to happen to you, pull yourself back together as you work in the Roman Catholic Church culture of the United States. Do not be judgmental. Yes, in as much as the soutane or cassock and the habits are good and are recommended for easy identification and could be seen as a constant reminder of who one is, they are not the yardsticks for measuring holiness. After all, it is said that: Cucullus non facit monachum, that is "a hood does not make a Monk."

SACRAMENTAL MINISTRATION AND ALTAR SERVERS

With regard to sacramental ministration, particularly the giving of Communion at Masses and taking same to the sick and the homebound, to the best of my knowledge, in Nigeria, these are the exclusive responsibilities of the priests. However, in cases of pastoral exigencies, catechists can conduct Communion services in the parishes and use the Hosts consecrated by a priest as Communion for the faithful. At Masses, when the need arises, senior seminarians and nuns can be asked to help in the distribution of Communion to the faithful. The giving of the cup to the faithful is not a common practice. There is nothing such as lay sacramental ministers, be they men or women, at least none that I know of. At Masses, the altar servers in the parishes are men, except in girls' schools where you can have girls serve at Mass.

The U.S. experience with regard to sacramental ministration and altar or Mass servers reveals a different picture. Over here, there are sacramental ministers as laymen and women. These people assist the priests during Masses in the distribution of Communion and in the giving of the "cup" (the blood of Christ) to the faithful, since Communion is usually in both species. They also bring Communion to the sick and the home-bound. Boys and girls serve at Masses in the parishes and in Schools where there still celebrate Masses.

SUNDAY OBLIGATION

In Nigeria, particularly in my home culture among the Etung people, Sundays are holy days of obligation. To this end, people do not go to their farms or businesses on this day, as is the case in so many parts of the Catholic world. However, every now and then you find some business shops opened by those who own them after coming back from church.

The Saturday Mass, no matter what time of the day, does not substitute for the Sunday Mass, and those who attend it would not see it as fulfilling the Sunday obligation of going to Mass, as a holy day of obligation. The readings for the Saturday Mass are from the Liturgical Calendar of Saturday of that particular year and week and not from the succeeding Sunday, which is the next day.

This Sunday obligation as observed among the Etung people, for the most part, seems to be a different practice in some parts of the United States among some Catholic Christians. Thus, for those concerned, first, business and commerce are open on Sunday almost like every other day, though in some places with shorter business hours. With the introduction of the Saturday vigil Mass, for some people, the Saturday Mass substitutes for the Sunday Mass, and those who attend it are considered as fulfilling their Sunday obligation. This reality becomes more justifiable when you also realize that the readings of the Saturday vigil Mass are that of the upcoming

Sunday, which is the next day, as contained in the Liturgical Calendar.

Unaware of these differences when I first arrived in the parish of my pastoral placement in the United States, I initially had some problems and confusion as I prepared my homilies for the Saturday vigil Masses and Sunday Masses. Thus, for the first two weekends, I prepared my homilies in accordance with the Liturgical Calendar of Saturday readings as different from Sunday readings. So, I had two sets of readings and homilies for the weekend Masses for Saturday and Sunday, respectively. During this time, I got to the church to celebrate the Saturday vigil Mass, only to hear the lectors reading from the Sunday readings of the next day. Not wanting to cause any embarrassment either to the lector or to myself, I listened to the readings attentively and gave my homily based on them. My well prepared and reflected homilies that I had taken so much time to prepare were left undelivered. In time, once I realized what was going on, I also adjusted to the expectations of my newfound Catholic culture regarding Sunday obligations.

Finally, constrained by the Catholic culture in my newfound world in terms of the length of time for Mass, I had to discipline myself to say a complete Mass within 40 to 45 minutes. This was such a difficult cultural adjustment from what I was used to doing in Nigeria, where one Mass can last for two, three or even four hours depending on what is being celebrated during the Mass and who the priest is. If he is a "singing priest" then be prepared to stay longer. In fact, in my home culture, people do not just go to or attend Mass, but they celebrate it.

This reminds me of the experience I had during on my first home visit (to Nigeria) after going to the U.S. Incidentally, I ar-

A HANDBOOK ON CULTURE SHOCK

rived my village on this visit on a Saturday. The next day being Sunday, I went to Church to celebrate a Mass with the people. Having just come from the U.S. and still very fresh from the U.S. liturgical culture, especially in terms of the length of time a Mass takes, I said to the people: "This Mass will last for not more than one hour. Today, I will celebrate an American Mass in this Church with you." The people looked at me with high expectancy. You could see the visible joy and touch the excitement on their faces that were beaming with smiles, especially for having me back home in one piece. Guess what! my plan did not work. By the time I began the Consecration, I looked at my wrist watch, we were already two hours into the Mass. I shook my head several times. And by the time I finished celebrating the Mass, two hours and forty-five minutes have gone by. It just could not work.

The questions that arise here are: What happened? Who was to take the blame? I must confess by admitting that, beginning from me, it was not possible to give a short homily as I had earlier planned to. Second, during the prayer of intercession, which is usually spontaneous from some people among the congregation, the lengthy prayers that could call down fire from heaven said by those concerned were seemingly endless with periodic interjections of "Amen" by some "spirit filled" (charismatic) people in the congregation. Then came the time for taking up the collection. This is the high point of the celebration. Yes, people who formed the congregation would not stop singing and dancing along, even forward and backward with the rhythm of the music to the collection box, (which is usually placed in front of the sanctuary), to throw in their coins and leave some foodstuffs right in front of the Altar.

The bottom line of the message here is that it would always be an uphill task that may look like forcing a round peg into a squared hole in your attempt to make the Mass shorter than necessary in most African cultures, not just Nigeria alone. And anything short of this would be counterproductive, spiritually and otherwise. Finally, on this note, if you think that the length of time for the Mass is too long in Nigeria, then, try some Pentecostal or new generation churches. In this latter group, if you are able to come out from a service after four hours, then, thank your God.

As I continued to reminisce on both my past and ongoing experiences, my reminiscence tells me to talk more on some issues that are not only worth knowing but may promise a new insight and possibly guide the decisions of those who may be concerned. And that is why this section on **FYI** goes beyond any exclusive benefit of people in a particular class, to the benefit of all (people), both in the ecclesiastical and secular works of life. May I then make bold to introduce the reflection on such areas as Importation or Exportation, Use of Western Union, Use of Courier service for mailing and the need to always Travel light, to mention but a few.

IMPORTATION AND EXPORTATION

Without intending to hurt anyone by belittling or underestimating your intelligence, for the benefit of emphasis, permit me to say that by importation here I mean, the act or business of bringing or carrying in goods from an outside source, such as a foreign country to another country for trade or sale. While exportation is the opposite of importation. In its own case, it is the act of sending or transporting a commodity abroad for sale

A HANDBOOK ON CULTURE SHOCK

or trade or for private consumption. Every now and then you find people involved in this business in one way or another.

In addressing more particularly the Nigerian audience living in America, in terms of exporting motor cars (for instance) to Nigeria, I say to you: "Be very careful. Weigh the options, by way of the merits and demerits of buying a car in the U.S. and exporting it to Nigeria or going to buy the same kind of car in Nigeria." Without attempting to discourage you from the first option (of buying a car in America and shipping to Nigeria), I would not want to fail in my duty to give you some information. I must also acknowledge the fact that this option (of exporting) seems to be better, especially because you'll be more certain of the good condition of the car. This is because before the car is sold to you, it would be brought to an auto inspection area where it is inspected, tested and guaranteed that it has all the requirements it takes to pass the test of roadworthiness according to the U.S. laws concerned. In spite of this, do not be too sure that you will pick up the car in Nigeria under the same good condition. Besides the possibility of the problems associated with containers that carry the car, and any accident along the way, the rough handling of it at the wharf is another issue to think about. But if it all works well, this option of exportation is the best not minding the cost of shipping. After all, the same kind of car plus the shipping cost may even sell higher in Nigeria.

While still in the U.S., I started thinking about the possibility of buying a car and shipping it to Nigeria, especially a car with an American "spec" (specification). One day, I decided to share my thoughts with a Nigerian friend of mind who has been in America for a good number of years. He sat me down and gave me a friendly advice born from his own personal experience. From what he said to me, he did not leave me in doubt about the ugly situation at some seaports in Nigeria. Thus, some bad guys working at the ports, popularly known as "wharf rats" sometimes while unloading a car, may loosen and do away with some original parts of the car, such as the lights (lamps and bulbs), factory fitted radios etc. He even talked about the possibility of the engine of the car being changed and replaced with another weaker or older one. Far from scaring you with these unhealthy possible developments, the point here is that, at the end of the day you may not pick up your car intact or all in one piece as it was when you exported it.

Fellow Nigerians, you would agree that this argument or suspicion holds much water when you go to some Nigerian automobile parts markets to buy some motor parts, and the dealer begins to tell and show you some original and fake parts. Wherever the slang came from, among Nigerian car parts dealers, the original parts are called, "Japan," while the fake parts are called, "Belgium," "Aba," or "Nnewi."

For anyone who has had this experience of market distinction of motor parts in Nigeria, the question is: Have you ever stopped to ask yourself where the dealers got the original parts? However, I do not doubt the fact that they can be imported. To avoid any nightmare and discomfort, my friend advised that, if any Nigerian-American must export a car to Nigeria, such a person should, in addition to paying for the actual shipping of the car, also pay for and leave the whole job of clearing the car at the Nigerian seaport to the transporting company or agent. Certainly, it will be more expensive to do this. But by so doing, you avoid the trouble and hazard you would have to go through in paying the tariff for the car and facing related custom "irregularities." Besides, you would be able to hold the agent responsible for any damage done to the car, especially if the car is insured. This arrangement seems to be the best bet in the business of car importation to Nigeria from America. Good luck to those of you who have the bucks.

USE WESTERN UNION MONEY TRANSFER

The heading "Use Western Union Money Transfer" speaks for itself. Without boring you with too many words, I dare to presume that you know what Western Union Money Transfer is all about. From my experience, I agree with its mission statement that seems to say something like: "The most trusted and fastest means to send money worldwide." According to the Union's statistics, Western Union Money Transfer service is available at more than 110,000 Agent locations in over 185 countries and territories worldwide, and nearly 40,000 U.S. Agent locations. The service guarantees that in most cases, your funds can be picked up anywhere in their network within minutes. With this service, you can send money to almost anywhere in the world from the convenience of your location, whether you live in a village, town or city, even from your home or office in United States. This Union is at your service 24 hours a day, 7 days a week.

You may wonder, from all I have said so far in praise of Western Union Money Transfer if I was paid some money by the Union to become one of their advertising agents. No! What I believe is that whatever is good news, should be shared with others. I also believe that the blind should not lead the blind. Rather, whoever has even one eye, has a responsibility to lead

FOR YOUR INFORMATION

and show the way to others who may be completely blind due to their ignorance or misinformation, especially as we live in an age of too much information with their related setbacks.

Not only to fellow Nigerians living in America, but also to all who may have the need to send money overseas or long distance, I passionately and strongly advise you to use Western Union Money Transfer. Avoid the temptation to send money by hand through anybody, or by regular mail. Many who have done this, have their share of stories to tell. I do not mean to say that, no one can be trusted. You know as well as I do, that money is very tempting. Raw cash in the hands of someone is even more tempting. Do not put your brother, sister or friend to the test by giving any of them raw cash to bring to your family overseas. However, in exceptional cases where the recipient of the money is in a village somewhere in Nigeria, for instance, where they are no Western Union services, then you may have no choice than to risk giving money to someone you personally trust would not disappoint you and make you lose the confidence you repose in him or her.

On the whole, what I am trying to say is that, for your own good and for the good of keeping unsoiled your brotherhood, sisterhood and friendship with all your loved ones, as much as possible, spare them the trouble of delivering raw cash on your behalf to anyone, when they go for vocation in Nigeria. Granted that temptation must come, Jesus Christ warns us in the Scriptures that – woe to him from whom it comes. Again, I emphasize that a blind man is bound to stumble and possibly fall, but do not put or place a stone in his way. Probably, you must be wondering why I am speaking in parables. Sometimes this means of talking helps to drive the message home better

A Handbook on Culture Shock

and faster. No wonder Christ used it several times in the Bible. What I am saying in effect is that – do not provide an occasion for your brother to be tempted beyond his power to resist (the temptation.) Use Western Union! It is fast, reliable and easy. Its flexibility, reliability, and convenience would allow you to live a life free of anxiety, speedily take care of the needs of your loved ones far away, and solve your financial problems. Yes, it would allow you to do the things you want to do that involve finance expertly, efficiently and everyday. A stitch in time, saves nine.

USE COURIER MAIL OR SERVICE

When I arrived the United States about two years ago, I wrote a couple of letters to some of my family members and friends in Nigeria. I sent them by regular mail. To this day, out of about five letters, only two have been received, and at different times, at a space of three and five months, respectively. Don't ask me of the other three, because I have no clue about where they are. After this experience, I did not need someone to tell me that I have to stop sending letters by regular mail from America to Nigeria. My only luck was that, the letters in question were just what some people call: "Hello! Hello! letters with no serious stuff enclosed.

When I shared this experience with another of my Nigerian friends resident, too, in the U.S., he said to me: "It is very risky, iffy, precarious and unsafe to send letters to Nigeria by regular mail because on arrival in Nigeria, such letters having the American stamp, are often suspected of containing dollars. And so, your guess as to what may become of those letters, will be as good as mind." But guess what! letters from Nigeria to the U.S. do arrive safely and they take between one to two weeks. I have received a couple of them. Now, where lies the problem?

Thanks to the invention of emails and telephone services in the world of communication technology to complement the information means of touching lives, bridging distances, healing rifts and building bonds of friendship. These two, from hence, became the only means of my keeping in-touch with some of my folks back home in Nigeria. But it is not always that emails and telephone services would carry the message you want to deliver. They can only convey written and spoken words, respectively. What about important letters, parcels and packages? How do you send these home when the need arises and be sure that they will reach their desired destinations, delivered to and received by their respective persons? These and similar questions with their related problems have a solution, and so, they can be fixed. It is simply this:

"Use Courier Mail such as UPS, DHL, FedEx, or Global Express (from the post office). These are the fastest and safer methods for sending your valuable material (important letters, parcels and packages). With the proper address, your message is sure to get "there" within a few days. And if it does not, you have the right to hold the staff of the particular courier service responsible for lost of package. To be able to do this, be advised to keep the duplicate of the form you filled when sending the message as a proof.

Do I need to tell you that, courier services are very expensive in sending messages overseas? If I need to, then know that, for instance, to mail just one letter (not a parcel) to Nigeria, from Upstate New York, the charge is $100.00 even. If you have a heavy parcel or some goods to send or ship, then be prepared to spend even more than you could imagine. And this is not all. If you ship a cargo home through this service, be ready also to pay the import or custom duties on the cargo when it arrives in Nigeria. Wow! This sounds really demanding and too much. Well, that is what it takes. So, if you want the courier service, then be ready to spend the money. By all means, especially for freights or cargoes to be shipped from America to Nigeria, courier is preferable to regular mail. The ball is in your court. Do not say that you were not warned when "it" happens.

TRAVEL LIGHT

Perhaps, you are familiar with the saying: "Usus, magister egregious," which means, "experience is the best teacher." The import of this saying cannot be overemphasized nor doubted by many people. Most times, the experience in question could be either a personal one or that of other people. In either case, every experience carries with it a message to give and a lesson to learn from. Depending on the intensity or gravity of a particular experience, one can learn a lesson the easy way or the hard way. In whichever way, Christian charity demands that we share our experiences with one another, especially those ones that teach a moral lesson. By my reflection, this sense of morale to share our experiences is for the benefit of the "community" in three ways: 1.) It helps other people to be aware of a situation and to avoid it, if it is an uncomfortable or inconveniencing one. 2.) It is highly informative to "Peter" not to provide occasions for similar stressful, tough and "impossible" experiences for "Paul," especially if "Peter" is unaware of the uncomfortable consequences of his act on "Paul." 3.) It

FOR YOUR INFORMATION

helps the one who may have had the "impossible" experience to politely shun or guard against its recurrence in the future.

If you are yet to get the message I am trying to put across, here is a personal experience to help hit the point home. It may interest you to know that my first trip home to visit with my family in Nigeria after staying 15 months in the United States was overly expensive. Before leaving Hudson Falls in Upstate New York, I was forced to eliminate some of my personal belongings in order to accommodate all the parcels and packages mailed to me from many of my Nigerian friends resident in many parts of the United States. Having known that I was traveling to Nigeria through my personal contacts with them and through other sources of information, many of these friends sent a lot of stuff to me to carry and bring to their families and friends in Nigeria. Even up to the morning of my departure, packages and parcels were still arriving from some of them. As I felt bound in conscience to help bring the "cargoes" to Nigeria for their families, I had to continue the mass elimination of my "personal effects," in order to have room for my friends' stuff.

In spite of all this, at the end of the day, I hate to recall what I went through at John F. Kennedy Airport (acronym JFK) in New York City. Besides the fact that some of the baggage were too big and I had to go buy some baggage at the airport to reload some of the items so as to reduce the cost for extra luggage, it still cost me $880.00 even, for extra luggage from JKF to Lagos in Nigeria. This experience is truly and indeed a typical case of learning one's lesson the very hard way. I guess, at this point you now know where I am coming from with the heading "**Travel Light.**"

A HANDBOOK ON CULTURE SHOCK

Against the backdrop of this experience therefore, I have the following points to make for your information. 1.) Always travel light. If possible and as needed, you can send whatever baggage or luggage you have ahead of you through any of the courier services. 2.) For those of you who are often fond of sending stuff to others to bring home to your families in Nigeria, for instance, put yourself in the shoes of those carrying the baggage in light of the experience I just shared with you. Certainly, you would not want to go through all that. It is no picnic. In conscience then, do not think of subjecting or making other people go through this tough and rough journey home.

The journey home should be easy, smooth, and free of hazards and other anxieties. 3.) Do also realize that by traveling too heavy, you expose yourself to the danger of being walloped or attacked by armed robbers or "people of the underworld" at your port of destination. With so much baggage around you, you cannot avoid drawing attention to yourself. Be very careful! 4.) In fact, why do you trouble yourself with shopping overseas to bring home to your people? After all, many of the very things you spend so much money buying overseas, and spend so much money transporting them home, can be found in and bought in your home country, Nigeria for instance. And for the most part, they could even be bought at a cheaper cost or rate. Unless you just want to show off with items, such as clothes that have an American spec, which of course, can also be found in Nigeria. 5.) By the way, do also consider the fact that, your friend who is going home to Nigeria on vacation, is going to his village not yours. In stead of resting with his family, he may end up delivering parcels from one village or town to another for so many days. And by the time he is done, his vacation is over and he is on his way back to America "prematurely," unfulfilled, tired and dissatisfied with his visit. It is unfair to turn anyone into a "mailman" during his or her well deserved rest or vacation time. Think about this!

Before I rest my case on this **FYI** section, I challenge you also to make bold to share your own experiences with others. Aside the fact that this would help to make the world go round, you may strike a new note that someone may not have heard before. By the same token, I agree that some people do not like sharing their painful experiences, especially those ones brought upon them by other people. If you are one of those persons who shy away from speaking up, this is for you: "Hurt not expressed becomes permanent sadness; anger not expressed becomes depression; fears not expressed becomes avoidance; inadequacies not expressed become phony smiles; and experiences not shared become selfishness and egocentric."

CULTURE OF DRUGS OR PILLS

Drugs in this context are chemical substances used as medicine in the treatment of illness or sickness or disease. While Pills are small, often coated tablets or pellets of medicine, taken by swallowing whole or chewing, for the purpose of curing an illness, sickness or disease. Medical and Chemical sciences have developed many of these drugs or pills taken by so many people all over the world whose health conditions allow them to do so. Thanks for this invention and the good it appears to be doing "to" its "victims."

At this point, I feel bound in conscience to brave up and talk

A Handbook on Culture Shock

about the reality of the culture of drugs or pills in today's modern world. Incidentally, this reality or culture seems to conflict with my personal "belief" and conviction. Remember, I did previously mention in this book that, some people in my foreign culture said that, what makes them look and keep young, in spite of the fact that they are actually advanced in years, is a good medical environment. This reasoning together with other realities, personal philosophy and perhaps theology, challenge me to extensively share my reflection on the culture of drugs or pills. From the start, please, do bear in mind that, my intention is not to upset anyone or turn anyone's world upside down. My aim is far from a deliberate intent to tread on anyone's dreams. Plus or minus, I believe in and salute the efficacy of some drugs or pills. In my pedagogic reasoning, as I attempt to expound below, I may be wrong and so you don't need to accept it or agree with me.

I believe that the miracle to good health condition is held by the body. Your body, my body and our bodies are constantly striving to heal whenever we become sick. The creator, God, created this wonderful body we have that way, to cure itself of all the various afflictions that come its way. The body, I will like to reemphasize is equipped with inbuilt natural immunities or abilities or antibodies to fight against foreign bodies. And the mind is the powerhouse of good health. You just gotta believe it! But the seed of the nightmare that people go through in health related issues is sown much early in life. People are taught from very young that *health* comes from the *outside.* To this end, many a person actually believes that good health comes in the form of a pill. Sad! I don't believe that.

According to Dr. Will Craig, D.C. who lives in Queensbury,

FOR YOUR INFORMATION

New York, in an insert in *The Post-Star* of March 7, 2005, titled: "Queensbury Doctor Regrets Unfortunate Mistake..." (and I agree with him): "Health is an inside-out process. Our bodies were designed to be self-healing." Health Physicians therefore, in plying their trade, should work with the body and not against it. This singular understanding will bring about profound results. People should not be talked into becoming slaves to drugs as the ultimate or only alternative to health. An excessive or over indulge in taking drugs and swallowing or chewing pills, has an adverse effect on the body cells. These cells become weak and eventually are rendered unable to perform one of their duties as antibodies meant to help the body fight against any interference. These antibodies are antidotes or various proteins in the blood that are generated in reaction to foreign proteins. They neutralize any foreign protein and produce immunity against certain microorganisms or their toxins.

For your own good, as much as you can resist the temptation, please, stay away from drugs or pills. These two,(which often go together) by my estimation constitute foreign bodies that are forcefully introduced or injected into the natural system of the body every so often, thereby gradually causing a paralysis in many parts of the body. They are therefore, palsies that have weakening or debilitating influence. In their slow and steady destructive tendencies, they put the body in an enfeebled condition or debilitated state. Yes, every drug you take has a side effect, which is of course, always unhealthy to the victim. Just trust in God and believe in the power of the mind!

A woman in Upstate New York shared an interesting experience with me. This experience may be of help to confirm my

A HANDBOOK ON CULTURE SHOCK

personal therapeutic philosophy. I know that some people who would read this experience may say that it is just one case, and so an "exception to the rule." To think this way amounts to debunking my argument and denying the import and the message it intends to put across. Just give it a fair hearing and do not sit in judgment against its relevance. We all have the freedom of expression to express our personal opinions on issue though without any coercion to its adherence:

Her (the woman's) experience was that, she was sick and went to see her family doctor. After the session, she was given a prescription to go to a drugstore and get a pallet or bundle of pills. Of course, she did go, but she did not take any of them. In spite of her not swallowing any of the pills, she was feeling mush better on each passing day. After one month, as suggested by the doctor, she went back for a checkup. The doctor, on seeing her said to her: "You look much more better than the last time you came in here. You have responded so well to the pills." At the end of his litany of praises, in which a feeling of pomposity was surging or beginning to manifest, the woman finally broke the balloon by simply saying to him: "But Doctor, I never took any of the pills that you prescribed for me. I have taken too much drugs in my life. This time around, I simply resigned to faith and kept praying to God, privately and with the community of believers in my church. I simply believed that I will be fine. And that is how I feel today, much better than "yesterday."

Do I need to tell you that the letting of the cat out of the bag by the woman sent some jitters that created a jinxing moment for the doctor? Yes, the woman said he (the doctor) felt visibly jittery. But with the power of professionalism and conviction of trade, he pulled himself together. The rest of the story does not really matter. The punch line of this experience is that, drugs or pills do not always have the answers. But your mind, working with your body immunities, does, more often than not. Again, I will say, little did the woman know that, while she shared her story with me, she was simply confirming my therapeutic ideology.

As I continue to agree with the "redeeming' thoughts of Dr. Craig, as previously cited, I also affirm that the present state of America's health is appalling. Much of that is due to people's faith in pills, and not taking responsibility for their health. They are so brainwashed; believing that the only way to health is through pills. Without any intention to sound offensive, "we" in America have become a people and a nation of pill-poppers and drug-freaks. It is indeed a culture of drugs or pills.

In his *The Post-Star* insert, Dr. Craig observes that in spite of the nation's good medical standing, the World Health Organization (WHO) in its recent study ranked the U.S. only 29th in health. Isn't this a startling statistic considering the fact that the U.S. is equipped with the most modern technology, and probably some of the finest and best medical doctors? The question that we cannot resist is this: Are drugs or pills and technology really the answer? In the same *Post-Star* insert Dr. Craig, reports that: "On July 26, 2000, The Journal of the American Medical Association reported that, according to Johns Hopkins, medical errors are the third leading causes of death in the U.S."

Generally speaking, the culture of drugs or pills could be like what I may called a culture of medical hypnosis, in which

A HANDBOOK ON CULTURE SHOCK

its hypnotic victims are hypnotized to a state of medical gullibility, and the society goes with the flow unquestionably. In fact, the healing arts – especially medicine and "religion, operate within society, not outside it. They are an important part of society. Today, as in the past, either of these institutions (medicine and religion) is used to mold society by supporting certain values and opposing others. Consequently, they reflect and promote the primary moral values of the community. Since the individual is denied any existence apart from the group, the equation of the one with the many in "dogmatically" accepting community values is quite logical. This status quo "fathers" the institutionalized and unconscious "community therapy." This is just another slogan in the profession's unremitting campaign to sell itself to the ready-to-consume public through peddling, or persuasive adverts.

Perhaps, you may be wondering what I mean by "community therapy" in this context. By this I mean that, we in the society or community collaborate within the framework of existing medical facilities, whose nature and achievements are but high-flown phrases, convoluted or obscure semantics, caste cacophonies and utopian promises. To substantiate the above statement, let us take sometime to examine the field of *psychiatry.*

In delving into the historical philosophy of psychiatry, Thomas Szasz, observes (and I agree with him) that: in the relatively short history of psychiatry, the condition now called mental illness has been labeled and relabeled as *madness, lunacy, insanity, idiocy, dementia, dementia praecox, neurasthenia, psychopathy, mania, schizophrenia, neurosis, psychoneurosis, psychosis, ego failure, ego dyscontrol, emotional illness, emotional disorder, psychiatric illness, psychiatric disorder, immaturity, social failure, social maladaptation, behavior disorder,* and so forth. Similarly, the institution for the confinement of such "patients" has been called *madhouse, lunatic asylum, insane asylum, state hospital, state mental hospital, mental hospital, psychopathic hospital, psychiatric hospital, psychiatric institute, psychiatric institute for research and training, psychiatric center, and community mental health center.* It then becomes clear at this point that no single term can fulfill these contradictory functions, except temporarily. With continuous or persistent usage, the pejorative meaning of the term becomes increasingly apparent, falls short of its coercive power, and its value as semantic camouflage diminishes and disappears. To fill the "void" or vacuum created by the contempt of familiarity, new psychiatric terms for mental illness and mental hospital are then coined, giving the public the impression that an important new psychiatric discovery has been made. And in what seems like begging the question, when the fresh terms become too familiar, they, in turn, are discarded and a new crop of therapeutic-sounding words is introduced.

Now, back to the community therapy – its main goal seems to be the dissemination of a collectivistic mental health ethic as a kind of secular religion. And knowingly or unknowingly, "we" have all become its agents and consultants. We do this by talking to people, who talk to other people, and finally someone talks to, or has some sort of contact with, someone who is considered a potentially sick person. According to Thomas S. Szasz, M.D. in his book *Ideology and Insanity:* "This scheme works in conformity with Parkinson's Law: the expert at the top of the pyramid is so important and so busy that he needs

A HANDBOOK ON CULTURE SHOCK

a huge army of subordinate to help him, and his subordinates need a huge army of second-order subordinates, and so on."

In a society, especially the western world, that is gradually facing large-scale unemployment due to automation and great technological advances, in addition to an astronomic increase in the number of retirees and the aged, the prospect of "medical industry," ready and able to absorb a vast amount of "manpower," should be very attractive. It is! It will be! It will be a statement of fact to rise to the occasion and say that, as industries move south in the United States and some go or are sold to overseas countries, the medical industry is an immovable "asset," and so it remains unmoved nationwide. The situation is susceptible to another (self)-employment for retirees who must go pick up their prescriptions everyday in the various drugstores or keep an "hourly," daily, weekly and monthly appointments with their personal or family doctors. Regardless of what we call it, "medicalization" today is a big, big business. The hospitals have come to resemble gigantic industrial plants. This is true in every modern society. What an irony!

Commenting on family doctor or "family clinic," Thomas Szasz again in his book *Ideology and Insanity,* quotes Kingsley Davis as suggesting that, "such agencies offer not medical treatment but moral manipulation: 'Before one can cure such patients, one must alter their purpose; in short, one must operate, not on their anatomy, but on their system of values." Believe it or not, the trouble is, that people usually do not want to change their ways, alter their values and goals. By all means, they want to attain them. Honesty and authenticity, therefore, demands that the thoughtful person who is content to teach by example of his own conduct must always be ready to acknowledge error and to change his ways. But this is not what the "medical worker" wants: he does not want to change his ways, values, and goals, but those of others.

It is a fact that many clients today are lured to family doctors and family clinics by deliberate and tactical misrepresentation. In quoting Davis again, Thomas Szasz says that: "David observed that the prospective clients of family clinics, 'are told in one way or another, through lectures, newspaper publicity, or discreet announcement, that the clinic exists for the purpose of helping individuals out of their troubles… Once lured to the clinic, the individual may suffer further deception in the form of propaganda to the effect that his own best interest lies in doing the thing he apparently does not want to do, as if a man's 'best interest' could be judged by anything than his own desires." Could this then be a systemic deceit or systematic deception? Judge for yourself! Without any intension to sound pessimistic, be reminded also on this note of luring, that, once lured to "it," there is no end to "it." And if you are a retiree – enjoy your new self-employment for the rest of your life of picking up drugs or pills from or at drugstores, keeping series of medical appointments, and obeying other therapeutic "summons."

Because of the rush for the dollar or pecuniary gains and other cloudy reasons, today, it is difficult if not impossible to make a distinction between physicians who exploit their professional knowledge in the service of the community and those who work in the community in order to achieve the goals of their profession. Indeed, this distinction is not that simple in practice. This crossroads leaves us with the option or temptation of labeling the practice of medical education and com-

A HANDBOOK ON CULTURE SHOCK

munity therapy as not medical practice, but moral suasion and psychological coercion. Health, therefore, has become associated with principles dependent upon the prevailing ideology of the community concerned. This is a vexing problem. "Progressively," the agents or promoters of community health therapy now emerge as social engineers on the grand scale: They will be satisfied with nothing less than gaining license to export their ideologies to the world market with the media acting as midwives.

In recognizing the familiar model of human relation between the "victim" and the "agent': The client (victim) is like the ignorant child who must be "protected," if need be autocratically and without his consent, by the "expert," who is like the omnipotent parent. Again, borrowing from the ideas of Thomas Szasz – the agent who subscribes to this point of view and engages in this kind of work adopts a condescending attitude toward his (unyielding or unwilling) clients: "he regards them, at best, as stupid children in need of education, and, at worse, as evil criminals in need of correction. All too often he seeks to impose value change through fraud and force, rather than truth and example. In brief, he does not practice what he preaches." While he practically stays away from or in reality avoids the drugs or pills, he compels his clients to consume them. His task, more or less amounts to a brainwashing medical indoctrination with drugs or pills as the only way to "salvation." Sorry that the term "brainwashing" probably must have been applied here with unfortunate connotations to "meditherapeutic" practice, interpreted so, especially by those who are hostile to it. But the lesson of this needs to be taken to heart by all who knowingly or unknowingly are responsible for securing, (by inducement and suasion), medical treatment of potential or real "patience," for any kind of sickness, disease or infection.

As I bring this argument to a close, permit me to appeal that individuals and persons should be allowed to be "man" in all their activities and desires as moral beings. By "man" I mean, a human being, who is so, to the extent that he makes free, uncoerced choices. Anything that decreases his freedom, decreases his manhood. Hence, freedom, independence, and responsibility lead to being a man; while progressive enslavement, dependence, and irresponsibility lead to being a thing.

Today, irrespective of its origins and aims, the concept of "medicine," for the most part, serves to enslave man. It does this by permitting – indeed empowering, commanding and authorizing one man to impose his will on another, advertently or inadvertently, knowingly or unknowingly, intentionally or unintentionally, culturally and otherwise. In the context of our therapeutic philosophy, community therapy becomes largely a means for controlling the one and the many. Far from adjudication, in a mass society, this is best accomplished by recognizing an individual's existence only as a member of a group never as an individual. Given this scenario, the question of freedom is questionable.

For an example, the thought of Thomas Szasz aptly captures the American culture in this regard, he says: "In America, when the ideology of totalitarianism is promoted as fascism or communism, it is coldly rejected. However, when the same idea is promoted under the guise of mental health care, it is warmly embraced." By way of a contextual application of Thomas' ideology, it thus seems possible that where fascism

A HANDBOOK ON CULTURE SHOCK

and communism have failed to collectivize American society, medical health ethic may have succeeded or may yet succeed.

Probably you may be wondering why I decided to go so extensive into the culture of drugs and pills achieved through an overblown concept of medical therapy. I did this for a number of reasons, first: To compare this particular aspect of life in the developed world with what plays out in the developing world. The latter, (especially in the Etung culture), does not really experience this culture as such. Besides the plague of poverty and the unavailability of medical facilities, comparatively speaking, its people are more inclined to resigning to faith, trusting in God and depending on the powerhouse of the mind, and so even the few hospitals or clinics that are, have not been industrialized.

Second: The newcomer from the developing world into the culture of the developed world, needs to be aware of this culture right from the start. He should then do everything possible to stay away from such practices as the only option or alternative to health, no matter how much the system talks him to it. This is not because the culture is bad, but more so because his body system may not be accepting of such a practice being not used to it. The fact that people of the host culture are accepting it and it works for them does not mean that the newcomer will have the same luck. The former's (host's) body system has, probably been conditioned to this way of life.

Third: Without discrediting the medical field or doubting the professionalism of its experts, the presentation seeks to instill into the minds of potential and real patients that the body is created to be self-healing; the mind is a powerhouse with enough energies, strength, and vitalities that can help us to keep and enjoy a steady health, with the help of God. Let us then work individually to check this "mandate" of the professionally loyal "dynamic" or progressive whose mission is to obscure, and indeed deny, the ethical dilemmas of life, and to transform this into "medicalized" and "technicalized" remaking of man into a medical robot through problems susceptible to professional solutions.

Finally, I must disclaim that this is not another gimmick or scheme with any hidden agenda or intention to exploit anyone by any form of suasion, coercion and indoctrination. It is rather a moral empowerment that craves for liberty and self-determination, which allows man to stand alone as a moral being, though united with his fellow men as a member of a group, particular in a "medicalized" culture. Aside my personal philosophy on health, I am making this disclaimer in view of what I intend to suggest. I must say that, at this time it is like *one of those moments I feel like not being a priest,* not just because of my admitted humanity, but also in proffering religious solutions to human problems.

By the way, are you surprised that at one time or another, we priests do feel like not being priests? Do not be surprised. It does happen. Among other things, this feeling always surges when priests are haunted and plagued by the Freudian desires of pleasure and related longings. Of course, they, too, are human beings – complete men. To this end, it was Tarsitus – a philosopher who once said: "I am a man, and nothing human is alien to me." To deny this (human) reality is to deny the ontological constitution of the human person. However, as a tranquilizing meditation, in his celebrated book titled, *The Holy Longing,* Ronald Rolheiser, while admitting these desires,

A HANDBOOK ON CULTURE SHOCK

seems to suggest that, such human desires are holy longings. Such longings are for a better connection with the Holy, the Sacred, and the Supreme Being to know Him, to understand Him and to accept His beautiful plan for each of us. What a daily challenging – my brother priests!

In the context in question, my feeling like not being a priest is because of the fact that, "nemo iudex in causa sua." Yes, "no one is a judge in his own case," especially in proffering a God-centered solution to the health issues in questions, because *I am involved*. True as this difficulty may be, I dare not shy away from some of the priestly duties of teaching, instructing, informing, educating and enlightening. Bolden by this conviction, and far from plying my trade or advertising the "business" of the church, I want to say that: *"If you want to enjoy a steady health condition, then, be sincere, be honest, believe in God, think/talk well of others and go to Church.* I say this for a fact and with a "burning passion."

To say that it is better to leave your health in the hands of God at all times by firmly believing that He will take care of you and fix every situation, is to tell you the priceless solution to maintaining good health. This is the magic to keeping well, being well and getting well. This solution has been tested by many and proven to work. Providentially, at the time of this reflection, I came across an article in *The Post-Star* of May 6, 2005 that aptly addresses the efficacy of belonging to and going to Church if you want to get healthy. You won't believe how I felt when I came across the article in question. It was such a big relief to me since I was having difficulties in my choice of words to proffer a God-centered therapy to health issues. It was like God telling me "I'll help you get the message across to those concerned and those who would listen. The article is titled: "Want to get healthy? Go to Church." I agree with this completely and so I wish to extensively quote and talk about it.

"A growing body of scientific evidence shows that Americans who attended religious services at least once a week enjoy better-than-average health and lower rates of illness including depression. Perhaps most important, the studies show that weekly attendance confers a significant reduction in mortality risk over a given period of time. These studies have received almost no attention, in part because there is skepticism among many medical scientists about the validity of these studies, as Dr. Linda Powell can attest...Powell was a nonchurch-goer who was very suspicious of such studies."

No doubt, in a global culture of medicalization or medicine as the only preventive measure to health related issues, linking religion to health is out of the question. But evidence prove the benefit of religion on illness and patients who use religion to cope with health issues, fare better or slightly worse that those who do not. Hence, the article further says that: "Religious people who become upset that God has abandoned them or who become dependent on their faith, rather than their medical treatment, for recovery may inadvertently subvert the success of their recovery."

Powell, who was initially suspicious of the studies showing the effect of church attendance on health, after seeing the data, said: "I think I should go to church." Again, the panel that examined the church vis-à-vis health issues, "reported that the studies showed a 25 percent lower mortality rate for those who attend religious services at least weekly." By and large, the ar-

A Handbook on Culture Shock

ticle concludes with this optimistic assertion: "Religious services at churches, temples and mosques boast various features
that can be beneficial to health-meditation, a social network,
a set of values that discourage smoking, infidelity and other
unhealthy behaviors. Many of the studies have found that the
health benefit of weekly attendance accrue more heavily to
women than to men, perhaps because women make greater
use of religious social networks." This article has said it all.
What else can I say? Believe in God! Go to church and enjoy
good health. A word is enough for the wise – so the saying
goes.

CONCLUSION

Guided by a sincere and honest approach, generous and
positive intention, this presentation is free of all biases and
prejudices. As much as possible, it is a transparent attempt,
informed by the clarity of a comparative experience, to call a
spade a spade in obedience to the law of truth.

From the onset, the primary intention of this reflection was
culturally to inform, educate, and create a wider awareness
of cultural differences and expose the shocks therein, in addition to highlighting some subtle similarities. It was also meant
culturally to appraise and possibly challenge my audience
through a comparative exposé and analysis of my personal
cross-cultural experiences. Following this intention, there was
an honest attempt not to deviate from this trend and line of
thought. However, I do not claim at this point to have done an
incontestable justice to my original goal and intention. Neither
do I claim to have said it all and so exhausted what could have
been said. I am not presuming to say I cannot be outdone in a

similar presentation. Far be it! I am conscious that in an exposé of this nature, there is no limit to its study and investigation for a better articulation and methodical presentation. There is still room, therefore, for a possible, more appealing and even more compelling scholastic and synthetic view of the subject matter in question, even in the same context.

Furthermore, being a work rooted, founded, and articulated based on my personal experience, it may have suffered the vice of subjectivism because of my personal perception of ideas and worldview. This tendency cannot be overlooked. Consequently, my understanding of ideas, my interpretation of facts, and my application of the comparative experiences, may have been thwarted and twisted at one point or another to satisfy my personal and emotional ego. Yes, I am aware of my own blindness. Like the legend about the three blind men who went to "see" the elephant, the one who touched the tail, said: "The elephant is very like a rope." The second who touched the ear, said: "The elephant is very like an umbrella." And the third who touched the back, said: "The elephant is very like a mat." This is what probably happens to all of us when we have the same experiences but in presenting our observations, we are affected by our personal blindness, hence, this explains why there are usually different views on the same issue.

No doubt, in looking at and talking about cultural differences, especially from a comparative perspective or analysis, there is a natural propensity that tends toward "judgmentalism." Cognizant of this tendency, in this reflection, there must have been some sentences, expressions, and phrases that sounded "judgmentalistic." I never intended to judge any culture or ways of life of people in any context. After all, "who are you to judge your neighbor?" Therefore, if my audience at any point feels a particular aspect of its culture was talked down or negatively blown out of proportion, or even belittled or made inferior, kindly excuse my language. Furthermore, I do not rule out the possibility of the problem of semantics, which, if any, was not intended to create whatever hurt it may do to you as a person or to any whole cultural bloc.

True as these disclaimers may be, rather than taking it so personal, I also passionately appeal to your generosity that this presentation, for the most part, should be taken as a wake-up call to take a second look regarding those cultural aspects that are unbecoming and are difficult to deal with. This appeal becomes more urgent in view of the benefits of globalization, respect for human dignity, freedom, job opportunity, incentive for hard work, reward for excellence, cultural appreciation, patriotism, pluralism, polarization, malleability, docility, and the recognition, acknowledgment and acceptance of what really matters, in spite of our differences. Plus or minus, excuse my excesses, but do take a second look on those areas of concern.

On the other hand, if my audience feels proud because this presentation exalts your culture, then thank your lucky stars and realize that you are challenged to a mission. Thus, moved by fraternal concern for your brothers and sisters in the other cultural divide, who are not as lucky and as privileged as you are, there is the missionary mandate to honestly contribute in assisting them in the global endeavor to better their lot.

For my audience that seeks to cross cultural lines, bear in mind that you are a missioner. Remember also that " culture shock" is an inevitable and an unavoidable experience, either in toto or in some aspects of life. Note also that the degree of this shock varies from person to person. They would never ever be the same. Thus, some people get used to the changes faster than others, while others may be nursing the cultural wounds for a longer time by nostalgically remaining attached to what they have been used to. This nostalgic feeling, more often than not, creates a funky and melancholic mood and an unwelcome atmosphere that do much injury to the physical and psychological composition of the neophyte. To such people I say: Do not be reluctant to change which is supportive of cultural inclusiveness. Be inclusive! Stand up to your new world and accept the newness with its attendant challenges. Do not remain frozen, rather be flexible and penetrable. This is a way of cultural growth and maturity based on your privileged opportunity to experience a new culture. Always remember that transition is a key concept in human development. After all, philosophers tell us that the only thing that remains unchangeable is change itself. Everything, therefore, according to Heraclitus, is in a state of flux, hence, the dynamism of culture, which gives rise to the saying that: "Culture is dynamic."

True as this recommendation may be and compelling as it may sound, it is important to know that the change recommended here is not one that advocates for unreasonable and unquestionable compromise of one's own cultural values. It is also far from campaigning or canvassing for an unbecoming gullibility in accepting one's newfound culture with its experiences. This recommendation is rather one that favors cultural adaptation, which consequently benefits the newcomer as one who becomes culturally adaptive and can easily inculcate into oneself a sense of belonging in his or her newfound cultural

A HANDBOOK ON CULTURE SHOCK

environment. In fact, to gullibly swallow one's new cultural experiences without critically viewing and weighing or possibly analyzing them alongside one's cradle culture may amount to cultural unrootedness. Always realize that uncritical acceptance of the status quo reflects an ideology of compliance by sinful silence.

The apt and timely wisdom of Bishop Howard Hubbard of the Albany Diocese, New York, as reported in *The Evangelist* of May 6, 2004, scholarly and more clearly articulates and properly addresses this situation. Thus, he says: "In today's global village,...we need not be afraid of these multicultural challenges; indeed, we can be tremendously enriched by them, and the whole process can be mutually beneficial. But, to do so, we must...muster up the humility, sensitivity and courage to put on new lenses that will enable us to correct our 'cultural' myopia." By my estimation, this cross-cultural philosophy of Bishop Hubbard is a sound contribution to cultural anthropology that is very much needed in today's global village. It properly targets as well as contextually arrests the situation of people who are so strongly attached to their native culture and would not be ready to defrost or loosen up. This tendency is a ghetto mentality that could be occasioned by culture phobia and related cultural complexes. As a way forward therefore, to adopt this existential and realistic philosophy of Bishop Hubbard is to ponder seriously and accept the lesson of cultural pluralism and tolerance. No doubt, this is a step in the right direction.

As you may have gathered, the information contained herein does not provide you with an escape route from culture shock. In fact, culture shock is a sine qua non for authentic acculturation response and for a proper immersion or integration into a foreign culture. It is an initiation process or a *breaking-in* experience that situates you into another cultural domain. Therefore, reading between the lines, with a proper and intellectual digestion, made good in a contextual application of the ideas this book addresses, you would be prepared not to remain culturally frozen but to cultivate an open-minded approach as you enter into another culture. This approach would reduce, control, and minimize the inevitable shocks that await you.

Based on my experience, this work would not be complete if I do not have a word or two of encouragement to newcomers into a foreign culture. To this end, I would like to encourage you by saying that: "Since I was able to make it so far in my own cultural adjustment, you, too, can make it. The speed and place of adjustment may be different, but be sure that although cultural adjustment or acclimatization could be a difficult exercise, it is not an impossible task. Just be patient, first with yourself and then with your particular cultural situation as you toddle along. Do not be in a rush, else you become overwhelmed by trying to walk faster than your shadow or biting off more than you can chew at a time, or chasing two rats at the same time.

Always have it at the back of your mind that cultural adjustment is a *gradual warming-up process*. No doubt, there would be the initial apprehension and fear, both of the known and the unknown. Whatever the case and however tough the challenges may be, do not quit, do not throw in the towel, do not walk away, do not feel unable, and do not back off completely. Just hang in there and pull through. All these runaway tendencies show that you have no confidence in yourself, no self-

A Handbook on Culture Shock

affirmation and no cultural "rootedness." Besides, they may amount to self-defeatism. Remember these sayings: 'Tough times don't last, but tough people do. 'He who fights and runs away, leaves/lives to fight another day.' 'It could be worse somewhere else.' 'Your brothers and sisters all over the world are suffering the same thing.'" The beginning is bound to be a little difficult. And remember the famous African sayings: "Whatever is hot, would cool off.' 'The start of weeping is always hard.'" The latter, not a particularly happy proverb, but nonetheless true.

Before I rest my case, permit me to sound more specific on my advice and encouragement to my fellow Nigerian missioners and missionaries. To all who are far away from "home" I say to you: "As you walk on and navigate your way on the U.S. soil, bear in mind that first impression matters. Besides the fact that it sticks, you may not have a second chance for a first impression or even another opportunity to correct the first one that was battered by you." Yes, you cannot eat your cake and keep it. Note also that no matter how perfect you think you are and that you have succeeded in giving a good account or impression about yourself within a length of time, do not relax because when all seems so well and you are sailing smoothly, you may be going down the cliff. Hence, I urge you to stay awake! Keep your focus! Remain alert! because it takes only one mistake and all the irreproachable and impeccable character you have toiled to build will crumble in less than a second. Yes, it takes a split second to destroy yourself.

Probably, you are curious about why I decided to more specifically address my Nigerian audience. Are you the only one who does not know that in most parts of the United States, the name Nigeria conjures up a lot of negative feelings of suspicion and apprehension? This is due to the many crimes, such as trafficking, scams, business frauds (christened 419), and related dishonesty perpetrated and perpetuated by some Nigerians, both home and abroad. To substantiate this "allegation," two brief examples should suffice here. Now, listen to these personal experiences that I had in America about what some people, in this case, Nigerians, can come up with, with an intention to defraud.

It was on a beautiful spring morning when I decided to leave my room to go out for a walk. As I climbed down the staircase, I peeped into my mailbox and saw a paper in it. It was a fax message from someone in Nigeria. The full content of the message reads: " Dear Sir, my name is Akintollo Obayo. I am a Nigerian. I work for and have a very strong connection with Liquefied Natural Gas Co. located in Nigeria. As a senior staff who has worked in this oil rich country for about 50 years, I am planning for my retirement. Because of my commitment, transparency, honesty and hard work, I am due for a huge retirement benefit of about five million US Dollars. Besides, taking you into confidence, during my years of service, I was able to save in a personal and private account about six million US Dollars. I am sending you this message because, I'll like to come to America and invest all this money while enjoying my retirement with my God given family in your country. Could you please, send me your bank account number, to enable me transfer this money into it. I promise to make sure that you have a handsome amount from it as your reward. God bless you! Yours sincerely, Akinto."

Can you imagine this bunch of crap, well constructed and

A Handbook on Culture Shock

very enticing articulated lies? It may be difficult for you to guess my reaction and what I did. Since the fax message had a telephone number and an email address, I did not waste my hard earned dollars to call "Akinto" on phone, I decided to reply his message by email. My reply reads:

"Good to hear from you, Akinto. I have a very useful advice to give to you. If you love your country so much, and I believe you do, please, use that money to help the many poor in your village and for the development of your country. Let me know how you are making out. I look forward to hearing from you soonest. Yours in Christ, Basilio." Guess what! My email must have been a death sentence to Akin. I never heard from him again.

Because I want to prove the Nigerian "factor" beyond some reasonable doubts, here is another experience for you to think about: It was in Hudson Falls, New York, where the parish of my apostolate is located that one day a dear parishioner who owns and runs a Bridal Shoppe came to tell me that she had a contract from somebody in Nigeria. This Nigerian was requesting from this parishioner 50 wedding dresses or gowns in view of a "National Wedding-Day" ceremony for all the would-be wives of the just elected politicians into various political offices or positions in the country. This wise parishioner, knowing that a Nigerian priest was in her parish, decided to come ask me all about "National Wedding-Day of politicians in Nigeria." To cut the long story short, I simply smiled and said to myself: "They are at it again." Finally, I said to the woman: "I'll give you my telephone number to give to your Nigerian business partner, and tell him that you have a Nigerian priest in your parish who would like to talk to you about

For Your Information

the "deal." What a fortunate coincidence for the woman and an unfortunate one for the Nigerian! Until this day, the woman and I never heard from the "wedding planner" in Nigeria again. These are a few instances to open your eyes to the reality of fraudulent gimmicks, swindles and scams by some of us – Nigerians.

The untold consequences and bad effects of these swindling maneuvers on *innocent* Nigerians abroad are very shameful, pitiful and constitute a sorry sight. Incidentally, those who plan and carry out these craps, are "insulated" somewhere. The Nigerian public figures who work in America are the ones who receive the "slap," the insults and related psychological sufferings and social injuries brought upon them by the "black sheep of the family."

In stating a practical instance of the suffering of some innocent Nigerians irking out a living in America, I'll like to ask you one particular question again: "Are you the only one who does not know that in some parts of America, people do not accept credit cards from Nigerians? The only way therefore, Nigerians in those places concerned can be trusted to do business is either by certified bank checks or better still, by cash. What a shame!

I cannot help not substantiating my arguments in this reflection with one or two experiential proofs. Now listen to this:

There was a day I drove from Hudson Falls to Clifton Park, all in Upstate New York, about 45 minutes drive apart to visit with one of my respected Nigerian friends. His name is Chike. At the time of my visit, Chike's wife was away to Nigeria for the funeral ceremony of her late mom. May God rest her soul! I met Chike in the process of trying to send some picture

A HANDBOOK ON CULTURE SHOCK

souvenir cards of his late mother-in-law to his wife in Nigeria through courier service. He was told by the agent of the particular courier that was to provide the service that, they do not accept credit cards from Nigerians. For the service to be provided, then, Chike has to pay either with a certified bank check or with raw cash. On hearing this, being a Nigerian myself, I was so ashamed. I looked at my friend and felt so sorry for him, not only because of the heartbroken and difficult time, but more so because, he, being in the secular world, must be encountering many of such situations more often.

In the course of our talking about this unfortunate development, my friend, without leaving me in doubt and in his characteristic realism and objectiveness, said to me: "Victor, don't blame the courier service. Rather, let's blame some Nigerians who have put us in this messy limelight." Having made this statement of fact, we dwelled on it for a little more time and then changed the subject of discussion. It was indeed, another shameful and shocking experience. Fellow Nigerian-Americans, believe it or not we have a heavy task in our hands at present and in the future to prove that "your stock" is different from that of the "other" bad elements. Good luck and God bless you as you plan for a better representation of trust, honesty, sincerity, accountability, transparency, and authenticity.

No doubt, this battered image could be blown out of proportion, especially by some mass media, and others who may be prejudiced. But come to think of it, in every rumor, there is an element of truth. There is no smoke without fire. Yes, when a child is crying and pointing its finger at a particular direction, there must be something in the "offing." Do not be defensive by believing or saying that, one bad apple spoils the rest.

For Your Information

Ours (Nigeria's) is therefore an image that stands in need of redemption and on you lies the shared onus and responsibility to prove "them" (outsiders or non-Nigerians) wrong. To this end, I challenge you (the newcomer) from the onset to do all you can to give a good account of yourself, knowing that the United States, particularly the Adirondacks culture, for the most part, does not judge anyone based on the history of others or on prejudice. You are the only one who holds your present and future life in your own hands. Whatever impression you give them about yourself is what they would take.

By the same token, especially to missionaries, do not try to sell yourself by any cheap means or through an exaggerated appeal to emotions. This may amount to putting the cart before the horse. Just be yourself and let the taste of the pudding be in the eating. Or as it is often said: "Prove yourself." Finally, do not end up becoming part of the problem, but strive to be one of the many sought-for-solutions. At the end of the day, let it be said to your credit, that one good apple repairs the rest. Remember, you are an ambassador, a representative, a missioner and above all a missionary sent forth to stand for, to speak on behalf of, to search out, to learn and to teach.

After all is said and done, I am glad to welcome you to your new culture. Be ready for some culture "damage," some disillusionments, some feelings of anxiety, and uncertainty, some isolation and funky or depressing nostalgia, and, of course, some overwhelming excitements that would reshape your entire worldview, hopefully for the better and common good. All these experiences constitute some of the contents and form the main core of "culture shock."

A HANDBOOK ON CULTURE SHOCK

NOTES

[1] Hunter, James Davison. *Culture Wars: The struggle to defend America making sense of the battles over family, art, education, law, and politics,* New York: BasicBooks, 1991, 44.

[2] Szasz, Thomas S. M.D. *Ideology and Insanity:* New York: Anchor Books, Doubleday & Company, Inc. 1970, 34, 40, 42, 38, 48.

[3] Craig, Will D.C. "Queensbury Doctor Regrets Unfortunate Mistake..." *The Post-Star* (Insert), March 7, 2005.

[4] The Wall Street Journal. "Want to get healthy? Go to church." *The Post-Star,* May, 6, 2005.

[5] *The Evangelist,* "Catholic Must Develop Concept of World Church," May 6, 2004, 12.

GLOSSARY

Abiku – An "ogbanje" child who torments its mother by being born and shortly thereafter dying, being born again and dying again, over and over again. It is literarily translated as coming-and-going. This belief is held among some Nigerian people and cultures.

Abon-Osenghe – A form of traditional or cultural dance in the Etung culture. The name literally means "suffering children."

Agaba – A form of traditional dance in the Etung culture that is mostly patronized by the young people. It is mostly instrumental with a few repeated chants by its members.

Aje butter – Slang for people, especially girls who seem to be demanding excessive tender loving care (TLC).

Aku-mbang – The kind of cream that is gotten from palm fruit kennel. It literally means kennel oil used mostly by the Etung people on young children as body cream and to ward off evil spirits from attacking them.

Americanas – Slang for American dwellers.

Amibo – One who is a gossip and a news peddler. Such a person in this context hears from or discusses with a second party about a third party, and the goes on to tell the third party the content of the discussion he had with the second party exonerating himself of the ills that were discussed. He is very treacherous – a traitor and a betrayer.

Argumentum ad bacculum – (Latin) Argument or question that attacks the person.

Argumentum ad misericordia – (Latin) Argument that appeals to self-pity.

Bouquet and **Garter** – A marriage tradition among the Adirondack people of knowing who next would be in line for marriage, usually performed at a wedding reception by the newly wedded couple.

Conditio sine qua non – (Latin) Necessary condition.

Cum grano salis – (Latin) With a grain of salt. It means to take something with a grain of salt or not too seriously.

De fide – (Latin) Accepted as an article of faith.

Dibias – The name for soothsayers used by some Nigerian people and cultures to refer to people who claim to foretell events or predict the future.

Ekpa – It is a kind of traditional dance that is usually performed by grownup women and at night, to ward off evil from the village.

Ekpe or Mgbe – It is a society whose members are mostly grownup men. Sometimes, women who have risen to positions of importance in the village become members, too. Originally, the Ekpe was a society that maintained law and order and settled disputes among disputing persons in the village.

Eneke – The name given to a particular bird by the Igbos in eastern Nigeria.

Fon Nneh – The equivalent of "Ima-madu," but this time used by and among the Etung people and their culture. It literarily means to have somebody.

Ifighe – A traditional dance with its main character as a very tall masquerade that becomes smaller as it goes vertically higher. It is amazingly flexible.

Ima-madu – An expression used by the Igbos in eastern Nigeria to express one's connection to another person that can influence and warrant some favorable treatment and attention.

In periculum mortis – (Latin) In danger of death.

Modus operandi – (Latin for): Plan of action.

Mbim – Etung name for "tattoo." It is a temporary or permanent body art or mark.

Moninkim – A cultural dance that is performed mainly by

the women. It originates from the traditional rite of female circumcision. And so, it is usually performed by women at the end of their fattening days during their first outing after circumcision.

Naira – The name for Nigerian currency.

Nchibeh – A traditional dance with a two-face or double-sided face masquerade made or carved from black ebony hard wood.

Non sequitur – (Latin) It does not follow.

Nshoong or **Ashoong** – The equivalent of the "Osu caste," but this time used in the Etung culture. The former connotation is singular, while the latter is plural. Such people also suffer some discriminatory looks like in the "Osu caste."

Ntufam – This is the title for a chief in the Etung culture.

Obam – A traditional dance that is mainly performed by men, during which, women are not supposed to be seen outside their houses. Its costumes are usually red, and members dance in line. Its announcer dresses almost nude like one who is mad. He goes ahead of the group crying for help and weeping for fallen heroes, at the same time, he reminisces on the past history of the village.

Ogbanje – An evil or water spirit that torments its victims, especially children even unto death. This belief is held and found among many Nigerian tribes and cultures.

Ogenes – Traditional metallic tinkles used as musical instruments.

Ojjeh or **Okpee-inon** – The equivalent of sorcery in the Etung dialect and culture, which has to do with the use of supernatural powers over others through the assistance of evil spirits or "water birds."

Okumingbe – A form of traditional dance that is performed by the members of the Ekpe society. It has a masquerade that is beautifully adorn with colorful cascading wears and a bell tied around its waist.

Osu caste – A system in eastern Nigeria that recognizes the historical fact of some people belonging to the slave category. Such people must be treated differently by way of segregation and marginalization, as well as discriminated against and denied certain privileges in the community or village.

Ottee –A traditional talk–truth ritual performed by its believers among the Etung people and believed to have the power to compel one to confess the truth of a particular matter in question.

Oval Office – The name of the office of the President of the United States of America.

Quarrangidas – An expression used in some parts of Nigeria to refer to late night-keepers and twilight risers who sleep outside their homes and must get home the next morning early enough in order not be seen by their neighbors, onlookers, or passersby.

Roman collar – A Roman Catholic clergy wear, having a white collar on his neck, tucked into a shirt.

Susu – The village system of daily banking used by the Etung people and its environs.

The knocking on door – The first step or introductory rite of marriage in the Etung culture.

Voodoo – A charm, fetish, spell, or curse thought by believers in voodoo to possess magic power that can be used to control someone, hypnotize people and even to change one's destiny.

ISBN 1-41206385-X